Other Books and Series by Jeff Bowen

Applications for Enrollment of Chickasaw Newborn Act of 1905
Volumes I thru VII

Cherokee Intermarried White 1906 Volume I

Visit our website at **www.nativestudy.com** to learn more about these and other books and series by Jeff Bowen

CHEROKEE INTERMARRIED WHITE 1906 VOLUME II

TRANSCRIBED BY
JEFF BOWEN
NATIVE STUDY
Gallipolis, Ohio
USA

Other Books and Series by Jeff Bowen

1901-1907 Native American Census Seneca, Eastern Shawnee, Miami, Modoc, Ottawa, Peoria, Quapaw, and Wyandotte Indians (Under Seneca School, Indian Territory)

1932 Census of The Standing Rock Sioux Reservation with Births And Deaths 1924-1932

Census of The Blackfeet, Montana, 1897- 1901 Expanded Edition

Eastern Cherokee by Blood, 1906-1910, Volumes I thru XIII

Choctaw of Mississippi Indian Census 1929-1932 with Births and Deaths 1924-1931 Volume I
Choctaw of Mississippi Indian Census 1933, 1934 & 1937, Supplemental Rolls to 1934 & 1935 with Births and Deaths 1932-1938, and Marriages 1936-1938 Volume II

Eastern Cherokee Census Cherokee, North Carolina 1930-1939 Census 1930-1931 with Births And Deaths 1924-1931 Taken By Agent L. W. Page Volume I
Eastern Cherokee Census Cherokee, North Carolina 1930-1939 Census 1932-1933 with Births And Deaths 1930-1932 Taken By Agent R. L. Spalsbury Volume II
Eastern Cherokee Census Cherokee, North Carolina 1930-1939 Census 1934-1937 with Births and Deaths 1925-1938 and Marriages 1936 & 1938 Taken by Agents R. L. Spalsbury And Harold W. Foght Volume III

Seminole of Florida Indian Census, 1930-1940 with Birth and Death Records, 1930-1938

Texas Cherokees 1820-1839 A Document For Litigation 1921

Choctaw By Blood Enrollment Cards 1898-1914 Volumes I thru XVII

Starr Roll 1894 (Cherokee Payment Rolls) Districts: Canadian, Cooweescoowee, and Delaware Volume One
Starr Roll 1894 (Cherokee Payment Rolls) Districts: Flint, Going Snake, and Illinois Volume Two
Starr Roll 1894 (Cherokee Payment Rolls) Districts: Saline, Sequoyah, and Tahlequah; Including Orphan Roll Volume Three

Cherokee Intruder Cases Dockets of Hearings 1901-1909 Volumes I & II

Indian Wills, 1911-1921 Records of the Bureau of Indian Affairs Books One thru Seven;
Native American Wills & Probate Records 1911-1921

Other Books and Series by Jeff Bowen

Turtle Mountain Reservation Chippewa Indians 1932 Census with Births & Deaths, 1924-1932

Chickasaw By Blood Enrollment Cards 1898-1914 Volume I thru V

Cherokee Descendants East An Index to the Guion Miller Applications Volume I
Cherokee Descendants West An Index to the Guion Miller Applications Volume II (A-M)
Cherokee Descendants West An Index to the Guion Miller Applications Volume III (N-Z)

Applications for Enrollment of Seminole Newborn Freedmen, Act of 1905

Eastern Cherokee Census, Cherokee, North Carolina, 1915-1922, Taken by Agent James E. Henderson   Volume I (1915-1916)
Volume II (1917-1918)
Volume III (1919-1920)
Volume IV (1921-1922)

Complete Delaware Roll of 1898

Eastern Cherokee Census, Cherokee, North Carolina, 1923-1929, Taken by Agent James E. Henderson   Volume I (1923-1924)
Volume II (1925-1926)
Volume III (1927-1929)

Applications for Enrollment of Seminole Newborn Act of 1905 Volumes I & II

North Carolina Eastern Cherokee Indian Census 1898-1899, 1904, 1906, 1909-1912, 1914 Revised and Expanded Edition

1932 Hopi and Navajo Native American Census with Birth & Death Rolls (1925-1931) Volume 1 - Hopi
1932 Hopi and Navajo Native American Census with Birth & Death Rolls (1930-1932) Volume 2 - Navajo

Western Navajo Reservation Navajo, Hopi and Paiute 1933 Census with Birth & Death Rolls 1925-1933

Cherokee Citizenship Commission Dockets 1880-1884 and 1887-1889 Volumes I thru V

Copyright © 2013
by Jeff Bowen

ALL RIGHTS RESERVED
No part of this publication may be reproduced
or used in any form or manner whatsoever
without previous written permission from the
copyright holder or publisher.

Originally published:
Baltimore, Maryland
2013

Reprinted by:

Native Study LLC
Gallipolis, OH
www.nativestudy.com
2020

Library of Congress Control Number: 2020917307

ISBN: 978-1-64968-071-6

Made in the United States of America.

**This series is dedicated to
Jerry Bowen
the Brave and the Strong.**

DEPARTMENT OF THE INTERIOR

Commissioner to the Five Civilized Tribes

Muskogee, Indian Territory, March 9, 1907.

NOTICE IS HEREBY GIVEN that the undersigned, the Commissioner to the Five Civilized Tribes, has been designated by the Secretary of the Interior, as the official to make and approve appraisals of the value of improvements upon land in the Cherokee Nation which were made prior to November 5, 1906, by white persons who intermarried with Cherokee citizens prior to December 16, 1895, and who have the right under the Act of Congress approved March 2, 1907 (Public 190), to sell improvements.

NOTICE IS FURTHER GIVEN that former claimants to citizenship by intermarriage who have made permanent and valuable improvements on lands of the Cherokee Nation and who claim the right to sell the same under and by virtue of said Act of Congress of March 2, 1907 (Public 180), must appear before the Commissioner to the Five Civilized Tribes prior to April 1, 1907, and designate the land upon which are located the improvements which they claim the right to sell by virtue of said Act; and if any such intermarried citizen shall fail to appear before the Commissioner to the Five Civilized Tribes prior to April 1, 1907, it will be considered that he makes no claim to the benefits conferred by said Act. Such appearance and designation of improvements must be made before the Commissioner at his office in Muskogee, Indian Territory, at any time between Monday, March 11th, 1907, and Saturday, March 30th, 1907, inclusive, or at any of the following named places between the dates named at which places the Commissioner will have a representative to receive said designations and hear testimony relative thereto:

Bartlesville, Ind. Ter., Monday March 18th, 1907, to Saturday March 23rd, 1907, inclusive.
Tulsa, Ind. Ter., Monday March 25th, 1907, to Saturday March 30th, 1907, inclusive.
Claremore, Ind. Ter., Monday March 18th, 1907, to Saturday March 23rd, 1907, inclusive.
Nowata, Ind. Ter., Monday March 25th, 1907, to Saturday March 30th, 1907, inclusive.
Vinita, Ind. Ter., Monday March 18th, 1907, to Saturday March 23rd, 1907, inclusive.
Pryor Creek, Ind. Ter., Monday March 25th, 1907, to Saturday March 30th, 1907, inclusive.
Tahlequah, Ind. Ter., Monday March 18, 1907, to Saturday March 23rd, 1907, inclusive.
Sallisaw, Ind. Ter., Monday March 25th, 1907, to Saturday March 30th, 1907, inclusive.

Designations must be made in person by the intermarried white claimant, or in case proper proof is made that he is physically unable to appear, by some adult member of his immediate family, or in case proper proof is made of the fact that the intermarried white claimant is physically unable to appear and has no adult member of his immediate family, by a person holding a properly executed power of attorney; provided, that in every case the designation must be made by a party familiar with the character, ownership, location and value of the improvements to be designated. At the time of said designation the testimony of any competent person will be taken by the Commissioner as to the location, character and value of said improvements.

No former intermarried white claimant will be permitted to designate improvements upon more land than he would have been entitled to take in allotment for himself had he been admitted to citizenship. If any intermarried white claimant has made a tentative selection of a full allotment he will not be allowed to designate improvements upon other land.

NOTICE IS FURTHER GIVEN that if any citizen of the Cherokee Nation entitled to select an allotment shall claim that the improvements on land tentatively selected by a former intermarried white claimant, or held by him, do not belong to said intermarried white claimant, or makes any adverse claim to said improvements, or to the right of the intermarried white claimant to sell said improvements under the Act approved March 2, 1907 (Public 190), said citizen must appear before the Commissioner to the Five Civilized Tribes either at Muskogee, Indian Territory, prior to April 1, 1907, or at one of the places above designated and within the dates above designated and make formal complaint before the Commissioner to the Five Civilized Tribes of his contention. At Muskogee, Indian Territory, between March 11th and March 30th, 1907, inclusive, and at the other places herein named during the hearings at said places as herein fixed, plats will be open for inspection showing the location of tentative allotments made by former claimants to citizenship by intermarriage and all other land on which such claimants claim improvements, so far as indicated by the records of this office.

All persons interested should take careful note of the limitation of time herein provided for, within which designations and complaints may be made, and that they must be made by appearance before the Commissioner.

TAMS BIXBY,
Commissioner.

This particular notice concerns the appraisals of improvements on properties held by Cherokee intermarried whites. You would have found notices like this throughout the Nation to bring in people to finalize the allotment question, of who belonged and who did not.

E.C.M.   Cherokee 58.

DEPARTMENT OF THE INTERIOR,
COMMISSIONER TO THE FIVE CIVILIZED TRIBES.

In the matter of the application for the enrollment of
ALBERTIN HAMPTON as a citizen by intermarriage of the Cherokee
Nation.

DECISION

THE RECORDS OF THIS OFFICE SHOW: That at Fairland, Indian
Territory, July 9, 1900, Albertin Hampton appeared before the Commission to the Five Civilized Tribes, and made application for the
enrollment of himself as a citizen by intermarriage, and for the
enrollment of his wife, Jane E. Hampton, et al. as citizens by
blood of the Cherokee Nation. The application for the enrollment of
the said Jane E. Hampton et al. as citizens by blood of the Cherokee
Nation has been heretofore disposed of, and their rights to enrollment will not be considered in this decision. Further proceedings
in the matter of said application were had at Muskogee, Indian
Territory, September 3, 1902, October 14, 1902, and January 2, 1907.

THE EVIDENCE IN THIS CASE SHOWS: That the applicant herein,
Albertin Hampton, a white man, was married, in accordance with
Cherokee law, January 20, 1874, to his wife, Jane E. Hampton, nee
Thomas, who was at the time of said marriage a recognized citizen
by blood of the Cherokee Nation, and whose name appears on the approved partial roll of citizens by blood of the Cherokee Nation,
opposite No. 195; that since said marriage the said Albertin Hampton
and Jane E. Hampton have resided together as husband and wife, and
have continuously lived in the Cherokee Nation. Said Albertin
Hampton is identified on the Cherokee authenticated tribal roll of
1880, and the Cherokee census roll of 1896, as "Bert Hampton", an
intermarried citizen of the Cherokee Nation.

IT IS, THEREFORE, ORDERED AND ADJUDGED: That in accordance with
the decision of the Supreme Court of the United States, dated November
5, 1906, in the case of Daniel Red Bird et al. vs. the United States,

E.C.M.   - 2 -   Cherokee 58.

under the provisions of Section twenty-one, of the Act of Congress approved June 28, 1898 (30 Stat., 495), Albertin Hampton is entitled to enrollment as a citizen by intermarriage of the Cherokee Nation, and his application for enrollment as such is accordingly granted.

                                                    Commissioner.

Dated at Muskogee, Indian Territory, this JAN 18 1907

The above is an accepted decision of the Commissioner to the Five Civilized Tribes. The Attorney for the Cherokee Nation had fifteen days after the date of Commissioner's decision in which to protest.

> Cherokee
> 58.
>
> W.W. HASTINGS, ATTORNEY
> H. M. VANCE, SECRETARY
>
> OFFICE OF
> **Attorney for the Cherokee Nation,**
> MUSKOGEE, I.T. January 18, 1907.
>
> The Commissioner to the Five Civilized Tribes,
>
> Muskogee, Indian Territory.
>
> Sir:
>
> Receipt is acknowledged of the testimony and of your decision enrolling Albertin Hampton, as a citizen by intermarriage of the Cherokee Nation. Time for protesting said decision is waived and I consent that said person may be placed upon the schedule immediately.
>
> Yours very truly,
>
> W. W. Hastings
>
> Attorney for Cherokee Nation.

The above is a notice of the Attorney waiving the time for protesting the Commissioner's decision (on the two previous pages) concerning Albertin Hampton's application and consenting to place the applicant upon schedule immediately.

INTRODUCTION

The *Cherokee Intermarried White*, National Archive film M-1301, Rolls 305-307, are found under the heading of Applications for Enrollment of the Commission to the Five Civilized Tribes. The genealogical value of this series concerning the relationships between many Cherokee tribesman and their marriages among another race is very important and virtually a treasure trove of information long sought after. While on the other hand what these cases are really about are the efforts of many to attain Cherokee land allotments. Referenced from the Supreme Court Decision, Cherokee Intermarriage Cases – 203 U.S. 76 (1906).

This collection of Intermarried claims involves two hundred and eighty-eight separate cases with a variety of scenarios from the divorced to the widowed to the deserving to the deceptive. During these times there were many that wanted what was rightfully only the Cherokees. You will see each case will be headed by the title from the first folder as an example: *Intermarried White I, Trans from Cher. 34*, the transfer number is the Dawes Commission number from the claimants spouse.

These cases are fascinating because of the generational bloodlines that can be verified by documentation rather than just word of mouth. From Kent Carter's book, *The Dawes Commission*, "The tribe also, continued to oppose the enrollment of whites who had married into the Cherokee tribe. That controversy dragged through the U.S. Court of Claims and then the Supreme Court, which finally ruled in favor of the tribe on November 05, 1906. The court upheld the Cherokee citizenship laws that denied rights to any white who had married into the tribe after November 1, 1877. It also upheld an 1839 law which stated that anyone who moved out of the nation lost their citizenship unless they were readmitted. The applications of 3,341 persons were rejected as a result of this ruling, and the allotment clerks were forced to undo a great deal of their work. With the issue finally settled by the courts, the commission was able to send the first schedule of Cherokees by intermarriage, containing fifty-five names, to the secretary of interior on June 10, 1907. Eventually only 286 people were enrolled as intermarried whites----far fewer than the number put on the rolls of the Choctaw and Chickasaw tribes, which had much more liberal laws on rights based on marriage." [1]

---

[1] The Dawes Commission and the Allotment of the Five Civilized Tribes, 1893-1914 by Kent Carter, pg. 121

In Cohen's Handbook of Federal Indian Law he states, "In the *Cherokee Intermarriage Cases,* the Supreme Court considered the claims of certain white persons, intermarried with Cherokee Indians, who wanted to participate in the common property of the Cherokee Nation. Such persons were permitted by tribal law to be tribal citizens with limited rights in tribal property. The tribe had also provided for the revocation of citizenship rights of a white person who intermarried with a Cherokee if the Cherokee spouse were abandoned or if a widower or widow married a non-Cherokee. The Court found that the Cherokee Nation had authority to qualify the rights of citizenship which it offered to its "naturalized citizens. Such tribal action defeated the claims of the plaintiffs:

The laws and usages of the Cherokees, their earliest history, the fundamental principles of their national policy, their constitution and statutes, all show that citizenship rested on blood or marriage; that the man who would assert citizenship must establish marriage; that when marriage ceased (with a special reservation in favor of widows or widowers) citizenship ceased; that when an intermarried white married a person having no rights of Cherokee citizenship by blood it was conclusive evidence that the tie which bound him to the Cherokee people was severed and the very basis of his citizenship obliterated."[2]

An important footnote that Cohen published within his pages for the above paragraph also needs to be studied. He noted, "Under Cherokee law white persons intermarrying with Cherokees before 1875 were tribal citizens for most purposes, including allotment of tribal land, but had no interest in tribal funds except those funds derived from tribal lands. A Cherokee law that became effective in 1875 provided that whites marrying Cherokees had no rights to tribal property but could obtain full citizenship by the payment of $500 to the tribe. In 1877 the tribe provided that no intermarried citizen could obtain any rights to tribal land or funds."[3]

During many years of study this author has found cases that should have been been accepted, especially with the particular documentation presented. All in all the outcome of the decision made should have rendered a different result. Also there have been many that numb the mind as to how they their cases were even considered. The years have given many the hopes that their ancestors were one of those that had a decent claim and an honest consideration. Like any time in history there are political struggles

---

[2] Felix S. Cohen's Handbook of FEDERAL INDIAN LAW 1982 ED. pgs 20-21.
[3] Felix S. Cohen's Handbook of FEDERAL INDIAN LAW 1982 ED. pg 21 footnote16.

and the human factor that points out man is not perfect. These pages were transcribed with the wish that another person somewhere along the line will find their relation from the past and give them the answers long hoped for.

Jeff Bowen
Gallipolis, Ohio
NativeStudy.com

Cherokee Intermarried White 1906
Volume II

Cher IW 36
Trans from Cher 3985   3-13-07

◇◇◇◇◇

E.C.M.

DEPARTMENT OF THE INTERIOR,

COMMISSIONER TO THE FIVE CIVILIZED TRIBES.

In the matter of the application for the enrollment of

MARY C. McGHEE

as a citizen by intermarriage of the Cherokee Nation.

CHEROKEE 3985.

◇◇◇◇◇

Department of the Interior,
Commission to the Five Civilized Tribes,
Vinita, I. T., October 2nd, 1900.

In the matter of the application of David A. McGee[sic] for the enrollment of himself, wife and children as Cherokee citizens; being sworn and examined by Commissioner Needles he testified as follows:

Q What is your name? A David A. McGee.
Q What is your age? A 51.
Q What is your post-office address? A Hill.
Q What district do you live in? A Delaware District.
Q Are you a citizen of the Cherokee Nation by blood? A Yes sir.
Q What degree of blood do you claim? A I don't know; my mother was about a half-breed; my father was a white man.
Q Who do you want to enroll? A Myself and family.
Q What is the name of your wife? A Mary C.
Q Is she a Cherokee citizen by blood? A White woman.
Q What is her age? A About 44 I believe.
Q Have you got a certificate of marriage? A No sir.
Q What was her name before you married her? A Lusk.
Q What are the name of your children? A Dennis B. 20; he will be 21 the 22nd of this month.
Eliza J., she is about 18 I guess; John Ross, about 17 I guess; Elizabeth B., she is about 15; Esther, she is about 12; Florence, she is about 9; Ambrose, he is about 6.

Cherokee Intermarried White 1906
Volume II

Q Are these children all alive and living with you at this time? A Yes sir.
Q You have always lived in the Cherokee Nation? A Yes sir.
1880 roll page 288 #1760 David McGee Delaware District;
1880 roll page 288 #1761 Mary C. McGee Delaware District
1880 roll page 288 #1765 Dennis Busheyhead McGee,   "
1896 roll page 500 #1943 David A. McGhee, Delaware District;
1896 roll page 581 #369 Mary C McGhee   "
1896 roll page 500 #1946 Dennis B. McGhee   "
1896 roll page 500 #1947 Eliza J. McGhee   "
1896 roll page 500 #1948 John R. McGhee   "
1896 roll page 500 #1949 Elizabeth B. McGhee   "
1896 roll page 500 #1950 Esther L. McGhee   "
Q Is that her name, Esther L.? A I believe it is.
1896 roll page 500 #1951 Florence E. McGhee Delaware District;
1896 roll page 500 #1952 Ambrose McGhee   "

Com'r Needles: The name os[sic] David A. McGee and Mary C. McGee his wife appear upon the authenticated roll of 1880 as well as the census roll of 1896; the name of his child, Dennis B. also appears upon the authenticated roll of 1880 as well as the census roll of 1896; name of Eliza J., John R., Elizabeth B., Esther L. Florence and Ambrose appear upon the census roll of 1896; they all being duly identified according to page and number of the rolls as indicated in the testimony, and having made satisfactory proof as to their residence, said David A. McGee will be duly listed for enrollment as a Cherokee citizen by intermarriage, and his wife, Mary C., and their children as enumerated in the testimony as Cherokee citizens by blood.

M.D. Green, being first duly sworn, states that as stenographer to the Commission to the Five Civilized Tribes he correctly recorded the testimony and proceedings in this case and that the foregoing is a true and complete transcript of his stenographic notes thereof.

                                                    MD Green
Subscribed and sworn to before me this 2nd October 1900.

                    CR Breckinridge   Commissioner.

◇◇◇◇◇

Cherokee Intermarried White 1906
Volume II

JOR.
Cher. 3985.

Department of the Interior,
Commission to the Five Civilized Tribes.
Tahlequah, I. T., October 28, 1902.

SUPPLEMENTAL TESTIMONY in the matter of the application for the enrollment of MARY C. McGHEE as a citizen by intermarriage of the Cherokee Nation.

MARY C. McGHEE?[sic] being first duly sworn, and being examined, testified as follows:

BY COMMISSION: What is your name? A Mary C. McGhee.
Q How old are you? A Forty-eight.
Q What is your post office address? A Dodge, Indian Territory.
Q What was your post office when application was made for your enrollment? A Hill.
Q Application was made for your enrollment as a citizen by intermarriage of the Cherokee Nation? A Yes sir.
Q What is the name of yur[sic] husband? A David A. McGhee.
Q Is he living? A Yes sir.
Q Is he a Cherokee by blood? A Yes sir.
Q When were you and he married? A We were married in 1873.
Q Does your name appear upon the roll of 1880? A Yes sir.
Q Were you ever married before you married your present husband? A No sir.
Q Was he ever married before he married you? A No sir.
Q You are his first wife and he is your first husband? A Yes sir
Q Have you and he lived together continuously since your marriage? A Yes sir.
Q Have you ever been separated at all? A No sir.
Q Have you resided in the Cherokee Nation continuously since you married your husband in 1873? A Yes sir.
Q How long has your husband resided in the Cherokee Nation? A He was born and raised here.
Q Resided here all of his life? A Yes sir.
Q Have either of you been outside the Cherokee Nation for any purpose within the past five years? No sir.
Q You have how many children that application was made for: A Seven.
Q Are all of those children living at this time? A Yes sir
Q You have had no children at all to die since you were enrolled? A No sir.

This testimony will be filed with and made a part of the record in the matter of the application for the enrollment of Mary C. McGhee as a citizen by intermarriage of the Cherokee Nation, Cherokee straight card field No. 3985.

Cherokee Intermarried White 1906
Volume II

Wm. Hutchinson, being first duly sworn, states that as stenographer to the Commission to the Five Civilized Tribes he correctly recorded the testimony and proceedings in this case, and that the foregoing is a true and complete transcript of his stenographic notes thereof.

Wm Hutchinson

Subscribed and sworn to before me this 14th day of November, 1902.

BC Jones
Notary Public.

◇◇◇◇◇

Cherokee No. 3985.

DEPARTMENT OF THE INTERIOR,

COMMISSIONER TO THE FIVE CIVILIZED TRIBES,

MUSKOGEE, INDIAN TERRITORY, JANUARY 4, 1907.

IN THE MATTER of the application for the enrollment of Mary C. McGee, as a citizen by intermarriage of the Cherokee Nation.

MARY C. McGEE, being first duly sworn by Walter W. Chappell, Notary Public in the Western District of the Indian Territory, testified as follows:

EXAMINATION

ON BEHALF OF THE COMMISSIONER:

Q What is your name? A Mary C. McGee.
Q Your age? A Fifty-three.
Q Your postoffice address? A Dodge, Indian Territory.
Q You claim to be a citizen of the Cherokee Nation by intermarriage, do you? A Yes sir.
Q Through whom do you claim your citizenship? A David A. McGee.
Q Is he living? A Yes sir.
Q What is his citizenship? A Cherokee by blood.
Q When were you and Mr. McGee married? A 1873, January.
Q Where were you married? A South West City, Missouri.
Q Who married you? A J. J. Shorthill, a Baptist minister.
Q Were you married under a Cherokee license? A No sir, we didn't have to have a license at the time.
Q You were not married under a license of any kind? A No sir.

Cherokee Intermarried White 1906
Volume II

Q Have you a certificate of your marriage? A No sir, I have not; I got one but I got it misplaced.
Q Do you know whether or not that has been recorded? A I don't know; I suppose it has.
Q Where would it be recorded? A I don't know.
Q You had that certificate in your possession at one time, did you? A Yes sir.
Q Do you know what became of it? A No, I don't know; I sent one to my mother, and I never did get it back.
Q Were wither you or Mr. McGee married prior to this marriage at South West City, Missouri, in 1873? A No sir.
Q Your husband at that time was a Cherokee citizen was he? A Yes sir.
Q Where was he born? A Born in Delaware District, Cherokee Nation.
Q Lived in the Cherokee Nation all his life, has he? A Yes.
Q Have you and your husband lived together continuously since your marriage? A Yes sir.
Q Where have you resided during that time? A Delaware District, Cherokee Nation
Q Were there any persons present at your marriage in 1873? A There was two, but I don't know where there is any of them living or not, one of them aint[sic] I know.
Q What was your maiden name? A Lusk.
Q What was your citizenship at the time of your marriage? A I was living in the Cherokee Nation.
Q Where were you born? A I was born in Arkansas.
Q You were a citizen of the State of Arkansas then at the time you married? A Yes sir.

(Witness dismissed).

DAVID A. McGEE, being first duly sworn by Walter W. Chappell, Notary Public in the Western District of the Indian Territory, testified as follows:

EXAMINATION

ON BEHALF OF THE COMMISSIONER:

Q What is your name, age and postoffice address?
A David A. McGee; Dodge, 58 years old.
Q You are the husband of the applicant, Mary C. McGee? A Yes sir.
Q When were you and she married? A January 29, 1873.
Q Married at South West City, Missouri, were you? A Yes sir.
Q You were not married under a Cherokee license? A No sir; didn't require it then.
Q Have you and the applicant lived together continuously since you married? A Yes sir.
Q Where have you resided during that time? A Near Dodge, right around in that settlement most of the time.
Q In the Cherokee Nation? A Yes sir.

Cherokee Intermarried White 1906
Volume II

ON BEHALF OF THE COMMISSIONER:

The witness, David A. McGee, is identified on the approved partial roll of citizens by blood of the Cherokee Nation the Cherokee Nation opposite No. 9630.
The applicant Mary C. McGee (nee Lusk) is identified on the authenticated Cherokee tribal roll of 1880 and Cherokee census roll of 1896 opposite Nos. 1760 and 369, respectively, as an intermarried white.

(Witness dismissed).

EZEKIEL FIELDS, being first duly sworn by Walter W. Chappell, Notary Public in the Western District of the Indian Territory, testified as follows:

EXAMINATION

ON BEHALF OF THE COMMISSIONER:
Q What is your name? A Ezekiel Fields.
Q Your postoffice address? A South West City, Missouri.
Q What is your citizenship? A Cherokee by blood.
Q Are you acquainted with the applicant, Mrs. McGee, and her husband David A. McGee? A Yes sir.
Q How long have you known them? A Known Mr. McGee ever since he was a little boy; known Mrs. McGee since they were married.
Q Do you know when they were married? A No sir.
Q About when? A Why, yes.
Q When was that? A I can't tell you that at all; I don't remember about the year; it has been sometime back.
Q Have you known them ever since their marriage? A Yes sir.
Q Have they lived together continuously since that time? A Yes sir.
Q And been living in the Cherokee Nation? A Yes sir.

(Witness dismissed).

MARGARET FIELDS, being first duly sworn by Walter W. Chappell, Notary Public in the Western District of the Indian Territory, testified as follows:

EXAMINATION

ON BEHALF OF THE COMMISSIONER:

Q What is your name, age and postoffice address? A Margaret Fields; fifty-nine; South West City, Missouri.
Q What is your citizenship, Mrs. Fields? A I don't know.
Q Are you a Cherokee by blood? A No sir.
Q You are the wife of Ezekiel Fields, are you, who has just testified? A Yes sir.

Cherokee Intermarried White 1906
Volume II

Q Are you acquainted with the applicant Mary C. McGee and her husband David A. McGee? A Yes sir.
Q How long have you known them? A Known Mr. McGee ever since he was a small boy, and knowed[sic] his wife awhile before they was married.
Q Do you know when they were married? A No sir.
Q About how many years ago was it, since they were married? A I guess about 23, some where along there.
Q You have known them ever since their marriage? A Yes sir.
Q They have lived together continuously since that time? A Yes sir.
Q And been living in the Cherokee Nation? A Yes sir.

(Witness dismissed).

I, S. T. Wright, stenographer to the Commissioner to the Five Civilized Tribes, on oath, state that I recorded the testimony and proceedings had in the above entitled cause on January 4th, 1907, and that the above and foregoing is a true and correct transcript of my stenographic notes thereof taken on said date.

S.T. Wright

Subscribed and sworn to before me this January 5th, 1907.

Edward Merrick
NOTARY PUBLIC.

◇◇◇◇◇

E.C.M.   Cherokee 3985.

DEPARTMENT OF THE INTERIOR,

COMMISSIONER TO THE FIVE CIVILIZED TRIBES.

In the matter of the application for the enrollment of MARY C. McGHEE as a citizen by intermarriage of the Cherokee Nation.

D E C I S I O N

THE RECORDS OF THIS OFFICE SHOW: That at Vinita, Indian Territory, October 2, 1900, David A. McGhee appeared before the Commission to the Five Civilized Tribes, and made application for the enrollment of his wife, Mary C. McGhee, as a citizen by intermarriage, and for the enrollment of himself et al. as citizens by blood of the Cherokee Nation. The application for the enrollment of the said David A. McGhee et al. as citizens by blood of the Cherokee Nation has been heretofore disposed of, and their rights to enrollment will not be considered in this decision. Further proceedings in

Cherokee Intermarried White 1906
Volume II

the matter of said application were had at Tahlequah, Indian Territory, October 28, 1902; and at Muskogee, Indian Territory, January 4, 1907.

THE EVIDENCE IN THIS CASE SHOWS: That the applicant herein, Mary C. McGhee, a white woman, married, January 29, 1873, one David A. McGhee in the State of Missouri, who was at the time of said marriage a recognized citizen by blood of the Cherokee Nation, and whose name appears on the approved partial roll of citizens by blood of the Cherokee Nation, opposite No. 9630; that from the time of said marriage the said David A. McGhee and the said Mary C. McGhee resided together as husband and wife, and continuously lived in the Cherokee Nation up to and including September 1, 1902. Said Mary C. McGhee is identified on the Cherokee authenticated tribal roll of 1880, and the Cherokee census roll of 1896, as an intermarried citizen of the Cherokee Nation.

IT IS, THEREFORE, ORDERED AND ADJUDGED: That in accordance with the decision of the Supreme Court of the United States, dated November 5, 1906, in the case of Daniel Red Bird et al. vs. the United States, under the provision of Section twenty-one, of the Act of Congress approved June 28, 1898 (30 Stat. 495), Mary C. McGhee is entitled to enrollment as a citizen by intermarriage of the Cherokee Nation, and her application for enrollment as such is accordingly granted.

Tams Bixby
Commissioner.

Dated at Muskogee, Indian Territory,
this   JAN 16 1907

◇◇◇◇◇

Cherokee
3985

Muskogee, Indian Territory, December 26, 1906.

Mary C. McGhee,
    Dodge, Indian Territory.

Dear Madam:

November 6, 1906, the United States Supreme Court held that white persons who intermarried with Cherokee citizens according to Cherokee law prior to November 1, 1875, are entitled to enrollment and allotments of land as citizens of the Cherokee Nation.

You are advised that to properly determine your right to enrollment as a citizen by intermarriage of the Cherokee Nation, it will be necessary for you to appear before the Commissioner for the purpose of giving testimony as to the date of your marriage and whether or not your husband, by reason of your marriage to whom you claim the right to

Cherokee Intermarried White 1906
Volume II

enrollment as a citizen by intermarriage of the Cherokee Nation, was a recognized Cherokee citizen at the time of your marriage to him.

You are, therefore, directed to appear before the Commissioner at Muskogee, Indian Territory, at 9 o'clock A. M., on Friday, January 4, 1907, and give testimony as above indicated.

Respectfully,

J.M.H   Acting Commissioner.

Cherokee 3985

Muskogee, Indian Territory, January 17, 1907.

W. W. Hastings,
    Attorney for the Cherokee Nation,
        Muskogee, Indian Territory.

Dear Sir:

There is enclosed herewith copy of the decision of the Commissioner to the Five Civilized Tribes, dated January 16, 1907, granting the application for the enrollment of Mary C. McGhee as a citizen by intermarriage of the Cherokee Nation.

Respectfully,

Encl. I-6   Commissioner.
RPI

| W.W. HASTINGS. | OFFICE OF | H.M. VANCE. |
| ATTORNEY. | | SECRETARY. |

Cherokee 3985

Attorney for the Cherokee Nation,
MUSKOGEE, I. T.

January 18, 1907.

The Commissioner
    to the Five Civilized Tribes,
        Muskogee, Indian Territory.

Sir:

Receipt is acknowledged of the testimony and of your decision enrolling Mary C. McGhee as a citizen by intermarriage of the Cherokee Nation. Time for protesting said

Cherokee Intermarried White 1906
Volume II

decision is waived and I consent that said person may be placed upon the schedule immediately.

W. W. Hastings
Attorney for Cherokee Nation.

◇◇◇◇◇

Cherokee
3985

Muskogee, Indian Territory, January 19, 1907.

Mary C. McGhee,
    Dodge, Indian Territory.

Dear Madam:

There is enclosed herewith copy of the decision of the Commissioner to the Five Civilized Tribes, dated January 16, 1907, granting the application for your enrollment of as a citizen by intermarriage of the Cherokee Nation.

You will be advised when your name has been placed upon the schedule of citizens of the Cherokee Nation and approved by the Secretary of the Interior.

Respectfully,

Commissioner.

Encl. I-50
  RPI

Cher IW 37
Trans from Cher 4052   3-13-07

◇◇◇◇◇

E.C.M.

DEPARTMENT OF THE INTERIOR,

COMMISSIONER TO THE FIVE CIVILIZED TRIBES.

In the matter of the application for the enrollment of

MARGARET FIELDS

as a citizen by intermarriage of the Cherokee Nation.

Cherokee Intermarried White 1906
Volume II

CHEROKEE 4052

◇◇◇◇◇◇

DEPARTMENT OF THE INTERIOR,
COMMISSION TO THE FIVE CIVILIZED TRIBES,
VINITA, I.T., OCTOBER 3d, 1900.

In the matter of the application of Ezekial Fields for the enrollment of himself, wife and children as citizens of the Cherokee Nation; said Fields being sworn by Commissioner T. B. Needles, testified as follows:

Q What is your name? A Ezekial Fields.
Q What is your age? A 57.
Q Your post office address? A Southwest City, Missouri.
Q What district do you live in? A Delaware.
Q Are you a recognized citizen of the Cherokee Nation? A Yes, sir.
Q Gy[sic] blood? A Yes, sir.
Q What degree of blood do you claim? A Quarter.
Q For whom do you apply? A Myself, wife and children.
Q What is the name of your wife? A Margarette.
Q When did you marry her? A 1863.
Q What is the name of your children under 21 years of age? A Ezekial Jr., 17.
Q What is the name of the next child? A Martha J.
Q How old is she? A 22.
Q What is the name of the next one? A Ella Zoe.
Q How old is Ella Z? A She is 15.
Q What is the name of the next one? A Maggie May.
Q How old is Maggie May? A 12 years old.
Q What is the name of the next one? A Lula Pearl, 19 years old.
Q These children alive and living with you? A Yes, sir.
Q You have always lived in the Cherokee Nation? A Yes, sir.

    1880 enrollment; page 258, #1050, Ezekiel[sic] Fields, Delaware.
    1880 enrollment; page 258, #1055, Martha J. Fields, Delaware.
    1880 enrollment; page 258, #1051, Margaret Fields, Delaware.
    1896 enrollment; page 470, #1128, Ezekial Fields, Delaware.
    1896 enrollment; page 572, #183, Margarette Fields, Delaware.
    1896 enrollment, page 470, #1130, Lula Pearl Fields, Delaware.
    1896 enrollment, page 470, #1129, Martha Jane Fields, Delaware.
    1896 enrollment, page 470, #1131, Ezekial Fields, Jr., Delaware.
    1896 enrollment; page 470, #1132, Ella Zoe   "   "
    1896 enrollment; page 470, #1133, Maggie Fields,   "

Cherokee Intermarried White 1906
Volume II

Com'r Needles:--The name of Ezecial[sic] Fields appears upon the authenticated roll of 1880, as well as the name of his wife, Margaret Fields, as an intermarried white. Their names also appears[sic] upon the census roll of 1896. The name of Martha Jane also appears upon the authenticated roll of 1880 and census roll of 1896. The names of Lule[sic] P., Maggie M. and Ella Z., appear upon the census roll of 1896. They all being duly identified according to the age and number of the rols[sic], and having made satisfactory proof as to their residence, said Ezekial Fieds[sic] and his children will be duly listed for enrollment as Cherokee citizens by blood, and his wife, Margaret, will be duly listed for enrollment as a Cherokee citizen by intermarriage.

---oooOOOooo---

J.O. Rosson, being first duly sworn, states that as stenographer to the Commission to the Five Civilized Tribes, he correctly recorded the testimony and proceedings in this case, and that the foregoing is a true and complete transcript of his stenographic notes thereof.

JO Rosson

Subscribed and sworn to before me this 8th day of October, 1900.

CR Breckinridge
Commissioner.

◇◇◇◇◇

JOR.
Cher. 4052.

Department of the Interior,
Commission to the Five Civilized Tribes.
Tahlequah, I. T., October 13, 1902.

SUPPLEMENTAL TESTIMONY AND PROCEEDINGS in the matter of the application for the enrollment of MARGARET FIELDS as a citizen by intermarriage of the Cherokee Nation.

MARGARET FIELDS, being first duly sworn, and being examined, testified as follows:

BY COMMISSION: What is your name? A Margaret Fields.
Q How old are you? A I am fifty-two, I think.
Q What is your post office address? A Dodge.
Q What was your post office address when you were enrolled?
A Southwest City, Missouri.
Q You are a white woman, are you? A Yes sir.
Q Has application heretofore been made to this Commission for your enrollment as a citizen by intermarriage of the Cherokee Nation? A Yes sir.
Q What is the name of your husband? A Bud Fields. I call him Bud Fields.
Q What is his correct name? A Ezekiel Fields.

Cherokee Intermarried White 1906
Volume II

Q Is h living? A Yes sir.
Q Is he a Cerokee[sic] by blood? A Yes sir.
Q Do you claim your right to enrollment by reason of your marriage to him? A Yes sir.
Q When were you and he married? A Married the time of the war.
Q Does your name appear upon the roll of 188L[sic] A I think so.
Q At the time application was made to the Commission for your enrollment, was satisfactory proof made of your marriage to your present husband? A Yes sir.
Q Have you and he lived together continuously since you were married? A Yes sir.
Q Were you living together on the 1st day of September, 1902? A Yes sir.
Q You have never been separated? A No sir.
Q Were you ever married before you married him? A No sir.
Q Was he ever married before he married you? A No sir.
Q You are his first wife and he is your first husband? A Yes sir.
Q Have you resided in the Cherokee Nation continuously since you and he married? A Yes sir.
Q Has he also? A Yes sir.
Q How many children have you that application was made for? A Five.
Q Are all those children living at this time? A Yes sir.

      This testimony will be filed with and made a part of the record in the matter of the application for the enrollment of Margaret Fields as a citizen by intermarriage of the Cherokee Nation, Cherokee straight card field No. 4052.

Wm. Hutchinson, being first duly sworn, states that as stenographer to the Commission to the Five Civilized Tribes he correctly recorded the testimony and proceedings in this case, and that the foregoing is a true and complete transcript of the stenographic notes thereof.

                                                        Wm Hutchinson

Subscribed and sworn to before me this 22d day of October, 1902.

                                                        John O Rosson
                                                        Notary Public.

◇◇◇◇◇

LGD   Cherokee 4052.

DEPARTMENT OF THE INTERIOR,
COMMISSIONER TO THE FIVE CIVILIZED TRIBES.

Muskogee, Indian Territory, January 3, 1907.

      In the matter of the application of MARGARET FIELDS for enrollment as a citizen by intermarriage of the Cherokee Nation.

Cherokee Intermarried White 1906
Volume II

Margaret Fields, being first duly sworn by B. P. Rasmus, a notary public, testified as follows:

Q What is your name? A Margaret Fields.
Q What is your age? A 59 years old.
Q What is your postoffice address? A Southwest City, Missouri.
Q You claim to be a citizen by intermarriage of the Cherokee Nation? A Yes sir.
Q Through whom do you claim your right to enrollment?
A My husband, Ezekiel Fields.
Q When were you married.[sic] A In 1863 I think, time of the war.
Q Where were you married? A In Arkansas.
Q Under the Arkansas law? A Yes sir.
Q Have you got a certificate? A No.
Q Who married you? A Woods.
Q Preacher? A Yes, claimed to be.
Q Were you ever married before you married Ezekiel Fields? A No sir.
Q Was he ever married before he married you? A No sir.
Q How long did you live in Arkansas after you were married? A About one year.
Q Have you lived together continuously as husband and wife ever since you were married? A Yes sir.
Q When did you come to Indian Territory? A Right after the war.
Q Have you lived here ever since? A Yes.
Q When was your husband first admitted to citizenship in the Cherokee Nation?
A I cant[sic] tell you. Always - ever since I knew him.

The applicant is identified on the 1880 Cherokee roll, Delaware District, opposite No. 1051. Her husband, through whom she claims her right to enrollment, is identified upon said roll in said district opposite No. 1050. He is also identified upon the final roll of citizens by blood of the Cherokee Nation opposite No. 8792.

Witness excused.

Ezekiel Fields, being first duly sworn by B. P. Rasmus, a notary public, testified as follows:

Q What is your name? A Ezekiel Fields.
Q What is your age? A 67 years old.
Q What is your postoffice address? A Southwest City, Missouri.
Q Are you a citizen of the Cherokee Nation? A Yes.
Q What relation are you to Margaret Fields? A She is my wife.
Q When were you married to her? A In 1863.
Q Where were you married? A In Arkansas.
Q Who married you? A A fellow by the name of Woods.
Q Preacher, was he? A He claimed to be.
Q Were you ever married before you married Margaret Fields? A No sir.
Q Was she ever married before she married you? A No.

Cherokee Intermarried White 1906
Volume II

Q Have you lived together continuously as husband and wife ever since 1863 up to the present time? [sic] Yes sir.
Q Is there anyone here today who knows of your marriage to Margaret Fields? A I dont[sic] know.

Witness excused.

Daniel K. Wetsel, being first duly sworn by B. P. Rasmus, a notary public, testified as follows:

Q What is your name? A Daniel K. Wetsel.
Q What is your age? A 63 years old.
Q What is your post office address? A Maysville, Arkansas.
Q Do you know Ezekiel Fields? A Yes sir.
Q Do you know Margaret Fields? A Yes sir.
Q How long have you known them? A 8 or 9 years.
Q Have they lived together as husband and wife ever since you have known them? A Yes sir.

Witness excused.

Demie T. Stubblefield, being first duly sworn, on oath, states that as stenographer to the Commissioner to the Five Civilized Tribes she reported the proceedings had in the above cause, and that the above and foregoing is a true and correct transcript of her stenographic notes thereof.

Demi T Stubblefield

Subscribed and sworn to before me this, January 4, 1907.

Edward Merrick
Notary Public.

◇◇◇◇◇

DEPARTMENT OF THE INTERIOR
COMMISSIONER TO THE FIVE CIVILIZED TRIBES
MUSKOGEE, IND. TER.
JAN. 4, 1907.

ooOoo

ADDITIONAL TESTIMONY IN THE MATTER OF THE APPLICATION FOR THE ENROLLMENT OF MARGARET FIELDS AS A CITIZEN BY INTERMARRIAGE OF THE CHEROKEE NATION.

CENSUS CARD NO. 4052.

DAVID A. McGEE BEING FIRST DULY SWORN TESTIFIED AS FOLLOWS:

Cherokee Intermarried White 1906
Volume II

EXAMINATION BY THE COMMISSIONER:

Q What is your name? A David A. McGee.
Q What is your age? A About fifty eight.
Q What is your post office address? A Dodge, Indian Territory.
Q Are you a citizen or non citizen.[sic] A Cherokee.
Q Cherokee citizen by blood? A Yes sir.
Q Do you know Ezekiel Fields? A Yes sir.
Q Are you acquainted with Margaret Fields? A Yes sir.
Q How long have you known her? A I've known Margaret Fields since about sixty one; I've known him all my life.
Q Do you know when they were married? During the war, I think along about sixty three.
Q Where were they married? A I don't know.
Q You didn't see them married? A No sir.
Q You know that they held themselves out as man and wife ever since the war.
A Yes sir.
Q Did you live in the same community with them? A Yes sir, raised together.

ooOoo

B. E. SLOAN BEING FIRST DULY SWORN TESTIFIED AS FOLLOWS:

EXAMINATION BY THE COMMISSIONER:

Q What is your name.[sic] A B. E. Sloan.
Q What is your post office address? A Big Cabin.
Q How old are you.[sic] A Fifty six.
Q Are you a citizen or non citizen of the Cherokee Nation.[sic] A Citizen.
Q Are you acquainted with Ezekiel Fields and Margaret Fields[sic] A Yes sir.
Q How long have you known them? A I've known them about forty, forty one or two years I reckon; ever since I was a little boy like.
Q Do you know when they were married? A No sir I dont[sic] know when they were married.
Q How long have they held themselves out as man and wife in the community in which they lived.[sic] A Thirty five or six as near as I can tell.
Q Thirtyfive or six years. A Years. I knew them when they was single.
Q So recognized in the community in which they lived? A Yes, sir.

ooOoo

Clara Mitchell Wood being first duly sworn upon her oath states that as stenographer for the Commissioner to the Five Civilized Tribes she reported the above and foregoing proceedings and that this is a correct transcript of her stenographic notes.

Clara Mitchell Wood

Cherokee Intermarried White 1906
Volume II

Subscribed and sworn to before me this 5th day of January 1907.

Chas E Webster
Notary Public.

◇◇◇◇◇◇

E.C.M.
Cherokee 4052

DEPARTMENT OF THE INTERIOR,
COMMISSIONER TO THE FIVE CIVILIZED TRIBES.

In the matter of the application for the enrollment of Margaret Fields as a citizen by intermarriage of the Cherokee Nation.

D E CI S IO N . [sic]

THE RECORDS OF THIS OFFICE SHOW: That at Vinita, Indian Territory, October 3, 1900, Ezekiel Fields appeared before the Commission to the Five Civilized Tribes and made application for the enrollment of his wife, Margaret Fields as a citizen by intermarriage, and for the enrollment of himself, et al. as citizens by blood of the Cherokee Nation. The application for the enrollment of the said Ezekiel Fields, et al. as citizens by blood of the Cherokee Nation has been heretofore disposed of, and their rights for enrollment will not be considered in this decision. Further proceedings in the matter of said application were had at Tahlequah, Indian Territory, October 13, 1902 and at Muskogee, Indian Territory, January 4, 1907.

THE EVIDENCE IN THIS CASE SHOWS: That the applicant herein, Margaret Fields, a white woman, married about the year 1863, one Ezekiel Fields, who was at the time of said marriage a recognized citizen by blood of the Cherokee Nation, and whose name appears upon the approved partial roll of citizens by blood of the Cherokee Nation opposite number 9782; that from the time of said marriage the said Ezekiel Fields and Margaret Fields resided together as husband and wife, and continuously lived in the Cherokee Nation up to and including September 1, 1902. Said Margaret Fields is identified on the Cherokee Authenticated Tribal Roll of 1880 and the Cherokee Census Roll of 1896 as an intermarried citizen of the Cherokee Nation.

IT IS THEREFORE ORDERED AND ADJUDGED: That in accordance with the decision of the Supreme Court of the United States, dated November 5, 1906, in the case of Daniel Red Bird et al., vs. the United States, under the provision of Section 21, of the Act of Congress approved June 28, 1898, (30th. Stat. 495) Margaret Fields is entitled to enrollment as a citizen by intermarriage of the Cherokee Nation, and her application for enrollment as such is accordingly granted.

Cherokee Intermarried White 1906
Volume II

Tams Bixby
Commissioner.

Dated at Muskogee, Indian Territory,
this   JAN 17 1907

◇◇◇◇◇

Cherokee
4052

Muskogee, Indian Territory, December 26, 1906.

Margaret Fields,
    Dodge, Indian Territory.

Dear Madam:

    November 6, 1906, the United States Supreme Court held that white persons who intermarried with Cherokee citizens according to Cherokee law prior to November 1, 1875, are entitled to enrollment and allotments of land as citizens of the Cherokee Nation.

    You are advised that to properly determine your right to enrollment as a citizen by intermarriage of the Cherokee Nation, it will be necessary for you to appear before the Commissioner for the purpose of giving testimony as to the date of your marriage and whether or not your husband, by reason of your marriage to whom you claim the right to enrollment as a citizen by intermarriage of the Cherokee Nation, was a recognized Cherokee citizen at the time of your marriage to him.

    You are, therefore, directed to appear before the Commissioner at Muskogee, Indian Territory, at 9 o'clock A. M., on Friday, January 4, 1907, and give testimony as above indicated.

Respectfully,

J.M.H.   Acting Commissioner.

◇◇◇◇◇

Cherokee Intermarried White 1906
Volume II

Cherokee
4052

Muskogee, Indian Territory, January 17, 1907.

W. W. Hastings,
    Attorney for the Cherokee Nation,
        Muskogee, Indian Territory.

Dear Sir:

    There is enclosed herewith a copy of the decision of the Commissioner to the Five Civilized Tribes, dated January 17, 1907, granting the application for the enrollment of Margaret Fields as a citizen by intermarriage of the Cherokee Nation.

        Respectfully,

Encl. H-38
JMH
                                          Commissioner.

Cherokee 4052   W.W. HASTINGS, ATTORNEY.   OFFICE OF   H.M. VANCE, SECRETARY.

Attorney for the Cherokee Nation,
MUSKOGEE, I. T.

January 18, 1907.

The Commissioner to the Five Civilized Tribes,
    Muskogee, Indian Territory.

Sir:

    Receipt is acknowledged of the testimony and of your decision enrolling Margaret Fields as a citizen by intermarriage of the Cherokee Nation. Time for protesting said decision is waived and I consent that said person may be placed upon the schedule immediately.

        Yours very truly,
            W. W. Hastings
            Attorney for Cherokee Nation.

Cherokee Intermarried White 1906
Volume II

Cherokee
4052

Muskogee, Indian Territory, January 19, 1907.

Margaret Fields,
    Dodge, Indian Territory.

Dear Madam:

    There is enclosed herewith a copy of the decision of the Commissioner to the Five Civilized Tribes, dated January 17, 1907, granting the application for your enrollment as a citizen by intermarriage of the Cherokee Nation.

    You will be advised when your name has been placed upon a schedule of citizens of the Cherokee Nation and approved by the Secretary of the Interior.

                      Respectfully,

Encl. H-89   Commissioner.
JMH

Cher IW 38
Trans from Cher 4102 3-13-07

                                                                         E.C.M.

DEPARTMENT OF THE INTERIOR,

COMMISSIONER TO THE FIVE CIVILIZED TRIBES.

In the matter of the application for the enrollment of

                      GARRETT G. JAMES

as a citizen by intermarriage of the Cherokee Nation.

                        CHEROKEE 4102

Cherokee Intermarried White 1906
Volume II

DEPARTMENT OF THE INTERIOR,
COMMISSION TO THE FIVE CIVILIZED TRIBES,
VINITA, I.T., OCTOBER 3d, 1900.

In the matter of the application of Garrett James for the enrollment of himself, wife and childrel[sic] as citizens of the Cherokee Nation; said James being sworn by Commissioner C. R. Breckinridge, testified as follows:

Q Give me your name, please? A Garrett James.
Q How old are you? A 49 years old.
Q What is your post office? A Fairland.
Q In what district do you live? A Delaware.
Q Who is it you want to have put on the roll? A Myself, wife and three children.
Q Are you Cherokee by blood? A No, sir.
Q White man? A Yes, sir.
Q What is your wife? A Cherokee.
Q Have you your marriage license and certificate? A Yes, sir.
Q You married in 1875? A Yes, sir.
Q To Miss Mary E. A. Hudson, is that right? A Yes, sir.
Q Have you lived in the Cherokee Nation ever since your marriage in 1875? A Yes, sir.
Q Is your wife still living? A Yes, sir.
Q What is her age? A She is 44.
Q What was her father's name? A James Hudson.
Q Dead or alive? A He is dead.
Q Has he been dead more than 20 years? A He has been dead about 14 years, I think.
Q Her mother's name, please? A Sallie Hudson.
Q Is she dead or alive? A She is living.
Q Give me the names of your children? A Houston Wyley.
Q Is is[sic] 19 years old? A Yes, sir.
[sic] Jesse Price, 15 years old? A Yes, sir.
Q Both living now are they? A Yes, sir
Q These are the ones you apply for--these two? A Yes, sir.

    1880 enrollment; page 273, #1410, Garret James, Delaware.
    1880 enrollment; page 273, #1411, Mary E. A. James, Delaware.
Page 578 1896 enrollment; page Q578[sic], #282, Garrett G. James, Delaware
    1896 enrollment; page 486, #1607, Mary Ann Elizabeth James, Delaware.
    1896 enrollment; page 486, #1610, Jesse Price James, Delaware.
    1896 enrollment; page 486, #1609, (Jouston) James, Delaware.
        (Houston)

  Com'r Breckinridge:--The applicant applies for the enrollment of himself, his wife and two children: His wife is identified on the rolls of 1880 and 1896 as a native Cherokee. She has lived in the Cherokee Nation ever since her enrollment in 1880 and she will be listed now for enrollment as a Cherokee by blood. The applicant is identified on the rolls of 1880 and 1io6[sic]. He has lived with her and in the Cherokee Nation ever since 1880, and he will be listed now for enrollment as a Cherokee by intermarriage. His

Cherokee Intermarried White 1906
Volume II

two children are both minors and are living now, and they are identified with their parents on the roll of 1896. They will be listed now for enrollment as Cherokees by blood.

---oooOOOooo---

J. O. Rosson, being first duly sworn, states that as stenographer to the Commission to the Five Civilized Tribes, he correctly recorded the testimony and proceedings in this case, and that the foregoing is a true and complete transcript of his stenographic notes thereof.

JO Rosson

Subscribed and sworn to before me this 8th day of October, 1900.

CR Breckinridge

Commissioner.

◇◇◇◇◇

Cherokee 4102.

Department of the Interior,
Commission to the Five Civilized Tribes,
Muskogee, I. T., September 22, 1902.

In the matter of the application of Garret G. James for the enrollment of himself as a citizen by intermarriage, and the enrollment of his wife, Mary E. A. James and children, Houston W. James and Jesse P. James, as citizens by blood of the Cherokee Nation.

Cherokee Nation appears by W. W. Hastings.

Francis M. Conner, being sworn and examined by the Commission, testified as follows:
Q State your name, age and postoffice address? A Francis M. Conner, age 50, postoffice Fairland, I.T.
Q Are you acquainted with Garret G. James? A Yes sir.
Q How long have you known him? A About twenty years.
Q Are you acquainted with his wife? A Yes sir.
Q How long have you known her? A About twenty-five years.
Q When were they married? A In '76 or '77.
Q Have they been living together continuously since that time as man and wife? A Yes sir.
Q Are they living together now? A Yes sir.
Q Where do they live? A About a mile north of me, about three and a half miles north of Fairland.
Q In the Cherokee Nation? A Yes sir.
Q How long have they lived there? A Ever since they married.
Q In the nation continuously? A Yes sir.

Cherokee Intermarried White 1906
Volume II

The undersigned, being duly sworn, states that as stenographer to the Commission to the Five Civilized Tribes he correctly recorded the testimony and proceedings in this case, and that the foregoing is a true and correct transcript of his stenographic notes thereof.

E.G. Rothenberger

Subscribed and sworn to before me this 24th day of September, 1902.

BC Jones
Notary Public.

◇◇◇◇◇

DEPARTMENT OF THE INTERIOR
COMMISSIONER TO THE FIVE CIVILIZED TRIBES
MUSKOGEE, IND. TER.
JAN. 3, 1907.

CHEROKEE 4102.

IN THE MATTER OF THE APPLICATION FOR THE ENROLLMENT OF GARRETT G. JAMES AS A CITIZEN BY BLOOD OF THE CHEROKEE NATION.

JESSE P. JAMES BEING FIRST DULY SWORN BY B.P. RASMUS A NOTARY PUBLIC TESTIFIED AS FOLLOWS:

EXAMINATION BY THE COMMISSIONER:

Q What is your name.[sic] A Jesse P. James/[sic]
Q What is your age.[sic] A Twenty one.
Q What is your post office address? A Fairland Indian Territory.
Q Are you a citizen by blood of the Cherokee Nation? A Yes sir.
Q You appear here today for the purpose of giving testimony relative to the right to enrollment of Garrett G. James as a citizen by intermarriage of the Cherokee Nation do you[sic] A Yes sir.
Q What relation are you to Garrett G. James.[sic] A I'm his son.
Q Is Garrett G. James living or dead.[sic] A Dead.
Q When did he die.[sic] A November 12, 1906.
Q Your father was not a Cherokee by blood. A No sir.
Q His only claim to the right to enrollment as a citizen of the Cherokee Nation is by virtue of his marriage to a citizen by blood of the nation is it.[sic] A Yes sir.
Q What is the name of the citizen thru whom he claims the right to enrollment as a citizen by intermarriage of the Cherokee Nation.[sic] A Her name was Mary E. Hudson or Mary E. James or Mary E. A. as some times appears. Hudson was her maiden name.

Cherokee Intermarried White 1906
Volume II

Q Are you informed as to when your father and mother married[sic] A Nothing only by the marriage certificate, is all the proof I have of it, the license whatever it may be.

The witness presents an original marriage license and certificate showing that on May 8, 1875 a license was issued in accordance with the law of the Cherokee Nation authorizing the marriage of Garrett James and Miss May[sic] Hudson and that said parties were united in marriage in accordance with the terms of said license May 13, 1875 by T. J. McGee Judge of the District Court Delaware District Cherokee Nation.

Q Is Mary E. A. James your mother? A Yes sir.
Q She is living at the present time is she not.[sic] A Yes sir she's living at the present time.
Q Why did she not appear here today.[sic] A Well the reason why she didn't appear she's hardly able to travel about.
Q Her health will not permit her to appear. A Well sometimes it will and sometimes it wont[sic]; it wouldn't at the present time is the reason she didn't want to come herself.
Q Did you ever hear that your father was married prior to his marriage to your mother.[sic] A No sir he was not that I ever heard of.
Q Was your mother married prior to her marriage to your father.[sic] A No sir she was not that I know of.
Q Did they live continuously in the Cherokee Nation as man and wife from the date of the marriage until the date of your father's death last December.[sic] A Yes sir they have been citizens of the Cherokee Nation and lived there.
Q You do not know of their ever having been absent for any length of time from the Cherokee Nation.[sic] A No sir.
Q Or that there's ever been any separation of any kind.[sic] A None whatever.

The applicant Garrett G. James is identified on Cherokee Authenticated Tribal Roll of 1880 Delaware District No. 1410; his wife Mary E. A. James is included in the approved partial roll of citizens by blood of the Cherokee Nation opposite No. 9909.

ooOoo

Clara Mitchell Wood being first duly sworn upon her oath states that as stenographer for the Commissioner to the Five Civilized Tribes she reported the above and foregoing proceedings and that this is a correct transcript of her stenographic notes.

Clara Mitchell Wood

Subscribed and sworn to before me this 3rd day of January 1907

B.P. Rasmus
Notary Public.

Cherokee Intermarried White 1906
Volume II

(The Marriage License and Certificate below typed as given.)

Cherokee Nation)
Delaware Dist)
                     To any Lawful Judge or Regular Minister of the Gospel of the Cherokee Nation
     Greeting
                In the name of the Cherokee Nation, you are hereby authorized and Empowered to Somnize the Rites of of Matrimony. According to the form Usually Observed and performed in Such Cases. Between Garett James a citizen of the U States and Miss Mary Hudson a citizens of the Cherokee Nation
Said Garett James having fully conformed to all laws passed By the National Counsil Regulating Entermarriages of Citizens the U States with citizens of the Cherokee Nation Here in fail Not
                              Given from under my hand Officially this the
                              8th Day of May A D 1875
                              J.E. Harlm Clk Del Dist C N.

Cherokee Nation (
Delaware District (
                this is to Certify by me that the marriage of ceremony was deuly performd By Me with the parties named in the within Licens this the 13th Day May A.D. 1875
                          (T.J. McGhee   Juge of the District Court
                          (In and for Delaware District Cherokee
                          (Nation

Cherokee Nation
Delaware Dist
                I Do hereby Certify that the within Licens was Duly granted to Garett James a citizen of the U States to Marry Miss Mary Hudson a citizen of the Chekee Nation. The Licens Return Executed and placed on Record in conformity with the act entitled an act Regulating Intermarrages of citizens of the U States with citizens of the Cherokee Nation   (
Approved Oct 15 the 1855   (In Testimony whereof I have here unto set my hand and seal of Del Dist on the 15 day of May 1875

                                          J E Harlm Ck Del Dit

     The undersigned being duly sworn states that as stenographer to the Commissioner to the Five Civilized Tribes, she made the above copy, and that the same is a true and correct copy of the instrument now on file in this office.

                                          Mary Tabor Mallory

Subscribed and sworn to before me the 15th.day of January 1907.
                                          Chas E Webster
                                                 Notary Public.

Cherokee Intermarried White 1906
Volume II

◇◇◇◇◇

E.C.M.   Cherokee 4102.

DEPARTMENT OF THE INTERIOR,

COMMISSIONER TO THE FIVE CIVILIZED TRIBES.

In the matter of the application for the enrollment of GARRETT G. JAMES as a citizen by intermarriage of the Cherokee Nation.

D E C I S I O N

THE RECORDS OF THIS OFFICE SHOW: That at Vinita, Indian Territory, October 3, 1900, application was received by the Commission to the Five Civilized Tribes for the enrollment of Garrett g. James as a citizen by intermarriage of the Cherokee Nation. Further proceedings in the matter of said application were had at Muskogee, Indian Territory, September 22, 1902, and January 3, 1907.

THE EVIDENCE IN THIS CASE SHOWS: That the applicant herein, Garrett G. James, a white man, was married in accordance with Cherokee law May 13, 1875, to his wife, Mary E. A. James, nee Hudson, who was at the time of said marriage a recognized citizen by blood of the Cherokee Nation, who is identified on the Cherokee authenticated tribal roll of 1880, Delaware District, at No. 1411, as a native Cherokee, and whose name appears on the approved partial roll of citizens by blood of the Cherokee Nation, opposite No. 9909. It is further shown that since said marriage the said Garrett G. James and Mary e. A. James have resided together as husband and wife, and continuously lived in the Cherokee Nation up to and including September 1, 1902. Said applicant is identified on the Cherokee authenticated tribal roll of 1880, and the Cherokee census roll of 1896, as an intermarried citizen of the Cherokee Nation.

IT IS, THEREFORE, ORDERED AND ADJUDGED: That in accordance with the decision of the Supreme Court of the United States, dated November 5, 1906, in the case of Daniel Red Bird et al., vs. the United States, Nos. 125, 126, 127 and 128, the said applicant, Garrett G. James is entitled, under the provision of Section twenty-one, of the Act of Congress approved June 28, 1898 (30 Stats., 495), to enrollment as a citizen by intermarriage of the Cherokee Nation, and his application for enrollment as such is accordingly granted.

                                         Tams Bixby
                                              Commissioner.

Dated at Muskogee, Indian Territory,
this   JAN 19 1907

◇◇◇◇◇

Cherokee Intermarried White 1906
Volume II

Department of the Interior.
COMMISSIONER TO THE FIVE CIVILIZED TRIBES.

In the matter of the death of **Garrett G. James** a citizen of the **Cherokee** Nation, who formerly resided at or near **Fairland**, Ind. Ter., and died on the **12** day of **November**, **1906**

AFFIDAVIT OF RELATIVE.

Indian Territory }
Western District

I, **Jesse P. James**, on oath state that I am **21** years of age and a citizen by **blood**, of the **Cherokee** Nation; that my postoffice address is **Fairland**, Ind. Ter.; that I am **Son** of **Garrett G. James** who was a citizen, by **intermarriage**, of the **Cherokee** Nation and that said **Garrett G. James** died on the **12** day of **November**, **1906**

                       Jesse P. James

WITNESSES TO MARK:

Subscribed and sworn to before me this **11** day of **May**, **1907**

                       CG James
      My Commission expires Sept 7th. 1908   Notary Public.

AFFIDAVIT OF ACQUAINTANCE.

Northern District }
Indian Territory

I, **Francis M Conner**, on oath state that I am **55** years of age, and a citizen by **intermarriage** of the **Cherokee** Nation; that my postoffice address is **FAIRLAND IND. TER.**, Ind. Ter.; that I was personally acquainted with **Garrett G James** who was a citizen, by **intermarriage**, of the **Cherokee** Nation; and that said **Garrett G. James** died on the **12** day of **November**, **1906**

                       Francis M Conner

WITNESSES TO MARK:

Cherokee Intermarried White 1906
Volume II

Subscribed and sworn to before me this **11**   day of **May**   , 1907

CG James

My Commission expires Sept 7th. 1908   Notary Public.

◇◇◇◇◇◇

Cherokee
4102

Muskogee, Indian Territory, December 27, 1906.

Garrett G. James,
    Fairland, Indian Territory.

Dear Sir:

    November 6, 1906, the United States Supreme Court held that white persons who intermarried with Cherokee citizens according to Cherokee law prior to November 1, 1875, are entitled to enrollment and allotments of land as citizens of the Cherokee Nation.

    You are advised that to properly determine your right to enrollment as a citizen by intermarriage of the Cherokee Nation, it will be necessary for you to appear before the Commissioner for the purpose of giving testimony as to the date of your marriage and whether or not your wife, by reason of your marriage to whom you claim the right to enrollment as a citizen of the Cherokee Nation, was a recognized citizen of the Cherokee Nation at the time of your marriage to her, and whether or not you were married to her in accordance with Cherokee laws.

    You are, therefore, directed to appear before the Commissioner at Muskogee, Indian Territory, at 9 o'clock A. M., on Friday, January 4, 1907, and give testimony as above indicated.

                      Respectfully,

JMH   Acting Commissioner.

◇◇◇◇◇◇

Cherokee Intermarried White 1906
Volume II

Cherokee
4102.

Muskogee, Indian Territory, January 19, 1907.

W. W. Hastings,
    Attorney for the Cherokee Nation,
        Muskogee, Indian Territory.

Dear Sir:

    There is enclosed herewith a copy of the decision of the Commissioner to the Five Civilized Tribes, dated January 19, 1907, granting the application for the enrollment of Garrett G. James, as a citizen by intermarriage of the Cherokee Nation.

Respectfully,

Commissioner.

Incl. C-23
LMC

◇◇◇◇◇◇

Cherokee 4102.   W.W. HASTINGS.   OFFICE OF   H.M. VANCE.
                             ATTORNEY.   SECRETARY.

Attorney for the Cherokee Nation,
MUSKOGEE, I. T.

January 19, 1907.

The Commissioner to the Five Civilized Tribes,
    Muskogee, Indian Territory.

Sir:

    Receipt is acknowledged of the testimony and of your decision enrolling Garrett G. James as a citizen by intermarriage of the Cherokee Nation. Time for protesting said decision is waived and I consent that said person may be placed upon the schedule immediately.

Respectfully,
W. W. Hastings
Attorney for Cherokee Nation.

◇◇◇◇◇◇

Cherokee Intermarried White 1906
Volume II

Cherokee
4102

Muskogee, Indian Territory, January 21, 1907.

Garrett G. James,
    Fairland, Indian Territory.

Dear Sir:

    There is enclosed herewith a copy of the decision of the Commissioner to the Five Civilized Tribes, dated January 19, 1907, granting the application for your enrollment as a citizen by intermarriage of the Cherokee Nation.

    You will be advised when your name has been placed upon the schedule of citizens of the Cherokee Nation and approved by the Secretary of the Interior.

                      Respectfully,

E.R.C.   Commissioner.
Enc. E.C. 5.

◇◇◇◇◇

Muskogee, Indian Territory, April 8, 1907.

Garrett G. James,
    Fairland, Indian Territory.

Dear Sir:

    Your marriage license and certificate filed in the matter of your application for enrollment as a citizen by intermarriage of the Cherokee Nation, is returned to you herewith, copies of the same being retained in this office.

                        Respectfully,

Incl. P-4-8   Acting Commissioner.
  MMP

Cherokee Intermarried White 1906
Volume II

Cher IW 39
Trans from Cher 4261 3-13-07

◇◇◇◇◇◇

E.C.M.

DEPARTMENT OF THE INTERIOR,

COMMISSIONER TO THE FIVE CIVILIZED TRIBES.

In the matter of the application for the enrollment of

ALMYRA V. TYNER

as a citizen by intermarriage of the Cherokee Nation.

CHEROKEE 4261

◇◇◇◇◇◇

_B_

DEPARTMENT OF THE INTERIOR,
COMMISSION TO THE FIVE CIVILIZED TRIBES,
BARTLESVILLE, IT., OCTOBER 9th, 1900.

In the matter of the application of Reuben R. Tyner for the enrollment of himself, wife and children as citizens of the Cherokee Nation; said Tyner being sworn by Commissioner C. R. Breckinridge, and examined by the Commission, testified as follows:

Q What is your name? A Reuben R. Tyner.
Q You making application for the enrollment of anybody besides yourself? A Family.
Q What does your family consist of? A Wife and children.
Q What is your wife's name? A Almyre[sic].
Q How many children have you? A We have with us five I beliee.
Q What is the name of the oldest one? A 19 is the oldest.
Q What is his name? A Weaver Tyner.
Q Girl or boy? A Boy.
Q Next one? A Laura.
Q How old is Laura? A 16.
Q Next one? A Next one is Maud.
Q How old is Maud? A She is 12.
Q The next one? [sic] Lew Wallace.
Q How old is that child? A He is 10.

31

Cherokee Intermarried White 1906
Volume II

Q Next one? A I belive[sic] that is all.
Q You are making application for your wife as a citizen by blood.[sic] A No, sir.
Q Citizen by intermarriage? A Yes, sir.
Q What is your age? A 59.
Q What is your post office address? A Austin.
Q Indian Territory? A Yes, sir.
Q Are you a resident of the Indian Territory? A Yes, sir.
Q How long have you resided in the Indian Territory? A All my life.
Q In the Cherokee nation? A Yes, sir.
Q Have you been outside of the Indian Territory for the past three years? A No, sir.
Q You make application for your wife as an intermarried citizen of the Cherokee Nation? A Yes, sir.
Q Is she a white woman? A Yes, sir.
Q When did you marry her? A I married her July 3d, 1868.
Q Where? A At Fort Gibson, Illinois District.
Q Married in accordance with the laws of the Cherokee Nation? [sic] Judge Thornton married us.
Q What is your father's name? A Jackson.
Q Is he living? A No, sir.
Q What is your mother's name? A Her name was Delila Seibolt.
Q Are they both citizens of the Cherokee Nation? A Yes, sir.
Q How long have they been dead? A My mother died when I was three years old; father died in '61 of[sic] 62.
Q What district in the Therokee[sic] Nation did they belong? A Put on the roll in Cooweescoowee, that is father, mother died in Going Snake.
Q How old is your wife? Almyra Tyner? A She is just 49.
Q What was her father's name? A William Irons.
Q Is he living? A No, sir.
Q What is your wife's mother's name? A Her mother's name is, I do not know what her name is.
Q Her maiden name was Irons, was it? A Yes, sir.
Q Her parents are both white people? A Yes, sir.
Q Never made any claims to Cherokee citizenship by blood? A Yes, sir.
Q You are the father of these four children? A Yes, sir.
Q Almyra Tyner is the mother of them? A Yes, sir.
Q They all live at your home? A Yes, sir.
Q Have you any evidence of your marriage to Almyra Tyner? A None whatever, except these documents I showed you.

    1880 enrollment; page 189, #2981, Reuben Tyner, (Big), Cooweeccowee[sic].
    1880 enrollment; page 189, #2982, A. V. Tyner, Cooweescoowee.
    1896 enrollment; page 271, #4877, Rheubin Tyner,   "
    1896 enrollment; page 326, #995, Almira V. Tyner, Cooweescoowee
    1896 enrollment; page 271, #4881, Weaver Tyner, Cooweescoowee.
    1896 enrollment; page 271, #4882, Laura Tyner, Cooweescoowee.
    1896 enrollment; page 271, #4993, Maud Tyner, Cooweescoowee.

Cherokee Intermarried White 1906
Volume II

1896 enrollment; page 271, #4884, Leaw W. Tyner, Cooweescoowee.

COMMISSION: The name of the applicatn[sic], Reuben R. Tyner, is found upon the 1880 and 1896 rolls of the Cherokee Nation as a native Cherokee. He is identified as the applicant, and his[sic] established satisfactory proof of his residence in the Indian territory The name of his wife, Almyra Tyner is also found upon the 1880 and 1896 rolls of the Cherokee Nation as an intermarried white. The names of his fur minor children for whom application has been made, is found upon the 1896 roll as citizens of the Cherokee Nation. Satisfactory proof has been offered as to their residence in the Indian Territory. The applicant and his four minor children will be listed for enrollment as citizens by blood of the Cherokee Nation, and his wife, Almyra Tyner, as an intermarried citizen of the Cherokee Nation.

---oooOOOooo---

J. O. Rosson, being first duly sworn, states that as stenographer to the Commission to the Five Civilized Tribes, he correctly recorded the testimony and proceedings in this case, and that the foregoing is a true and complete transcript of his stenographic notes thereof.

J O Rosson

Subscribed and sworn to before me this 10th day of October, 1900.

CR Breckinridge

Commissioner.

◇◇◇◇◇

Cher # 4261

Department of the Interior,
Commission to the Five Civilized Tribes,
Muskogee, I. T., October 10, 1902.

In the matter of the application of REUBEN R. TYNER, for the enrollment of himself and his four children, WEAVER, LAURA, MAUD, and LEW WALLACE TYNER, as citizens by blood, and his wife ALMYRA V. TYNER, as a citizen by intermarriage, of the Cherokee Nation.

ALMYRA V. TYNER, called as a witness, being duly sworn and examined by the Commission, testified as follows:

Q Your full name is Almyra V. Tyner ? A Yes sir.
Q How old are you ? A I will be fifty three in December.
Q What is your post office ? A Ochelata.
Q It used to be Austin, did it ? A Yes sir.
Q You are a white woman ? A Yes sir.
Q You are on the roll of 1880 as an intermarried white ? A Yes sir.

Cherokee Intermarried White 1906
Volume II

Q What was your husband's name at that time ? A Reuben R. Tyner.
Q Have you and your husband Reuben R. Tyner been living together in the Cherokee Nation ever since 1880 ? A Yes sir.
Q Were you living together on the first day of last September ? A No sir; he is dead.
Q When did he die ? A 24th of July last.
Q You lived with him then up to the time of his death ? A Yes sir.
Q You were never married but the once ? A No sir.
Q Was your husband ever married before he married you ? A No sir.
Q You[sic] four children are living at home with you ? A Yes sir. The youngest one Lew Wallace is dead.
Q When did he die ? A Last December.
Q The others are at home with you ? A Yes sir.
Q There are three at home with you ? A Yes sir.

E. C. Bagwell, on oath states that, as stenographer to the Commission to the Five Civilized Tribes, he correctly recorded the testimony and proceedings had in the above entitled cause, and that the foregoing is an accurate transcript of his stenographic notes thereof.

E.C. Bagwell

Subscribed and sworn to before me this October 17, 1902.

BC Jones
Notary Public.

◇◇◇◇◇

Cherokee No. 4261.

DEPARTMENT OF THE INTERIOR,

COMMISSIONER TO THE FIVE CIVILIZED TRIBES,

MUSKOGEE, INDIAN TERRITORY, JANUARY 4, 1907.

IN THE MATTER of the application for the enrollment of Almyra V. Tyner, as a citizen by intermarriage of the Cherokee Nation.

ALMYRA V. TYNER, being first duly sworn by Walter W. Chappell, Notary Public in the Western District of the Indian Territory, testified as follows:

EXAMINATION

ON BEHALF OF THE COMMISSIONER:

Cherokee Intermarried White 1906
Volume II

Q What is your name? A Almyra V. Tyner.
Q Your age, Mrs. Tyner? A Fifty-six, this last December.
Q What is your postoffice address? A Ochelata.
Q Is that in the Cherokee Nation? A Yes sir.
Q You claim to be a citizen of the Cherokee Nation by intermarriage, do you?
A Yes sir.
Q Through whom do you claim that right? A Reuben R. Tyner.
Q Is Reuben R. Tyner living? A No sir.
Q When did he die? A 1902, July 24th.
Q What was his citizenship? A Cherokee by blood.
Q When were you and he married? A I can't recollect the date.
Q Were you married under a Cherokee license?
A Married by a Judge, - Amos Thornton married us.
Q Did you secure a Cherokee license? A No sir, - he was a Cherokee citizen by blood.
Q What was your maiden name? A Almyra Irons.

ON BEHALF OF THE COMMISSIONER:

The applicant offers in evidence a marriage certificate which has been kept as a family record and which shows "that R. R. Tyner and Almira Irons were united by me in holy matrimony at my residence on the 3rd day of July in the year of our Lord 1868, in presence of my family.

(Signed) Amos Thornton,
Judge of Illinois District, C. N."
Same will be filed herewith and made a part of the records in this case.
The applicant also offers in evidence the affidavits of George B. Keeler and George W. Tyner, executed on the 8th day of October, 1900, and same will be filed herewith and made part of the records in this case, and considered for what they are worth?[sic]

Q When was this marriage certificate you offer in evidence made? A I don't know just what year it was written, - I think it was, - -
Q About how many years ago? A I think in 1880 sometime, - about 1881.
Q Who filled it out? A My husband did. It is his writing.
Q Did he copy this from the original? A I don't know.
Q Did you ever see the original certificate that was issued by Judge Amos Thornton?
A Why, there wasn't anything issued as I know of, because he told us when we were married that he would put it on record.
Q Had either you or your husband been married prior to your marriage in 1868?
A No sir.
Q After your marriage where did you and your husband live? A Lived on Bird Creek three years, and then moved on Caney and lived there on the place we are now living on 32 years.
Q Have you lived continuously in the Cherokee Nation since that marriage? A Yes sir.
Q You lived together then continuously up until his death? A Yes sir.

Cherokee Intermarried White 1906
Volume II

ON BEHALF OF THE COMMISSIONER:

Said Reuben R. Tyner, is identified on the authenticated Cherokee tribal roll of 1880 and Cherokee census roll of 1896, Coowees Coowee District, opposite Nos. 2981 and 4877, respectively, as a Cherokee by blood.
The record of marriage certificates for Illinois District furnished this office by the Cherokee authorities does not cover the year 1868, and no record of the certificate of marriage issued by Amos Thornton, Judge of Illinois District, Cherokee Nation, can be found.

Q Have you married since the death of your husband? A No sir.

ON BEHALF OF THE COMMISSIONER:

The applicant is identified on the authenticated Cherokee tribal roll of 1880 and Cherokee census roll of 1896, Coowees Coowee District, opposite No. 2982 and 995, respectively, as an intermarried white.

(Witness dismissed).

GEORGE B. KEELER, being first duly sworn by Walter W. Chappell, Notary Public in the Western District of the Indian Territory, testified as follows:

EXAMINATION
ON BEHALF OF THE COMMISSIONER:

Q What is your name? A George B. Keeler.
Q Age and postoffice address? [sic] Fifty-six; Bartlesville, I.T.
Q Are you a citizen of the Cherokee Nation? A I am.
Q Are you acquainted with the applicant, Almyra V. Tyner? A I am.
Q Were you acquainted with her husband Reuben R. Tyner, now deceased? A I was.
Q When did you first become acquainted with them? A Lived on Caney River in Coowees Coowee District, about eight miles south of Bartlesville, where Bartlesville is now; at that time there was no Bartlesville.
Q Did they live continuously together until Mr. Tyner's death? A Yes sir.
Q Lived in the Cherokee nation during that time? A Yes sir.
Q You were not acquainted with them at the time of their marriage? A No sir.

(Witness dismissed).

I, S. T. Wright, stenographer to the Commissioner to the Five Civilized Tribes, on oath, state that I recorded the testimony and proceedings had in the above entitled cause on January 4, 1907, and that the above and foregoing is a true and correct transcript of my stenographic notes thereof taken on said date.

Cherokee Intermarried White 1906
Volume II

               S.T. Wright

Subscribed and sworn to before me this January 5, 1907.

               Edward Merrick
               NOTARY PUBLIC.

◇◇◇◇◇

4261

(CERTIFIED COPY)

"What therefore God hath joined together, let not man put asunder."

THIS IS TO CERTIFY

That R. R. Tyner & Almira Irons

      were united by me, in

HOLY MATRIMONY

At My Residence on the 3rd day of July, in the year of our Lord 1868.

In Presence of My Family

Signed Amos Thornton

    Judger of Illinois District C. N.

Therefore shall a man leave his father and his mother and shall cleave unto his wife and they shall be one flesh. Gen. II, 24.

 (Back)

BIRTHS.

R. R. Ryner[sic], Dec. 17th, 1840
Almira Tyner, " 5th, 1850
Fannie Tyner, Nov. 26th, 1869
Emma Tyner, May 2nd, 1871
T. J. Tyner, June 27th, 1873
G. E. Tyner, April 1st, 1875
Flora May Tyner, Jan. 31st, 1877
Leonard P. Tyner, May 29th, 1879

Cherokee Intermarried White 1906
Volume II

James B. W. Tyner, July 28th, 1881
Laura A. Tyner, April 29th, 1884
Frank P. Tyner, May 11th, 1886.
Lula Maud Tyner, Sept. 18th, 1888
Lew Wallace Tyner, Aug. 3rd, 1890.

I, S. T. Wright, on oath, state that the above is a true and correct copy of marriage certificate, purporting to be the family record, and to show the date of the marriage of R. R. Tyner and Almira Irons on July 3, 1868, and which was filed for consideration in connection with the application of Almyra Tyner for enrollment as a citizen of the Cherokee Nation by intermarriage. (Original of this certificate was returned to the applicant).

ST Wright

Subscribed and sworn to before me
this 5th day of January, 1907.

Edward Merrick
NOTARY PUBLIC.

◇◇◇◇◇

United States of America) ss
Indian Territory)
Northern District) ss

George B. Keeler of lawful age who after being duly sworn according to, law says that he is well and personally acquainted with R. R. Tyner and his wife Elmira[sic] who are Citizens of the cherokee[sic] Nation and has known them for the last 29 years past having lived in same vicinity with them during all of said time and knows that said R.R. Tyner and Elmira Tyner have lived together as man and wife for 29 years last past in the Cherokee Nation Indian Territory

Geo B Keeler

Subscribed and sworn to before me this 8th day of October 1900

CR Keeler
My Commission Expires Mch 25" 1901   Notary Public

◇◇◇◇◇

United States of America)
)
Indian Territory) ss
)
Nortern[sic] District)
)
)

George Tyner of lawful age) who after being duly sworn according to law says that he is well and personally acquainted with R. R. Tyner and his wife Emira[sic] Tyner and has

Cherokee Intermarried White 1906
Volume II

known them and lived in the same neighborhood with them for the 29 years last past, and knows that said R. R. Tyner and Elmira Tyner has lived together as man and wife for 29 years last past in the Cherokee Nation, Indian Territory

Geo W Tyner

Subscribed and sworn to before me this 8th day of October 1900

My Commission Expires
Mch 25" 1901

CR Keeler
Notary Public

◇◇◇◇◇

E C M   Cherokee 4261

DEPARTMENT OF THE INTERIOR,
COMMISSIONER TO THE FIVE CIVILIZED TRIBES.

In the matter of the application for the enrollment of Almyra V. Tyner as a citizen by intermarriage of the Cherokee Nation.

D E C I S I O N.

THE RECORDS OF THIS OFFICE SHOW: That at Bartlesville, Indian Territory, October 9, 1900, Reuben R. Tyner appeared before the Commission to the Five Civilized Tribes, and made application for the enrollment of his wife, Almyra V. Tyner, as a citizen by intermarriage, and for the enrollment of himself, et al. as citizens by blood of the Cherokee Nation. The application for the enrollment of the said Reuben R. Tyner, et al. as citizens by blood of the Cherokee Nation has been heretofore disposed of, and their rights to enrollment will not be considered in this decision. Further proceedings in the matter of said application were had at Muskogee, Indian Territory, October 10, 1902 and January 4, 1907.

THE EVIDENCE OF THIS CASE SHOWS: That the applicant herein, Almyra V. Tyner, a white woman, married on July 3, 1868, one Reuben R. Tyner, who was at the time of said marriage a recognized citizen by blood of the Cherokee Nation, and whose name appears upon the Cherokee Authenticated Tribal Roll of 1880, and the Cherokee Census Roll of 1896; that from the time of said marriage until the death of the said Reuben R. Tyner, which occurred July 24, 1902, the said Reuben R. Tyner and Almyra V. Tyner resided together as husband and wife in the Cherokee Nation; that since the death of the said Reuben R. Tyner, the said Almyra V. Tyner has remained unmarried and continuously lived in the Cherokee Nation up to and including September 1, 1902. Said Almyra V. Tyner is identified on the Cherokee Authenticated Tribal Roll of 1880 and the Cherokee Census Roll of 1896 as an intermarried citizen of the Cherokee Nation.

Cherokee Intermarried White 1906
Volume II

IT IS THEREFORE ORDERED AND ADJUDGED: That in accordance with the decision of the Supreme Court of the United States dated November 5, 1906, in the case of Daniel Red Bird, et al. vs. the United States under the provision of Section 21, of the Act of Congress approved June 28, 1898, (30th. Stat. 495) Almyra V. Tyner is entitled to enrollment as a citizen by intermarriage of the Cherokee Nation, and her application for enrollment as such is accordingly granted.

              Tams Bixby
                Commissioner.

Dated at Muskogee, Indian Territory,
this JAN 16 1907

◇◇◇◇◇

Cherokee
4261

           Muskogee, Indian Territory, December 27, 1906.

Almyra V. Tyner,
  Ochelata, Indian Territory.

Dear Madam:

  November 6, 1906, the United States Supreme Court held that white persons who intermarried with Cherokee citizens according to Cherokee law prior to November 1, 1875, are entitled to enrollment and allotments of land as citizens of the Cherokee Nation.

  You are advised that to properly determine your right to enrollment as a citizen by intermarriage of the Cherokee Nation, it will be necessary for you to appear before the Commissioner for the purpose of giving testimony as to the date of your marriage and whether or not your husband, by reason of your marriage to whom you claim the right to enrollment as a citizen by intermarriage of the Cherokee Nation, was a recognized Cherokee citizen at the time of your marriage to him.

  You are, therefore, directed to appear before the Commissioner at Muskogee, Indian Territory, at 9 o'clock A. M., on Friday, January 4, 1907, and give testimony as above indicated.

              Respectfully,

J.M.H.   Acting Commissioner.

◇◇◇◇◇

Cherokee Intermarried White 1906
Volume II

Cherokee 4261

Muskogee, Indian Territory, January 17, 1907.

W. W. Hastings,
    Attorney for the Cherokee Nation,
        Muskogee, Indian Territory.

Dear Sir:

    There is enclosed herewith copy of the decision of the Commissioner to the Five Civilized Tribes, dated January 16, 1907, granting the application for the enrollment of Almyra V. Tyner as a citizen by intermarriage of the Cherokee Nation.

        Respectfully,

Encl. I-5   Commissioner.
RPI

◇◇◇◇◇

| W.W. HASTINGS. ATTORNEY. | OFFICE OF | H.M. VANCE. SECRETARY. | Cherokee 4261. |

Attorney for the Cherokee Nation,
MUSKOGEE, I. T.

January 18, 1907.

The Commissioner
    to the Five Civilized Tribes,
        Muskogee, Indian Territory.

Sir:

    Receipt is acknowledged of the testimony and of your decision enrolling Almyra V. Tyner as a citizen by intermarriage of the Cherokee Nation. Time for protesting said decision is waived and I consent that said person may be placed upon the schedule immediately.

                              W. W. Hastings
                              Attorney for Cherokee Nation.

◇◇◇◇◇

Cherokee Intermarried White 1906
Volume II

Cherokee
4261

Muskogee, Indian Territory, January 19, 1907.

Almyra V. Tyner,
    Ochelata, Indian Territory.

Dear Madam:

There is enclosed herewith copy of the decision of the Commissioner to the Five Civilized Tribes, dated January 16, 1907, granting the application for your enrollment as a citizen by intermarriage of the Cherokee Nation.

Respectfully,

Commissioner.

Encl. I-40

RPI

Cher IW 40
Trans from Cher 4391 3-13-07

◇◇◇◇◇

E.C.M.

DEPARTMENT OF THE INTERIOR,

COMMISSIONER TO THE FIVE CIVILIZED TRIBES.

In the matter of the application for the enrollment of

WILLIAM MARTIN

as a citizen by intermarriage of the Cherokee Nation.

CHEROKEE 4391.

◇◇◇◇◇

Cherokee Intermarried White 1906
Volume II

Department of the Interior,
Commission to the Five Civilized Tribes,
Nowata, I. T. October, 15th 1900.

In the matter of the application of Sarah E. Martin for the enrollment of herself, husband and two children. She having been duly sworn before the Commission testified as follows:

Q What is your name[sic] [sic] Sarah E. Martin.
Q How old are you? A. 43.
Q What is your post office address? A. Coffeyville
Q What district do you live in? A. Cooweescoowee.
Q Are you a recognized citixen[sic] of the Cherokee Nation? [sic] Yes sir.
Q By blood? A. Yes sir.
Q What degree of blood do your[sic] cliam[sic]? A. My mother and foather[sic] were both Cherokee Indians.
Q Are you a full blood? A. No sir a 1/4
Q For whom do you apply? A. Myself, my husband and two children.
Q What is your husbands[sic] name? A. William Martin.
Q White man? A. Yes sir.
Q Why is he not here himself? A. He is at home.
Q How old is he? A. 70.
Q When were you married to him? A Been married 28 years.
His name is on the 1880 authenticated roll is it? A Yes sir.
Q What is the name of your children? A. William Penn.
Q How old is he? [sic] 17
Q You say that you have one in jail? A. Yes sir.
Q Who is it? A. Joel.
Q How old is Joel? A. 24.
Q Is he married? A Yes sir.
Q Is he and his wife living together? A. No sir they are seperated[sic].
Q Does he live with you? A. Yes sir he did before he was arrested.
Q Has he any middle name? A. Yes sir Joel T.
Q Are these the only two children that you have? A. Yes sir.
Q. How long hve[sic] you lived in the Cherokee Nation? A. Born and raised here.
Q Lived here all your life? A. Yes sir.
Q Have you and your husband lived together since your marriage? A. Yes sir.
Q Has he any middle name? A. Just William.

1880 roll, page 136, No. 1789, Bill Martin, Cooweescoowee,
1880	"	"	136	"	1790	Sarah Martin,	Do	N. C.
1896	"	"	315	"	678	Bill Martin	"	
1896	"	"	214	"	3243	Sarah Martin	"	
1896	"	"	214	"	3244	Joel T. Martin	"	
1880	"	"	136	"	1792	Joel Martin	"	
1896	"	"	214	"	3246	Wm. P. Martin	"	

Cherokee Intermarried White 1906
Volume II

Q You say that the reason that Joel T. Martin is not here to enter his own application for enrollment is because he is in prison at Muskogee and cannot come? A. Yes sir.
The name of the applicant Sarah E. Martin appears on the 1880 authenticated roll and on the census roll of 1896 as Sarah Martin a Cherokee by blood. The name of William Martin, her husband appears on the 1880 authenticated roll and the census roll of 1896 as Bill Martin and the name of her oldest son Joel T. Martin appears on the 1880 authenticated roll as Joel T. Martin and on the census roll of 1896 as Joel T Martin; and the son William P. Martin also appears on the census roll of 1896 as William P. Martin. The[sic] all being duly identified according to the page and number of the roll as indicated in the testimony, and having made satisfaoctry[sic] proof as to their residence, Sarah E. Martin, William P. Martin and Joel T. Martin will be listed for enrollment as Cherokees by blood and the name of her husband, William Martin will be listed for enrollment as a citizen by intermarriage.

Chas. von Wewie[sic] being dult[sic] sworn states that as stenographer to the Commission to the five[sic] Civilized Tribes he reported in full all the proceedings had in the above entitled cause and that the foregoing is a true, correct and full transcript of his stenographic notes of said proceedings.

Chas von Weise

Subscribed and sworn to before me this the 15th Of October, 1900.

TB Needles
Commissioner.

◇◇◇◇◇

Cher-4391

DEPARTMENT OF THE INTERIOR,
Commission to the Five Civilized Tribes,
Muskogee, I.T., October 23, 1902.

In the matter of the application of William Martin for enrollment as a citizen by intermarriage of the Cherokee nation[sic], and for the enrollment of his wife Sarah E., and his children William P. and Joel T., as citizens by blood of the Cherokee Nation.

William Martin being first duly sworn and examined by the Commission, testified as follows:

Q William Martin is your name? A Yes sir.
Q How old are you? A 72 years old.
Q What is your postoffice address? A Coffeyville, Kansas.
Q Are you a white man? A Yes sir.
Q Is your name on the 1880 roll as an adopted citizen? A I am on all the rolls that's here.
Q Is your name on the 1880 Cherokee roll as an adopted white citizen? A I expect it is.
Q What is your wife's name? A Sarah E.

Cherokee Intermarried White 1906
Volume II

Q Was she you wife in 1880? A I was married in 1873.
Q To Sarah? A Yes sir.
Q Is Sarah the wife through whom you claim citizenship? A Yes sir.
Q Have you and your wife Sarah E. been living together ever since you were married? A Yes sir.
Q You never have been separated, have you? A No sir.
Q You are living together now? A Yes sir.
Q Have you lived in the Cherokee nation[sic] during all that time? A Ever since 1867.
Q You never lived anywhere else during that time? A No.
Q How many children have you? A Six-one dead; five living.
Q How many have you at home with you? A Two.
Q William P. and Joel T? A Yes, and James Robert.
Q How old is James Robert? A He is 23.
Q He enrolled himself didn't he? A Yes sir.
Q Where is Joel T. Martin? A At home.
Q How long has Joel T. resided in the Cherokee nation[sic]? A Born and raised here.
Q Has he lived in the Cherokee nation all his life? A All his life.
Q Joel is married isn't he A He was, but he isn't now; he has a child.
Q Is his wife dead? A No, she left him and married another man.
Q What is his child's name? A William Argent.
Q Your son got a letter from the Commission asking him to send his marriage license and certificate to the Commission, and also the birth affidavit for his child William Argent. Do you know whether he did it? A I don't know whether he die it or not.
Q Will you tell him about it when you get home? A Yes sir.

-----o---

Frances R. Lane upon oath states that as stenographer to the Commission to the Five Civilized Tribes she correctly recorded the testimony in the above cause, and that the foregoing is an accurate transcript of her stenographic notes thereof.

Frances R Lane

Subscribed and sworn to before me this November 3, 1902.

BC Jones
Notary Public.

Cherokee Intermarried White 1906
Volume II

CHEROKEE NO. 4391

DEPARTMENT OF THE INTERIOR
Commissioner to the Five Civilized Tribes
Muskogee, Indian Territory

In the matter of the application for the enrollment of William Martin as a citizen by intermarriage of the Cherokee Nation

The applicant being first duly sworn by Walter W. Chappell a Notary Public for the Western District, testified as follows:

Q What is your name? A William Martin
Q Your age? A I am going on 77
Q Your postoffice address? A Childers
Q Is that in the Cherokee Nation? A Yes sir.
Q What district[sic] A Nowata--Cooweescoowee District
Q You claim to be a citizen by intermarriage of the Cherokee Nation[sic] A. Yes sir.
Q Through whom do you claim that right? A By my wife
Q What is her name? A Sarah E. Walker, daughter of George Walker.
Q Is she living? A Yes sir
Q What is her citizenship? A She's a Cherokee
Q Cherokee by blood? A Yes sir, born and raised there.
Q When were you and she married?

The applicant offers in evidence an instrument which shows that he was married under Cherokee license on March 13, 1873, same being filed herewith and made a part of the record in this case

On Page 10, Book A, Record of Marriage Licenses Cooweescoowee District, appears the following:
"Mch. Issued license to Wm. Martin citizen of the U.S. to marry Sarah Walker, citizen of the Cherokee Nation
Issued by John Myers, District Clerk. Married by Rev. W. N. Adams, March 13, 1873"

The said Sarah E. Martin nee Walker, is included in the partial approved roll of citizens by blood of the Cherokee Nation opposite No. 10488

Q Were either you or your wife married prior to the time you intermarried? A No sir.
Q Where did you live subsequent to your marriage? A I lived down on Big Creek.
Q That is in the Cherokee Nation is it? A Yes sir.
Q Did you continuously live there until September 1, 1902[sic] A I have been there ever since I have been in the Nation--'67
Q You have lived together continuously since you were married have you? A Yes sir.

Cherokee Intermarried White 1906
Volume II

The applicant William Martin is identified on the authenticated Cherokee tribal roll of 1880 and Cherokee Census roll of 1896, Cooesscoowee[sic] District, opposite Nos. 1789 and 678 as an intermarried white.

Witness excused

Gertrude Hanna, being first duly sworn states on oath that she reported the proceedings had in the above numbered case and that the above and foregoing is a true and correct transcript of her stenographic notes thereof stenographic notes taken therein, on January 3, 1907.

Gertrude Hanna

Subscribed and sworn to before me this 4th day of January, 1907

Walter W. Chappell
Notary Public.

◇◇◇◇◇

UNITED STATES OF AMERICA	I
	I
INDIAN TERRITORY	I (-: : ss : :-)
	I
NORTHERN DISTRICT	I

Mch.

Issued License to Wm Martin, citizen of the U.S. to marry Sarah Walker citizen of the C.N.
Issued by John Mayes, Dist. Clerk.

Married by Rev. Wm Adams, Mch. 13th" 1873.

Cherokee Nation, I.T.)
)
Coo-wee-scoo-wee District.)

This is to certify that the above is a true copy of the original record as found on page 10 in Book "A" Records of Marriage in the District of Coo-wee-scco-wee[sic].

In witness whreof[sic] I hereunto set my
hand and seal of office on this the 19th
day of July, A.D. 1897.

Joe M. Lahay, Clerk

Cherokee Intermarried White 1906
Volume II

(SEAL)   Coo-wee-scoo-wee District, C.N.

I, W.S. Stanfield a ~~duly commissioned~~ and acting Notary Public within and for the Northern District of the Indian Territory do hereby certify that the above and foregoing is a true and correct copy of the original certificate as made by Joe M. Lahay and filed in my office. That the original has been misplaced in my office some place, but that I preserved a copy and do now certify that the above and foregoing is a true and correct copy of the original certificate.
(SEAL)
In witness whereof I have hereunto set my hand and affixed my Notorial[sic] seal this the 5th day of Oct., 1900.   W. S. Stanfield
                                       Notary Public, My Commission
                                       expires Aug.2nd,1903. P.O.
                                                 Vinita, I.T.

This is to certify that the undersigned, being duly sworn, states that as stenographer to the Commissioner to the Five Civilized Tribes, she made the above and foregoing copy of certified copy of original record as found on page 10 in Book "A" Records of Marriage in the District of Coo-wee-scoo-wee, and that the same is a full, true and correct copy of the said certified copy of record now on file in this office.

                                         Sarah Waters

Subscribed and Sworn to before me this 15th day of January, 1907.

                                         Chas E Webster
                                         Notary Public.

                         ◇◇◇◇◇

E.C.M.   Cherokee 4391.

DEPARTMENT OF THE INTERIOR,

COMMISSIONER TO THE FIVE CIVILIZED TRIBES.

In the matter of the application for the enrollment of William Martin, as a citizen by intermarriage of the Cherokee Nation.

D E C I S I O N

THE RECORDS OF THIS OFFICE SHOW: That at Nowata, Indian Territory, October 14, 1900, application was received by the Commission to the Five Civilized Tribes, for the enrollment of William Martin as a citizen by intermarriage of the Cherokee Nation. Further proceedings in the matter of said application were had a Muskogee, Indian Territory, October 23, 1902, and January 3, 1907.

Cherokee Intermarried White 1906
Volume II

THE EVIDENCE IN THIS CASE SHOWS: That the applicant herein, William Martin, a white man, was married in accordance with Cherokee law March 13, 1873, to his wife, Sarah E. Martin, nee Walker, a recognized citizen by blood of the Cherokee Nation, who is identified on the Cherokee authenticated tribal roll of 1880, Cooweescoowee District, at No. 1790, as a native Cherokee, and whose name is included in the approved partial roll of citizens by blood of the Cherokee Nation, opposite No. 10488. It is further shown that since said marriage the said William Martin and Sarah E. Martin have resided together as husband and wife, and continuously lived in the Cherokee Nation up to and including September 1, 1902. Said applicant is identified on the Cherokee authenticated tribal roll of 1880, and the Cherokee census roll of 1896, as an intermarried citizen of the Cherokee Nation.

IT IS, THEREFORE, ORDERED AND ADJUDGED: That in accordance with the decision of the Supreme Court of the United States, dated November 5, 1906, in the cases of Daniel Red Bird et al., vs. the United States, Nos. 125, 126, 127 and 128, the said applicant, William Martin, is entitled, under the provision of Section 21, of the Act of Congress approved June 28, 1898 (30 Stat., 495), to enrollment as a citizen by intermarriage of the Cherokee Nation, and his application for enrollment as such is accordingly granted.

                                            Tams Bixby
                                            Commissioner.

Dated at Muskogee, Indian Territory,
this   JAN 19 1907

◇◇◇◇◇

Cherokee
4391

                                      Muskogee, Indian Territory, December 27, 1906

William Martin,
        Ruby, Indian Territory.

Dear Sir:

        November 6, 1906, the United States Supreme Court held that white persons who intermarried with Cherokee citizens according to Cherokee law prior to November 1, 1875, are entitled to enrollment and allotments of land as citizens of the Cherokee Nation.

        You are advised that to properly determine your right to enrollment as a citizen by intermarriage of the Cherokee Nation, it will be necessary for you to appear before the Commissioner for the purpose of giving testimony as to the date of your marriage and whether or not your wife, by reason of your marriage to whom you claim the right to enrollment as a citizen of the Cherokee Nation, was a recognized citizen of the Cherokee

Cherokee Intermarried White 1906
Volume II

Nation at the time of your marriage to her, and whether or not you were married to her in accordance with Cherokee laws.

You are, therefore, directed to appear before the Commissioner at Muskogee, Indian Territory, at 9 o'clock A. M., on Friday, January 4, 1907, and give testimony as above indicated.

Respectfully,

JMH

Acting Commissioner.

◇◇◇◇◇

Cherokee
4391

Muskogee, Indian Territory, January 19, 1907.

W. W. Hastings,
    Attorney for the Cherokee Nation,
        Muskogee, Indian Territory.

Dear Sir:

There is enclosed herewith a copy of the decision of the Commissioner to the Five Civilized Tribes, dated January 19, 1907, granting the application for the enrollment of William Martin, as a citizen by intermarriage of the Cherokee Nation.

Respectfully,

Commissioner.

Incl. C-13
LMC

◇◇◇◇◇

Cherokee 4391.   W.W.HASTINGS, ATTORNEY.   OFFICE OF   H.M. VANCE, SECRETARY.

Attorney for the Cherokee Nation,
MUSKOGEE, I. T.

January 19, 1907.

The Commissioner to the Five Civilized Tribes,
    Muskogee, Indian Territory.

Sir:

Receipt is acknowledged of the testimony and of your decision enrolling William Martin as a citizen by intermarriage of the Cherokee Nation. Time for protesting said

Cherokee Intermarried White 1906
Volume II

decision is waived and I consent that said person may be placed upon the schedule immediately.

Respectfully,
W. W. Hastings
Attorney for Cherokee Nation.

◇◇◇◇◇

Cherokee
4391

Muskogee, Indian Territory, January 21, 1907.

William Martin,
    Ruby, Indian Territory.

Dear Sir:

    There is enclosed herewith a copy of the decision of the Commissioner to the Five Civilized Tribes, dated January 19, 1907, granting the application for your enrollment as a citizen by intermarriage of the Cherokee Nation.

    You will be advised when your name has been placed upon a schedule of citizens of the Cherokee Nation and approved by the Secretary of the Interior.

Respectfully,

E.R.C.   Commissioner.
Enc. E.C. 7.

◇◇◇◇◇

Muskogee, Indian Territory, April 8, 1907.

William Martin,
    Childers, Indian Territory.

Dear Sir:

    Your marriage license and certificate, filed in connection with your application for enrollment as a citizen by intermarriage of the Cherokee Nation, is returned to you herewith, copies of the same being retained in this office.

Respectfully,

Incl. P-4-9   Acting Commissioner.
MMP

Cherokee Intermarried White 1906
Volume II

Cher IW 41
Trans from Cher 4393 3-13-07

E.C.M.

DEPARTMENT OF THE INTERIOR,

COMMISSIONER TO THE FIVE CIVILIZED TRIBES.

In the matter of the application for the enrollment of

JAMES M. CHANEY

as a citizen by intermarriage of the Cherokee Nation.

CHEROKEE 4393.

Department of the Interior,
Commission to the Five Civilized Tribes,
Nowata, I.T., October 15, 1900.

In the matter of the application of James W[sic]. Chaney for the enrollment of himself, wife and 6 children as Cherokee citizens being sworn and examined by Commissioner Breckinridge he testified as follows:

Q What is your full name? A James M. Chaney.
Q How old are you? A 51.
Q What is your post-office? A Ruby.
Q In what district do you live, Cooweescoowee? A Yes sir/[sic]
Q Who is it you want to have enrolled, yourself and family? A Wife and children.
Q How many children? A 9 of them but some of them will have to come themselves I suppose.
Q How many have you got under 21 and unmarried? A I have got 6
Q Are you a Cherokee by blood? A Yes sir.
Q Let me see your marriage license and certificate A I have not got any.
Q When were you married? A 1874.
Q Have you been living with that wife ever since you were married to her? A Yes sir.
Q You are on the roll of 1880 them? A Yes sir
Q Give me your wife's name? A Julia. She may be on the roll Pinkie
Q How old is she? [sic] 44 years old.
Q She has no middle name? A I think there is an A but I'm not positive.

Cherokee Intermarried White 1906
Volume II

Q They come[sic] times call her Pinkie? A Yes sir.
Q But her real name is Julia? A Yes sir
Q Was she born in the Cherokee Nation? A Yes sir
Q Lived here all her live? A Yes sir/[sic]
Q And married you in 1874? A Yes sir
Q Give me the name of her father? A John Brown.
Q Is he dead? A Yes sir.
Q Give me the name of her mother? A Sarah.
Q Is she dead? A Yes sir.
Q Now give me the names of your children? A These six children and their ages?
A (Produces list and hands to com'r)
Q The oldest one of these 6 is Eliza, 16 years old? A Yes sir
Q The next one is Mamie, she is 14 years old? A Yes sir
Q Next one is Della? A Yes sir
Q She is 12 years old? A Yes sir
Q Next one is Ethel? QA[sic] She is 9 years old? A Yes sir.
Q And then the next one? A Lou Ella.
Q Lou Ella is six years old? A Yes sir.
Q And then George W. is four years old? A Yes sir/[sic]
Q They are all living now? A Yes sir/[sic]
1880 roll page 80 #521 James Chaney Cooweescoowee, adopted white;
1880 roll page 80 #522 as Pinkey Chaney Cooweescoowee District, native Cherokee;
1896 roll page 299 #245 James M. Chaney Cooweescoowee;
1896 roll page 136 #1106 as Pinky Chaney   "
1896 roll page 136 #1109 Eliza Chaney   "
1896 roll page 136 #1110 as Mama Chaney   "
1896 roll page 136 #1111 Della Chaney   "
1896 roll page 136 #1112 Ethel Chaney   "
1896 roll page 136 #1113 Luella Chaney   "
1896 roll page 136 #1114 George W. Chaney   "

    Com'r Breckinridge: The applicant applies for the enrollment of himself, his wife and six minor children; his wife is identified on the rolls of 1880 and 1896 as a native Cherokee; she has lived in the Cherokee Nation all her life and she will be listed for enrollment as a Cherokee by blood;
    The applicant states that he married his wife in 1874, and that they have lived together in the Cherokee Nation ever since their marriage; he is identified with his wife on the rolls of 1880 and 1896 and he will be listed now for enrollment as a Cherokee by intermarriage.
    His six minr[sic] children named in the testimony are all identified with their parents on the roll of 1896; they are living at this time and they will be listed for enrollment as Cherokees by blood.

    M.D. Green, being first duly sworn, states that as stenographer to the Commission to the Five Civilized Tribes he correctly recorded the testimony and proceedings in this case and that the foregoing is a true and complete transcript of his stenographic notes thereof.

Cherokee Intermarried White 1906
Volume II

MD Green

Subscribed and sworn to before me this 15th day of October 1900.

TB Needles
Commissioner.

◇◇◇◇◇

Cherokee 4393.

DEPARTMENT OF THE INTERIOR,
COMMISSION TO THE FIVE CIVILIZED TRIBES.
Muskogee, I. T., October 25, 1902.

In the matter of the application of James M. Chaney for the enrollment of himself as a citizen by intermarriage, and for the enrollment of his wife, Julia Chaney, and his seven minor children, Eliza, Mamie, Della, Ethel, Lou E., George W. and Florence E. Chaney, as citizens by blood, of the Cherokee Nation.

SUPPLEMENTAL PROCEEDINGS.

JAMES M. CHANEY, being sworn, testified as follows:

By the Commission,

Q What's your name? A J. M. Chaney.
Q What's your age? A Fifty-three or four, born in '49.
Q What's your postoffice? A Ruby, I. T.
Q Are you the same James M. Chaney that made application for enrollment as an intermarried citizen in October, 1900? A I think so.
Q What's your wife's name? A Julia.
Q Is she a Cherokee citizen by blood? A Yes, sir.
Q When were you married to your wife, Julia? A 15th[sic] of February, '74.
Q Do you appear on the '80 roll with her? A Yes, sir.
Q Had you ever been married before you married your wife, Julia? A No, sir.
Q Had she ever been married before her marriage to you? A No, sir.
Q Have you and your wife, Julia, lived together as husband and wife all the time since '80 up to the present time? A Yes, sir.
Q Never have been separated since '80? A No, sir.
Q Living together on the first day of September, 1902? A Yes, sir.
Q Have you and your wife lived in the Cherokee Nation all the time since 1880 up to the present time? A Yes, sir.
Q Are these children, Eliza, Mamie, Della, Ethel, Lou E., George W. and Florence E., you children by your wife, Julia? A Yes, sir.
Q Lived in the Cherokee Nation all their lives? A Yes, sir, Florence is one year old.
Q Has that been recorded? A Yes, sir.

Cherokee Intermarried White 1906
Volume II

Retta Chick, being first duly sworn, states that, as stenographer to the Commission to the Five Civilized Tribes, she recorded the testimony and proceedings in the matter of the foregoing application, and that the above is a true and complete transcript of her stenographic notes thereof.

Retta Chick

Subscribed and sworn to before me this 29th day of November, 1902.

PG Reuter
Notary Public.

◇◇◇◇◇

Cherokee No.
4393.

DEPARTMENT OF THE INTERIOR,

COMMISSIONER TO THE FIVE CIVILIZED TRIBES,

MUSKOGEE, INDIAN TERRITORY, JANUARY 4, 1907.

IN THE MATTER of the application for the enrollment of James M. Chaney as a citizen by intermarriage of the Cherokee Nation.

JAMES M. CHANEY, being first duly sworn by Walter W. Chappell, Notary Public in the Western District of the Indian Territory, testified as follows:

EXAMINATION

ON BEHALF OF THE COMMISSIONER:

Q State your name, age and postoffice address? A James M. Chaney; Ruby, Indian Territory, 58 years old past.
Q You claim to be a citizen by intermarriage of the Cherokee Nation? A Yes sir, according to the decision of the Supreme Court.
Q Through whom do you claim that right? A By intermarriage with my wife.
Q Is she living? A Yes sir.
Q What is her name? A Julia A. Chaney.
Q What was her maiden name? A Julia Brown.
Q What was her citizenship? A Cherokee by blood.
Q Where was she born? A On Grand river[sic].
Q In the Cherokee Nation? A Yes sir, I think in Coowees Coowee District.
Q Lived in the Cherokee Nation all her life? A Yes sir.
Q When were you and Julia Brown married? A Fifth day of February 1874.
Q Where? A About four and a half miles south east of where Nowata is now.

Cherokee Intermarried White 1906
Volume II

Q Were you married under a Cherokee license? A Yes sir.
Q Where was that license secured? A Near Claremore; Mr. Link Foreman was clerk at the time.
Q Had either you or your wife been married prior to that time? A No sir.
Q You have lived together continuously since your marriage, have you? A Yes sir.
Q Where have you resided during that time? A Near Coodys Bluff.
Q Is that in the Cherokee Nation? A Yes sir.

ON BEHALF OF THE COMMISSIONER:

    The said Julia Chaney (nee Brown), is included in an approved partial roll of citizens by blood of the Cherokee Nation opposite No. 10495.
    The applicant James M. Chaney is identified on the authenticated Cherokee tribal roll of 1880 and Cherokee census roll of 1896, Coowees Coowee District, opposite Nos. 521 and 245, respectively, as an intermarried white.

Q From whom did you secure your license to marry under the Cherokee law? A Link Foreman was clerk at the time.
Q Who performed the ceremony? A Dempsey Coker, a Cherokee preacher.
Q Was your wife ever known by any other name than Julia? A Yes sir, Pinkey; the Dawes Commission changed it and put her proper name down.

ON BEHALF OF THE COMMISSIONER:

    On Page 13, Book A, "Record Marriage License Coowees Cowee[sic]sic] District", the following appears: (or J)
    "January 28, issued married license to I. M. Chaney to marry Pinkey Brown, citizen of the C. N., issued by H. L. Foreman, District Clerk; married by Rev. Dempy[sic]sic] Caker[sic]sic], February 5, 1874."

(Witness dismissed).

I, S. T. Wright, stenographer to the Commissioner to the Five Civilized Tribes, on oath, state that I recorded the testimony and proceedings had in the above entitled cause on January 4, 1907, and that the above and foregoing is a true and correct transcript of my stenographic notes thereof taken on said date.
                                                     S.T. Wright

Subscribed and sworn to before me this January 4th, 1907.

                                                  Edward Merrick
                                                  NOTARY PUBLIC.

Cherokee Intermarried White 1906
Volume II

E.C.M. Cherokee 4393.

DEPARTMENT OF THE INTERIOR,

COMMISSIONER TO THE FIVE CIVILIZED TRIBES.

In the matter of the application for the enrollment of JAMES M. CHANEY as a citizen by intermarriage of the Cherokee Nation.

D E C I S I O N

THE RECORDS OF THIS OFFICE SHOW: That at Nowata, Indian Territory, October 15, 1900, James M. Chaney appeared before the Commission to the Five Civilized Tribes, and made application for the enrollment of himself as a citizen by intermarriage, and for the enrollment of his wife, Julia Chaney et al. as citizens by blood of the Cherokee Nation. The application for the enrollment of the said Julia Chaney et al. as citizens by blood of the Cherokee Nation has been heretofore disposed of, and their rights for enrollment will not be considered in this decision. Further proceedings in the matter of said application were had at Muskogee, Indian Territory, October 25, 1902, and January 4, 1907.

THE EVIDENCE IN THIS CASE SHOWS: That the applicant herein, James M. Chaney, a white man, was married, in accordance with Cherokee law, February 5, 1874, to his wife, Julia Chaney, nee Brown, who was at the time of said marriage a recognized citizen by blood of the Cherokee Nation and whose name appears on the approved partial roll of citizens by blood of the Cherokee Nation, opposite No. 10495; that since said marriage the said James M. Chaney and the said Julia Chaney have resided together as husband and wife, and have continuously lived in the Cherokee Nation. The said James M. Chaney is identified on the Cherokee authenticated tribal roll of 1880, and the Cherokee census roll of 1896, as an intermarried citizen of the Cherokee Nation.

IT IS, THEREFORE, ORDERED AND ADJUDGED: That in accordance with the decision of the Supreme Court of the United States, dated November 5, 1906, in the case of Daniel Red Bird et al. vs. the United States, under the provision of Section 21, of the Act of Congress approved June 28, 1898 (30 Stat., 495), James M. Chaney is entitled to enrollment as a citizen by intermarriage of the Cherokee Nation, and his application for enrollment as such is accordingly granted.

Tams Bixby
Commissioner.

Dated at Muskogee, Indian Territory,
this   JAN 12 1907

Cherokee Intermarried White 1906
Volume II

Cherokee
4393

Muskogee, Indian Territory, December 27, 1906.

James M. Chaney,
    Ruby, Indian Territory.

Dear Sir:

    November 6, 1906, the United States Supreme Court held that white persons who intermarried with Cherokee citizens according to Cherokee law prior to November 1, 1875, are entitled to enrollment and allotments of land as citizens of the Cherokee Nation.

    You are advised that to properly determine your right to enrollment as a citizen by intermarriage of the Cherokee Nation, it will be necessary for you to appear before the Commissioner for the purpose of giving testimony as to the date of your marriage and whether or not your wife, by reason of your marriage to whom you claim the right to enrollment as a citizen of the Cherokee Nation, was a recognized citizen of the Cherokee Nation at the time of your marriage to her, and whether or not you were married to her in accordance with Cherokee laws.

    You are, therefore, directed to appear before the Commissioner at Muskogee, Indian Territory, at 9 o'clock A. M., on Friday, January 4, 1907, and give testimony as above indicated.

                Respectfully,

JMH   Acting Commissioner.

◇◇◇◇◇

(COPY)

D.C.2191-1907.

Washington, D. C. January 9, 1907.

The Honorable Secretary of the Interior,
    Washington, D.C.

Sir:

    We are in receipt of a communication from E. B. Lawson, Attorney at Law, Nowata, Indian Territory, who states that James M. Chaney, is entitled under the decision, known as Intermarried White's case, to an allotment of land in the Cherokee Nation, said Chaney having married a Cherokee citizen prior to 1875. Mr. Chaney is a white man and has

Cherokee Intermarried White 1906
Volume II

selected an allotment of land in the Cherokee Nation, but prior to such selection lf[sic] as an allotment this land was filed upon by another citizen of the Cherokee Nation and Mr. Chaney is thus forced to contest the filing made by the other citizen.

Mr. Lawson states that the land involved is surrounded by oil wells and that these wells are now being pumped to the great damage and detriment of the lands owned by Mr. Chaney. It is further stated by Mr. Lawson that Mr. Chandy[sic] owns all of the improvements on the lands in question and it will be necessary for his citizenship to be passed upon before there can be a trial by the Commissioner to the Five Civilized Tribes of the contest over the land in question.

Mr. Lawson states that Mr. Chaney has already given his testimony before the Commissioner relating to his marriage and that so far as testimony is concerned the citizenship case is closed and is awaiting decision of the Commissioner to the Five Civilized Tribes.

In view of the facts set out by Mr. Lawson, showing that delay in a decision of the citizenship case will work serious damage to Mr. Chaney we very respectfully request that you may direct the Commissioner to the Five Civilized Tribes to make this citizenship case special in order that a decision may be had without delay, thus enabling Mr. Chaney to prosecute his contest case to a prompt conclusion.

A decision of the contest case over the land involved is to be desired as much by one of the contending parties as the other, since injury to the land will necessarily be injury to the successful claimant, and there can be no decision in the contest case until Mr. Chaney's citizenship is passed upon.

Very respectfully,

James K. Jones.

Cherokee Intermarried White 1906
Volume II

(COPY)

D.C.2190-1907.　　　　　　　　　　　　　　　　　　　　　　　　　W.H.M.

DEPARTMENT OF THE INTERIOR
WASHINGTON.

I.T.D.357-1907.　　　　　　　　　　　　　　　　　　　　　　　January 10, 1907.

L.R.S.

The Commissioner to the Five Civilized Tribes,
　　Muskogee, Indian Territory.

Sir:

　　There is enclosed a letter from Mr. James K. Jones, relative to the allotment case of James M. Chaney. If the statements made by the attorney are true, it would appear that this citizenship case should [sic] made special, and you are requested to take immediate action thereon unless there is some good reason why such procedure should not be had, in which case you will report direct to the Department.

　　　　　　　　　　　　　　Respectfully,

　　　　　　　　　　　　　　Thos. Tyan[sic]

1 enclosure.　　　　　　　　　　　　　　　　　First Assistant Secretary.

◇◇◇◇◇

Cherokee
4393.

　　　　　　　　　　　　Muskogee, Indian Territory, January 12, 1907.

W. W. Hastings,
　　Attorney for the Cherokee Nation,
　　　　Muskogee, Indian Territory.

Dear Sir:

　　There is enclosed herewith a copy of the decision of the Commissioner to the Five Civilized Tribes, dated January 12, 1907, granting the application for the enrollment of James M. Chaney as a citizen by intermarriage of the Cherokee Nation.

　　Under date of January 10, 1907 (I.T.D.357-1907), the Department directed that this case be made special, and you are requested to asvise[sic] this office by return mail whether or not you desire to file protest against the Commissioner's action.

Cherokee Intermarried White 1906
Volume II

Respectfully,

Encl. H-21   Commissioner.
JMH

◇◇◇◇◇◇

Muskogee, Indian Territory, January 14, 1907.

<u>DIRECT</u>.

The Honorable,
    The Secretary of the Interior.

Sir:

    Receipt is acknowledged of Departmental letter of January 10, 1907 (I.T.D.357-1907), sent direct, marked "Special", inclosing a letter from Mr. James K. Jones, relative to making special the case of James M. Chaney, an applicant for enrollment as a citizen by intermarriage of the Cherokee Nation. This office is directed to take immediate action on the case unless there is some good reason why such procedure shoule[sic] not be had.

    In reply you are respectfully advised that said case was submitted to the Commissioner for a decision on January 4, 1907, and that a copy of the decision of the Commissioner, dated January 12, 1907, granting the application for the enrollment of James M. Chaney as a citizen by intermarriage of the Cherokee Nation was on that date forwarded the Attorney for the Cherokee Nation for such protest as he may desire to make against the action of the Commissiones[sic]. Said attorney was requested to advise the Commissioner by return mail if he did not desire to enter a protest against the Commissioner's action in this case. In case the Attorney for the Nation enters no protest the name of James M. Chaney will be included in the first schedule of intermarried white citizens found to be entitled of enrollment, which schedule it is expected will be forwarded for Departmental approval in a few days. Mr. Jones' letter is returned herewith.

                                                           Respectfully,

Encl. HJ-1.
  HJC

                                                                                   Commissioner.

◇◇◇◇◇◇

Cherokee Intermarried White 1906
Volume II

Cherokee
4393

Muskogee, Indian Territory, January 21, 1907.

James M. Chaney,
    Ruby, Indian Territory.

Dear Sir:

    There is enclosed herewith a copy of the decision of the Commissioner to the Five Civilized Tribes, dated January 12, 1907, granting the application for your enrollment as a citizen by intermarriage of the Cherokee Nation.

    You will be advised when your name has been placed upon a schedule of citizens of the Cherokee Nation and approved by the Secretary of the Interior.

                  Respectfully,

E.R.C.   Commissioner.
Enc E.C.S.

◇◇◇◇◇

Cherokee 4393   W.W. HASTINGS.   OFFICE OF   H.M. VANCE.
                               ATTORNEY.   SECRETARY.

Attorney for the Cherokee Nation,
MUSKOGEE, I. T.

                                                            January 18, 1907.

The Commissioner to the Five Civilized Tribes,
    Muskogee, Indian Territory.

Sir:

    Receipt is acknowledged of the testimony and of your decision enrolling James M. Chaney as a citizen by intermarriage of the Cherokee Nation. Time for protesting said decision is waived and I consent that said person may be placed upon the schedule immediately.

                    Yours very truly,
                    W. W. Hastings
                    Attorney for Cherokee Nation.

Cherokee Intermarried White 1906
Volume II

Cher IW 42
Trans from Cher 4412 3-13-07

◇◇◇◇◇

DEPARTMENT OF THE INTERIOR,

COMMISSIONER TO THE FIVE CIVILIZED TRIBES.

In the matter of the application for the enrollment of

JAMES THORNBRUGH[sic]

as a citizen by intermarriage of the Cherokee Nation.

CHEROKEE 4412.

◇◇◇◇◇

Department of the Interior.
Commission to the Five Civilized Tribes.
Nowata, I. T., October 15, 1900.

In the matter of the application of James Thornbrough[sic] for the enrollment of himself and wife as Cherokee citizens; he being sworn and examined by Commission[sic] T. B. Needles, testified as follows:

Q What's your name? A James Thornbrough.
Q What is your age? A 56.
Q What is your postoffice address? A Coffeyville, Kans.
Q What district do you live in? A Cooweescoowee.
Q Are you a recognized citizen of the Cherokee Nation? A Yes.
Q By blood or intermarriage? A Intermarriage.
Q For whom do you apply for enrollment? A Me and my wife.
Q What is your wife's name? A Hortense.
Q What was he name before you married her? A Hortense Walker.
Q Her age? A 44.
Q When did you marry her? A 1874,
Q Your name and hers both on the roll of 1880? A Yes, sir.
Q How long have you lived in the Cherokee Nation? A 27 years this fall.
Q Continuously? A Yes, sir, ever since.
Q Is your wife a Cherokee by blood? A Yes, sir.
   1880 roll ;page 185, #2887, James Thornburgh, Cooweescoowee.
   1880 roll; page 185, #2888, Hortenuse[sic] Thornburgh,
   1896 roll; page 326, #1009, James Thornbrough,

Cherokee Intermarried White 1906
Volume II

1896 roll; page 267, #4745, Hortense Thornbrough.

Commissioner-
The name of James Thornbrough and his wife, Hortense, are found upon the authenticated roll of 1880 as well as the Census Roll of 1896 as Cherokee citizens by blood. Having made satisfactory proof as to their residence, and being fully identified according to page and number of the roll, they will both be duly listed for enrollment by this Commission as Cherokee citizens by blood.

E. G. Rothenberger, being first duly sworn, states that as stenographer to the Commission to the Five Civilized Tribes, he reported in full all proceedings in the above case, and that the foregoing is a true and complete translation of his stenographic notes in said case.

E.G. Rothenberger

Subscribed and sworn to before me this 15th day of October, 1900.

CR Breckinridge
Commissioner.

Cherokee 4412.

Department of the Interior,
Commission to the Five Civilized Tribes,
Muskogee, I. T., October 6, 1902.

In the matter of the application of James Thornbrugh for the enrollment of himself as a citizen by intermarriage, and for the enrollment of his wife, Hortense D. Thornbrugh, as a citizen by blood of the Cherokee Nation; he being sworn and examined by the Commission, testified as follows:

Q What is your name? A James Thornbrugh.
Q What is your age at this time? A Fifty-eight.
Q What is your postoffice? A Coffeyville, Kansas.
Q Are you the same James Thornbrugh that made application to this Commission for enrollment as an intermarried citizen on October 15, 1900? A Yes sir.
Q What is your wife's name? A Hortense D.
Q Is she a citizen by blood? A Yes sir.
Q Is she living at this time? A Yes sir.
Q When were you and she married? A In March, 1874.
Q Were you ever married before you married this wife? A Yes sir.
Q How many times before? A Once before.
Q Was that wife living or dead when you married this wife? A Dead.
Q Was she a white woman or Cherokee? A White woman.
Q Were you married to this wife under a Cherokee license? A Yes sir.

Cherokee Intermarried White 1906
Volume II

Q Was she ever married prior to her marriage to you? A No sir.
Q You are her first husband? A Yes sir.
Q She is your second wife? A Yes sir.
Q Have you and she lived together continuously from the time of your marriage as husband and wife up to the present time? A Yes sir.
Q You never married any other woman since you married, Hortense? A No sir.
Q You and she were living together on the first day of September, 1902? A Yes sir.
Q Have you lived in the Cherokee Nation ever since 1880 up to the present time? A Yes sir.
Q Has you wife lived in the Cherokee Nation all the time since 1880? A Yes sir.

The undersigned, being duly sworn, states that as stenographer to the Commission to the Five Civilized Tribes he correctly recorded the testimony and proceedings in this case, and that the foregoing is a true and complete transcript of his stenographic notes thereof.

E.G. Rothenberger

Subscribed and sworn to before me this 28th day of October, 1902.

BC Jones
Notary Public.

◇◇◇◇◇

Cherokee 4412.

DEPARTMENT OF THE INTERIOR,
COMMISSION TO THE FIVE CIVILIZED TRIBES.
Muskogee, Indian Territory, January 4, 1907.

In the Matter of the Application for the Enrollment of James Thornbrugh as a citizen by intermarriage of the Cherokee Nation.

APPEARANCES:
Applicant appears in person.
Cherokee Nation represented by H. M. Vance, in behalf of W. W. Hastings, Attorney.

James Thornbrugh being first duly sworn by B. P. Rasmus, Notary Public, testitied as follows:

ON BEHALF OF COMMISSIONER.

Q What is your name? A James Thornbrugh.
Q What is your age
A I will be 64 the 28th of January.

Cherokee Intermarried White 1906
Volume II

Q What is your post office address?
A Coffeyville, Kansas.
Q Are you an applicant for enrollment as a citizen by intermarriage of the Cherokee Nation?
A Yes sir.
Q You have no Cherokee blood?
A No sir.
Q Your only claim to the right to enrollment as a citizen of the Cherokee Nation is by virtue of your marriage to a citizen by blood of the Nation?
A Yes sir.
Q You are a resident now of the Cherokee Nation, are you not?
A Yes sir.
Q What is the citizen's name through whom you claim the right to enrollment?
A Hortensia Walker.
Q Is she living or dead?
A She is living.
Q She was a recognized citizen of the Cherokee Nation at the time you married her?
A Yes sir.
Q Living in the Cherokee Nation?
A Yes sir.
Q When did you marry her?
A March 30, '74.
Q Was she your first wife?
A No, my second wife.
Q Was your former wife living or dead at the time you married her?
A Dead.
Q Were you her first husband?
A Yes, she had never been married.
Q Since your marriage, have you and she continuously lived together as husband and wife?
A Yes sir.
Q And have lived in the Cherokee Nation all the time?
A Yes sir.
Q Did you marry your wife in accordance with the laws of the Cherokee Nation?
A Yes sir.
Q You secured a license, did you?
A Yes sir.
Q Have you any documentary evidence showing your marriage to your wife?
A Yes sir.

The applicant presents a certified copy of marriage license showing that March 26, 1874, license was issued to James Thornbrugh, citizen of the United States, to marry Hortensia Walker, citizen of the Cherokee Nation, by D. W. Lipe, clerk Cooweescoowee District. This is filed herewith and made a part of the record in this case.

Cherokee Intermarried White 1906
Volume II

Q You were married in accordance with the terms of this license?
A Yes sir.
Q Have you a copy of the certificate of marriage?
A Yes sir.

Applicant present a certificate of marriage showing that the parties named in the above mentioned license were united in marriage March 30, 1874, by Hamilton Balentine, officiating clergyman. The applicant is identified on the Cherokee Authenticated Tribal Roll of 1880, Cooweescoowee District, No. 2878. The name of his wife, Hortensia B. Thornbrugh, is included in the approved partial roll of citizens by blood of the Cherokee Nation opposite No. 10550.

The undersigned being first duly sworn states that as stenographer to the Commission to the Five Civilized Tribes, she correctly recorded the testimony taken in this case and that the foregoing is a full, true and correct transcript of her stenographic notes thereof.

Myrtle Hill

Subscribed and sworn to before me this the 5th day of January, 1907.

John E. Tidwell
Notary Public.

◇◇◇◇◇

CERTIFIED COPY.

Cherokee Nation, Cooweescoowee District.

Issued License of Marriage to James Thornbrough, citizen of the U. S., to marry Hortensia Walker, citizen Cherokee Nation.

Issued by D. W. Lipe, Clerk of Cooweescoowee District, Mch. 26, 1874.

Married by Rev. Hameltine Balentine, on the 30 Mch. 1874.

I hereby certify that the above is a true copy of the original as on file in this office this the 29 of March 1880.

C. C. Lipe, Clerk,
Cooweescoowee
District.

(SEAL).

I further certify that I have a very distinct recollection of issuing the above license to James Thornbrough citizen U. S. to marry Hortensia Walker, and that the original were misplaced or lost.

Cherokee Intermarried White 1906
Volume II

Cooweescoowee Dist., C. N.,
March 29th, 1880.

D. W. Lipe, late,
Clk C. D. C. N.

Endorsed:
Marriage certificate
of
James Thornbrough.

I, Frances R. Lane, a stenographer to the Commissioner to the Five Civilized Tribes, do hereby certify that the above and foregoing is a complete copy of a certified copy of a marriage license (and statement as to same) issued to James Thornbrough to marry Hortensia Walker, now on file with the records of the Commissioner to the Five Civilized Tribes in the matter of the application for the enrollment of James Thornbrough as a citizen by intermarriage of the Cherokee Nation, -Cherokee 4412.

Frances R Lane

Subscribed and sworn to before me this January 15, 1907.

Edward Merrick
Notary Public.

◇◇◇◇◇

(The below typed as given.)

Cherokee Nation, Cooweescoowee District

I send License of marriage to James Thornbrough citizen of the U. S. to marry Hortensia Walker, a citizen Cherokee Nation.

Issued by D. W. Lipe Clerk of Cooweescoowee District. March 26, 1874. Married by Rev. Hameltin, Balentine on the 30 Mch 1874.

I hereby certify that the above is a true copy of the original as on file in this office this the 29 of March 1880.

(Signed) C. C. Lipe Clerk
SEAL   Cooweescoowee District.

I further certify that I have a very distinct recollection of issuing the above license to James Thornbrough citizen U. S. to marry Hortensia Walker, and that the original were misplaced or lost.

Cherokee Intermarried White 1906
Volume II

Cooweescoowee Dist. C. N.

March 29th 1880

(Signed) D. W. Lipe, late
Clk C. D. C N

The undersigned, being first duly sworn, states that as stenographer to the Commissioner to the Five Civilized Tribes, she made the above copy and that the same is a full, true and correct copy of the instrument now on file in this office.

Mattie M. Pace

Subscribed and sworn to before me this April 6, 1907.

B.P. Rasmus
Notary Public.

◇◇◇◇◇

THIS CERTIFIES

That Mr. James Thornbrugh of Cooweeskoowee[sic] District, Cherokee Nation AND Miss Hortensia D. Walker of Cooweeskoowee District Cherokee Nation, were united in HOLY MATRIMONY According to the Ordinance of GOD and the laws of the Cherokee Nation at Pheasant Hill on the Thirtieth day of March in the year of OUR LORD, One Thousand Eight Hundred and Seventy four

Witnesses Anna H. Balentine   Hamilton Balentine,

J. A. A. Balentine.   Officiating Clergyman

The undersigned, being first duly sworn, states that as stenographer to the Commissioner to the Five Civilized Tribes, she made the above copy, and that the same is a full, true and correct copy of the original marriage certificate now on file in this office.

Mattie M Pace

Subscribed and sworn to before me this April 6, 1907.

B. P. Rasmus
Notary Public.

◇◇◇◇◇

Cherokee Intermarried White 1906
Volume II

F.R.

Cherokee 4412.

DEPARTMENT OF THE INTERIOR,

COMMISSIONER TO THE FIVE CIVILIZED TRIBES.

In the matter of the application for the enrollment of JAMES THORNBRUGH as a citizen by intermarriage of the Cherokee Nation.

D E C I S I O N

THE RECORDS OF THIS OFFICE SHOW: That at Nowata, Indian Territory, October 15, 1900, application was received by the Commission to the Five Civilized Tribes for the enrollment of James Thornbrugh as a citizen by intermarriage of the Cherokee Nation. Further proceedings in the matter of said application were had at Muskogee, Indian Territory, October 6, 1902, and January 4, 1907.

THE EVIDENCE IN THIS CASE SHOWS: That the applicant herein, James Thornbrugh, a white man, was married, in accordance with Cherokee law, March 30, 1874, to his wife, Hortense Thornbrugh, who was at the time of said marriage a recognized citizen by blood of the Cherokee Nation, who is identified on the Cherokee authenticated tribal roll of 1880, Cooweescoowee District, No. 2888, as a native Cherokee, and whose name appears opposite No. 10550 on the approved partial roll of citizens by blood of the Cherokee Nation. It is further shown that since said marriage the said James and Hortense Thornbrugh have resided together as husband and wife, and have continuously lived in the Cherokee Nation.

IT IS, THEREFORE, ORDERED AND ADJUDGED: That in accordance with the decision of the Supreme Court of the United States, dated November 5, 1906, in the case of Daniel Red Bird et al. vs. the United States, Nos. 125, 126, 127 and 128, the said applicant, James Thornbrugh, is entitled, under the provision of Section 21, of the Act of Congress approved June 28, 1898 (30 Stats., 495), to enrollment as a citizen by intermarriage of the Cherokee Nation, and his application for enrollment as such is accordingly granted.

Tams Bixby
Commissioner.

Dated at Muskogee, Indian Territory,
this   JAN 19 1907

Cherokee Intermarried White 1906
Volume II

Cherokee
4412

Muskogee, Indian Territory, December 27, 1906.

James Thornbrugh,
    Coffeyville, Kansas.

Dear Sir:

    November 6, 1906, the United States Supreme Court held that white persons who intermarried with Cherokee citizens according to Cherokee law prior to November 1, 1875, are entitled to enrollment and allotments of land as citizens of the Cherokee Nation.

    You are advised that to properly determine your right to enrollment as a citizen by intermarriage of the Cherokee Nation, it will be necessary for you to appear before the Commissioner for the purpose of giving testimony as to the date of your marriage and whether or not your wife, by reason of your marriage to whom you claim the right to enrollment as a citizen of the Cherokee Nation, was a recognized citizen of the Cherokee Nation at the time of your marriage to her, and whether or not you were married to her in accordance with Cherokee laws.

    You are, therefore, directed to appear before the Commissioner at Muskogee, Indian Territory, at 9 o'clock A. M., on Friday, January 4, 1907, and give testimony as above indicated.

                    Respectfully,

JMH   Acting Commissioner.

Cherokee
4412.

Muskogee, Indian Territory, January 19, 1907.

W. W. Hastings,
    Attorney for the Cherokee Nation,
        Muskogee, Indian Territory.

Dear Sir:

    There is enclosed herewith a copy of the decision of the Commissioner to the Five Civilized Tribes, dated January 17, 1907, granting the application for the enrollment of James Thornbrugh, as a citizen by intermarriage of the Cherokee Nation.

Cherokee Intermarried White 1906
Volume II

Respectfully,

Commissioner.

Incl. C-16
LMC

◇◇◇◇◇

Cherokee 4412 W.W. HASTINGS. OFFICE OF H.M. VANCE.
ATTORNEY. SECRETARY.

Attorney for the Cherokee Nation,
MUSKOGEE, I. T.

January 19, 1907.

The Commissioner to the Five Civilized Tribes,
Muskogee, Indian Territory.

Sir:

Receipt is acknowledged of the testimony and of your decision enrolling James Thornbrugh as a citizen by intermarriage of the Cherokee Nation. Time for protesting said decision is waived and I consent that said person may be placed upon the schedule immediately.

Respectfully,
W. W. Hastings
Attorney for Cherokee Nation.

◇◇◇◇◇

Cherokee
4412

Muskogee, Indian Territory, January 21, 1907.

(No name given)
Coffeyville, Kansas.

Dear Sir:

There is enclosed herewith a copy of the decision of the Commissioner to the Five Civilized Tribes, dated January 17, 1907, granting the application for your enrollment as a citizen by intermarriage of the Cherokee Nation.

You will be advised when your name has been placed upon a schedule of citizens of the Cherokee Nation and approved by the Secretary of the Interior.

Cherokee Intermarried White 1906
Volume II

Respectfully,

E.R.C.   Commissioner.
Enc. E.C. 9

◇◇◇◇◇◇

Muskogee, Indian Territory, April 8, 1907.

James Thornbrugh,
      Coffeyville, Kansas.

Dear Sir:

      Your marriage license and certificate filed in connection with your application for enrollment, as a citizen by intermarriage of the Cherokee Nation, is returned to you herewith, copies of the same being retained in this office.

Respectfully,

Incl. P-4-10   Acting Commissioner.
  MMP

Cher IW 43
Trans from Cher 4427 3-13-07

◇◇◇◇◇◇

L.G.D.   Cherokee 4427.

DEPARTMENT OF THE INTERIOR,
COMMISSIONER TO THE FIVE CIVILIZED TRIBES.
MUSKOGEE, I. T., JANUARY 4, 1907.

      In the matter of the application for the enrollment of Holland L. Parrish as a citizen by intermarriage of the Cherokee Nation.

      APPEARANCES: Applicant appears in person.

HOLLAND L. PARRISH, being first duly sworn by John E. Tidwell, Notary Public, testified as follows:

ON BEHALF OF THE COMMISSIONER:

Q What is your name? A Holland L. Parrish.

Cherokee Intermarried White 1906
Volume II

Q What is your age? A I am 58.
Q What is your post office address? A Coodys Bluff.
Q You claim the right to be enrolled as a citizen by intermarriage of the Cherokee Nation? A Yes sir.
Q Through whom do you claim the right to enrollment as a citizen by intermarriage of the Cherokee Nation? A Cyntha Jane Daniel.
Q When were you married? A 28th of December, 1869.
Q Were you married under Cherokee license? A Yes sir.
Q Where were you married? A At John Coker's; not far from Coodys Bluff.
Q That is in the Cherokee Nation? A Yes sir.

Book "A", records of marriage licenses for Cooweescoowee District, on page 4, contains the following entry:- "December 25, issued license of marriage to Holland L. Parrish, citizen of the U. S., to marry Cyntha J. Daniel, a citizen of the Cherokee Nation. Issued by J. B. Mayes, District Clerk; marriage solemnized by Dempy F. Coker on the 28th day of December, 1869."

Q Who was J. B. Mayes? A Well sir, he was a Cherokee fellow that lived up there in Cooweescoowee District; he was elected Clerk of Cooweescoowee District in August, 1869.
Q Who married you? A Demps[sic] Coker.
Q What was he? A He was a Primitive Baptist preacher, a Cherokee man.
Q Is Cyntha Jane Parrish living? A No sir.
Q When did she die? A In '93.
Q Have you maried[sic] since her death? A No sir.
Q Were you married prior to your marriage to Cyntha Jane Parrish? [sic] No sir.
Q Was she ever married prior to her marriage to you? A No sir.
Q You both lived together as husband and wife from the time of your marriage in 1869 up to the time of her death in 1893? A Yes sir.
Q You have lived continuously in the Cherokee Nation since her death? A Yes sir.

The applicant is identified on the 1880 roll, Cooweescoowee District, opposite No. 2165.

The undersigned, being first duly sworn, states that as stenographer to the Commissioner to the Five Civilized Tribes, she correctly recorded the above and foregoing testimony, and that the same is a full, true and correct transcript of her stenographic notes thereof.

Sarah Waters

Subscribed and sworn to before me this 4th day of January, 1907.

John E. Tidwell
Notary Public.

Cherokee Intermarried White 1906
Volume II

Cherokee 4427

Muskogee, Indian Territory, December 27, 1906.

Holland L. Parrish,
    Coodys Bluff, Indian Territory.

Dear Sir:

    November 6, 1906, the United States Supreme Court held that white persons who intermarried with Cherokee citizens according to Cherokee law prior to November 1, 1875, are entitled to enrollment and allotments of land as citizens of the Cherokee Nation.

    You are advised that to properly determine your right to enrollment as a citizen by intermarriage of the Cherokee Nation, it will be necessary for you to appear before the Commissioner for the purpose of giving testimony as to the date of your marriage and whether or not your wife, by reason of your marriage to whom you claim the right to enrollment as a citizen of the Cherokee Nation, was a recognized citizen of the Cherokee Nation at the time of your marriage to her, and whether or not you were married to her in accordance with Cherokee laws.

    You are, therefore, directed to appear before the Commissioner at Muskogee, Indian Territory, at 9 o'clock A. M., on Friday, January 4, 1907, and give testimony as above indicated.

                                    Respectfully,

JMH   Acting Commissioner.

◇◇◇◇◇

(Handwritten note difficult to read)

                                Record & Dec,
                                not in jacket
                                when papers
                                were transferred
                                          CFB
                                Apr 6, 1907

Cherokee Intermarried White 1906
Volume II

Cher IW 44
Trans from Cher 4503   3-13-07

◇◇◇◇◇

E.C.M.

DEPARTMENT OF THE INTERIOR,

COMMISSIONER TO THE FIVE CIVILIZED TRIBES.

In the matter of the application for the enrollment of

JAMES G. MEHLIN

as a citizen by intermarriage of the Cherokee Nation.

CHEROKEE 4503.

◇◇◇◇◇

Department of the Interior,
Commission to the Five Civilized tribes,
Nowata, I. T. October, 17th 19oo.[sic]

In the matter of the application of Ja,es[sic] G. Mehlin for the enrollment of himself and wife as Cherokee citizens. He being duly sworn before the Commission testified as follows-

Q What is your name? A. James G. Mehlin.
Q What is your age? [sic] 58.
Q What is your post office Address? A. Allowee[sic].
Q What district do you live in? A. Cooweescoowee.
Q Are you a recognized citizen of the Cherokee Nation? A. Yes sir.
Q By blood or intermarriage? A. Intermarriage.
Q For whom do you apply for enrollment? A. Myself and wife.
Q What is her name? A. Elizabeth.
Q What was her name before you married her? A. Ratteling-goard[sic].
Q How old is she? A. 54.
Q Have you a certificate of your marriage? A. Yes sir.
Applicant presents satisfactory proof as to his marriage to his wife Elizabeth Rattlengoard[sic] in 1868'[sic]
1880 roll page 138, No. 1860, James Mghealen, Cooweescoowee, Adpt. White
1880   138   1861   Elizabeth Mghealen   "   N. C.
1896   317   735   James G. Mehlin   "

Cherokee Intermarried White 1906
Volume II

1896   214#3238(3248) Elizabeth Mehlin   "

Q How long have you lived in the Cherokee Nation? A. Since 58.
Q Lived with you[sic] wife ever since your marriage? A. Yes sir.
Q She is living now? A. Yes sir.
The name of James G. Mehlin is found on the authenticated roll of 1880 as James Mghealen and on the census roll of 1896 as James C. Mehlin. The name of his wife Elizabeth is found on on[sic] the 1880 authenticated roll and on the census roll of 1896 as a native Cherokee. They having made satisfactory proof as to their marriage and residence, and both being identified according to the page and number of the rolls as indicated in the testimony the said James G. Mehlin will be listed for enrollment as a Cherokee by intermarriage and his wife Elizabeth will be listed for enrollment as a Cherokee by blood.

Chas. von Weise being sworn states that as stenographer to the Commission to the Five Civilized tribes[sic] he reported in full all the prooceedings[sic] in the above cause and that the foregoing is a true, correct and full transcript of his stenographic notes in said proceedings.

Chas von Weise

Subsceibed[sic] and sworn to before me this the 18th of October, 1900.

TB Needles
Commissioner.

◇◇◇◇◇

Cherokee 4503.

Department of the Interior,
Commission to the Five Civilized Tribes,
Muskogee, I. T., October 3, 1902.

In the matter of the application of James G. Mehlin for the enrollment of himself as a citizen by intermarriage, and for the enrollment of his wife, Elizabeth Mehlin, as a citizen by blood of the Cherokee Nation; he being sworn and examined by the Commission, testified as follows:

Q What is your name? A James G. Mehlin.
Q What is your age at this time? A About sixty years old.
Q What is your postoffice address? A Alluwe.
Q Are you the same James G. Mehlin for whom application was made as an intermarried citizen to this Commission on October 17 1900? A Yes sir.
Q What is your wife's name? A Elizabeth.
Q What was her maiden name? A Rattlingourd.
Q She is living at this time? A Yes sir.
Q When were you and Elizabeth married? A In '68.
Q Were you ever married prior to your marriage to your wife, Elizabeth? A No sir.

Cherokee Intermarried White 1906
Volume II

Q Was she ever married prior to her marriage to you? A No sir.
Q You her first husband and she your first wife? A Yes sir.
Q Have you and she lived together continuously from the time of your marriage up until the present time as husband and wife? A Yes sir.
Q Never been separated during that time? A Never.
Q Living together on the first day of September 1902, as husband and wife were you? A Yes sir.
Q How long have you lived in the Cherokee Nation? A I come here in '59 or '60.
Q Have you lived here all the time since '60, in the Cherokee Nation? A Yes sir.
Q Has your wife lived here all the time since 1860 with you? A Yes sir, she was born and raised here, lived here all her life.
Q You have no children under 21 years of age? A Only one, and he is of age.

The undersigned, being duly sworn, states that as stenographer to the Commission to the Five Civilized Tribes he correctly recorded the testimony and proceedings in this case, and that the foregoing is a true and complete transcript of his stenographic notes thereof.

E.G. Rothenberger

Subscribed and sworn to before me this 17th day of October, 1902.

BC Jones
Notary Public.

◇◇◇◇◇

DEPARTMENT OF THE INTERIOR
COMMISSIONER TO THE FIVE CIVILIZED TRIBES
MUSKOGEE IND. TER.
JAN. 4, 1907.

IN THE MATTER OF THE APPLICATION FOR THE ENROLLMENT OF JAMES E[sic]. MEHLIN AS A CITIZEN BY INTERMARRIAGE OF THE CHEROKEE NATION.

CHEROKEE CENSUS CARD NO. 4503.

JAMES T[sic]. MEHLIN BEING FIRST DULY SWORN TESTIFIED AS FOLLOWS:

EXAMINATION BY THE COMMISSIONER:

Q What is your name.[sic] A James T[sic]. Mehlin.
Q What is your age. A I was born in '42.
Q What is your post office address? A Alluwe.
Q Do you claim to be a citizen by intermarriage of the Cherokee Nation? A Yes sir.

Cherokee Intermarried White 1906
Volume II

Q Thru whom do you claim your intermarried rights. A Thru my wife.
Q What's her name? A Elizabeth R. Gourd.
Q When were you married to Eliza beth[sic] R. Gourd. A In '68.
Q By whom were you married? A John B. Jones, Baptist Missionary in the Cherokee Nation.
Q Where were you married? A Tahlequah
Q Were you married in accordance with the Cherokee laws governing intermarriage between whites and citizens? A Yes, sir.
Q Did you get a license. A Yes.
Q Who did you get a license from. A William Turner. District Clerk.
Q Have you got a copy of that. A No, the preacher got that
A Have you got a certificate of the preacher who married you. A Yes sir.
Q Is this it? A Yes sir.
Q Do you want to leave this with the records in this case? A Yes sir.

Applicant offers in evidence a certificate of John B. Jones showing that he was married to Elizabeth R. Gourd on the 29th day of February 1868 under a license issued by William H. Turner Clerk of the District Court Tahlequah District. The same will be filed with the records in this case and made a part thereof.

Q Were you ever married before you married Elizabeth R. Gourd[sic] A No sir
Q Was she ever married before she married you. A No sir.
Q Have you lived together continuously as husband and wife since you married, 1868 up to and including the present time. A Yes sir.
Q In the Cherokee Nation. A Yes sir.

The applicant is identified on the 1880 Cherokee Roll Coo-wee-scoo-wee District opposite 1860; his wife thru whom he claims intermarriage rights is identified on said roll of said district opposite No. 1861; she is also identified on the final roll of citizens by blood of the Cherokee Nation opposite No. 10801.

Q Has your wife taken her allotment yet. A O yes, long ago.
Q Are you and your wife living together and have you lived together continuously since that time as husband and wife. A Yes sir.
Q What became of the license that was issued to you at the time you married your wife.
A Why I turned it over to Mr. Jones and I dont[sic] know what he done with it.
Q You never have seen it since. A No.

Clara Mitchell Wood being first duly sworn upon her oath states that as stenographer for the Commissioner to the Five Civilized Tribes she reported the above and foregoing proceedings and that this is a correct transcript of her stenographic notes thereof stenographic notes.

Clara Mitchell Wood

Cherokee Intermarried White 1906
Volume II

Subscribed and sworn to before me this 8th day of January 1907.

(No Signature Given)
Notary Public.

◇◇◇◇◇

Record of License issued for Marriages to Citizens of the
United States.

4th   James Mehlin issued Feb'y 25th 1868.

    Married to Miss Betsy R. Gourd, -

    Ceremony by Jno. B. Jones, March 9th 1868.

This is to certify that the foregoing is a true and correct copy of marriage license, No. 4, appearing in the District Court Records and the Records of Marriage License of the Tahlequah District, for the years 1868 to 1872.

Sarah Waters

Subscribed and sworn to before me this 12th day of January, 1907.

B. P. Rasmus
Notary Public.

◇◇◇◇◇

COPY

Tahlequah Cherokee Nation
March 9 1868

TO WHOM IT MAY CONCERN

    Be it known that in accordance with a lisence[sic] issued by William H. Turner, Clerk of the District Court of Tahlequah District on the 29th day of February 1868 I have this day joined in the holy bands of marriage Mr James G. Mehlin a citizen of the United States & Miss Elizabeth R. Goard[sic] of the Cherokee Nation.

(Signed)   John B. Jones
Minister of the Gospel

Cherokee Intermarried White 1906
Volume II

Witnesses:

Wm. R. Lotta
Anna J. Lotta

The undersigned being first duly sworn states that as stenographer to the Commissioner to the Five Civilized Tribes, she made the above and foregoing copy and that the same is a true and correct copy of the original marriage certificate.

Lola M. Champlin

Subscribed and sworn to before me this 15 day of January 1907.

Chas E Webster
Notary Public.

◇◇◇◇◇

(The Marriage Certificate above given again.)

◇◇◇◇◇

E.C.M. Cherokee 4503.

DEPARTMENT OF THE INTERIOR,

COMMISSIONER TO THE FIVE CIVILIZED TRIBES.

In the matter of the application for the enrollment of JAMES G. MEHLIN as a citizen by intermarriage of the Cherokee Nation.

D E C I S I O N

THE RECORDS OF THIS OFFICE SHOW: That at Nowata, Indian Territory, October 17, 1900, James G. Mehlin appeared before the Commission to the Five Civilized Tribes, and made application for the enrollment of himself as a citizen by intermarriage, and for the enrollment of his wife, Elizabeth Mehlin, as a citizen by blood of the Cherokee Nation. The application for the enrollment of the said Elizabeth Mehlin as a citizen by blood of the Cherokee Nation has been heretofore disposed of and her right to enrollment will not be considered in this decision. Further proceedings in the matter of said application were had at Muskogee, Indian Territory, October 3, 1902, and January 4, 1907.

THE EVIDENCE IN THIS CASE SHOWS: That the applicant herein, James G. Mehlin, a white man, in accordance with Cherokee law, March 9, 1868, to his wife, Elizabeth Mehlin, nee R. Gourd, who was at the time of said marriage a recognized

81

Cherokee Intermarried White 1906
Volume II

citizen by blood of the Cherokee Nation, and whose name appears on the approved partial roll of citizens by blood of the Cherokee Nation, opposite No. 10801; that since said marriage the said James G. Mehlin and the said Elizabeth Mehlin have resided together as husband and wife, and have continuously lived in the Cherokee Nation. Said James G. Mehlin is identified on the Cherokee authenticated tribal roll of 1880, and the Cherokee census roll of 1896, as an intermarried citizen of the Cherokee Nation.

IT IS, THEREFORE, ORDERED AND ADJUDGED: That in accordance with the decision of the Supreme Court of the United States, dated November 5, 1906, in the case of Daniel Red Bird et al. vs. the United States, under the provision of Section 21, of the Act of Congress approved June 28, 1898 (30 Stat., 495), James G. Mehlin is entitled to enrollment as a citizen by intermarriage of the Cherokee Nation, and his application for enrollment as such is accordingly granted.

Tams Bixby
Commissioner.

Dated at Muskogee, Indian Territory,
this   JAN 18 1907

◇◇◇◇◇

Cherokee
   4503.

Muskogee, Indian Territory, December 27, 1906.

James G. Mehlin,
      Alluwe, Indian Territory.

Dear Sir:

November 6, 1906, the United States Supreme Court held that white persons who intermarried with Cherokee citizens according to Cherokee law prior to November 1, 1875, are entitled to enrollment and allotments of land as citizens of the Cherokee Nation.

You are advised that to properly determine your right to enrollment as a citizen by intermarriage of the Cherokee Nation, it will be necessary for you to appear before the Commissioner for the purpose of giving testimony as to the date of your marriage and whether or not your wife, by reason of your marriage to whom you claim the right to enrollment as a citizen of the Cherokee Nation, was a recognized citizen of the Cherokee Nation at the time of your marriage to her, and whether or not you were married to her in accordance with Cherokee laws.

Cherokee Intermarried White 1906
Volume II

You are therefore directed to appear before the Commissioner at Muskogee, Indian Territory, at 9 o'clock A. M., on Friday, January 4, 1907, and give testimony as above indicated.

Respectfully,

H.J.C.   Acting Commissioner.

◇◇◇◇◇

Cherokee
4503.

Muskogee, Indian Territory, January 18, 1907.

W. W. Hastings,
      Attorney for the Cherokee Nation,
            Muskogee, Indian Territory.

Dear Sir:

There is enclosed herewith a copy of the decision of the Commissioner to the Five Civilized Tribes, dated January 17, 1907, granting the application for the enrollment of James G. Mehlin, as a citizen by intermarriage of the Cherokee Nation.

Respectfully,

Encl. HJ-22.
H.J.C.   Commissioner.

◇◇◇◇◇

Cherokee 4503   W.W.HASTINGS.   OFFICE OF   H.M. VANCE.
                       ATTORNEY.   SECRETARY.

Attorney for the Cherokee Nation,
MUSKOGEE, I. T.

January 18, 1907.

The Commissioner to the Five Civilized Tribes,
        Muskogee, Indian Territory.

Sir:

Receipt is acknowledged of the testimony and of your decision enrolling James G. Mehlin as a citizen by intermarriage of the Cherokee Nation. Time for protesting said decision is waived and I consent that said person may be placed upon the schedule immediately.

Yours very truly,
W. W. Hastings
Attorney for Cherokee Nation.

Cherokee Intermarried White 1906
Volume II

◇◇◇◇◇

Cherokee
4503

Muskogee, Indian Territory, January 21, 1907.

James G. Mehlin,
    Alluwe, Indian Territory.

Dear Sir:

    There is enclosed herewith copy of the decision of the Commissioner to the Five Civilized Tribes, dated January 18, 1907, granting the application for your enrollment as a citizen by intermarriage of the Cherokee Nation.

        Respectfully,

Encl. M - 19   Commissioner.
M.T.M.

◇◇◇◇◇

Muskogee, Indian Territory, April 8, 1907.

James G. Mehlin,
    Alluwe, Indian Territory.

Dear Sir:

    Your marriage license and certificate filed in connection with your application for enrollment as a citizen by intermarriage of the Cherokee Nation, is returned to you herewith, copies of the same being retained in this office.

        Respectfully,

Incl. P-4-11   Acting Commissioner.
  MMP

Cherokee Intermarried White 1906
Volume II

Cher IW 45
Trans from Cher 4761 3-13-07

◇◇◇◇◇

C.E.W.

DEPARTMENT OF THE INTERIOR,

COMMISSIONER TO THE FIVE CIVILIZED TRIBES.

In the matter of the application for the enrollment of

ALFRED FOYIL

as a citizen by intermarriage of the Cherokee Nation.

CHEROKEE 4761

◇◇◇◇◇

Doubtful as to Minnie Buckner.

Department of the Interior,
Commissioner to the Five Civilized Tribes,
Claremore, I.T., October 23, 1900.

In the matter of the application of Alfred Foyil for the enrollment of himself, wife, child and an adopted orphan child, Minnie Buckner, as Cherokee citizens; being sworn and examined by Com'r Needles he testified as follows:

Q What is your name? A Alfred Foyil.
Q How old are you? A 58 years old.
Q What is your post-office address? A Foyil.
Q In what district do you live? A Cooweescoowee.
Q Are you a recognized citizen of the Cherokee Nation? A Yes sir.
Q By blood or intermarriage? A Intermarriage.
Q Who do you desire to enroll? A Myseself[sic], wife and one child and I have got an adopted child that is living with me, but she is not at home now; she is at school at Tahlequah.
Q What is the name of your wife? A Charlotte.
Q When did you marry her? A 1874.
Q What is the name of your child? A Milo.
Q What is his age? A 14
Q What is the name of the adopted child which you want to enroll? A Minnie Buckner.

Cherokee Intermarried White 1906
Volume II

Q How old is Minnie? A She is 18 years old.
Q What is the name of her father? A I couldn't tell you.
Q You know the name of her mother? A Yes sir.
Q What was her name? A Her maiden name was Cindy Hampton.
Q Is she a Cherokee by blood? A Yes sir.
Q Is she living? A Yexxxx[sic] No sir
Q The child living with you? A Yes sir.
Q Are you her legal guardian? A I guess so, I have never been so appointed by law, I raised her ever since her mother died.
Q You have always lived in the Cherokee Nation since your marriage? A Yes sir.
Q Your wife too? A Yes sir.
Q She is living now? A Yes sir.
Q Your first wife? A No sir.
Q Was your former wife dead when you married Charlotte? A Yes sir.
Q Are you her first husband? A Yes sir.
Q What was her name before you married her? A Choate.
1880 roll page 695 #458 Alfred Foil Sequoyah Dist; adopted white;
1880 roll page 695 #459 Charlotte Foil Sequoyah Dist; native Cher;
1896 roll page 304 #350 Alford Foyil Cooweescoowee Dist;
1896 roll page 156 #1677 Charlotte Foyil Cooweescoowee Dist.
1896 roll page 156 #1678 Milo Foyil   "
1896 roll examined for orphan child and name not found.
1894 roll page 1049 Minnie B. Buckner Orphan roll, Cooweescoowee Dist
Q Is her name Minnie B? A No sir.
Q How long has Cynthia Hampton been dead? A About 7 or 8 years.
Q What was her name in 1880? A She was called Everett then.
Q Did she ever marry Buckner? A Yes sir.
1880 roll examined for Minnie Buckner's mother and name not found;

Com'r Needles: The name of Alfred Foyil is found upon the authenticated roll of 1880 as well as the census roll of 1896; and the name of his wife, Charlotte, is also found upon the authenticated roll of 1880 as well as the census roll of 1896, he as an intermarried citizen, and she as a Cherokee by blood; the name of his child is also found upon the 1896 census roll; they having made satisfactory proof as to residence, and being duly identified, said applicant will be duly listed for enrollment as a Cherokee citizen by intermarriage and his wife Charlotte and his child Milo as Cherokee citizens by blood.

He also applies for Minnie Buckner, an orphan child which he has raised; the name of Minnie Buckner is found upon the pay roll of 1894, her name cannot be found upon the census roll of 1896; he avers that her mother is one Cynthia Hampton, or Cynthia Buckner, but the name of Cynthia Hampton or Cynthia Buckner is not found upon the Authenticated roll of 1880; no proof is presented to the Commission as to the citizenship of said Minnie Buckner; applicant avers that she is a Cherokee citizen by blood; consequently final judgment as to the enrollment of said Minnie Buckner will be suspended, and her name will be placed upon a doubtful card, awaiting proof as to the citizenship of her mother, Cynthia.

Cherokee Intermarried White 1906
Volume II

M.D. Green, being first duly sworn states that as stenographer to the Commission to the Five Civilized Tribes he correctly recorded the testimony and proceedings in this case and that the foregoing is a true and complete transcript of his stenographic notes thereof.

MD Green

Subscribed and sworn to before me this 23 day of Oct. 1900.

CR Breckinridge

Commissioner.

◇◇◇◇◇

Cherokee 4761.

Department of the Interior,
Commission to the Five Civilized Tribes,
Muskogee, I. T., October 16, 1902.

In the matter of the application of Alfred Foyil for the enrollment of himself as a citizen by intermarriage, and for the enrollment of his wife, Charlotte, and child, Milo Foyil, as citizens by blood of the Cherokee Nation; he being sworn and examined by the Commission, testified as follows:

Q What is your name? A Alfred Foyil.
Q How old are you? A Sixty years old.
Q What is your postoffice address? A Foyil.
Q Are you a white man? A Yes sir.
Q Does your name appear on the roll of 1880 as an adopted white citizen? A Yes sir.
Q What is the name of your wife? A Charlotte Choate.
Q Was she your wife in 1880? A Yes sir.
Q Is she the wife through whom you claim your citizenship? A Yes sir.
Q Have you and your wife, Charlotte, been living together ever since 1880? A Yes sir.
Q Have you ever been separated at any time? A No sir.
Q You are living together now are you? A Yes sir.
Q Have you been residing and making your home in the Cherokee Nation ever since 1880? A Yes sir.
Q How many children have you? A One.
Q Milo? A Yes sir.
Q Is that child living with you? A Yes sir.

The undersigned, being duly sworn, states that as stenographer to the Commission to the Five Civilized Tribes he correctly recorded the testimony and proceedings in this case, and that the foregoing is a true and correct transcript of his stenographic notes thereof.

E.G. Rothenberger

Cherokee Intermarried White 1906
Volume II

Subscribed and sworn to before me this 13th day of November, 1902.

BC Jones
Notary Public.

◇◇◇◇◇

DEPARTMENT OF THE INTERIOR
COMMISSIONER TO THE FIVE CIVILIZED TRIBES
MUSKOGEE, IND. TER.
JAN. 4, 1907

IN THE MATTER OF THE APPLICATION FOR THE
ENROLLMENT OF ALFRED FOYIL AS A CITIZEN
BY INTERMARRIAGE OF THE CHEROKEE NATION

CENSUS CARE NO. 4761.

ALFRED FOYIL BEING FIRST DULY SWORN TESTIFIED AS FOLLOWS:

EXAMINATION BY THE COMMISSIONER:

Q What is your name.[sic] A Alfred Foyil.
Q How old are you.[sic] A Sixty four years old.
Q What is your post office address? A Foyil, Indian territory.
Q You claim to be a citizen by intermarriage of the Cherokee Nation? A Yes sir.
Q Thru whom do you claim your intermarried rights. A I married Charlotte Choate.
Q When was you married to Charlotte Choate.[sic] A The 15th day of August 1874.
Q Where? A Sweet town, Cherokee nation.
Q Were you ever married before you married Charlotte Foyil. A Yes sir
Q What was your first wife's name? A Cabin.
Q Was she a citizen or non citizen of the Cherokee Nation? A Non citizen
Q Was she living or dead at the time you married Charlotte Foyil. A Dead.
Q Was Charlotte Foyil ever married before she married you[sic] A No sir
Q Are you and Charlotte Foyil living together at this time[sic] A Yes sir
Q Have you lived together continuously since you married in 1874. A Yes sir.
Q Were you married under Cherokee license. A Yes sir.
Q Have you got that license with you. A Yes sir.

The applicant offers in evidence the marriage license issued to him on the 14th day of August 1874 by R. R. Taylor Clerk of Sequoyah District to marry Miss Charlotte Choate a Cherokee citizen and also the certificate that he was married under said license on the 15th day of August 1874; the certificate being signed by Franklin Faulker[sic] Judge of Sequoyah District Cherokee Nation.

Applicant is identified on the 1880 Cherokee Roll Sequoyah District opposite No. 458; his wife thru whom he claims his right to enrollment is identified on said roll

Cherokee Intermarried White 1906
Volume II

and said district opposite No. 459; she is also identified on the final roll of citizens by blood of the Cherokee Nation opposite No. 11409.

Clara Mitchell Wood being first duly sworn upon her oath states that as stenographer for the Commissioner to the Five Civilized Tribes she reported the above and foregoing proceedings and that this is a correct transcript of her stenographic notes.

Clara Mitchell Wood

Subscribed and sworn to before me this 8th day of January 1907

B.P. Rasmus
Notary Public.

◇◇◇◇◇

(COPY)

Cherokee Nation I Mr. Alfred Foyl[sic] a whiteman and a citizen of the United
                I States, having already complied with the law respecting inter-
Sequoyah Dist I marriage with white men by presenting a petition with the requisite number of signers, to marry Charlotte Choate a Cherokee, License is hereby granted to the Mr. Foyl to marry the said Miss Choate Now, therefore, To Any of the Judges of the Cherokee Nation or Any regularly ordained Minister of the Gospel, "Greeting" You are hereby Authorized by virtue of this license to join in the hold bonds of matrimony, by solemnizing the rights usually observed in such cases between the above named Alfred Foyl and Charlotte Choate Given from under my hand officially on this 14th day of Aug. 1874

R.R. Taylor Clk. Seq. Dist.

I do hereby certify that I performed the mariage[sic] ceremony Between the within named couple on this the 15th day of August 1874

Franklin Falkner, Judge
Sequoyah Dist. C.N.

Clerks, Office. I
Sequoyah District I
Cherokee Nation I I hereby certify that the within Marriage License and certificate were recorded by me in BookA. Page (124) Records of Marriage License in this office this September 3rd 1890

J.H. Adair, Clerk
Sequoyah District
C.N.

(SEAL)

Cherokee Intermarried White 1906
Volume II

The undersigned being first duly sworn states, that as stenographer to the Commissioner to the Five Civilized Tribes, he made the above and foregoing copy, and that the same is a true and correct copy of the marriage license and certificate now on file in this office.

Robt P. Ironside

Subscribed and sworn to before me the 12 day of January, 1907.

Chas E Webster

My Comm Ex_____   Notary Public

◇◇◇◇◇

C.E.W.   Cherokee 4761

DEPARTMENT OF THE INTERIOR,

COMMISSIONER TO THE FIVE CIVILIZED TRIBES.

In the matter of the application for the enrollment of Alfred Foyil, as a citizen by intermarriage of the Cherokee Nation.

D E C I S I O N

THE RECORDS OF THIS OFFICE SHOW: That at Claremore, Indian Territory, October 23, 1900, Alfred Foyil appeared before the Commission to the Five Civilized Tribes, and made application for the enrollment of himself, as a citizen by intermarriage, and for the enrollment of his wife, Charlotte Foyil, and his son Milo Foyil, as citizens by blood of the Cherokee Nation. The application for the enrollment of the said Charlotte Foyil and her son, Milo Foyil, as citizens by blood of the Cherokee Nation has been heretofore disposed of and their rights to enrollment will not be considered in this decision. Further proceedings in the matter of said application were had at Muskogee, Indian Territory, October 16, 1902, and January 4, 1907.

THE EVIDENCE IN THIS CASE SHOWS: That the applicant herein Alfred Foyil, a white man, was married in accordance with Cherokee law August 15, 1874 to his wife, Charlotte Foyil, nee Choate, who was at the time of said marriage a recognized citizen by blood of the Cherokee Nation, and whose name appears upon the approved partial roll of citizens by blood of the Cherokee Nation, opposite Number 11409; that since said marriage the said Alfred Foyil and Charlotte Foyil have resided together as husband and wife and have continuously lived in the Cherokee Nation. Said Alfred Foyil is identified on the Cherokee Authenticated tribal roll of 1880, and the Cherokee Census Roll of 1896 as an intermarried citizen of the Cherokee Nation.

Cherokee Intermarried White 1906
Volume II

IT IS, THEREFORE, ORDERED AND ADJUDGED: That in accordance with the decision of the Supreme Court of the United States, dated November 5, 1906, in the case of Daniel Red Bird et al., vs. the United States under the provision of Section 21 of the Act of Congress approved June 28, 1898, (30 Stat. 495), Alfred Foyil is entitled to enrollment as a citizen by intermarriage of the Cherokee Nation, and his application for enrollment as such is accordingly granted.

Tams Bixby
Commissioner.

Dated at Muskogee, Indian Territory,
this   JAN 17 1907

◇◇◇◇◇

Cherokee
4761.

Muskogee, Indian Territory, December 28, 1906.

Alfred Foyil,
    Foyil, Indian Territory.

Dear Sir:

    November 6, 1906, the United States Supreme Court held that white persons who intermarried with Cherokee citizens according to Cherokee law prior to November 1, 1875, are entitled to enrollment and allotments of land as citizens of the Cherokee Nation.

    You are advised that to properly determine your right to enrollment as a citizen by intermarriage of the Cherokee Nation, it will be necessary for you to appear before the Commissioner for the purpose of giving testimony as to the date of your marriage and whether or not your wife, by reason of your marriage to whom you claim the right to enrollment as a citizen of the Cherokee Nation, was a recognized citizen of the Cherokee Nation at the time of your marriage to her, and whether or not you were married to her in accordance with Cherokee laws.

    You are therefore directed to appear before the Commissioner at Muskogee, Indian Territory, at 9 o'clock A. M., on Friday, January 4, 1907, and give testimony as above indicated.

Respectfully,

H.J.C.   Acting Commissioner.

◇◇◇◇◇

Cherokee Intermarried White 1906
Volume II

Cherokee 4761

Muskogee, Indian Territory, January 17, 1907.

W. W. Hastings,
    Attorney for the Cherokee Nation,
        Muskogee, Indian Territory.

Dear Sir:

There is enclosed herewith copy of the decision of the Commissioner to the Five Civilized Tribes, dated January 17, 1907, granting the application for the enrollment of Alfred Foyil as a citizen by intermarriage of the Cherokee Nation.

Respectfully,

Encl. I-14
RPI

Commissioner.

◇◇◇◇◇

Cherokee 4761.   W.W.HASTINGS.   OFFICE OF   H.M. VANCE.
                ATTORNEY.   SECRETARY.

Attorney for the Cherokee Nation,
MUSKOGEE, I. T. January 18, 1907.

The Commissioner to the Five Civilized Tribes,
    Muskogee, Indian Territory.

Sir:

Receipt is acknowledged of the testimony and of your decision enrolling Alfred Foyil as a citizen by intermarriage of the Cherokee Nation. Time for protesting said decision is waived and I consent that said person may be placed upon the schedule immediately.

Yours very truly,
W. W. Hastings
Attorney for Cherokee Nation.

◇◇◇◇◇

Cherokee Intermarried White 1906
Volume II

Cherokee
4761

Muskogee, Indian Territory, January 19, 1907.

Alfred Foyil,
    Foyil, Indian Territory.

Dear Sir:

    There is enclosed herewith a copy of the decision of the Commissioner to the Five Civilized Tribes, dated January 18, 1907, granting your application for enrollment as a citizen by intermarriage of the Cherokee Nation.

                  Respectfully,

Encl. H-84   Commissioner.
JMH

◇◇◇◇◇

Muskogee, Indian Territory, April 8, 1907.

Alfred Foyil,
    Foyil, Indian Territory.

Dear Sir:

    Your marriage livense[sic] and certificate filed in connection with your application for enrollment as a citizen by intermarriage of the Cherokee Nation, is returned to you herewith, copies of the same being retained in this office.

                  Respectfully,

Incl. P-4-12   Acting Commissioner.
MMP

Cherokee Intermarried White 1906
Volume II

Cher IW 46
Trans from Cher 4906 3-13-07

Department of the Interior,
Commission to the Five Civilized Tribes,
Claremore, I. T. October, 25th 1900.

In the matter of the application of Murdock McLeod for enrollment as a Cherokee Citizen. He being sworn testified before the Commission as follows:

Q What is your name? A. Murdoch McLeod.
Q What is your age? A. 66.
Q What is your post office? A. Claremore.
Q What district do you live in? A. Cooweescoowee.
Q Who is it that you want enrolled? A. Just myself.
Q Are you a Cherokee by blood? A. No sir.
Q When were you married? A. In 1869.
Q To whom were you married? A. Annie H. Brown.
Q She was a Cherokee was she? A. yes sir.
Q Is she alive? A. No sir.
Q When did she die? A. In 1876.
Q Did you and she live together from the time you were married until her death?
A. Yes sir.
Q Have you ever married since her death? A. No sir.

1880 roll, page 143, No. 1977, M. McLeord[sic], Cooweescoowee, Adpt. White
1896   315   656, Murdoc McCloud   "

Q Have you lived in the Cherokee Nation ever since 1880? A. I moved here in 1859 and have never been out but twice when I went to Fort Smith on a visit.

The applicant is identified on the roll of 1880 and 1896 as an adopted Cherokee. He has lived in the Cherokee Nation ever since the death of his Cherokee wife. He has lived in the Cherokee Nation since 1859. He has never married since the death of his Cherokee wife and he will be listed for enrollment as a Cherokee by adoption.

§§*§*§*§*§*§*§*§*§*§*§*§*§*§*§*§*§*

Chas. von Weise being sworn states that as stenographer to the Commission to the Five Civilized Tribes he reported in full all the proceedings had in the above entitled cause and that the foregoing is a full, true and correct transcript of his stenographic notes in said proceeding.

                                        Chas vonWeise

Cherokee Intermarried White 1906
Volume II

Subscribed and sworn to before me this the 26th of October, 1900.

MD Green
Notary Public.

◇◇◇◇◇

COOWEESCOOWEE.
Statement of Applicant Taken Under Oath.

CHEROKEE BY BLOOD AND ADOPTION.

66   Date   OCT 25 1900   1900.
Name   Murdoch McLeod
District   COOWEESCOOWEE.   Year   1880   Page   143   No.   1977
Citizen by blood   No   Mother's citizenship
Intermarried citizen   Yes
Married under what law   Date of marriage   1869
License   Certificate
Wife's name
District   Year   Page   No.
Citizen by blood   Mother's citizenship
Intermarried citizen
Married under what law   Date of marriage
License   Certificate

Names of Children:

Dist.   Year   Page   No.   Age
Dist.   Year   Page   No.   Age
Dist.   Year   Page   No.   Age
Dist.   Year   Page   No.   Age
Dist.   Year   Page   No.   Age

On 1880 Roll as M. McLeord.

◇◇◇◇◇

Cher-4906

DEPARTMENT OF THE INTERIOR.
Commission to the Five Civilized Tribes.
Muskogee, I.T., October 21, 1902.

In the matter of the application of Murdock McLeod for enrollment as a citizen by intermarriage of the Cherokee Nation.

Murdock McLeod, called as a witness, being first duly sworn by the Commission, testified as follows:

Cherokee Intermarried White 1906
Volume II

Q What is your name? A Murdock McLeod.
Q How old are you? A 68 years.
Q What is your postoffice address? A Clarmore[sic], I.T.
Q You are a white man are you? A Yes sir.
Q Have you been enrolled on the 1880 roll as an adopted white citizen? A Yes sir.
Q What was your wife's name in 1880? A Her name was Annie Henry.
Q Is she the wife through whom you claim citizenship? A Yes, she has been dead some years.
Q Was she dead in 1880? A I believe so.
Q Was she the first wife you ever had? A Yes sir.
Q And the only wife you ever had? A Yes sir.
Q You think she died about twenty years ago? A Yes, I don't recollect the date; between 1870 and 1880.
Q You lived with her from the time you married her up to the time she died? A Yes sir.
Q You have been residing in the Cherokee nation[sic] since 1880? A Yes sir.
Q Never lived anywhere else? A I have never been out of the Cherokee nation since 1859, only just across the line.
Q You say you just married the one time? A Yes sir.
Q You are a widower now? A Yes sir.

---------o---------

Frances R. Lane upon oath states that as stenographer to the Commission to the Five Civilized Tribes she correctly recorded the testimony in the above entitled cause, and that the foregoing is an accurate transcript of her stenographic notes thereof.

Frances R Lane

Subscribed and sworn to before me this 28th day of October, 1902.

BC Jones
Notary Public.

BCJ

Cherokee 4906					Cherokee Allotment 24746

Department of the Interior,
Commission to the Five Civilized Tribes,
Cherokee Land Office,
Tahlequah, I.T., August 19, 1903.

In the matter of the application of Murdoch McLeon[sic] for enrollment as a citizen by intermarriage of the Cherokee Nation.

Cherokee Intermarried White 1906
Volume II

SUPPLEMENTAL TESTIMONY.

NELLIE C. ROSS, being duly sworn and examined by the Commission, testified as follows:

Q What is your name? A Nellie C. Ross.
Q How old are you? A 31.
Q What is your postoffice address? A Claremore.
Q You are enrolled by this Commission as a citizen by blood of the Cherokee Nation, are you? A Yes sir.
Q You present here a power of attorney signed by Murdoch McLeod, authorizing you to select the allotment to which he is entitled in the Cherokee Nation; why is Murdoch McLeod not here to select his own allotment? A He is not able to make the trip.
Q Why isn't he able to? A He is feeble from old age.
Q Is there any special illness or is he just infirm from old age? A Just general inform condition.
Q You state that on account of his age he is not able to make the trip to Tahlequah from Claremore? A Yes sir.
Q Are you any relation of his? A He is my father.

      Commission: It appearing that Murdoch McLeod is infirm and unable to make personal selection of his allotment in the Cherokee Nation, his daughter, Nellie C. Ross, will be permitted to represent him by poser of attorney in selection of said allotment.

++++++++++++++++++++++++++

Mabel F. Maxwell, being duly sworn, states that, as stenographer to the Commission to the Five Civilized Tribes, she correctly recorded the supplemental testimony in this case, and that the above is a true and complete transcript of her stenographic notes thereof.

                                            Mabel F Maxwell

Subscribed and sworn to before me
this 19th day of August, 1903.

                                            Samuel Foreman
MFM   Notary Public.

Cherokee Intermarried White 1906
Volume II

Cherokee 4906

DEPARTMENT OF THE INTERIOR
COMMISSIONER TO THE FIVE CIVILIZED TRIBES
MUSKOGEE, INDIAN TERRITORY
January 3, 1907

In the matter of the application for the enrollment of Murdoch McLeod as a citizen by intermarriage of the Cherokee Nation.

The applicant being first duly sworn by Walter W. Chappell a notary for the Western District testified as follows:

Q What is your name? [sic] Murdoch McLeod
Q What is your age? A Seventy-two
Q What is your postoffice address? A Claremore
Q Do you claim to be a citizen by intermarriage of the Cherokee Nation? A Yes sir.
Q Through whom do you claim that right? A I married a girl by the name of Annie Henry Brown
Q Is she living at the present time? A No sir.
Q When did she die? A She died in 1875
Q What was her citizenship at the time of her marriage to you? A She was a one quarter or one half Cherokee.
Q Where were you married? A Tahlequah
Q Were you married under Cherokee license? A Yes sir.
Q What was the date of this marriage? A February 8, 1868
Q Was the license under which you were married issued by the authorities of the Tahlequah district? A Yes sir, by the clerk of the District, Robert Ross
Q Have you a certified copy of that license? A No sir.

Opposite No. 11 under the head of "Record of Licenses issued for marriages to citizens of the United States", of the "District Court Records and of marriage licenses Tahlequah District 1868--72", now in the custody of this office, appears the following:

"Murdoch McLeod issued February 8, 1869 to marry Miss Ann Henry Brown. Ceremony by John B. Jones February 10, 1869"

Q Had either you or your wife been married prior to your marriage in 1869? A No sir
Q Did you live together continuously from that time till her death in 1875? A Yes sir.
Q Where did you reside? A In Tahlequah at that time
Q Did you live there continuously up to her death? A Yes sir.
Q Where have you lived since that time[sic]A Well in different parts of the Nation, I am a carpenter by trade, so work around
Q Have you ever lived outside the Cherokee Nation since her death[sic] A No sir.
Q Have you since her death married again? A No sir.

Cherokee Intermarried White 1906
Volume II

The applicant is identified on the authenticated Cherokee Roll of 1880 and Cherokee Census Roll of 1896, Cooesscoowee[sic] District, opposite numbers 1977 and 656, respectively, as an intermarried white.

Q Did you have any children by your wife? A Yes sir, one living yet
Q What is its name? A She's Mrs. Ross now, married. She's a widow, Nellie Ross, her name was Nellie Catherine McLeod before she married
Q Was she married prior to September 1, 1902? A I can't say
Q Has she made application for enrollment as a Cherokee? A Oh yes She's got deeds to her land. She's a Cherokee all right.
Q Do you know under what name she made application? A Nellie K Ross or Nellie C Ross, sometime C and sometimes K

Witness excused

Gertrude Hanna, being duly sworn, states on oath that as stenographer to the Commissioner to the Five Civilized Tribes she reported the proceedings in the above case on January 3, 1907 and that the above and foregoing is a true and correct transcript of her stenographic notes taken therein.

Gertrude Hanna

Subscribed and sworn to before me this 4th day of January, 1907

Walter W Chappell
Notary Public

◇◇◇◇◇

C.F.B. Cherokee 4906.

DEPARTMENT OF THE INTERIOR,

COMMISSIONER TO THE FIVE CIVILIZED TRIBES.

In the matter of the application for the enrollment of MURDOCH McLEOD as a citizen by intermarriage of the Cherokee Nation.

D E C I S I O N

THE RECORDS OF THIS OFFICE SHOW: That at Claremore, Indian Territory, October 25, 1900, Murdoch McLeod appeared before the Commission to the Five Civilized Tribes, and made application for his enrollment as a citizen by intermarriage of the Cherokee Nation. Further proceedings in the matter of said application were had at Muskogee, Indian Territory, October 21, 1902, at Tahlequah, Indian Territory, August 19, 1903, and at Muskogee, Indian Territory, January 3, 1907.

Cherokee Intermarried White 1906
Volume II

THE EVIDENCE IN THIS CASE SHOWS: That the applicant herein, Murdoch McLeod, a white man, married February 10, 1869, one Ann Henry Brown, a citizen by blood of the Cherokee Nation, in accordance with Cherokee law. Said applicant and his wife resided together as husband and wife until the death of the said Ann Henry McLeod, which occurred in 1875; that since the death of his said wife said Murdoch McLeod has not married and that his residence has been continuously in the Cherokee Nation since 1869. Said applicant is identified on the Cherokee authenticated tribal roll of 1880, and the Cherokee Census Roll of 1896 as an intermarried citizen of the Cherokee Nation.

IT IS, THEREFORE, ORDERED AND ADJUDGED: That in accordance with the decision of the Supreme Court of the United States, dated November 5, 1906, in the case of Daniel Red Bird et al. vs. the United States, under the provisions of Section 21, of the Act of Congress approved June 28, 1898 (30 Stats., 495), Murdoch McLeod is entitled to enrollment as a citizen by intermarriage of the Cherokee Nation, and his application for enrollment as such is accordingly granted.

                Tams Bixby
                      Commissioner.

Dated at Muskogee, Indian Territory,
this JAN 17 1907

◇◇◇◇◇

Cherokee
 4906.

             Muskogee, Indian Territory, December 28, 1906.

Murdoch McLeod,
  Claremore, Indian Territory.

Dear Sir:

  November 6, 1906, the United States Supreme Court held that white persons who intermarried with Cherokee citizens according to Cherokee law prior to November 1, 1875, are entitled to enrollment and allotments of land as citizens of the Cherokee Nation.

  You are advised that to properly determine your right to enrollment as a citizen by intermarriage of the Cherokee Nation, it will be necessary for you to appear before the Commissioner for the purpose of giving testimony as to the date of your marriage and whether or not your wife, by reason of your marriage to whom you claim the right to enrollment as a citizen of the Cherokee Nation, was a recognized citizen of the Cherokee Nation at the time of your marriage to her, and whether or not you were married to her in accordance with Cherokee laws.

Cherokee Intermarried White 1906
Volume II

You are therefore directed to appear before the Commissioner at Muskogee, Indian Territory, at 9 o'clock A. M., on Friday, January 4, 1907, and give testimony as above indicated.

Respectfully,

H.J.C.   Acting Commissioner.

◇◇◇◇◇

Cherokee
    4906

Muskogee, Indian Territory, January 17, 1907.

W. W. Hastings,
    Attorney for the Cherokee Nation,
        Muskogee, Indian Territory.

Dear Sir:

There is enclosed herewith a copy of the decision of the Commissioner to the Five Civilized Tribes, dated January 18, 1907, granting the application for the enrollment of Murdoch McLeod as a citizen by intermarriage of the Cherokee Nation.

Respectfully,

E.R.C.   Commissioner.
Enc. E.C.-3

◇◇◇◇◇

Cherokee 4906.   W.W.HASTINGS.   OFFICE OF   H.M. VANCE.
                        ATTORNEY.   SECRETARY.

Attorney for the Cherokee Nation,
MUSKOGEE, I. T.

January 18, 1907.

The Commissioner to the Five Civilized Tribes,
    Muskogee, Indian Territory.

Sir:

Receipt is acknowledged of the testimony and of your decision enrolling Murdoch McLeod as a citizen by intermarriage of the Cherokee Nation. Time for protesting said decision is waived and I consent that said person may be placed upon the schedule immediately.

Yours very truly,
        W. W. Hastings
            Attorney for Cherokee Nation.

Cherokee Intermarried White 1906
Volume II

Cherokee
4906

Muskogee, Indian Territory, January 19, 1907.

Murdoch McLeod,
    Claremore, Indian Territory.

Dear Sir:

    There is enclosed herewith a copy of the decision of the Commissioner to the Five Civilized Tribes, dated January 18, 1907, granting your application for enrollment as a citizen by intermarriage of the Cherokee Nation.

    You will be advised when your name has been placed upon a schedule of citizens of the Cherokee Nation and approved by the Secretary of the Interior.

                      Respectfully,

Encl.H-79   Commissioner.
  JMH

Cher IW 47
Trans from Cher 5154 3-13-07

                                                               C.F.B.

DEPARTMENT OF THE INTERIOR,

COMMISSIONER TO THE FIVE CIVILIZED TRIBES.

In the matter of the application for the enrollment of

                Greenville P. Hefflefinger

as a citizen by intermarriage of the Cherokee Nation.

                      Cherokee 5154.

Cherokee Intermarried White 1906
Volume II

◇◇◇◇◇

R

Department of the Interior,
Commission to the Five Civilized Tribes,
Claremore, I. T., October 30, 1900.

In the matter of the application of Elizabeth Hefflefinger for the enrollment of herself and husband as Cherokee citizens; being sworn by Commissioner Brecinridge[sic] and examined by the Commission she testified as follows:

Q What is your name? A Elizabeth Hefflefinger
Q How old are you? A I guess I am about 48
Q What is your post-office address? A Dawson
Q Do you make application for enrollment as a citizen by blood of the Cherokee Nation? A Yes sir.
Q What degree of Cherokee blood do you claim? A Quarter I guess, or over a quarter, my father was half.
Q Who do you want to have enrolled? A Myself and my husband.
Q No children? A No sir.
Q What district ware you living in? A Coowee coowee[sic]
Q How long have you lived in the Cherokee Nation? A All my live.
Q Have you been outside of the Cherokee Nation at any time during the past three years? A Only right there at Tulsa, Indian Territory Creek Nation, I had children there going to school.
Q What is the name of your father? A Jesse Cochran.
Q Was he a Cherokee by blood? A Yes sir.
Q Is he living or dead? A Dead.
Q What is the name of your mother? A Betsy.
Q Your mother living? A Ye No sir.
Q Was she a Cherokee? A Yes sir.
Q Are you married? A Yes sir.
Q What is the name of your husband? A Pace Hefflefinger.
Q Has he any middle name? A Greenville Pace.
Q We had better enroll him as Greenville Pace hadn't we? A Yes sir, I guess so.
Q Is your husband living? A Yes sir.
Q What is his age? A 52 I believe.
Q Is he a Cherokee citizen by blood or adoption? A By adoption
Q What is the name of his father? A His name was the same Greenville Hefflefinger.
Q Is his father living or dead? A Dead.
Q Was he a Cherokee or a white man? A White man.
Q What is the name of your husband's mother? A Nancy.
Q Is she living? No sir.
Q Were the parents of your husband ever recognized as citizens of the Cherokee Nation? A No sir.

Cherokee Intermarried White 1906
Volume II

Q When were you married to your husband? A In 1872
Q You have been living with him continuously since that time? A Yes sir.
Q Were you ever married before? A No sir.
Q Was he ever married before? A No sir.
Q What district did you live in in 1880? A Cooweescoowee.
Q In what district did you liv in 1896? A Cooweescoowee
1880 roll page 119 #1462 as Pace Hefferfinger[sic] Cooweescoowee adopted white
1880 roll page 119 #1464 Lizzie Hefferfinger Cooweescoowee native Ch
1896 roll page 309 #512 Pace Hefflefinger Cooweescoowee
1896 roll page 182 #2408 Lizzie Hefflefinger Cooweescoowee
Q Have you any evidence of your marriage to your husband? A No sir.

Commission: The applicant applies for the enrollment of herself and husband; she is identified on the authenticated roll of 1880 as well as the census roll of 1896 as a native Cherokee; she has lived in the Cherokee Nation all her live and will be listed for enrollment by this Commission as a Cherokee citizen by blood.

She avers that she was married to her husband in 1872, and that neither she nor he had been married previous to that time; they have lived together continuously since that time as man and wife; he is identified with her on the authenticated roll of 1880 as an adopted white, and upon the census roll of 1896 as an adopted white; satisfactory proof as to his residence in the Cherokee Nation having been made, he will be listed for enrollment as a citizen by intermarriage of the Cherokee Nation.

M.D. Green, being first duly sworn, states that as stenographer to the Commission to the Five Civilized Tribes he corrected recorded the testimony and proceedings in this case and that the foregoing is a true and complete transcript of his stenographic notes thereof.

                     MD Green

Subscribed and sworn to before me this 31 day of Oct., 1900.

           CR Breckinridge
                    Commissioner.

Cherokee Intermarried White 1906
Volume II

DEPARTMENT OF THE INTERIOR.
Commission to the Five Civilized Tribes.
Muskogee, Indian Territory, October 7th, 1902.

In the matter of the applicantion[sic] of Greenville P. Hefflefinger for the enrollment of himself as a citizen by intermarriage of the Cherokee Nation and for the enrollment of his wife, Elizabeth Hefflefinger, as a citizen by blood of the Cherokee Nation.

Supplemental to #5154.

Applicant appears in person.
Cherokee Nation by J. C. Starr.

GREENVILLE P. HEFFLEFINGER, being duly sworn, testified as follows:
Examined by the Commission.
Q. State your full name? A. Greenville P. Hefflefinger.
Q. How old are you? A. I am 53--this last March.
Q. What is your post office? A. Dawson.
Q. You are a white man? A. Yes, sir.
Q. Are you the Greenville P. Hefflefinger who made application in 1900 to be enrolled as a citizen of the Cherokee Nation by intermarriage? A. Yes, sir.
Q. What is the name of the wife through whom you claim? A. Elizabth[sic].
Q. Is she your first wife? A. Yes, sir.
Q. You were never married before? A. Oh, no.
Q. Was she ever married before she married you? A. No, sir.
Q. How long have you lived in the Cherokee Nation? A. I been here ever since '71.
Q. Continuously? A. Yes, sir; only just to make a visit.
Q. But your home has been in the Cherokee Nation? A. Yes, sir.
Q. When did you marry your wife Elizabeth? A. Spring of '72, I think.
Q. You are both on the roll of eighty? A. Yes, sir.
Q. Have you been living together in the Cherokee Nation ever since that time? A. Yes, sir.
Q. Living together now? A. Yes, sir.
Q. Never been separated? A. No, sir.
Q. You have no children? A. Yes, I have two children.
Q. But they are married? A. Yes, sir.
Q. No children living with you? A. No, sir.

++

Cherokee Intermarried White 1906
Volume II

Jesse O. Carr, being first duly sworn, states that as stenographer to the Commission to the Five Civilized Tribes he reported the above entitled case and that the foregoing is a true and complete transcript of his stenographic notes thereof.

Jesse O. Carr

Subscribed and sworn to before me this 15$^{\underline{th}}$ day of November, 1902.

BC Jones
Notary Public.

◇◇◇◇◇

Cherokee-5154.

DEPARTMENT OF THE INTERIOR,
COMMISSIONER TO THE FIVE CIVILIZED TRIBES.
Muskogee, I.T., January 4, 1907.

In the matter of the application for the enrollment of GREENVILLE P. HEFFLEFINGER as a citizen by intermarriage of the Cherokee Nation.

Elizabeth Hefflefinger, being first duly sworn, testified as follows: The oath being administered by B. P. Rasmus, a Notary Public for the Western District, Indian Territory.

By the Commissioner:
Q What is your name? A Elizabeth Hefflefinger.
Q What is your age? A Fifty-four, I think is my age.
Q Are you a citizen by blood of the Cherokee Nation? A yes sir.
Q Are you married? A Yes sir.
Q What is your husband's name? A Greenville P. Hefflefinger.
Q Is he living? A Yes sir.
Q Is he a Cherokee by blood? A No sir.
Q He claims the right to enrollment as a citizen of the Cherokee nation[sic] by virtue of his marriage to you, does he? A Yes sir.
Q When were you married to him? A In 1872.
Q Were you a recognized citizen of the Cherokee nation at the time of your marriage? A Yes sir.
Q And living in the Cherokee country, were you? A Yes sir- I was born there.
Q Since your marriage have you and he continuously resided together as husband and wife? A Yes sir.
Q And lived continuously in the Cherokee nation, have you? A Yes sir.
Q In what district were you married? A Cooweescoowee.
Q Did he marry you in accordance with the Cherokee law? A Yes sir.
Q Obtained a license from the Cherokee authorities? A Yes sir
Q Who married you? A Jim Teacher, a full blood Cherokee preacher.

Cherokee Intermarried White 1906
Volume II

Q Have you any documentary evidence to show your marriage? Have you a license?
A No, I haven't got it.
Q It was recorded was it? A Yes sir.
Q In Cooweescoowee District? A Yes sir, when Myers was clerk

> The original marriage records, Cooweescoowee District, Book C., which is in the possession of this office, page 9, shows the following entry:
> "   May ___, issued license of marriage to G. P. Hefflefinger, a citizen of the United Stares, to marry Elizabeth Cochran, a citizen of the Cherokee nation. Issued by John Mayes, District Clerk. Married by Rev. James Teacher, May 11, 1872."
>
> The applicant Greenville P. Hefflefinger, is identified on the authenticated Cherokee tribal roll of 1880 Cooweescoowee District, No. 1462.
> The name of his wife, Elizabeth Heflefinger[sic], is included in the approved partian roll of citizens by blood of the Cherokee Nation the Cherokee Nation opposite No. 12368.

Q Have you ever been married more than the one time? A No
Q Was your husband ever married prior to his marriage to you? A No sir.

Frances R. Lane upon oath states that as stenographer to the Commissioner to the Five Civilized Tribes she reported the testimony in the above entitled cause and that the above and foregoing is an accurate transcript of her stenographic notes thereof.

Frances R Lane

Subscribed and sworn to before me this January 5, 1907.

Edward Merrick
Notary Public.

◇◇◇◇◇

Cherokee Intermarried White 1906
Volume II

C. F. B. Cherokee 5154.

DEPARTMENT OF THE INTERIOR,

COMMISSIONER TO THE FIVE CIVILIZED TRIBES.

In the matter of the application for the enrollment of Greenville P. Hefflefinger, as a citizen by intermarriage of the Cherokee Nation.

D E C I S I O N

THE RECORDS OF THIS OFFICE SHOW: That at Claremore, Indian Territory, October 30, 1900, Elizabeth Hefflefinger appeared before the Commission to the Five Civilized Tribes and made application for the enrollment of herself as a citizen by blood, and for the enrollment of her husband, Greenville P. Hefflefinger, as a citizen by intermarriage of the Cherokee Nation. The application for the enrollment of said Elizabeth Hefflefinger has been heretofore disposed of and her rights to enrollment will not be considered in this decision. Further proceedings in the matter of said application were had at Muskogee, Indian Territory, October 7, 1902, and January 4, 1907.

THE EVIDENCE IN THIS CASE SHOWS: That the applicant herein, Greenville P. Hefflefinger, a white man, married on May 11, 1872, his wife Elizabeth Hefflefinger, nee Cochran, in accordance with Cherokee law, and who was at the time of said marriage, a recognized citizen by blood of the Cherokee Nation, and whose name appears upon the approved partial roll of citizens of the Cherokee Nation opposite nimber[sic] 12368; that from the time of said marriage, the said Greenville P. and Elizabeth Hefflefinger have resided together as husband and wife and have continuously lived in the Cherokee Nation. Said applicant is duly identified on the Cherokee authenticated tribal roll of 1880 and the Cherokee census roll of 1896, as an intermarried citizen of the Cherokee Nation.

IT IS, THEREFORE, ORDERED AND ADJUDGED: That in accordance with the decision of the Supreme Court of the United States, dated November 5, 1906, in the case of Daniel Red Bird, et al., vs. the United States, under the provision of Section 21 of the Act of Congress approved June 28, 1898, (30 Stat., 495), Greenville P. Hefflefinger is entitled to enrollment as a citizen by intermarriage of the Cherokee Nation and his application for enrollment as such is accordingly granted.

Tams Bixby
Commissioner.

Dated at Muskogee, Indian Territory,
this   JAN 16 1907

Cherokee Intermarried White 1906
Volume II

Cherokee
5154.

Muskogee, Indian Territory, December 29, 1906.

Greenville P. Hefflefinger,
    Dawson, Indian Territory.

Dear Sir:

    November 6, 1906, the United States Supreme Court held that white persons who intermarried with Cherokee citizens according to Cherokee law prior to November 1, 1875, are entitled to enrollment and allotments of land as citizens of the Cherokee Nation.

    You are advised that to properly determine your right to enrollment as a citizen by intermarriage of the Cherokee Nation, it will be necessary for you to appear before the Commissioner for the purpose of giving testimony as to the date of your marriage and whether or not your wife, by reason of your marriage to whom you claim the right to enrollment as a citizen of the Cherokee Nation, was a recognized citizen of the Cherokee Nation at the time of your marriage to her, and whether or not you were married to her in accordance with Cherokee laws.

    You are, therefore, directed to appear before the Commissioner at Muskogee, Indian Territory, at 9 o'clock A. M., on Friday, January 4, 1907, and give testimony as above indicated.

                            Respectfully,

H.J.C.   Commissioner.

◇◇◇◇◇

Cherokee 5154

Muskogee, Indian Territory, January 17, 1907.

W. W. Hastings,
    Attorney for the Cherokee Nation,
        Muskogee, Indian Territory.

Dear Sir:

    There is enclosed herewith copy of the decision of the Commissioner to the Five Civilized Tribes, dated January 16, 1907, granting the application for the enrollment of Greenville P. Hefflefinger as a citizen by intermarriage of the Cherokee Nation.

Cherokee Intermarried White 1906
Volume II

Respectfully,

Enc I-3
RPI
Commissioner.

◇◇◇◇◇

Cherokee 5154.   W.W. HASTINGS.   OFFICE OF   H.M. VANCE.
ATTORNEY.   SECRETARY.

Attorney for the Cherokee Nation,
MUSKOGEE, I. T.

January 18, 1907.

The Commissioner to the Five Civilized Tribes,
    Muskogee, Indian Territory.
Sir:

    Receipt is acknowledged of the testimony and of your decision enrolling Greenville P. Hefflefinger as a citizen by intermarriage of the Cherokee Nation. Time for protesting said decision is waived and I consent that said person may be placed upon the schedule immediately.

Yours very truly,
W. W. Hastings
Attorney for Cherokee Nation.

◇◇◇◇◇

Cherokee
5154

Muskogee, Indian Territory, January 19, 1907.

Greenville P. Hefflefinger,
    Dawson, Indian Territory.

Dear Sir:

    There is enclosed herewith copy of the decision of the Commissioner to the Five Civilized Tribes, dated January 16, 1907, granting the application for your enrollment as a citizen by intermarriage of the Cherokee Nation.

    You will be advised when your name has been placed upon a schedule of citizens of the Cherokee Nation and approved by the Secretary of the Interior.

Respectfully,

Enc I-2
RPI
Commissioner.

Cherokee Intermarried White 1906
Volume II

Cher IW 48
Trans from Cher 5393   3-13-07

C.E.W..

DEPARTMENT OF THE INTERIOR,

COMMISSIONER TO THE FIVE CIVILIZED TRIBES.

In the matter of the application for the enrollment of

JOHN H. BAKER

as a citizen by intermarriage of the Cherokee Nation.

CHEROKEE 5393

DEPARTMENT OF THE INTERIOR,
COMMISSION TO THE FIVE CIVILIZED TRIBES,
CLAREMORE, I.T., NOVEMBER 14th, 1900.

    In the matter of the application of John H. Baker for the enrollment of himself, wife and children as citizens of the Cherokee Nation; said Baker being sworn and examined by Commissioner Needles, testified as follows:

Q What is your name? A John H. Baker.
Q What is your age? A 54 years old, 26th of this month.
Q What is your post office address? A Tulsa.
Q What district do you live in? A Cooweescoowee.
Q Are you a recognized citizen of the Cherokee Nation? A Yes, sir.
Q By blood or intermarriage? A Intermarriage
Q For whom do you apply for enrollment? A I want to enroll Elizabeth Baker.
Q Who, your wife and children? A Wife and children.
Q What is the name of your wife? A Elizabeth.
Q Have you any certificate of marriage? A Yes, sir.
Q When were you married? A '74.
Q Her name is Elizabeth? A Yes, sir.
Q What is the name of your children? A The two living at home, Sarah Anna Eliza.
Q How old is Eliza? A She is 16 years old I guess.
Q What is the name of the next child? A Webster Cleveland.
Q How old is Webster? A He will be 13 years old the 30th of this month.

Cherokee Intermarried White 1906
Volume II

1880 Roll; page 74, #394, John Baker, Cooweescoowee.
1880 Roll; page 74, #395, Lizzie Baker, "
1896 Roll; page 296, #120, John Baker, "
1896 Roll; page 118, #585, Elizabeth Baker, "
1896 Roll; page 118, #587, Annie E. Baker, "
1896 Roll; page 118, #388, Webster C Baker, "
Q Are these children alive and living with you? A Yes, sir.
Q Your wife is living is she? A Yrs, sir.

Com'r Needles:--The name of John Baker appears upon the authenticated roll of 1880 as John Baker and upon the census roll of 1896, and he will be duly listed for enrollment as a Cherokee citizen by intermarriage, having been fully identified. The name of his wife, Lizzie appears upon the authenticated roll of 1880 as Lizzie Baker, and the census roll of 1896 as Elizabeth. The names of his two children, Sarah A. E. and Webster C., appears upon the census roll of 1896. They all being duly identified and having made satisfactory proof as to their residence, they will be duly listed for enrollment as Cherokee citizens by blood.

---oooOOOooo---

J. O. Rosson, being first duly sworn, states as stenographer to the Commission to the Five Civilized Tribes, he correctly recorded the testimony and proceedings in this case, and that the foregoing is a true and complete transcript of his stenographic notes thereof.

JO Rosson

Subscribed and sworn to before me this 15th day of November, 1900.

CR Breckinridge
Commissioner

◇◇◇◇◇

Cherokee 5393.

DEPARTMENT OF THE INTERIOR,
COMMISSION TO THE FIVE CIVILIZED TRIBES.
Muskogee, I. T., October 14, 1902.

In the matter of the application of John H. Baker for the enrollment of himself as a citizen by intermarriage, and for the enrollment of his wife Elizabeth Baker, and his two children, Sarah A. E. Jackson and Webster C. Baker, as citizens by blood, of the Cherokee Nation.

SUPPLEMENTAL PROCEEDINGS.

JOHN H. BAKER, being sworn, testified as follows:

Cherokee Intermarried White 1906
Volume II

By the Commission,
Q What's your name, Mr. Baker? A John Harvey Baker.
Q What's your age? A Fifty-five.
Q What's your postoffice? A Collinsville.
Q Collinsville, Indian Territory? A Yes, sir.
Q Are you the same John H. Baker that applied to the Commission for enrollment as an intermarried citizen in November, 1900? A Yes, sir.
Q What's your wife's name? A Elizabeth Baker.
Q Is she a citizen by blood of the Cherokee Nation? A Yes, sir.
Q When were you married to your wife, Elizabeth? A August, 1874.
Q She's your first wife? A Yes, sir.
Q Was she ever married before you married her? A No, sir.
Q You're her first husband? A Yes, sir.
Q Have you and she lived together ever since your marriage up until the present time? A Yes, sir.
Q Living together as husband and wife on the first day of September, 1902? A Yes, sir.
Q Never been separated? A No, sir.
Q Have you and she lived in the Cherokee Nation all the time since 1880 up to the present time? A Yes, sir.
Q Are these children, Sarah A. E. Jackson and Webster C. Baker, your children by your wife, Elizabeth? A Yes, sir.
Q Both living now? A Yes, sir.
Q Have they lived in the Cherokee Nation all their lived? A Yes, sir.
Q Is this child, Sarah A. E., married? A Yes, sir.
Q Sarah E. has married since the original application? A Yes, sir, since last January.
Q What's her husband's name? A Jackson.
Q What his given name? A They call him Nat, I don't know whether his name is Nathan or not.
Q What is his postoffice? A Collinsville.

Retta Chick, being first duly sworn, states that, as stenographer to the Commission to the Five Civilized Tribes, she recorded the testimony and proceedings in the matter of the foregoing application, and that the above is a true and complete transcript of her stenographic notes thereof.

Retta Chick

Subscribed and sworn to before me this 31st day of October, 1902.

BC Jones
Notary Public.

◇◇◇◇◇

Cherokee Intermarried White 1906
Volume II

DEPARTMENT OF THE INTERIOR
COMMISSIONER TO THE FIVE CIVILIZED TRIBES
MUSKOGEE, IND. TER
JAN. 4, 1907

IN THE MATTER OF THE APPLICATION FOR THE ENROLLMENT AS A CITIZEN BY INTERMARRIAGE OF THE CHEROKEE NATION OF JOHN H. BAKER.

CENSUS CARD NO. 5393.

JOHN HARVEY BAKER BEING FIRST DULY SWORN TESTIFIED AS FOLLOWS:

EXAMINATION BY THE COMMISSIONER:

Q What is your name.[sic] A John Harvey Baker.
Q How old are you Mr Baker.[sic] A I was born in 1846,
Q What is your post office address. A Collinsville.
Q Do you claim to be an intermarried citizen of the Cherokee Nation. A Yes sir.
Q Thru whom do you claim your intermarried rights? A Elizabeth Buffington.
Q When did you marry Elizabeth Buffington. A Sixth day of August 1874.
Q Where. A At a place about four miles northeast of where Claremore is today.
Q In the Cherokee Nation. A Yes sir.
Q You married under a Cherokee license. A Yes sir.
Q Have you got that license. A I did have them and turned them here when I came to enroll; that's the last I recollect of them.
Q Was Elizabeth Buffington a citizen of the Cherokee Nation at the time you married her. A Yes sir.
Q Recognized citizen by blood. A Yes sir.
Q Were here[sic] parents citizens by blood. A Yes sir both of them.
Q She was living in the Cherokee nation at that time A Yes sir
Q Always had? A Always had; born and raised here.
Q Were you ever married before you married Elizabeth Buffington A No sir.
Q Was she ever married before she married you? A No sir.
Q Have you lived together continuously as husband and wife in the Cherokee Nation from the date of your marriage in 1874 up to the present time? A Yes sir.

The applicant is identified on the 1880 Cherokee Roll Coo-wee-scoo-wee District opposite No. 394. His wife thru whom he claims his right to enrollment is identified on said roll in said district opposite No. 395; she is also identified upon the final roll of citizens by blood of the Cherokee Nation opposite No. 24919.

Q Has your wife taken her allotment yet? A Yes sir.
Q Are you living on her allotment at this time. A We are not living on it; we live in Collinsville but we have it rented out; have for three years.

Cherokee Intermarried White 1906
Volume II

Page 19 of Book "A" of marriage licenses of Coo-wee-scoo-wee District shows that the applicant herein was issued a license to marry Lizzie Buffington on the first day of August 1874 and that he was married under said license on the 6th day of August 1874 the same being certified to by D. W. Lipe Clerk of Coo-we--escoo-wee[sic] District.

Clara Mitchell Wood being first duly sworn upon her oath states that as stenographer for the Commissioner to the Five Civilized Tribes she reported the above and foregoing proceedings and that this is a correct transcript of her stenographic notes.

Clara Mitchell Wood

Subscribed and sworn to before me this 8th day of January 1907

B.P. Rasmus
Notary Public.

◇◇◇◇◇

C.E.W.   Cherokee 5393

DEPARTMENT OF THE INTERIOR,

COMMISSIONER TO THE FIVE CIVILIZED TRIBES.

In the matter of the application for the enrollment of John H. Baker, as a citizen by intermarriage of the Cherokee Nation.

D E C I S I O N

THE RECORDS OF THIS OFFICE SHOW: That at Claremore, Indian Territory, November 14, 1900, John H. Baker appeared before the Commission to the Five Civilized Tribes and made application for the enrollment of himself, as a citizen by intermarriage, and for the enrollment of his wife, Elizabeth Baker, et al., as citizens by blood of the Cherokee Nation has been heretofore disposed of and their rights to enrollment will not be considered in this decision. Further proceedings in the matter of said application were had at Muskogee, Indian Territory, October 14, 1902, and January 4, 1907.

THE EVIDENCE IN THIS CASE SHOWS: That the applicant herein, John H. Baker, a white man, was married in accordance with Cherokee law August 6, 1874 to his wife, Elizabeth Baker, nee Buffington, who was at the time of said marriage a recognized citizen by blood of the Cherokee Nation, and whose name appears upon the approved partial roll of citizens by blood, opposite number 24919; that since said marriage the said John H. Baker and Elizabeth Baker have resided together as husband and wife and have continuously lived in the Cherokee Nation. Said John H. Baker is identified on the

Cherokee Intermarried White 1906
Volume II

Cherokee Authenticated tribal roll of 1880, and the Cherokee Census Roll of 1896 as an intermarried citizen of the Cherokee Nation.

IT IS, THEREFORE, ORDERED AND ADJUDGED: That in accordance with the decision of the Supreme Court of the United States, dated November 5, 1906, in the case of Daniel Red Bird et al., vs. the United States under the provision of Section 21 of the Act of Congress approved June 28, 1898, (30 Stat., 495), John H. Baker is entitled to enrollment as a citizen by intermarriage of the Cherokee Nation, and his application for enrollment as such is accordingly granted.

Tams Bixby
Commissioner.

Dated at Muskogee, Indian Territory,
this   JAN 18 1907

◇◇◇◇◇◇

Cherokee
5393.

Muskogee, Indian Territory, December 29, 1906.

John H. Baker,
    Collinsville, Indian Territory.

Dear Sir:

November 6, 1906, the United States Supreme Court held that white persons who intermarried with Cherokee citizens according to Cherokee law prior to November 1, 1875, are entitled to enrollment and allotments of land as citizens of the Cherokee Nation.

You are advised that to properly determine your right to enrollment as a citizen by intermarriage of the Cherokee Nation, it will be necessary for you to appear before the Commissioner for the purpose of giving testimony as to the date of your marriage and whether or not your wife, by reason of your marriage to whom you claim the right to enrollment as a citizen of the Cherokee Nation, was a recognized citizen of the Cherokee Nation at the time of your marriage to her, and whether or not you were married to her in accordance with Cherokee laws.

You are, therefore, directed to appear before the Commissioner at Muskogee, Indian Territory, at 9 o'clock A. M., on Friday, January 4, 1907, and give testimony as above indicated.

Respectfully,

H.J.C. Commissioner.

◇◇◇◇◇◇

Cherokee Intermarried White 1906
Volume II

Cherokee 5393.

Muskogee, Indian Territory, January 18, 1907.

W. W. Hastings,
    Attorney for the Cherokee Nation,
        Muskogee, Indian Territory.

Dear Sir:

There is enclosed herewith copy of the decision of the Commissioner to the Five Civilized Tribes, dated January 18, 1907, granting the application for the enrollment of John H. Baker as a citizen by intermarriage of the Cherokee Nation.

        Respectfully,

Encl. W-1.   Commissioner.
S.W.

◇◇◇◇◇

Cherokee 5383.   W.W.HASTINGS.   OFFICE OF   H.M. VANCE.
                      ATTORNEY.   SECRETARY.

Attorney for the Cherokee Nation,
MUSKOGEE, I. T.

                                                                          January 18, 1907.

The Commissioner to the Five Civilized Tribes,
        Muskogee, Indian Territory.

Sir:

Receipt is acknowledged of the testimony and of your decision enrolling John F[sic]. Baker as a citizen by intermarriage of the Cherokee Nation. Time for protesting said decision is waived and I consent that said person may be placed upon the schedule immediately.

                        Yours very truly,
                        W. W. Hastings
                        Attorney for Cherokee Nation.

◇◇◇◇◇

Cherokee Intermarried White 1906
Volume II

Cherokee
5393

Muskogee, Indian Territory, January 19, 1907.

John H. Baker,
    Collinsville, Indian Territory.

Dear Sir:

There is enclosed herewith a copy of the decision of the Commissioner to the Five Civilized Tribes, dated January 18, 1907, granting your application for enrollment as a citizen by intermarriage of the Cherokee Nation.

You will be advised when your name has been placed upon a schedule of citizens of the Cherokee Nation and approved by the Secretary of the Interior.

Respectfully,

Encl. H-82
JMH

Commissioner.

Cher IW 49
Trans from Cher 5471 3-13-07

◇◇◇◇◇

E.C.M.

DEPARTMENT OF THE INTERIOR,

COMMISSIONER TO THE FIVE CIVILIZED TRIBES.

In the matter of the application for the enrollment of

JOHN POLK DRAKE

as a citizen by intermarriage of the Cherokee Nation.

CHEROKEE 5471.

◇◇◇◇◇

Cherokee Intermarried White 1906
Volume II

Department of the Interior,
Commission to the Five Civilized Tribes,
Chelsea, I.T., November 16, 1900.

In the matter of the application of John Polk Drake for the enrollment of himself as a Cherokee by intermarriage, and his wife and children as Cherokees by blood: being sworn and examined by Commissioner Breckinridge, he testified as follows:

Q Give me your full name, please? A John Polk Drake.
Q How old are you? A I am 56 years old.
Q What is your post office? A Chelsea.
Q Do you live in Cooweescoowee district? A Yes, sir.
Q Do you apply for the enrollment of yourself and family? A Yes, sir.
Q Have you a wife? A Yes, sir.
Q How many children have you? A I think there is four; I have five, but I have a married daughter.
Q You have four unmarried? A Yes, sir.
Q Are they all under 21 years of age, these four? A I will have to see (examins[sic] paper). The oldest was born in 1881.
Q Are you a Cherokee by blood? A Yes, sir.
Q When were you married to your wife? A U[sic] was married, I was married twice, I was married to my first wife in 1871 I believe.
Q How long did your first wife life[sic]? A I think she died in 1876.
Q When did you remarry? A In 1877
Q Is the wife you married in 1877 still living? A Yes, sir.
Q You are with her on the roll of 1880 are you? A Yes, sir.
Q Give me the name of your present wife? A Emily Jane Drake, she was a Walker.
Q How old is she? A She is 56 years old.
Q What was her maiden name? A Walker.
Q You were married only once previous to this marriage? A Yes, sir.
Q And then this wife was dead before you married your present wife? A Yes, sir.
Q Your present wife was never married except to you? A No, sir.
Q Give me the name of her father? A T. M. Walker.
Q Is he dead? A Yes, sir.
Q Give me the name of her mother? A E. M. Walker.
Q Is she dead? A Yes, sir.
Q Give me the names of these four children, please? A Bessie Walker Drake, she was born June 22, 1881.
Q The next child? A John Ella.
Q That is a girl? A Yes, sir, I have no boys.
Q How old is she? A She was born in 1883, 17 years old.
Q The next child? A Emma Lane Drake, she was born in 1886.
Q Now the next child? A Nannie E., she was born in 1888, 12 years old.
Q These children are all living, are they? A Yes, sir.
(John P. Drake on 1880 roll, page 92, No. (1875), Cooweescoowee #875 district, adopted white. Emily J. Drake on 1880 roll, page 92, No. 876, Emma Drake, Cooweescoowee

Cherokee Intermarried White 1906
Volume II

district. John P. Drake on 1896 roll, page 301, No. 304, Cooweescoowee district. Emily J. Drake on 1896 roll, page 148, No. 1482, Betsy W. Drake, Cooweescoowee district. John Ella Drake on 1896 roll, page 148, No. 1483, Cooweescoowee district. Emma L. Drake on 1896 roll, page 148, No. 1484, Cooweescoowee district. Nannie E. Drake on 1896 roll, page 148, No. 1485, Cooweescoowee district.)
Q Has your wife lived in the Cherokee Nation all her live? A Yes, sir.
Q Have you lived in the Cherokee Nation ever since you married her in 1877? A Yes, sir, been here all the time.

The applicant applies for the enrollment of himself, his wife and four minor children. His wife is identified on the rolls of 1880 and 1896 as a native Cherokee, she has lived in the Cherokee Nation all her life, and she will be listed for enrollment as a Cherokee by blood. The applicant is identified with his wife on the roll of 1880, and on the roll of 1896, they have lived together ever since their marriage in 1877, and he will be listed for enrollment as a Cherokee by intermarriage. The four children named in the testimony are all identified with their parents on the roll of 1896, they are all living now, and will be listed for enrollment as Cherokees by blood.

--------o--------

Bruce C. Jones, being duly sworn, says that as stenographer to the Commission to the Five Civilized Tribes he correctly recorded the proceedings and testimony in the above case, and the foregoing is a true and complete transcript of his stenographic notes thereof.

Bruce C Jones

Sworn to and subscribed before me this the 16th of November, 1900.

CR Breckinridge

Commissioner.

◇◇◇◇◇

DEPARTMENT OF THE INTERIOR.
Commission to the Five Civilized Tribes.
Muskogee, Indian Territory, October 1st, 1902.

In the matter of the application of John P. Drake for the enrollment of himself as a citizen by intermarriage of the Cherokee Nation and for the enrollment of his wife, Emily J. Drake, and his children, Bessie W., John E., Emma L. and Nannie E. Drake, as citizens by blood of the Cherokee Nation.

Supplemental to #5471.

Cherokee Intermarried White 1906
Volume II

Appearances:

Applicant appears in person.
Cherokee Nation by J. C. Starr.

JOHN P. DRAKE, being duly sworn, testified as follows:--
Examination by the Commission.
Q. What is your name? A. John P. Drake,
Q. What is your age at this time? A. I am 68 years old.
Q. What is your post office? A. Chelsea.
Q. Are you the same John P. Drake foe[sic] whom application was made for enrollment as an intermarried citizen on November 16, 19oo[sic]? A. Yes, sir.
Q. What is your wife's name, Mr. Drake? A. Emma J. or Emily J. I don't remember.
Q. Emily J/[sic], it is on the card? A. Yes, sir.
Q. Is she living at this time? A. Yes, sir.
Q. When were you and she married? A. I believe in '76.
Q. Were you married prior to your marriage to this wife? A. Yes, sir.
Q. How many times were you married prior to your marriage to this wife? A. Just once.
Q. Was that wife living or dead? A. Dead.
Q. Was Emily J. ever married prior to her marriage to you? A. No, sir.
Q. You are her first husband? A. Yes, sir.
Q. She is your second wife? A. Yes, sir.
Q. Were you married under a Cherokee license? A. Yes, sir.
Q. Have you and Emily J. lived together continuously from the time of your marriage up to the present time? A. Yes, sir.
Q. Living together on the first of September, 1902? A. Yes, sir.
Q. Never separated? A. No, sir.
Q. How long have you lived in the Cherokee Nation? A. 31 years.
Q. Have you lived all the time in the Cherokee Nation for the last 31 years? A. Yes, sir.
Q. How long has your wife lived in the Cherokee Nation? A. Born and raised here.
Q. Has she lived in the Cherokee Nation all her life? A. Yes, sir. I think she was out a while during the war.
Q. Are these children, Bessie W., John E., Amma[sic] L. and Nannie E., your children by your wife Emily J.? A. Yes, sir.
Q. And are they all living at this time? A. Yes, sir.
Q. Have they lived in the Cherokee Nation all their lives? A. Yes, sir.

Jesse O. Carr, being first duly sworn, states that as stenographer to the Commission to the Five Civilized Tribes he reported the above entitled case and that the foregoing is a true and complete transcript of his stenographic notes thereof.

Jesse O. Carr

Cherokee Intermarried White 1906
Volume II

Subscribed and sworn to before me this 20th day of October, 1902.

                        BC Jones
                        Notary Public.

◇◇◇◇◇

Cherokee 5471.

DEPARTMENT OF THE INTERIOR,
COMMISSIONER TO THE FIVE CIVILIZED TRIBES.
Muskogee, Indian Territory, January 2, 1907.

In the Matter of the Application for the Enrollment of John P. Drake as a citizen by intermarriage of the Cherokee Nation.

John P. Drake being first duly sworn by Walter W. Chappell, Notary Public, testified as follows:

Q What is your name?   A John P. Drake.
Q Your age?   A 62.
Q Your post office address?   A Chelsea, Indian Territory.
Q You claim citizenship by intermarriage, of the Cherokee Nation, do you?
A Yes sir.
Q Through whom do you claim?   A Joanna McNair.
Q Is she living?   A No sir; she's dead.
Q What was her citizenship?   A She was Cherokee.
Q When were you married to her?   A December 17, 1871.
Q Where were you married?
A Illinois District, Cherokee Nation.
Q Were you married under a Cherokee license?
A Yes sir.
Q Have you a copy of that license with you?
A Yes sir, I have.

The applicant offers in evidence the certificate of W. H. Turner, Clerk of the District Court for Talequah[sic] District, Cherokee Nation under date of July 30, 1872, wherein it is certified that "J. P. Drake, a white man and citizen of the United States, has complied with the laws of the Cherokee Nation, regulating intermarriage with white men, and married Joanna McNair, Cherokee:, and that the ceremony of marriage between the above named parties was "solemnized by Judge T. M. Walker of Illinois District", the same being filed herewith and made a part of the record in this case. Book "B District Court Records and of Marriage License, Talequah[sic] District, 1868-72" recites under the head of "Record of Licenses issued for Marriages to Citizens of the United States", the following: "John P. Drake, issued December 15, 1981, to marry Joanna McNair".

Q Were you ever married prior to your marriage to Joanna McNair? A No sir.

Cherokee Intermarried White 1906
Volume II

Q Had she ever been married prior to that time? A No sir.
Q How long did you live together as husband and wife? A She died I think in '76 probably; that would be about 5 years.
Q Where did you live during that time? A Near Fort Gibson.
Q Well, after her death, did you marry again? A Yes sir.
Q What was the date of your second marriage? A I think it was February 11, 1877.
Q Is your second wife living? A Yes sir.
Q What is her citizenship? A Cherokee by blood; raised here.
Q What was her name? A Emily J. Walker.
Q Has she been enrolled? A Yes sir.
Q Received her allottment[sic]? A Yes sir; she has no deed for it.
Q Did you marry your second wife under a Cherokee license?
A The second marriage, I didn't have to get a license. I was told by the District Judge that we wasn't required to get a license; that citizens didn't have to.
Q Your second marriage was in accordance with the Cherokee customs at that time?
A Yes sir; I went and inquired about that and they said I didn't have to get a license; they were not issuing licenses then. We were married by a regular ordained minister in the presence of witnesses.
Q Did you have any children by your first wife?
A Yes sir
Q Are they living? A No sir.
Q Have you any children by your second wife? A Yes sir.
Q What are their names?
A Mary B. Drake, Bessie W., John E., Emma L. and Nannie E.

The said Emily J., Bessie W., John E., Emma L. and Nannie E. Drake are included on a partial roll of citizens by blood of the Cherokee Nation, opposite numbers 13106 to 13110 inclusive.

Q How long have you lived in the Cherokee Nation, Mr. Drake?
A I have lived here ever since '71; 36 years.

The applicant is identified on the authenticated Cherokee Tribal Roll of 1880 and on the Cherokee Census Roll of 1896, opposite numbers 875 and 304 respectively, ICoo. District, as an intermarried white.

WITNESS DISMISSED.

The undersigned being first duly sworn states that as stenographer to the, she correctly recorded the testimony taken in this case and that the foregoing is a full, true and correct transcript of her stenographic notes thereof.

Myrtle Hill

Cherokee Intermarried White 1906
Volume II

Subscribed and sworn to before me this the 3rd day of January, 1907.

              B.P. Rasmus
              Notary Public.

◇◇◇◇◇

            Office Dist Ct. Tahlequah
            Cherokee Nation July 30th/72

  This certifies J.P. Drake a white man and formerly citizen of the U.S. has complied with the laws of the Cherokee Nation, "Regulating Intermarriage with Whitemen" and married Joannah[sic] former McNair a Cherokee, & a certificate of the Ceremony Solennized[sic] by Judge T.M. Walker of Illinois Dist. on file in my office. Thereby entitles Mr. J. P. Drake to full rights of Cherokee Citizenship under said law. And on Record in Office of the Dist Court for Tahlequah Dist Cherokee Nation.

              W.H. Turner
              Clk D.C for Tah Dist
This the 30th day of July 1872   Cherokee Nation

  The undersigned being duly sworn states that as stenographer to the Commissioner to the Five Civilized Tribes, she made the above copy, and that the same is a true and correct copy of the instrument now on file in this office.

              Mary Tabor Mallory

Subscribed and sworn to before me this the 15 day of January 1907

              Chas E Webster
              Notary Public.

◇◇◇◇◇

E.C.M.   Cherokee 5471

DEPARTMENT OF THE INTERIOR,

COMMISSIONER TO THE FIVE CIVILIZED TRIBES.

  In the matter of the application for the enrollment of John Polk Drake as a citizen by intermarriage of the Cherokee Nation.

D E C I S I O N

  THE RECORDS OF THIS OFFICE SHOW: That at Chelsea, Indian Territory, November 16, 1900, application was received by the Commission to the Five Civilized

Cherokee Intermarried White 1906
Volume II

Tribes, for the enrollment of John Polk Drake, as a citizen by intermarriage of the Cherokee Nation. Further proceedings in the matter of said application were had at Muskogee, Indian Territory, October 1, 1902, and January 2, 1907.

THE EVIDENCE IN THIS CASE SHOWS: That the applicant herein, John Polk Drake, a white man, was married in accordance with Cherokee law December 17, 1871, to his deceased wife, Joanna Drake, nee McNair, who was at the time of said marriage, a recognized citizen by blood of the Cherokee Nation; that from the time of said marriage until the death of said Joanna Drake, which occurred about the year 1876, the said John Polk and Joanna Drake resided together as husband and wife, and continuously lived in the Cherokee Nation; that on or about February 11, 1877, the said John Polk Drake married his wife Emily Jane Drake, nee Walker, who was, at the time of said marriage, a recognized citizen by blood of the Cherokee Nation, and whose name appears on the approved partial roll of citizens by blood of the Cherokee Nation as Emily J. Drake, opposite No. 13106; that since said marriage the said John Polk Drake and Emily Jane Drake have resided together as husband and wife, and that the residence of John Polk Drake has been continuously in the Cherokee Nation since December 17, 1871. Said applicant is identified on the Cherokee authenticated tribal roll of 1880, and the Cherokee census roll of 1896 as an intermarried citizen of the Cherokee Nation.

IT IS, THEREFORE, ORDERED AND ADJUDGED: That in accordance with the decision of the Supreme Court of the United States, dated November 5, 1906, in the cases of Daniel Red Bird, et al., vs. the United States, Nos. 125, 216[sic], 127 and 128, the said applicant, John Polk Drake is entitled under the provisions of Section twenty-one of the Act of Congress approved June 28, 1898 (30 Stat. 495), to enrollment as a citizen by intermarriage of the Cherokee Nation, and his application for enrollment as such is accordingly granted.

                Tams Bixby
                  Commissioner.

Dated at Muskogee, Indian Territory,
this   JAN 19 1907

◇◇◇◇◇◇

Cherokee
 5471.

             Muskogee, Indian Territory, January 19, 1907.

W. W. Hastings,
  Attorney for the Cherokee Nation,
    Muskogee, Indian Territory.

Dear Sir:

  There is enclosed herewith a copy of the decision of the Commissioner to the Five Civilized Tribes, dated January 19, 1907, granting the application for the enrollment of John Polk Drake, as a citizen by intermarriage of the Cherokee Nation.

Cherokee Intermarried White 1906
Volume II

Respectfully,

Incl. C-18
LMC
Commissioner.

◇◇◇◇◇

Cherokee 5471.   W.W. HASTINGS.   OFFICE OF   H.M. VANCE.
ATTORNEY.   SECRETARY.

Attorney for the Cherokee Nation,
MUSKOGEE, I. T.

January 19, 1907.

The Commissioner to the Five Civilized Tribes,
   Muskogee, Indian Territory.

Sir:

   Receipt is acknowledged of the testimony and of your decision enrolling John Polk Drake as a citizen by intermarriage of the Cherokee Nation. Time for protesting said decision is waived and I consent that said person may be placed upon the schedule immediately.

Respectfully,
W. W. Hastings
Attorney for Cherokee Nation.

◇◇◇◇◇

Cherokee
   5471

Muskogee, Indian Territory, January 21, 1907.

John Polk Drake,
   Chelsea, Indian Territory.

Dear Sir:

   There is enclosed herewith copy of the decision of the Commissioner to the Five Civilized Tribes, dated January 19, 1907, granting the application for your enrollment as a citizen by intermarriage of the Cherokee Nation.

   You will be advised when your name has been placed upon a schedule of citizens of the Cherokee Nation and approved by the Secretary of the Interior.

Respectfully,

Enc. M - 20
M.T.M.
Commissioner.

Cherokee Intermarried White 1906
Volume II

Muskogee, Indian Territory, April 8, 1907.

John Polk Drake,
    Chelsea, Indian Territory.

Dear Sir:

    Your marriage license and certificate, filed in connection with your application for enrollment as a citizen by intermarriage of the Cherokee Nation, is returned to you herewith, copies of the same being retained in this office.

Respectfully,

Incl. P-4-13   Acting Commissioner.
MMP

Cher IW 50
Trans from Cher 5515 3-13-07

C.E.W.

DEPARTMENT OF THE INTERIOR,

COMMISSIONER TO THE FIVE CIVILIZED TRIBES.

In the matter of the application for the enrollment of

JOHN A. SMITH

as a citizen by intermarriage of the Cherokee Nation.

CHEROKEE 5515

Cherokee Intermarried White 1906
Volume II

DEPARTMENT OF THE INTERIOR,
COMMISSION TO THE FIVE CIVILIZED TRIBES,
CHELSEA, I.T., NOVEMBER 17th, 1900.

In the matter of the application of John Addison Smith for the enrollment of himself and wife as citizens of the Cherokee Nation; said Smith being sworn and examined by Commissioner Breckinridge, testified as follows:

Q Give me your full name, please? A John Addison Smith.
Q How old are you? A 54.
Q What is your post office? A Chelsea.
Q Do you live in Cooweescoowee district? A Yes, sir.
Q You want to enroll yourself and family? A Yes, sir.
Q You have a wife have you? A Yes, sir.
Q How many children? A One, she is married
Q Are you a Cherokee by blood? A No, sir.
Q White man? A Yes, sir.
Q What is your wife? A She is a Cherokee.
Q When were you married to her? A '74.
Q You are on the 1880 roll then? A Yes, sir.
Q Have you and she lived together ever since you married in 1874? A Yes, sir.
Q Lived all the time in the Cherokee Nation? A Yes, sir.
Q Give me your wife's name, please? A Susan C. Smith.
Q How old is she? A 60 years old the first of last August.
Q Give me the name of her father? A L. B. Williams.
Q Is he dead? A Yes, sir.
Q Give me the name of her mother? A Sallie Williams.
Q Is she dead? A Yes, sir.
      1880 Roll; page 184, #2857, John Smith, Cooweescoowee.
      1880 Roll; page 184, #2858, Susan Smith, Cooweescoowee.
      1896 Roll; page 324, #948, John A. Smith, Cooweescoowee.
      1896 Roll; page 258, #4485, Susan C. Smith, Cooweescoowee.
Q Has she lived in the Cherokee Nation all her life? A Yes, sir.

    Com'r Breckinridge:--The applicant states that he was married to his wife in 1874. He is a white man. He is identified on the rolls of 1880 and 1896, and he states that he and his wife have lived together and in the Cherokee Nation ever since their marriage in 1874. He will now be listed for enrollment as a Cherokee by intermarriage. His wife is identified on the rolls of 1880 and 1896 as a native Cherokee. She has lived in the Cherokee Nation all her life and she will be listed now for enrollment as a Cherokee by blood.

---oooOOOoo---

    J. O. Rosson, being first duly sworn, states that as stenographer to the Commission to the Five Civilized Tribes, he correctly recorded the testimony and proceedings in this

Cherokee Intermarried White 1906
Volume II

case, and that the foregoing is a true and complete transcript of his stenographic notes thereof.

JO Rosson

Subscribed and sworn to before me this 17th day of November, 1900.

MD Green
Notary Public.

◇◇◇◇◇

DEPARTMENT OF THE INTERIOR.
Commission to the Five Civilized Tribes.
Muskogee, Indian Territory, October 1st, 1902.

In the matter of the application of John A. Smith for the enrollment of himself as a citizen by intermarriage of the Cherokee Nation and for the enrollment of his wife Susan C. Smith as a citizen by blood of the Cherokee Nation.

Supplemental to #5515.

Appearances:
Applicant appears in person.
Cherokee Nation by J. C. Starr.

JOHN A. SMITH, being duly sworn, testified as follows:
Examination by the Commission.
Q. What is your name? A. J. A. Smith.
Q. John A.? A. Yes, sir.
Q. Age, please, at this time? A. 57.
Q. Post office? A. Chelsea.
Q. Are you the same John A. Smith for whom application was made to this Commission for enrollment as an intermarried citizen on October 17th, 1900? A. Yes, sir.
Q. What is your wife's name? A. Susan Smith.
Q. Citizen by blood of the Cherokee Nation? A. Yes, sir.
Q. Is she living? A. Yes, sir.
Q. When were you and she married? A. It was either '73 or '74.
Q. Were you married under a Cherokee license? A. Yes, sir.
Q. Were you ever married prior to your marriage to this wife? A. No, sir.
Q. Was she ever married before? A. Yes, sir.
Q. How many times had she been married? A. Once.
Q. Was her first husband living or dead when you married? A. Dead.

Cherokee Intermarried White 1906
Volume II

Q. Have you and she lived together from the time you were married continuously? A. Yes, sir.
Q. Were you living together on the first of September, 1902? A. Yes, sir.
Q. Never been separated? A. No, sir.
Q. How long have you lived in the Cherokee Nation? A. Sinve[sic] '70.
Q. All the time since 1870? A. Yes, sir.
Q. How long has your wife lived in the Cherokee Nation? A. She was born and raised here.
Q. Lived here all her life? A. I think they went to Fort Scott during the war.
Q. She has lived here all the time since 1880? A. Yes, sir.

Jesse O. Carr, being first duly sworn, states that as stenographer to the Commission to the Five Civilized Tribes he reported the above entitled case and that the foregoing is a true and complete transcript of his stenographic notes thereof.

Jesse O. Carr

Subscribed and sworn to before me this 18th day of October, 1902.

BC Jones
Notary Public.

◇◇◇◇◇

CHEROKEE-5515.

DEPARTMENT OF THE INTERIOR,
COMMISSIONER TO THE FIVE CIVILIZED TRIBES.
Muskogee, Indian Territory, January 5, 1907.

In the matter of making proof of the marriage of John A. Smith to his Cherokee wife, prior to November 1, 1875.

John A. Smith, after having first been duly sworn by B. P. Rasmus, a Notary Public, testified as follows:

COMMISSIONER:

Q. What is your name? A. John A. Smith
Q. What is your age? A. 60.
Q. What is your post office address? A. Chelsea.
Q. Do you claim to be a citizen by intermarriage of the Cherokee Nation? A. Yes sir.
Q. Through whom do you claim your rights? A. Susan C. Williams.

Cherokee Intermarried White 1906
Volume II

Q. When were you married to her? A. On the 27th. of December, 1874. The record shows about March, 1875.
Q. Where were you married to her? A. At Fort Gibson.
Q. Under a Cherokee license? A. Yes sir.
Q. Have you your license? A. I have a certified copy of it here in the Commission. It was sent here about a month ago.
Q. In what District? A. Illinois District.

(Commissioner -- Page 37 of book "A" of marriage register for Illinois District shows that a license was issued to John A. Smith, a citizen of the United States, to marry a Cherokee citizen, on the 28th. day of December, 1874. Said page also contains the certificate of T. M. Walker, Judge of the Court for said District, dated March 25, 1875, stating that he married the parties under the said license.)

Q. Were you ever married before you married Susan C. Williams? A. No sir.
Q. Was she ever married before she married you? A. Yes sir.
Q. What was the name of her first husband? A. Dillon.
Q. Was he living or dead at the time of her marriage to you? A. He was dead.
Q. Are you living together at the present time as husband and wife? A. Yes sir.
Q. Have you lived together continuously since 1874 up to and including the present time? A. Yes sir.

(Commissioner -- The applicant is identified upon the 1880 roll, Cooweescoowee District, opposite No. 2857. His wife, through whom he claims his rights, is identified on said roll opposite No. 2858. She is also identified upon the final roll of citizens by blood of the Cherokee Nation opposite No. 13244.)

Witness excused.

Eula Jeanes Branson, being sworn, states that she correctly reported the proceedings had in the above and foregoing on the 5th. day of January, 1907.

Eula Jeanes Branson

Subscribed and sworn to before me this the 7th. day of January, 1907.

Walter W. Chappell
Notary Public.

Cherokee Intermarried White 1906
Volume II

C.E.W.   Cherokee 5515

DEPARTMENT OF THE INTERIOR,

COMMISSIONER TO THE FIVE CIVILIZED TRIBES.

In the matter of the application for the enrollment of John A. Smith, as a citizen by intermarriage of the Cherokee Nation.

D E C I S I O N

THE RECORDS OF THIS OFFICE SHOW: That at Chelsea, Indian Territory, November 17, 1900, John A. Smith appeared before the Commission to the Five Civilized Tribes and made application for the enrollment of himself, as a citizen by intermarriage, and for the enrollment of his wife, Susan C. Smith, as a citizen by blood of the Cherokee Nation. The application for the enrollment of the said Susan C. Smith, as a citizen by blood of the Cherokee Nation has been heretofore disposed of and her rights to enrollment will not be considered in this decision. Further proceedings in the matter of said application were had at Muskogee, Indian Territory,, October 1, 1902, and January 5, 1907.

THE EVIDENCE IN THIS CASE SHOWS: That the applicant herein, John A. Smith, a white man, was married in accordance with Cherokee law March 25, 1875, to his wife Susan C. Smith, nee Williams, who was at the time of said marriage a recognized citizen by blood of the Cherokee Nation, and whose name appears upon the approved partial roll of citizens by blood of the Cherokee Nation, opposite number 13244; that since said marriage the said John A. Smith and Susan C. Smith have resided together as husband and wife and have continuously lived in the Cherokee Nation. Said John A. Smith is identified on the Cherokee Authenticated tribal roll of 1880, and the Cherokee Census Roll of 1896 as an intermarried citizen of the Cherokee Nation.

IT IS, THEREFORE, ORDERED AND ADJUDGED: That in accordance with the decision of the Supreme Court of the United States, dated November 5, 1906, in the case of Daniel Red Bird et al., vs. the United States, under the provision of Section 21 of the Act of Congress approved June 28, 1898, (30 Stat., 495), John A. Smith is entitled to enrollment as a citizen by intermarriage of the Cherokee Nation, and his application for enrollment as such is accordingly granted.

                                            Tams Bixby
                                                Commissioner.

Dated at Muskogee, Indian Territory,
this   JAN 16 1907

Cherokee Intermarried White 1906
Volume II

Cherokee
5515

Muskogee, Indian Territory, December 27, 1906.

John A. Smith,
    Chelsea, Indian Territory.

Dear Sir:

November 6, 1906, the United States Supreme Court held that white persons who intermarried with Cherokee citizens according to Cherokee law prior to November 1, 1875, are entitled to enrollment and allotments of land as citizens of the Cherokee Nation.

You are advised that to properly determine your right to enrollment as a citizen by intermarriage of the Cherokee Nation, it will be necessary for you to appear before the Commissioner for the purpose of giving testimony as to the date of your marriage and whether or not your wife, by reason of your marriage to whom you claim the right to enrollment as a citizen of the Cherokee Nation, was a recognized citizen of the Cherokee Nation at the time of your marriage to her, and whether or not you were married to her in accordance with Cherokee laws.

You are, therefore, directed to appear before the Commissioner at Muskogee, Indian Territory, at 9 o'clock A. M., on Saturday, January 5, 1907, and give testimony as above indicated.

                Respectfully,

S.W.   Acting Commissioner.

◇◇◇◇◇◇

Cherokee 5515

Muskogee, Indian Territory, January 17, 1906.

W. W. Hastings,
    Attorney for the Cherokee Nation,
        Muskogee, Indian Territory.

Dear Sir:

There is enclosed herewith copy of the decision of the Commissioner to the Five Civilized Tribes, dated January 16, 1907, granting the application for the enrollment of John A. Smith as a citizen by intermarriage of the Cherokee Nation.

Cherokee Intermarried White 1906
Volume II

Respectfully,

Enc I-10   Commissioner.
RPI

◇◇◇◇◇

Cherokee 5515.   W.W. HASTINGS,   OFFICE OF   H.M. VANCE,
                      ATTORNEY.   SECRETARY.

Attorney for the Cherokee Nation,
MUSKOGEE, I. T.

January 18, 1907.

The Commissioner to the Five Civilized Tribes,
       Muskogee, Indian Territory.

Sir:

       Receipt is acknowledged of the testimony and of your decision enrolling John A. Smith as a citizen by intermarriage of the Cherokee Nation. Time for protesting said decision is waived and I consent that said person may be placed upon the schedule immediately.

Yours very truly,
W. W. Hastings
Attorney for Cherokee Nation.

◇◇◇◇◇

Cherokee
5515

Muskogee, Indian Territory, January 19, 1907.

John A. Smith,
       Chelsea, Indian Territory.

Dear Sir:

       There is enclosed herewith a copy of the decision of the Commissioner to the Five Civilized Tribes, dated January 16, 1907, granting your application for enrollment as a citizen by intermarriage of the Cherokee Nation.

       You will be advised when your name has been placed upon a schedule of citizens of the Cherokee Nation and approved by the Secretary of the Interior.

Respectfully,

Encl. H-76   Commissioner.
JMH

Cherokee Intermarried White 1906
Volume II

Cher IW 51
Trans from Cher 5934   3-13-07

C.E.W.

DEPARTMENT OF THE INTERIOR,

COMMISSIONER TO THE FIVE CIVILIZED TRIBES.

In the matter of the application for the enrollment of

MARTIN A. WALLACE

as a citizen by intermarriage of the Cherokee Nation.

CHEROKEE 5934.

Department of the Interior,
Commission to the Five Civilized Tribes.
Tahlequah, I. T. December 1st, 1900

In the matter of the application of Martin A. Wallace for the enrollment of himself, wife and five children as Cherokee citizens. He being sworn before Commissioner Needles testified as follows-

Q What is your name? A. Martin A. Wallace.
Q How old are you? A. 54.
Q What is your post office address? A. Tahlequah.
Q What district do you live in? A. Tahlequah.
Q Are you a recognized citizen of the Cherokee Nation? A. Yes sir
Q By blood or inter-marriage? A. Inter-marriage.
Q For whom do you apply? A. Myself and family.
Q Have you a certificate of your marriage? A. No sir.
Q When were you married? A. In 1869.
Q What is you wifes[sic] name? A. Julie.
Q How old is she ? A. 53.
Q What are the names of your children? A. Lu Lu.
Q How old? A. 19.
Q What is the next child named? A. Grace.
Q How old? A. 16.
Q Next child? A. Martha.

Cherokee Intermarried White 1906
Volume II

A[sic] How old? A. 14.
Q Next child? A. Julius M.
Q What age? A. 12.
Q Next child? Anna Alice E.
Q How old? A. 7.
Q That makes five? A. Yes sir.

1880 roll, page 490, No 1969, Martin Wallace, Going Snake dist.
1880	490	1970	Julia Wallace	"
1896	1291	291	Martin Wallace, Tahlequah	
1896	1266	3669	Julia Wallace,	"
1896	1266	3673	Lulu Wallace	"
1896	1266	3674	Grace Wallace	"
1896	1266	3675	Martha Wallace	" "
1896	1266	3676	Monroe Wallace	"
1896	1266	3677	Ailsy Wallace	"

Q Are these children all alive and living with you at this time? A. Yes sir.
Q Have you always lived in the Cherokee Nation ever since 1880? A. Yes sir since 1871.
Q Have you been living with you wife continuously since your marriage to her? A. Yes sir.

The name of Martin A. Wallace appears on the authenticated 1880 roll as Martin Wallace and on the census roll of 1896 as Martin Wallace, an adopted white. The name of his wife Julia appears on the authenticated 1880 roll and the census roll of 1896 as a Cherkee[sic] by blood. The names of his children Lu Lu, Grace, Martha, Julius M., and Alcie E. Wallace appear on the census roll of 1896. They all being duly identified according to the page and number of the roll as indicated in the testimony, and having made satisfactory proof as to residence, consequently the said Martain[sic] A. Wallace will be duly listed for enrollment as a Cherokee by intermarriage, and his wife Julie Wallace and the children named herein will be listed for enrollment as Cherokee citizens by blood.

Chas. von Weise, being sworn states, that as stenographer to the Commission to the Five Civilized Tribes he reported in full the above proceedings and that the foregoing is a full, true and correct transcript of his stenographic notes therein.

Chas von Weise

Subscribed and sworn to before me this the 3rd of December, 1900.

TB Needles
Commissioner

Cherokee Intermarried White 1906
Volume II

R.
Cher. 5934.

Department of the Interior.
Commission to the Five Civilized Tribes.
Tahlequah, I. T., September 30, 1902.

SUPPLEMENTAL TESTIMONY AND PROCEEDINGS in the matter of the application for the enrollment of MARTIN A. WALLACE as a citizen by intermarriage of the Cherokee Nation.

MARTIN A. WALLACE, being first duly sworn, and being examined, testified as follows:

BY COMMISSION: What is your name? A Martin A. Wallace.
Q How old are you? A Fifty-six.
Q What is your post office address? A Tahlequah.
Q You are a white man, are you? A Yes sir.
Q Have you heretofore made application to this Commission for enrollment as a citizen by intermarriage of the Cherokee Nation? A Yes sir.
Q What is the name of your wife? A Julia.
Q Is she living? A Yes sir.
Q Is she a Cherokee by blood? A Yes sir.
Q Do you claim your right to enrollment by reason of your marriage to her? A Yes sir.
Q When were you married? A Married in 1869.
Q Have you lived together continuously since that time? A Yes sir.
Q Are you living together now? A Yes sir.
Q Have you resided in the Cherokee Nation continuously since the date of your application for enrollment? A Yes sir, since 1871.
Q Were you ever married before you married your present wife? A No sir.
Q Was she ever married before she married you? A No sir.

This testimony will be filed with and made a part of the record in the matter of the application for the enrollment of Martin A. Wallace as a citizen by intermarriage of the Cherokee Nation, Cherokee straight card field No. 5934.

Wm. Hutchinson, being first duly sworn, states that as stenographer to the Commission to the Five Civilized Tribes he correctly recorded the testimony and proceedings in this case, and that the foregoing is a true and complete transcript of his stenographic notes thereof.

Wm Hutchinson

Cherokee Intermarried White 1906
Volume II

Subscribed and sworn to before me this 30th day of September, 1902.

>>>>John O Rosson
Notary Public.

◇◇◇◇◇

Cherokee No.
5934.

DEPARTMENT OF THE INTERIOR,

COMMISSIONER TO THE FIVE CIVILIZED TRIBES,

MUSKOGEE, INDIAN TERRITORY, JANUARY 5, 1907.

IN THE MATTER of the application for the enrollment of Martin A. Wallace, as a citizen by intermarriage of the Cherokee Nation.

MARTIN A. WALLACE, being first duly sworn by B. P. Rasmus, Notary Public, testified as follows:

EXAMINATION

ON BEHALF OF THE COMMISSIONER:

Q What is your name? A Martin A. Wallace.
Q What is your age? A Sixty.
Q Your postoffice? A Tahlequah, Cherokee Nation.
Q You are an applicant for enrollment as a citizen by intermarriage of the Cherokee Nation? A I am.
Q You have no Cherokee blood? A Don't claim any.
Q The only claim you make to citizenship in the Cherokee Nation is by virtue of your marriage to a citizen by blood of the Nation? A Yes sir.
Q What is the name of the citizen through whom you claim that right? A Her maiden name?
Q I want to know her full name? A Julia A. Wallace.
Q What was her maiden name? A Julia Raper.
Q Was she recognized as a citizen of the Cherokee Nation the Cherokee Nation at the time you married her? A Yes sir.
Q Living in the Cherokee Nation? A Yes sir.
Q When did you marry her? A Spring of 1872.
Q Is she living now? A Yes sir.
Q Since your marriage to her in 1872, have you and she lived together continuously as husband and wife? A Yes sir.
Q And have always lived in the Cherokee Nation? A Yes sir.
Q Is she your first wife? A Yes sir.

Cherokee Intermarried White 1906
Volume II

Q You were her first husband? A Yes sir.
Q You married her in accordance with Cherokee laws? A. Yes sir.
Q In what District was the license issued authorizing your marriage?
   A Tahlequah District.
Q The license then was issued in Tahlequah District about the year 1872?
   A In the spring of 1872.
Q Who married you? A Steven Foreman.
Q Who was he, a judge of the court?
   A. He was a Prebyterian[sic] preacher.

ON BEHALF OF THE COMMISSIONER:

        The applicant Martin A. Wallace, is identified on the 1880 Cherokee authenticated tribal roll, Going Snake District, opposite No. 1969. The name of his wife, Julia Wallace, is included in an approved partial roll of citizens by blood of the Cherokee Nation opposite No. 14174.

Q Was your wife born in the Cherokee Nation? A Born in South Carolina. I first married her in South Carolina in 1869, and we came here in the fall of '71, and I established her citizenship as a Cherokee and I then got license from the Court and married her by the Cherokee Law. Married her twice.

ON BEHALF OF THE COMMISSIONER:

        The original marriage record, Tahlequah District, Cherokee Nation, Book "C", which is in the possession of this office, No. 29, shows the following entry; "M. A. Wallace, white, citizen of the U. S. to marry Julia A. Wallace, formerly Raper, a Cherokee. Issued January 31, 1872, married by Rev. Steven Foreman, February 8th, 1872."

        (Witness Dismissed)

I, S. T. Wright, stenographer to the Commissioner to the Five Civilized Tribes, on oath, state that I reported the testimony and proceedings had in the above entitled cause on January 5th, 1907, and that the above and foregoing is a true and correct transcript of my stenographic notes thereof, taken on said date.

                                                           ST Wright

Subscribed and sworn to before me this 5th day of January, 1907.

                                                    Edward Merrick
                                                    Notary Public.

Cherokee Intermarried White 1906
Volume II

C.E.W. Cherokee 5934.

DEPARTMENT OF THE INTERIOR,

COMMISSIONER TO THE FIVE CIVILIZED TRIBES.

In the matter of the application for the enrollment of Martin A. Wallace, as a citizen by intermarriage of the Cherokee Nation.

D E C I S I O N

THE RECORDS OF THIS OFFICE SHOW: That at Tahlequah, Indian Territory, December 1, 1900, application was received by the Commission to the Five Civilized Tribes for the enrollment of Martin A. Wallace, as a citizen by intermarriage of the Cherokee Nation. Further proceedings in the matter of said application were had at Tahlequah, Indian Territory, September 30, 1901, and at Muskogee, Indian Territory, January 5, 1907.

THE EVIDENCE IN THIS CASE SHOWS: That the applicant herein, Martin A. Wallace, a white man, was married in accordance with Cherokee law February 8, 1872, to his wife, Julia Wallace, nee Raper, who was at the time of said marriage a recognized citizen by blood of the Cherokee Nation, and who is identified on the Cherokee authenticated tribal roll of 1880, Going Snake District, page 490, number 1970, as a native Cherokee, and whose name appears upon the approved partial roll of citizens by blood of the Cherokee Nation, opposite number 14174; that since marriage the said Martin A. Wallace and Julia Wallace have resided together as husband and wife and have continuously lived in the Cherokee Nation. Said applicant is identified on the Cherokee authenticated tribal roll of 1880, and the Cherokee census roll of 1896 as an intermarried citizen of the Cherokee Nation.

IT IS, THEREFORE, ORDERED AND ADJUDGED: That in accordance with the decision of the Supreme Court of the United States, dated November 5, 1906, in the cases of Daniel Red Bird et al., vs. the United States, Nos. 125, 126, 127 and 128, the said applicant Martin A. Wallace is entitled, under the provision of Section 21 of the Act of Congress approved June 28, 1898, (30 Stat., 495), to enrollment, as a citizen by intermarriage of the Cherokee Nation, and his application for enrollment as such is accordingly granted.

Tams Bixby
Commissioner.

Dated at Muskogee, Indian Territory,
this   JAN 19 1907

Cherokee Intermarried White 1906
Volume II

Cherokee
5934

Muskogee, Indian Territory, December 11, 1906.

Martin A. Wallace,
    Tahlequah, Indian Territory.

Dear Sir:

    In reply to your letter of December 6, 1906, in reference to your right to enrollment as a citizen of the Cherokee Nation, under the recent decision of the United States Supreme Court in the case involving the rights of intermarried white persons to be enrolled as citizens of the Cherokee Nation, you are advised that decisions will be rendered by this office in the cases of intermarried white persons, at the earliest practicable date.

                                  Respectfully,

L M B   Commissioner

◇◇◇◇◇

Cherokee
5934

Muskogee, Indian Territory, December 27, 1906.

Martin A. Wallace,
    Tahlequah, Indian Territory.

Dear Sir:

    November 6, 1906, the United States Supreme Court held that white persons who intermarried with Cherokee citizens according to Cherokee law prior to November 1, 1875, are entitled to enrollment and allotments of land as citizens of the Cherokee Nation.

    You are advised that to properly determine your right to enrollment as a citizen by intermarriage of the Cherokee Nation, it will be necessary for you to appear before the Commissioner for the purpose of giving testimony as to the date of your marriage and whether or not your wife, by reason of your marriage to whom you claim the right to enrollment as a citizen of the Cherokee Nation, was a recognized citizen of the Cherokee Nation at the time of your marriage to her, and whether or not you were married to her in accordance with Cherokee laws.

    You are therefore directed to appear before the Commissioner at Muskogee, Indian Territory, at 9 o'clock A. M., on Saturday, January 5, 1907, and give testimony as above indicated.

Cherokee Intermarried White 1906
Volume II

Respectfully,

S.W.   Acting Commissioner.

⋄⋄⋄⋄⋄

Cherokee
5934.

Muskogee, Indian Territory, January 19, 1907.

W. W. Hastings,
    Attorney for the Cherokee Nation,
        Muskogee, Indian Territory.

Dear Sir:

There is enclosed herewith a copy of the decision of the Commissioner to the Five Civilized Tribes, dated January 19, 1907, granting the application for the enrollment of Martin A. Wallace, as a citizen by intermarriage of the Cherokee Nation.

Respectfully,

Incl. C-21   Commissioner.
LMC

⋄⋄⋄⋄⋄

Cherokee 5934.   W.W.HASTINGS.   OFFICE OF   H.M. VANCE.
                                ATTORNEY.   SECRETARY.

Attorney for the Cherokee Nation,
MUSKOGEE, I. T.

January 19, 1907.

The Commissioner to the Five Civilized Tribes,
    Muskogee, Indian Territory.

Sir:

Receipt is acknowledged of the testimony and of your decision enrolling Martin A. Wallace as a citizen by intermarriage of the Cherokee Nation. Time for protesting said decision is waived and I consent that said person may be placed upon the schedule immediately.

Respectfully,
W. W. Hastings
Attorney for Cherokee Nation.

⋄⋄⋄⋄⋄

Cherokee Intermarried White 1906
Volume II

Cherokee
5934

Muskogee, Indian Territory, January 21, 1907.

Martin A. Wallace,
    Tahlequah, Indian Territory.

Dear Sir:

There is enclosed herewith a copy of the decision of the Commissioner to the Five Civilized Tribes, dated January 19, 1907, granting the application for your enrollment as a citizen by intermarriage of the Cherokee Nation.

You will be advised when your name has been placed upon a schedule of citizens of the Cherokee Nation and approved by the Secretary of the Interior.

Respectfully,

E.R.C.   Commissioner.
Enc. E.C. 10

Cher IW 52
Trans from Cher card 5957 3-13-07

◇◇◇◇◇◇

C.E.W.

DEPARTMENT OF THE INTERIOR,

COMMISSIONER TO THE FIVE CIVILIZED TRIBES.

In the matter of the application for the enrollment of

CHARLOTTE C. MANN

as a citizen by intermarriage of the Cherokee Nation.

CHEROKEE 5957

◇◇◇◇◇◇

Cherokee Intermarried White 1906
Volume II

Department of the Interior,
Commission to the Five Civilized Tribes,
Tahlequah, I.T., December 3, 1900.

In the matter of the application of Robert J. Mann for the enrollment of himself, wife and children as Cherokee citizens; being sworn and examined by Commissioner Needles he testified as follows:

Q What is your name? A Robert J. Mann.
Q What is your age? A 59.
Q What is your post-office address? A Oaks.
Q In what district do you live? A Saline.
Q Are you a recognized citizen of the Cherokee Nation? A I am.
Q By blood or intermarriage? A By blood.
Q Who do you desire to enroll? A Myself and family.
Q What is the name of your wife? A Charlotte C. Mann.
Q Is she a citizen by blood? A No sir, adopted.
Q When did you marry her? A In 1874
Q What is her age? A About 42 I think.
Q What is the name of your oldest child at home under 21? A About 14.
Q What is its name? A Narcissa.
Q Any middle name? A No sir.
Q What is the name of the next child? A Robert L.
Q How old is Robert? A 11
Q The full name of the next child now? A Galilee.
Q How old is Galilee? A About 6.
Q Have you got any more children? A Yes sir.
Q Well what are their names? A Ruth.
Q How old is Ruth? A About 4 I think.
Q The next child? A Gertrude.
Q How old is Gertrude? A 2
Q Any more? A John Davis.
Q How old is he? A About 6 months.
1880 roll page 454 #1157 Robert Man[sic] Goingsnake Dist native Cher 37 years old;
1880 roll page 454 as Catherine Man Goingsnake, as native Cher; 21 years old;
1896 roll page 1006 #797 Robert J. Man Saline Dist
Q Is your wife a Cherokee by blood? A No sir.
1896 roll page 1034 #23 Charlotte Mann Saline Dist as intermarried white;
1896 roll page 1007 #800 Narcissa Mann Saline Dist
1896 roll page 1007 #801 Robert L. Mann Jr   "
1896 roll page 1007 #802 Charlotte G. Mann   "
Q What is the name of this child? A Charlotte Galilee, that's her name.
1896 roll page 1007 #803 Ruth L. Mann Saline Dist
Q How long have you lived in the Cherokee Nation, lived here ever since 1880?
A I have been here all my life.
Q Your wife also? A No sir, she come here just before she was married.

Cherokee Intermarried White 1906
Volume II

Q Has she been living with you continuously since 1880? A Yes sir, 1874.
Q She is your first wife is she? A No sir.
Q Was your first wife living when you married Charlotte? A No sir.
Q Dovirced[sic] from her? A No, she was dead.
Q Are you her first husband? A Yes sir.

Com'r Needles: The name of Robert J. Mann appears upon the authenticated roll of 1880 and the census roll of 1896, as Robert J. Man, a Cherokee by blood; the name of his wife Charlotte C. appears upon the authenticated roll of 1880 as Catherine Man and upon the census roll of 1896 as Charlotte Mann, intermarried white; the names of his children, Narcissa, Robert L., Charlotte G. and Ruth L. appear upon the census roll of 1896/[sic] and he makes satisfactory proof of the birth of his two younger children Gertrude E. and John D., whose names do not appear upon the census roll of 1896; they all being fully identified and having made satisfactory proof as to residence, said Robert L. Mann and his said children as enumerated herein will be duly listed for enrollment as Cherokee citizens by blood, and his wife, Charlotte C., as a Cherokee citizen by intermarriage.

M.D. Green, being first duly sworn, states that as stenographer to the Commission to the Five Civilized Tribes he correctly recorded the testimony and proceedings in this case and that the foregoing is a true and complete transcript of his stenographic notes thereof.

MD Green

Subscribed and sworn to before me this 3rd day of December 1900.

CR Breckinridge

Commissiner[sic].

◇◇◇◇◇

JOR.
Cher. 5957.

Department of the Interior.
Commission to the.
Tahlequah, I. T., October 22, 1902.

SUPPLEMENTAL TESTIMONY in the matter of the application for the enrollment of CHARLOTTE C. MANN as a citizen by intermarriage of the Cherokee Nation.

CHARLOTTE C. MANN, being first duly sworn, and being examined, testified as follows:

BY COMMISSION: What is your name? A Charlotte C. Mann.
Q How old are you? A Fortt[sic]-four.
Q What is your post office address? A Oaks.

Cherokee Intermarried White 1906
Volume II

Q Are you a white woman? A Yes sir.
Q Has application been made to this Commission for your enrollment as a citizen by intermarriage of the Cherokee Nation? A Yes sir.
Q What is the name of your husband? A Robert J. Mann.
Q Is he living? A Yes sir.
Q Is he a Cherokee by blood? A Yes sir.
Q Do you claim your right to enrollment by reason of your marriage to him? A Yes sir.
Q When were you and he married? A 1874.
Q Does your name appear upon the roll of 1880? A Yes sir.
Q Were you ever married before you married him? A No sir.
Q Was he ever married before he married you? A Yes sir.
Q What was the name of his first wife? A I don't know, Julia something?
Q Is she living? A No sir, she is dead.
Q Was she living when you and him married? A No sir.
Q Have you and your present husband lived together continuously since your marriage? A Yes sir.
Q Were you living together on the 1st day of September, 1902? A Yes sir, we have been living together ever since we have been married.
Q Never been separated? A No sir.
Q How long have you resided in the Cherokee Nation? A I don't know how long that has been. I have been here ever since I was twelve years old.
Q Have your resided here continuously since that time? A Yes sir.
Q How long has your husband resided in the Cherokee Nation? A He has been born and raised here.
Q Resided here all his life continuously? A Yes sir, all his life, I reckon.
Q Has he resided here continuously while you have known him? A Been in the Cherokee Nation ever since me and him have been together?
Q How many children did you make application for? (No response)
Q Have you had any children die since you were enrolled by this Commission? A No sir.
Q All of your children that were enrolled by the Dawes Commission are living, are they? A Yes sir.
Q You don't now how many you had enrolled? Got one named Bertha E.? A It is Effie, its name is Effie.
Q What is that child's full name? A Effie Viola Mann. I haven't got any named Bertha.
Q Was this child born since your application for enrollment? A Yes sir, we sent her name in.
Q Have you a child named Charlotte G.[sic] A Charlotte Galilee is all I know.

ROBERT J. MANN, being first duly sworn, and being examined, testified as follows:

BY COMMISSION: What is your name? A Robert J. Mann.
Q How old are you? A I will be sixty this fall.
Q You are a Cherokee by blood? A Yes sir.
Q Are you the husband of Charlotte C. Mann? A Yes sir.

Cherokee Intermarried White 1906
Volume II

Q Were you ever married before you married her? A Yes sir.
Q What was the name of your first wife? A My first wife was before the war. I guess you don't want to know that far back. My wife before I married this one was Wilson.
Q Did you have any wife living when you married this one? A Not that I know of, no sir.
Q What was the name of the first wife that you had? A Julia.
Q Is she living? A No sir, she died the time of the war.
Q She died before you married your present wife? A Yes sir.
Q Were you married to any other woman besides her before you married your present wife? A Before I married this woman I was married to that Wilson girl.
Q What was her given name? A Ella.
Q Was Ella Wilson living when you married your present wife? A No sir.
Q Were those the only two times you have been married? A No, I was married the time of the war in Texas, you call it married. I got married in the Chickasaw Nation. I was living with a woman about a month. She is dead.
Q Was she dead before you married your present wife? A Yes sir.
Q Were those three the only women to whom you were ever married? A Yes sir, that is all.
Q You had no wife living when you marred[sic] your present wife? A No sir
Q Are all you children living at this time that you made application for? A They are all living. I had one enrolled by a Notary Public.
Q You had no children die since you were enrolled? A No sir.

   This testimony will be filed with and made a part of the record din the matter of the application for the enrollment of Charlotte C. Mann as a citizen by intermarriage of the Cherokee Nation, Cherokee straight card field No. 5957.

Wm. Hutchinson, being first duly sworn, states that as stenographer to the Commission to the Five Civilized Tribes he correctly recorded the testimony and proceedings in this case, and that the foregoing is a true and complete transcript of his stenographic notes thereof.

                       Wm Hutchinson

Subscribed and sworn to before me this 11th day of November, 1902.

                          BC Jones
                          Notary Public.

Cherokee Intermarried White 1906
Volume II

Cherokee 5957.

DEPARTMENT OF THE INTERIOR,
COMMISSIONER TO THE FIVE CIVILIZED TRIBES.
Muskogee, I. T., January 5, 1907.

In the matter of the application for the enrollment of Charlotte C. Mann for enrollment as a citizen by intermarriage of the Cherokee Nation.

Charlotte C. Mann, being first duly sworn by John E. Tidwell, a Notary Public for the Western District of Indian Territory, testified as follows:

By the Commissioner:
Q What is your name? A Charlotte C. Mann.
Q What is your age? A Forty-eight last August.
Q What is your postoffice address? A Oaks I. T.
Q Is that in the Cherokee Nation? A Yes sir.
Q You claim to be a citizen by intermarriage of the Cherokee Nation? A Yes sir.
Q Through whom do you claim that right? A Robert J. Mann.
Q What is his citizenship? A Cherokee by blood.
Q Is he a native born citizen of the Cherokee Nation? A Yes
Q Lived there all his life? A Yes, born and raised close to Oaks.
Q Is Robert J. Mann living at the present time? A Yes, he is living now.
Q Have you and he been married? A Yes sir.
Q When? A July 14, 1874.
Q Where were you married? A Married close to Oaks, at the Mission.
Q In what district of the Cherokee nation[sic]? A Going Snake.
Q Was[sic] you married under a license? A No, Women didn't get licenses.
Q Who performed the marriage ceremony between you? A Parson Mack.
Q What was his office? Was he a minister of the gospel or official of the Cherokee nation? A Minister.
Q Did he issue a certificate of marriage when he performed the ceremony? A No sir.
Q There was no marriage certificate issued that you know of? A No, he gave us nothing, no certificate or nothing. I think it is recorded.
Q Where is it recorded? A I couldn't tell that. My witness I guess can tell better than I can.
Q Were either you or Robert J. Mann ever married prior to your marriage in 1874? A He was married before. I never was
Q Was his wife living at the time you married him? A No, she was dead.
Q Where have you resided since your marriage in 1874? A Right there at Oaks; never moved more than four miles from there.
Q You lived continuously in the Cherokee nation[sic] since 1874? A Yes, never was out of the nation but once since I was married, when I went to do some trading.
Q Were there any witnesses present when you and Mr. Mann were married? A My brother-in-law here was present, Dave Mann.

Cherokee Intermarried White 1906
Volume II

Q He saw the marriage ceremony performed between you and your husband? A Yes sir.
Q Have you any children by your present husband? A Yes sir.
Q[sic] I have got 13. Three dead and four married.
Q What are the names of these children beginning with the youngest? A Effie V., John D., Gertrude, Ruth L., Charlotta G., Robert L and Narcissa.
Q Those older than these you have named are married are they? A Yes, three dead and four married older than that.

> Robert J. Mann, together with the above named children of the applicant are identified on the approved partial roll of Cherokees by blood opposite Nos. 14243 to 14250 inclusive.
>
> The applicant is identified on the authenticated Cherokee tribal roll of 1880, Going Snake District, and Cherokee Census Roll, 1896, Saline District, opposite No. 1158 and 1034 respectively.[sic] as an intermarried white.

David Mann being first duly sworn by Frances R. Lane, a Notary Public for the Western District of Indian Territory, testified as follows:

By the Commissioner:
Q What is your name? A David Mann.
Q What is your age? A Fifty-seven.
Q Your postoffice address? A Oaks, I. T.
Q Are you a Cherokee by blood? A Yes sir.
Q Have you been enrolled? A Yes sir.
Q Are you acquainted with the applicant in this case, Charlotte C. Mann? A Yes sir.
Q Do you know her husband, Robert J. Mann? A Yes sir.
Q Are you and he related? A Brothers.
Q How long have you known the applicant, Charlotte C. Mann? A About 32 years.
Q Did you know her prior to her marriage? A No, that was my first acquaintance with her when they got married.
Q Were you present when she and her husband were married? A Yes sir.
Q Where were they married? A Near Oaks, at the Moravian Mission.
Q When were they married? A They was married in 1874.
Q Were they married in accordance with the Cherokee laws and customs in effect at that time? A They was married under the custom for white women marrying in the Cherokee nation. They didn't have to get a license.
Q Who performed the marraige[sic] ceremony? A Parson Mack of the Moravian Mission.
Q Do you know whether or not he issued a certificate of marriage after he performed the ceremony? A I don't think he did. If he did I didn't know it. He generally did, but I never saw such a certificate.
Q Was that ceremony performed in the Going Snake District? A Yes sir.
Q If such a certificate was issued it would be recorded in the marriage records of Going Snake District? A Yes, sometimes and sometimes he had his business before the Tahlequah District. It might in in Tahlequah.

Cherokee Intermarried White 1906
Volume II

Q Have the applicant and her husband lived together continuously since their marriage in 1874? A Yes, up to and including the present time.
Q Living in the Cherokee nation during all that time, have they? A Yes, never lived anywhere else.
Q How do you identify the date of their marriage as being in the year 1874? Can you call anything to mind that would indicate that was the year? A I don't know as there is anything, exactly.
Q Do you remember when the bread payment was made in the Cherokee nation? A Yes sir.
Q With reference to that payment when were they married? Was it before or after? A The bread payment was made after I think.
Q About how long after? A To the best of my recollection I think 3 or 4 years. I would not be positive.
Q Are you married? A Yes sir.
Q When were you married? A I was married in 1869.

Frances R. Lane upon oath states that as stenographer to the Commissioner to the Five Civilized Tribes she reported the testimony in the above entitled cause and that the foregoing is an accurate transcript of her stenographic notes therein.

Frances R Lane

Subscribed and sworn to before me this January 7, 1907.

Edward Merrick
Notary Public.

◇◇◇◇◇

C.E.W.   Cherokee 5957

DEPARTMENT OF THE INTERIOR,

COMMISSIONER TO THE FIVE CIVILIZED TRIBES.

In the matter of the application for the enrollment of Charlotte C. Mann, as a citizen by intermarriage of the Cherokee Nation.

D E C I S I O N

THE RECORDS OF THIS OFFICE SHOW: That at Tahlequah, Indian Territory, December 3, 1900, Robert J. Mann appeared before the Commission to the Five Civilized Tribes, and made application for the enrollment of his wife, Charlotte C. Mann, as a

Cherokee Intermarried White 1906
Volume II

citizen by intermarriage, and for the enrollment of himself, et al., as citizens by blood of the Cherokee Nation. The application for the enrollment of the said Robert J. Mann, et al., as citizens by blood of the Cherokee Nation has been heretofore disposed of and their rights to enrollment will not be considered in this decision. Further proceedings in the matter of said application were had at Tahlequah, Indian Territory, October 22, 1902, and at Muskogee, Indian Territory, January 5, 1907.

THE EVIDENCE IN THIS CASE SHOWS: That the applicant herein, Charlotte C. Mann, a white woman, married July 14, 1874, one Robert J. Mann, who was at the time of said marriage a recognized citizen by blood of the Cherokee Nation, and whose name appears upon the approved partial roll of citizens by blood of the Cherokee Nation, opposite number 14243; that since said marriage the said Robert J. Mann and Charlotte C. Mann have resided together as husband and wife and have continuously lived in the Cherokee Nation. Said Charlotte C. Mann is identified on the Cherokee authenticated tribal roll of 1880, and the Cherokee Census Roll of 1896 as an intermarried citizen of the Cherokee Nation.

IT IS, THEREFORE, ORDERED AND ADJUDGED: That in accordance with the decision of the Supreme Court of the United States, dated November 5, 1906, in the case of Daniel Red Bird et al., vs. the United States under the provision of Section 21 of the Act of Congress approved June 28, 1898, (30 Stat., 495), Charlotte C. Mann is entitled to enrollment as a citizen by intermarriage of the Cherokee Nation, and her application for enrollment as such is accordingly granted.

           Tams Bixby
            Commissioner.

Dated at Muskogee, Indian Territory,
this JAN 16 1907

◇◇◇◇◇

Charlotte
5957

          Muskogee, Indian Territory, December 27, 1906.

Charlotte C. Mann,
  Oaks, Indian Territory.

Dear Madam:

November 6, 1906, the United States Supreme Court held that white persons who intermarried with Cherokee citizens according to Cherokee law prior to November 1, 1875, are entitled to enrollment and allotments of land as citizens of the Cherokee Nation.

You are advised that to properly determine your right to enrollment as a citizen by intermarriage of the Cherokee Nation, it will be necessary for you to appear before the

Cherokee Intermarried White 1906
Volume II

Commissioner for the purpose of giving testimony as to the date of your marriage and whether or not your husband, by reason of your marriage to whom you claim the right to enrollment as a citizen by intermarriage of the Cherokee Nation, was a recognized Cherokee citizen at the time of your marriage to him.

You are therefore directed to appear before the Commissioner at Muskogee, Indian Territory, at 9 o'clock A. M., on Saturday, January 5, 1907, and give testimony as above indicated.

Respectfully,

S.W.   Acting Commissioner.

Cherokee
5957

Muskogee, Indian Territory, January 19, 1907.

Charlotte C. Mann,
    Oaks, Indian Territory.

Dear Madam;

There is enclosed herewith copy of the decision of the Commissioner to the Five Civilized Tribes, dated January 17, 1907, granting the application for your enrollment as a citizen by intermarriage of the Cherokee Nation.

You will be advised when your name has been placed upon a schedule of citizens of the Cherokee Nation and approved by the Secretary of the Interior.

Respectfully,

Enc I-70   Commissioner.
RPI

Cherokee Intermarried White 1906
Volume II

Cherokee 5957

Muskogee, Indian Territory, January 17, 1907.

W. W. Hastings,
    Attorney for the Cherokee Nation,
        Muskogee, Indian Territory.

Dear Sir:

    There is enclosed herewith copy of the decision of the Commissioner to the Five Civilized Tribes, dated January 16, 1907, granting the application for the enrollment of Charlotte C. Mann as a citizen by intermarriage of the Cherokee Nation.

        Respectfully,

Enc I-8   Commissioner.
RPI

◇◇◇◇◇

W.W. HASTINGS. ATTORNEY.	OFFICE OF	H.M. VANCE. SECRETARY.

Cherokee 5957 :

Attorney for the Cherokee Nation,
MUSKOGEE, I. T.

January 18, 1907.

The Commissioner,
    to the Five Civilized Tribes,
        Muskogee, Indian Territory.

Sir:

    Receipt is acknowledged of the testimony and of your decision enrolling Charlotte C. Mann as a citizen by intermarriage of the Cherokee Nation. Time for protesting said decision is waived and I consent that said person may be placed upon the schedule immediately.

                                            W. W. Hastings
                                            Attorney for Cherokee Nation.

Cherokee Intermarried White 1906
Volume II

Cher IW 53
Trans from Cher 6258 3-13-07

◇◇◇◇◇

C.E.W.

DEPARTMENT OF THE INTERIOR,

COMMISSIONER TO THE FIVE CIVILIZED TRIBES.

In the matter of the application for the enrollment of

HARRIS A. LOFLIN

as a citizen by intermarriage of the Cherokee Nation.

CHEROKEE 6258

◇◇◇◇◇

Department of the Interior,
Commission to the Five Civilized Tribes,
Tahlequah, I.T., December 7, 1900.

In the matter of the application of Harris Asberry Loflin for the enrollment of himself, wife and children as Cherokee citizens; beig[sic] sworn and examined by Commissioner Needles h[sic] testified as follows:

Q What is your name? A Harris Asberry Loflin.
Q How old are you? A 60
Q What is your post-office address? A Siloam Springs, Arkansas
Q In what district to you live? A Gongsnake[sic].
Q Are you a citizen of the Cherokee Nation? A Yes sir, by adoption.
Q Who do you want to enroll? A I want to enroll my family.
Q What is the name of your wife? A Rebecca Jane.
Q Were you married to her before 1880? A Yes sir.
Q How old is your wife? A She is 46.
Q What are the names of your children? A Ada A.
Q How old is Ada? A 18.
Q The next child? A Vaul D.
Q How old is he? A 16.
Q The next child? A Chester C.
Q How old is Chester C.? A 14.

Cherokee Intermarried White 1906
Volume II

Q The next child? A Harris A., Jr.
Q How old is he? A 11.
Q The next child? A Clarence Robert.
Q How old is Clarence? A 8.
Q The next one? A Oscar M.
Q How old is he? A 2 years old.
Q Are these children alive and living with you at the present time? A Yes sir, all of them.
Q Rebecca J. your first wife? A Yes sir.
Q You her first husband? A Yes sir.
Q Have you lived with her continuously since you married her in the Cherokee Nation? A Yes sir.
Q Living with her now? A Yes sir.
1880 roll page 450 #1064 A.J. (H.A.([sic] Loflan[sic] Goingsnake, adopted white
1880 roll page 450 #1065 Beckey Loflan Goingsnake, native Cher;
1896 roll page 824 #111 Harris A. Loflin Goingsnake Dist.
1896 roll page 763 #1239 Rebecca J. Loflin Goingsnake.
1896 roll page 763 #1240 Ada A Loflin   "
1896 roll page 763 #1241 Vol D. Loflin   "
1896 roll page 763 #1242 Chester C. Loflin   "
1896 roll page 763 #1243 Harris A. Loflin   "
1896 roll page 763 #1244 Clarence R. Loflin "
Q You have never separated from your wife during this time? A No sir.

    Com'r Needles: The name of Harris A. Loflin appears upon the authenticated roll of 1880 and the census roll of 1896 as an intermarried white; the name of his wife, Rebecca J. appears upon the authenticated roll of 1880 as Beckey and upon the census roll of 1896 as Rebecca J., as a Cherokee citizen by blood;
    The names of his children, Ada A., Vaul D., Chester C., Harris A., Jr, and Clarence R. appear upon the census roll of 1896, and he makes satisfactory proof of birth as to the younger child, Oscar M. whose name does not appear upon said roll; they all being duly identified according to page and number of the rolls as indicated in the testimony, and having made satisfactory proof as to residence, said Harris A. Loflin will be duly listed for enrollment as a Cherokee citizen by intermarriage, and his wife Rebecca J. and their children enumerated herein will be duly listed for enrollment as Cherokee citizen[sic] by blood.

    M.D. Green, being first duly sworn, states that as stenographer to the Commission to the Five Civilized Tribes he correctly recorded the testimony and proceedings in this case and that the foregoing is a true and complete transcript of his stenographic notes thereof.

MD Green

Subscribed and sworn to before me this December 8, 1900.

C R Breckinridge
Commissioner.

Cherokee Intermarried White 1906
Volume II

Cherokee 6258.

Department of the Interior,
Commission to the Five Civilized Tribes.
Muskogee, I. T., October 6, 1902.

In the matter of the application of Harris A. Loflin for the enrollment of himself as a citizen by intermarriage, and for the enrollment of his wife, Rebecca J., and children, Ada A. Winstead, Vaul D., Chester C., Harris A. Jr., Clarence R. and Oscar M. Loflin and grandchild, Florence E. Winstead, as citizens by blood of the Cherokee Nation: he being sworn and examined by the Commission, testified as follows:

Q What is your name? A Harris A. Loflin.
Q What is your age at this time? A Sixty-two.
Q What is your postoffice? A Siloam Springs, Arkansas.
Q Are you the same Harris A. Loflin that made application to this Commission for enrollment as an intermarried citizen on December 7, 1900? A Some time about that time.
Q What is your wife's name? A Rebecca J.
Q Was she a Cherokee by blood? A Yes sir.
Q Is she living? A Yes sir.
Q When were you and she married? A In '74.
Q Were you ever married prior to your marriage to her? A No sir.
Q Was she ever married before? A No sir.
Q You her first husband and she your first wife? A Yes sir.
Q Have you and she lived together from the time of your marriage as husband and wife up until the present time? A Yes sir.
Q Never separated? A No sir.
Q Living together on the first day of September, 1902? A Yes sir.
Q How long have you lived in the Cherokee Nation? A About thirty-three years.
Q Have you lived here all the time since 1880? A Yes sir.
Q Living in the nation now? A Yes sir.
Q Has your wife, Rebecca J., lived in the Cherokee Nation all the time since 1880? A Yes sir.
Q Are these children, Ada A., Vaul D., Chester C., Harris A. Jr., Clarence R. and Oscar M., your children by your wife, Rebecca J.? A All my children by my wife, Rebecca J.
Q Are they all living at this time? A Yes sir.
Q Have they lived in the Cherokee Nation all their lives? A Yes sir, all their lives.
Q Who is this other child, Florence E. Winstead? A That is Ada A's; she has married since the enrollment; that is her daughter.

Cherokee Intermarried White 1906
Volume II

The undersigned, being duly sworn, states that as stenographer to the Commission to the Five Civilized Tribes he correctly recorded the testimony and proceedings in this case, and that the foregoing is a true and complete transcript of his stenographic notes thereof.

E.G. Rothenberger

Subscribed and sworn to before me this 28th day of October, 1902.

BC Jones
Notary Public.

◇◇◇◇◇

Cherokee No 6258.

DEPARTMENT OF THE INTERIOR,

COMMISSIONER TO THE FIVE CIVILIZED TRIBES,

MUSKOGEE, INDIAN TERRITORY, JANUARY 5, 1907.

IN THE MATTER of the application for the enrollment of Harris A. Loflin as a citizen by intermarriage of the Cherokee Nation.

HARRIS A. LOFLIN, being first duly sworn by B. P. Ramus[sic], Notary Public, testified as follows:

EXAMINATION

ON BEHALF OF THE COMMISSIONER:

Q What is your name? A Harris Asbury[sic] Loflin.
Q What is your age? A Sixty-six.
Q Your postoffice address? A Siloam Springs, Arkansas.
Q Are you an applicant for enrollment as a citizen by intermarriage of the Cherokee Nation? A I am.
Q You have no Cherokee by blood? A Not that I know of, no sir.
Q The only claim you make to the right to enrollment as a citizen of the Cherokee Nation is by virtue of your marriage to a citizen by blood of the Cherokee Nation, is it? A Yes.
Q What is the name of the citizen through whom you claim that right?
A Rebecca Loflin.
Q Is she living or dead? A Living, was yesterday morning.
Q When did you marry her? A 15th day of July, 1874.
Q Was she a recognized citizen of the Cherokee Nation at that time? [sic] She was, sir.
Q Residing in the Cherokee Country, was she? A Yes sir.

Cherokee Intermarried White 1906
Volume II

Q Did you marry her in accordance with the laws of the Cherokee Nation? A I did.
Q Did you secure a license? A Yes I procured a license.
Q In what district was that license secured? A Saline.
Q Since your marriage to your wife in 1874, have you and she continuously lived together as husband and wife? A We have.
Q And have always lived in the Cherokee Nation? A Always.
Q Was she your first wife? A First and only wife.
Q Were you her first husband? A Yes sir.

ON BEHALF OF THE COMMISSIONER:

    The applicant, Harris A. Loflin, is identified on the authenticated Cherokee tribal roll of 1880, Going Snake District, opposite No. 1064.

    The name of his wife, Rebecca J. Loflin, is enrolled on the approved partial roll of citizens by blood of the Cherokee Nation, opposite No. 14906.

    The applicant presents an original marriage license and certificate showing that on the 12th day of July, 1874, a license was issued in accordance with Cherokee law by J. M. Ross, Clerk of Saline District, authorizing the marriage of Harris C. Loflin, a citizen of the United States, and Rebecca J. Dial, a citizen of the Cherokee Nation, and that said parties were united in marriage in accordance with the terms of said license July 15, 1874, by A. J. Estes, Minister. Certified copy of this marriage license and certificate will be made and filed with and made a part of the record in this case.

    (Witness dismissed).

 I, S. T. Wright, stenographer to the Commissioner to the Five Civilized Tribes, on oath, state that I recorded the testimony and proceedings had in the above entitled cause on January 5, 1907, and that the above and foregoing is a true and correct transcript of my stenographic notes thereof taken on said date.

                  S.T. Wright

Subscribed and sworn to before me this January 5, 1907.

                  Edward Merrick
                  NOTARY PUBLIC.

Cherokee Intermarried White 1906
Volume II

(CERTIFIED COPY)

Saline District)
            (
Cherokee Nation)

Know all men by these presents: that marriage License are hereby granted Harris A. Loflin, a <u>white</u> <u>man</u> and a citizen of the <u>United</u> <u>States</u> to marry Rebecca J. Dial, a citizen of the Cherokee Nation, the said Harris A. Loflin having complied with the Laws and Customs of the Cherokee People, and any of the Judges of the Several Courts of this Nation, or any Ordained Minister of the Gosple[sic] having the care of souls, are hereby authorised[sic] and required to perform the marriage ceremony and return the same with a certificate of service as the Law directs.

Given from under my hand in office this the 12th day of July, 1874.

J. M. Ross, Clerk Saline District C. N.

MARDGE[sic] SERTIFICATE[sic].

Know all men that the parties above named was dewly[sic] maried[sic] on the fifteenth of July, 1874 by the undersigned, a Minister of the Gospel living in Benton County, State of Ark., as witnes[sic] my hand tthe[sic] day and dat[sic] in this certificate.

A. J. Bates. (Mins)

(Back)

Recorded in Clerk office, Saline Dist., C. N.

-------------------oOo-------------------

I, S. T. Wright, upon oath, state that the above is a true and correct copy of what purports to be the original marriage license and certificate of Harris A. Loflin and Rebecca J. Dial. Filed with application of Harris A. Loflin for enrollment as a citizen by intermarriage of the Cherokee Nation. (Original returned to applicant.)

S.T. Wright

Subscribed and sworn to before me this 5th day of January, 1907.

Edward Merrick
Notary Public.

Cherokee Intermarried White 1906
Volume II

C.E.W.   Cherokee 6258

DEPARTMENT OF THE INTERIOR,

COMMISSIONER TO THE FIVE CIVILIZED TRIBES

In the matter of the application for the enrollment of Harris L. Loflin, as a citizen by intermarriage of the Cherokee Nation.

D E C I S I O N

THE RECORDS OF THIS OFFICE SHOW: That at Tahlequah, Indian Territory, December 7, 1900, Harris A. Loflin appeared before the Commission to the Five Civilized Tribes, and made application for the enrollment of himself, as a citizen by intermarriage, and for the enrollment of his wife, Rebecca J. Loflin, as a citizen by blood of the Cherokee Nation. The application for the enrollment of the said Rebecca J. Loflin, et al., as citizens by blood of the Cherokee Nation has been heretofore disposed of and their rights to enrollment will not be considered in this decision. Further proceedings in the matter of said application were had at Muskogee, Indian Territory, October 6, 1902, and January 5, 1907.

THE EVIDENCE IN THIS CASE SHOWS: That the applicant herein, Harris A. Loflin, a white man, was married in accordance with Cherokee law July 15, 1874, to his wife, Rebecca J. Loflin, nee Dial, who was at the time of said marriage a recognized citizen by blood of the Cherokee Nation, and whose name appears upon the approved partial roll of citizens by blood of the Cherokee Nation, opposite number 14906; that since said marriage the said Harris A. Loflin and Rebecca J. Loflin have resided together as husband and wife and have continuously lived in the Cherokee Nation. Said Harris A. Loflin is identified on the Cherokee authenticated tribal roll of 1880, and the Cherokee census roll of 1896 as an intermarried citizen of the Cherokee Nation.

IT IS, THEREFORE, ORDERED AND ADJUDGED: That in accordance with the decision of the Supreme Court of the United States, dated November 5, 1906, in the case of Daniel Red Bird et al., vs. the United States under the provision of Section 21 of the Act of Congress approved June 28, 1898, (30 Stat., 495), Harris A. Loflin is entitled to enrollment as a citizen by intermarriage of the Cherokee Nation, and his application for enrollment as such is accordingly granted.

                                                                  Tams Bixby
                                                                   Commissioner.

Dated at Muskogee, Indian Territory,
this   JAN 17 1907

Cherokee Intermarried White 1906
Volume II

Cherokee 6258

Muskogee, Indian Territory, January 17, 1907

W. W. Hastings,
    Attorney for the Cherokee Nation,
        Muskogee, Indian Territory.

Dear Sir:

There is enclosed herewith copy of the decision of the Commissioner to the Five Civilized Tribes, dated January 17, 1907, granting the application for the enrollment of Harris A. Loflin as a citizen by intermarriage of the Cherokee Nation.

        Respectfully,

Enc I-1   Commissioner.
RPI

◇◇◇◇◇◇

Cherokee
  6258

Muskogee, Indian Territory, January 21, 1907.

Harris A. Loflin,
    Siloam Springs, Arkansas.

Dear Sir:

    There is enclosed herewith a copy of the decision of the Commissioner to the Five Civilized Tribes, dated January 17, 1907, granting the application for your enrollment as a citizen by intermarriage of the Cherokee Nation.

You will be advised when your name has been placed upon a schedule of citizens of the Cherokee Nation and approved by the Secretary of the Interior.

        Respectfully,

E.R.C.   Commissioner.
Enc. E.C. 11.

◇◇◇◇◇◇

Cherokee Intermarried White 1906
Volume II

Cherokee 6258   W.W.HASTINGS. ATTORNEY.   OFFICE OF   H.M. VANCE. SECRETARY.

Attorney for the Cherokee Nation,
MUSKOGEE, I. T.

January 18, 1907.

The Commissioner to the Five Civilized Tribes,
Muskogee, Indian Territory.

Sir:

Receipt is acknowledged of the testimony and of your decision enrolling Harris A. Loflin as a citizen by intermarriage of the Cherokee Nation. Time for protesting said decision is waived and I consent that said person may be placed upon the schedule immediately.

Yours very truly,
W. W. Hastings
Attorny[sic] for Cherokee Nation.

Cher IW 54
Trans from Cher 9999 3-13-07

◇◇◇◇◇

C.E.W.

DEPARTMENT OF THE INTERIOR,

COMMISSIONER TO THE FIVE CIVILIZED TRIBES.

In the matter of the application for the enrollment of

FLEMING H. WASSON

as a citizen by intermarriage of the Cherokee Nation.

CHEROKEE 9999

◇◇◇◇◇

Cherokee Intermarried White 1906
Volume II

Cher D 465

Department of the Interior,
Commission to the Five Civilized Tribes,
Muskogee, I. T., October 2, 1902.

In the matter of the application of FLEMING H. WASSON, for the enrollment of himself as a citizen by intermarriage of the Cherokee Nation.

FLEMING H. WASSON, called as a witness, being duly sworn and examined by the Commission, testified as follows:

Q What is your name ?   A Fleming H. Wasson.
Q What is your age at this time ?   A Sixty six.
Q What is your post office address ?   A My post office address now is Welch.
Q Are you the same Fleming H. Wasson who made application to the Commission for enrollment as an intermarried citizen on September 28, 1900 ?   A Yes sir.
Q What was your Cherokee wife's name ?   A Catherine Goddard.
Q Is she living ?   A Yes sir.
Q When were you and she married ?   A About 1877, I think.
Q Were you ever married prior to your marriage to her ?   A Yes sir.
Q How many times were you married before you married her ?   A Only once.
Q Was your first wife a white woman ?   A No sir, a Cherokee.
Q Were you married to your first wife under a Cherokee license ?   A Yes sir.
Q What was her name ?   A Her name was Millie Van Norman.
Q Was your first wife ever married prior to her marriage to you ?
A Yes sir, she was married to a man named Van Norman.
Q Was he living or dead when you married her ?   A Dead.
Q Did you and your first wife live together from the time you were married up till her death ?   A Yes sir.
Q After her death you married your last wife ?   A Yes sir.
Q Did you marry your last wife under a Cherokee license ?   A No sir. We married up in Chetopa.
Q Just married by a preacher ?   A Yes sir.
Q You and your last wife have lived together from the time you were married to the present time ?   A Yes sir.
Q Were living together as husband and wife on the first day of September, 1902 ?
A Yes sir.
Q How long have you lived in the Cherokee Nation ?   A Ever since about a year before I married my first woman. I moved out when I married my second woman; we went out with the children; we moved to Chetopa to school them, she had two children.
Q When did you move to Chetopa ?   A The next year after I married her.
Q When did you marry her ?   A In 1877.
Q You married your last wife in 1877 ?   A Yes sir.
Q How long after you married before you went to Chetopa, Kansas ?   A About a year.
Q Did you take your wife and her children there ?   A Yes sir.

Cherokee Intermarried White 1906
Volume II

Q How long did you stay in Chetopa, Kansas ? A Eight or ten years.
Q You were living there when the 1880 roll was made ? A Yes sir.
Q You were not on the 1880 roll ? A No sir.
Q Was your wife on the 1880 roll ? A I think so; I am not certain.
Q About what year did you come back to the Cherokee Nation ? A I don't remember, about ten or twelve years ago.
Q Have you lived in the Cherokee Nation all the time for the past ten years ? A Yes sir.
Q Has your last wife lived here in the Cherokee Nation with you for the past ten years ? A Yes sir.
Q Have you and she got any children ? A Yes sir.
Q How many children ? A Two.
Q They are your children by her ? A Yes sir.
Q Are they still under age ? A No sir, they are both grown. One is twenty one and the other is eighteen.

E. C. Bagwell, on oath states that, as stenographer to the Commission to the Five Civilized Tribes, he correctly recorded the testimony and proceedings had in the above entitled cause, and that the foregoing is an accurate transcript of his stenographic notes thereof.

E.C. Bagwell

Subscribed and sworn to before me this October 11, 1902.

BC Jones
Notary Public.

◇◇◇◇◇

"R"

Cherokee D 465

Department of the Interior,
Commission to the Five Civilized Tribes,
Muskogee, I. T., February 25, 1902.

SUPPLEMENTAL TESTIMONY AND PROCEEDINGS in the matter of the application of Fleming H. Wasson for the enrollment of himself as a Cherokee citizen.

Appearances:
  Applicant in person;
  W. W. Hastings, Attorney for the Cherokee Nation.

BY COMMISSION: The applicant was notified by registered letter February 11, 1902 that his case would be taken up for final consideration by the Commission on

Cherokee Intermarried White 1906
Volume II

the 27th day of February 1902. He this day appears before the Commission and requests that same be taken up and by agreement with the representative of the Cherokee Nation present the same is done.

FLEMING H. WASSON, being first duly sworn and being examined testified as follows:
BY COMMISSION:
Q What is your name? A Fleming H. Wasson.
Q How old are you? A 66.
Q Where do you live? A I live at Wasson post-office, about 6 miles this side of the line.
Q You are an applicant before the Commission for enrollment as a citizen of the Cherokee Nation? A Yes sr.
Q Do you submit your case to the Commission for final consideration? A Yes sir.

BY COMMISSION: The applicant and the representative of the Cherokee Nation present submit this case to the Commission and same is ordered closed and reported to the Commission for final decision, based upon the evidence of record.

M.D. Green, being first duly sworn, states that as stenographer to the Commission to the Five Civilized Tribes he correctly recorded the testimony and proceedings in this case and that the foregoing is a true and complete transcript of his stenographic notes thereof.

MD Green

Subscribed and sworn to before me this February 27, 1902.

TB Needles
Commissioner.

◇◇◇◇◇

Department of the Interior,
Commission to the Five Civilized Tribes,
Vinita, I.T., September 28, 1900.

In the matter of the application of Catherine Wasson for the enrollment of herself and child as Cherokees by blood and her husband as a Cherokee by intermarriage; being sworn and examined by Commissioner Breckenridge[sic], she testified as follows:

Q Give your full name, please? A Catherine Wasson.
Q How old are you? A 45.
Q What is your post office? A Wasson.
Q In what district do you live? A Cooweescoowee.
Q Who is it now you want to have put on the roll, yourself? A Myself and three children, I reckon, if I can enroll for one that is married.

Cherokee Intermarried White 1906
Volume II

Q You can't enroll one that is married, you can apply for the other. A Well I want to apply for myself and husband and one child.
Q Do you apply for yourself as a Cherokee by blood? A Yes, sir.
Q What proportion of Cherokee blood do you claim? [sic] / .1/16 I think.
Q Your husband a Cherokee or a white man? A White man.
Q How long have you lived in the Cherokee Nation? A All my live except I was back and forth sending me children to school.
Q Only in a temporary way? A Yes, sir.
Q What was your father's name? A William England.
Q He dead or alive? A He is dead.
Q Your mother's name? A Elizabeth.
Q She dead or alive? A She is dead.
Q When did you marry? A I married in 1869 first.
Q Is your husband the father of the children you apply for now? A No, sir, he is dead.
Q When did he die? A He died in 1873 or 1874.
Q When did you marry again? A I married in 1875.
Q Is your husband dead? A No, sir, he is alive.
Q Your present husband? A Yes, sir.
Q You married in 1875 to whom? A Fleming H. Wasson.
Q And he is still living? A He is living.
Q Then you are on the roll of 1880 as a Wasson? A Yes, sir; yesterday they couldn't find it.
Q From what district were you enrolled in 1880? A Cooweescoowee, it ought to be.
Q How old is your husband now? A 65.
Q He has lived with you ever since you were married, has he? A Yes, sir.
Q Where is he at this time, at home? A He is at home, he is at the post office down in town.
Q Give me now the name of your child? A Nettie May, 17 years old.
Q Living now, is she? A Yes, sir.
Q You are now on the roll of 1880? A I don't think we are, we ought to be, I don't know what reason we were not, my husband I thought enrolled us; he came down here for that purpose.
(On 1896 roll, page 553, No. 3430, Catherine Wasson, Delaware district. Fleming H. Wasson on 1896 roll, page 593, No. 584, Fleming H. Warsan[sic], Delaware district. Nettie May Wasson on 1896 roll, page 553, No. 3432, Nattie May Wassan[sic], Delaware district.)
Q If you were absent in 1880, where could you have been and for what purpose? A I guess that was when I would be out sending the children to school.
Q How long an absence did you make about that time? A We were in and out I guess for four or five years.
Q Where did you go? A About six miles from where we lived, moved into Chetopa.
Q Across the Kansas line? A Yes, sir, to send the children to school.
Q Did you keep your property back in the Territory? A Yes, sir.
Q You then just stayed there for the time being? A Yes, sir.
Q When did you move out of the Territory in order to school your children? A I guess it was in 1890, we came back here.

Cherokee Intermarried White 1906
Volume II

Q And you have been staying all the time in the Nation since 1890? A Yes, sir.
Q Did you derive your income from your property back in the Nation? A Yes, sir.
Q You never moved out to live at any time? A No, sir.
Q So that waht[sic] you lived on when you were outside was the income you derived from that property? A Yes, sir.
Q Your husband vote on the outside or do anything of that sort? A No, sir.
Q Did he engage regularly in business? A No, sir, he had a business in the Territory.
Q Who here now knew you all that time and knew that you lead that kind of live[sic]?
A Claud Shelton for one; he knows (indicating.)

    Randolph Ballard, being sworn and examined by Commissioner Breckenridge[sic], testified as follows:
Q Give you name, please? A Randolph Ballard.
Q Your age? A 46.
Q You are one of the witnesses here of the Cherokee Nation? A Yes sir.
Q How long have you lived in the Cherokee Nation? A All my life.
Q You know this lady here, Mrs. Wasson? A Yes, sir.
Q And her husband? A Yes, sir, I have seen him.
Q How long since you first knew them? A I expect it has been about twenty years, I reckon.
Q Did you ever hear that they had taken the children over across the Kansas line at any time? A No, sir, I didn't. I just heard them talking about them moving across over to Chetopa.
Q Does that mean across the Kansas line? A Yes, sir.
Q Did they keep their property, sell out here, and go there like they had abandoned the Territory? A No, sir, not that I know of.
Q Then later when the children has[sic] grown up did they all move back again?
A I don't know.
Q They are back here? A I see them now.
Q They kept property all the time, did they, in the Cherokee Nation? A Yes, sir, I guess they did, that is, a farm.
Q You just heard of their going over there, you didnt hear of their breaking up there[sic] possessions here and abandoning the country? A Yes, sir, I didn't hear of anything of that kind.

    Catherine Wasson, recalled, testified.
Mr. J.L. Baugh, representative of the Cherokee Nation: Where were you married at?
A I was living in the nation and we went to Chetopa and got married.
Q Your husband a white man? A Yes, sir.
Q Married under the Cherokee law? A I wasn't for he is a citizen; Jeff McGee married us, he was a citizen and I was.
Q Was he a citizen prior to your marriage? A Yes, sir.
Q Was he married to another Cherokee lady? A Yes, sir.
Q Has he got his license for the former marriage? A He sent for it at Tahlequah, Indian Territory but he didn't get them when I left home.

Cherokee Intermarried White 1906
Volume II

Commissioner Breckenridge[sic]: You say you and your husband were married according to law? A Not this husband, he was married to a former wife according to Cherokee law.
Q You haven't the Cherokee license for his first marriage with you? A No, sir.
Q Do you think your husband got it? A Yes, sir.
Q Was your husband's former wife dead when you and he married? A Yes, sir.
Q Were you ever married before you married him? A Yes, sir.
Q Your former husband was dead, was he? A Yes, sir.
Q Did either you or your husband have children by your first marriages when you first went up to Kansas? A I did.
Q So that you went up with children of your own? A Yes, sir, my children.

The applicant applies for the enrollment of herself, her husband and one child, a minor. She states that she is a native of the Cherokee Nation and has lived in the Cherokee Nation all her life except when living a few miles across the Kansas line beginning some twenty years or such matter ago, and they were temporarily domiciled there in order to educate their children. They retained their property here and her husband continued to cross and look after his Cherokee property. She was married to her present husband in 1875, and they returned permanently to the Cherokee Nation about 1890 and have lived here without interruption since. It appears from her own and other testimony set forth in the record that she failed to be recorded in 1880 through no fault of her own, and the same is doubtless true of her husband. She is identified on the roll of 1896, and she will be listed now for enrollment as a Cherokee by blood. Her child, Nettie May, is identified with her on the roll of 1896, is living now, and this child will be listed for enrollment as a Cherokee by blood. The claim of her husband for enrollment is based upon the alleged previous marriage to a Cherokee woman, at which time he procured a license and certificate. His present marriage did not, of course, require that ceremony. He is identified on the roll of 1896, but to await the production of the original or an official copy of his Cherokee license and certificate of marriage, he will at present be placed upon a doubtful card.

----------0-----------

Bruce C. Jones, being duly sworn, says that as stenographer to the Commission to the Five Civilized Tribes he correctly recorded the proceedings and testimony in the above case, and the foregoing is a true and complete transcript of his stenographic notes thereof.

Bruce C Jones

Sworn to and subscribed before me this the 1st of October, 1900.

CR Breckinridge

Commissioner.

Cherokee Intermarried White 1906
Volume II

DEPARTMENT OF THE INTERIOR.
COMMISSION TO THE FIVE CIVILIZED TRIBES.

In the matter of the death of **Fleming H. Wasson,** a citizen of the **Cherokee** Nation, who formerly resided at or near **Welch**, Ind. Ter., and died on the **10th** day of **April**, **1905**.

AFFIDAVIT OF RELATIVE.

UNITED STATES OF AMERICA, Indian Territory,
Northern DISTRICT.

I, **Catherine Wasson,** , on oath state that I am **49** years of age and a citizen by **blood**, of the **Cherokee** Nation; that my postoffice address is **Welch**, Ind. Ter.; that I am **the wife** of **Fleming H. Wasson** who was a citizen, by **Adoption**, of the **Cherokee** Nation and that said **Fleming H. Wasson** died on the **10th** day of **April**, **1905**.

Catherine Wasson

Witnesses To Mark:

Subscribed and sworn to before me this **16th** day of **June**, **1905**

JO Rosson

Notary Public.

AFFIDAVIT OF ACQUAINTANCE.

UNITED STATES OF AMERICA, Indian Territory,
.... DISTRICT.

I,.., on oath state that I am .... years of age, and a citizen by .... of the .... Nation; that my postoffice address is ...., Ind. Ter.; that I was personally acquainted with .... who was a citizen, by ...., of the ....Nation; and that said.. died on the ....day of ...., 1...................

Witnesses To Mark:

Cherokee Intermarried White 1906
Volume II

Subscribed and sworn to before me this .... day of ...., 190....

Notary Public.

<><><><><>

Cherokee No. 9999.

DEPARTMENT OF THE INTERIOR,
COMMISSIONER TO THE FIVE CIVILIZED TRIBES.

Muskogee, Indian Territory. January 2, 1907.

In the matter of the application for the enrollment of Fleming H. Wasson as a citizen by intermarriage of the Cherokee Nation.

Katherine[sic] Wasson being first duly sworn by W. W. Chappell, a Notary Public, testifies as follows:

BY THE COMMISSIONER:

Q State your name, age and postoffice address? [sic] Katherine Wasson; 52; Muskogee.
Q What is your citizenship? [sic] Cherokee by blood.
Q Are you married? A No, sir not now.
Q You have been married have you? A Yes, sir.
Q What was the name of your husband? A Fleming H. Wasson.
Q Is he living at this time? A No, sir.
Q When did he die? A He died two years ago in April.
Q Died in April 1905? A Yes, sir.
Q What was the citizenship of your husband? A Claimed to be a citizen by intermarriage of the Cherokee Nation.
Q When were you married? A We was married in '74.
Q Where were you married? A We was married in Chetopa, Kansas.
Q Were you married under a Cherokee license? A He was a citizen by intermarriage when I married him.
Q He was a citizen by his first marriage? A His first wife was a Cherokee by blood.
Q Was his first wife dead at the time you and he married?
A Yes sir.
Q Were you ever married prior to that time? A Yes, sir.
Q Was your husband dead at the time of your marriage to Fleming H. Wasson?
A Yes, sir.
Q You claim to be a citizen by blood of the Cherokee Nation do you not.[sic]
A Yes , sir.

Cherokee Intermarried White 1906
Volume II

Q   At the time of your marriage to Fleming H. Wasson he claimed to be a citizen by intermarriage of the Cherokee Nation? A Yes, sir.

The witness Katherine Wasson, is identified on Cherokee Straight Card No. 3704 as a citizen by blood of the Cherokee Nation, and is on the approved roll of citizens by blood of the Cherokee Nation opposite No. 27622.

Q   Was your husband married to his first wife in accordance with the Cherokee law? A Yes, sir.
Q   Married under a Cheeokee[sic] license? A Yes, sir.
Q   Have you a copy of that license? A No, sir, it got burned when our house burned.
Q   Do you know where he was married to his first wife? A Yes, sir he stopped at my house on his way to get married
Q   In what district was that? A Delaware district, Cherokee Nation; down on Honey Creek.
Q   Do you know who issued the license under which he was married? A Jeff McGhee and Jim Harland-- one was the clerk and the other a Judge, I don't know which one it was.
Q   That was sometime during the year 1870.[sic] A Yes, sir.
Q   Now then you were married to Fleming H. Wasson in 1874? A Yes, sir.
Q   At Chetopa, Kansas? A Yes, sir.
Q   Under what authority were you married? A We were married by the magistrate.
Q   Were you married under a license issued by the State? A It was just put on record we didn't get any license; we were both citizens of the Territory you know, and we didn't get any license there, but we put them on record at the Court house in Oswego.
Q   Where were you living at the time of your marriage? A In the Territory, up here on Russell Creek, about six miles this side of Chetopa.
Q   You were both living in the Cherokee Nation at the time of your marriage? A Yes, sir.
Q   Did you continue to live there up until his death in 1905? A We went up to Chetopa to send our children to school part of the time, but we had a farm in the Territory.
Q   You owned property in the Cherokee Nation ever since you were married? A Yes, sir.
Q   And were never absent except during the time you were sending your children to school in Chetopa, Kansas? A No, sir.
Q   Do you know who performed the marriage ceremony between your late husband and his first wife? A Jeff McGhee or Jim Harland I don't know which. One was a clerk and the other a Judge.
Q   Were you acquainted with your husband's first wife? A Yes, sir slightly. She was a cousin to my first husband.
Q   What was her name at the time of her marriage? A Mary Bly.
Q   She was a Cherokee by blood was she? A Yes, sir.
Q   When did she die? A She died along about '72.
Q   When were you married the first time? A In the winter of '69.

Cherokee Intermarried White 1906
Volume II

Q   Was your first husband a citizen of the Cherokee Nation?
A   Yes, sir a Cherokee by blood.
Q   When did he die? A He died in '73.
Q   You never married Mr. Wasson under a Cherokee license? A No, sir.
Q   He simply claims by virtue of his marriage to his first wife.[sic]
A   Yes, sir to his first wife.
Q   You say that your deceased husband claims his rights to citizenship in the Cherokee Nation by virtue of his marriage to one Mary Bly under a license issued by the Cherokee Nation, Delaware district, in 1870.[sic] A Yes, sir.
Q   What was the name of your husband's first wife at the time he was married to her.[sic] A She has been married before. Her maiden name was Mary Bly, but her name was Mary Van Armon when he married her.

Book "S" of the original marriage records, Delaware District, Cherokee Nation, now in the possession of this office shows that on June 23, 1873 a Cherokee marriage license was issued to Fleming H. Wasson, a citizen of the United States to Marry Mary Van Normian, a citizen of the Cherokee Nation, and that said license was "executed and returned June 23, 1873" and that said marriage was in "accordance to the Act passed by the National Council regulating intermarriages of the United States with citizens of this nation."

WITNESS EXCUSED.

F. Elma Lane upon oath states that she reported the proceedings in the above entitled cause and that the forgoeing[sic] is a true and correct transcript of her stenographic notes therein.

F. Elma Lane

Subscribed and sowrn[sic] to before me this 2nd day of January 1907.

Walter W. Chappell
Notary Public.

◇◇◇◇◇

Cherokee D 465

EXECUTIVE OFFICE CHEROKEE NATION,
Tahlequah, I. T.

I, B. W. Alberty, assistant Executive secretary of the Cherokee Nation do hereby certify that the Marriage record of Delaware District Cherokee Nation shows, that a marriage license was issued to F. H. Wasson to marry Mary Varnerman, June 25th 1873 and that they were married on the same day; that said marriage record has been filed in this office by law and is in my custody.

Cherokee Intermarried White 1906
Volume II

Given under my hand and the seal of the Cherokee Nation this the 31st day of October 1900.

(S E A L)

B. W. Alberty
Assistant Executive Secretary
Cherokee Nation.

I, the undersigned, as stenographer to the Commission to the Five Civilized Tribes do certify that the above is a full and correct copy of the certificate - - on file in this office.

Ella Mielenz

◇◇◇◇◇

C.E.W.

Cherokee 9999

DEPARTMENT OF THE INTERIOR,

COMMISSIONER TO THE FIVE CIVILIZED TRIBES.

In the matter of the application for the enrollment of Fleming H. Wasson, as a citizen by intermarriage of the Cherokee Nation.

D E C I S I O N

THE RECORDS OF THIS OFFICE SHOW: That at Vinita, Indian Territory, September 28, 1900, Catherine Wasson appeared before the Commission to the Five Civilized Tribes and made application for her husband, Fleming H. Wasson, as a citizen by intermarriage, and for the enrollment of herself, et al., as citizens by blood of the Cherokee Nation. The application for the enrollment of the said Catherine Wasson, et al., as citizens by blood of the Cherokee Nation has been heretofore disposed of and their rights to enrollment will not be considered in this decision. Further proceedings in the matter of said application were had at Muskogee, Indian Territory, February 25, 1902, October 2, 1902, and January 2, 1907.

THE EVIDENCE IN THIS CASE SHOWS: That the applicant herein, Fleming H. Wasson, a white man, was married in accordance with Cherokee law June 25, 1873 to his wife, Mary Wasson, nee Vannorman, since deceased, who was at the time of said marriage a recognized citizen by blood of the Cherokee Nation. Said Fleming H. Wasson and Mary Wasson resided together as husband and wife and continuously lived in the Cherokee Nation until the death of Mary Wasson in the year 1874; that the said Fleming H. Wasson subsequent to her death, was married to his present wife, Catherine Wasson, nee England, who was at the time of said marriage a recognized citizen by blood of the Cherokee Nation, and whose name appears upon the approved partial roll of citizens by blood of the Cherokee Nation, opposite number 27622. The evidence further shows that the name of said Fleming H. Wasson and his wife, Catherine Wasson cannot be found

Cherokee Intermarried White 1906
Volume II

upon the Cherokee Authenticated tribal roll of 1880, for the reason that at the time said roll was made and at various other times for short periods the said Fleming H. Wasson was in the State of Kansas educating his children, but retained his property in the Cherokee Nation, and derived his income from his business in the Indian Territory. The said Fleming H. Wasson and his wife, Catherine Wasson are identified on the Cherokee Census roll of 1896.

IT IS, THEREFORE, ORDERED AND ADJUDGED: That in accordance with the decision of the Supreme Court of the United States, dated November 5, 1906, in the case of Daniel Red Bird et al., vs. the United States under the provision of Section 21 of the Act of Congress approved June 28, 1898, (30 Stat., 495), Fleming H. Wasson is entitled to enrollment as a citizen by intermarriage of the Cherokee Nation, and his application for enrollment as such is accordingly granted.

Tams Bixby
Commissioner.

Dated at Muskogee, Indian Territory,
this   JAN 16 1907

◇◇◇◇◇

COMMISSIONERS:
HENRY L. DAWES,
TAMS BIXBY,
THOMAS B. NEEDLES,
C. R. BRECKINRIDGE.

DEPARTMENT OF THE INTERIOR,
COMMISSION TO THE FIVE CIVILIZED TRIBES.

ALLISON L. AYLESWORTH,
SECRETARY.

ADDRESS ONLY THE
COMMISSION TO THE FIVE CIVILIZED TRIBES.

Muskogee, Indian Territory,   **February 11,**   1902

Mrs. Catherine Wasson,
    Wasson, Indian Territory,

Madam:-

You are hereby notified that the application of   **Fleming H. Wasson**

for enrollment as ....citizen..... of the Cherokee Nation will be taken up for final consideration by the Commission to the Five Civilized Tribes, at its office in Muskogee, Indian Territory, on the   **27th**   day of   **February**   , 1902.

On said date, you may, if you desire, appear before the Commission, in person or by attorney, when an opportunity will be given you to introduce any additional testimony affecting your application.

You are further notified that the Representatives of the Cherokee Nation will also, at the same time, be afforded an opportunity to introduce testimony tending to disprove your

Cherokee Intermarried White 1906
Volume II

right to enrollment, but said Representatives will be required to notify you of their intention to introduce such testimony before they will be permitted to do so.

You are required to supply the Commission with certified copy of marriage license issued to Fleming H. Wasson and his first wife Mary Varnorman.

Yours truly,

Cherokee D-465
Register.

Acting Chairman.

◇◇◇◇◇

COPY

Cherokee D-465.

Muskogee, Indian Territory, December 15, 1902.

W. W. Hastings,
      Attorney for the Cherokee Nation,
            Muskogee, Indian Territory.

Dear Sir:

There is herewith inclosed a copy of the decision of the Commission to the Five Civilized Tribes, dated December 10, 1902, granting the application of Catherine Wasson for the enrollment of her husband, Fleming H. Wasson, as a citizen by intermarriage of the Cherokee Nation.

You are advised that you will be allowed fifteen days from date hereof in which to file such protest as you desire to make against the action of the Commission in this case, a copy of which protest you will be required to serve upon the applicant. If you fail to file protest within the time allowed this decision will be considered final.

Respectfully,
Tams Bixby.
Acting Chairman.

Enc. H-218.

◇◇◇◇◇

Cherokee Intermarried White 1906
Volume II

Cherokee D-465

Muskogee, Indian Territory, January 15, 1903.

Catherine Wasson,
    Welch, Indian Territory.

Dear Madam:-

There is herewith enclosed a copy of the decision of the Commission to the Five Civilized Tribes, dated December 15, 1902, granting your application for the enrollment of your husband, Fleming H. Wasson, as a citizen by intermarriage of the Cherokee Nation.

Respectfully,

Acting Chairman.

Enc. M-465

Register.

◇◇◇◇◇

Cherokee
3704

Muskogee, Indian Territory, December 21, 1906.

Catherine Wasson,
    Welch, Indian Territory.

Dear Madam:

November 6, 1906, the United States Supreme Court held that white persons who intermarried with Cherokee citizens according to Cherokee law prior to November 1, 1875, are entitled to enrollment and allotments of land as citizens of the Cherokee Nation.

You are advised that to properly determine the right to enrollment as a citizen by intermarriage of the Cherokee Nation, of your husband, Fleming H. Wasson, deceased, it will be necessary for you to appear before the Commissioner for the purpose of giving testimony as to the date of his marriage and whether or not his wife, by reason of his marriage to whom he claims the right to enrollment as a citizen of the Cherokee Nation, was a recognized citizen of the Cherokee Nation at the time of his marriage to her, and whether or not he was married to her in accordance with Cherokee laws.

Cherokee Intermarried White 1906
Volume II

You are, therefore, directed to appear before the Commissioner at Muskogee, Indian Territory, at 9 o'clock A. M., on Wednesday, January 2, 1907, and give testimony as above indicated.

Respectfully,

J.M.H.   Acting Commissioner.

◇◇◇◇◇

Cherokee 9999

Muskogee, Indian Territory, January 17, 1907.

W. W. Hastings,
    Attorney for the Cherokee Nation,
        Muskogee, Indian Territory.

Dear Sir:

There is enclosed herewith copy of the decision of the Commissioner to the Five Civilized Tribes, dated January 16, 1907, granting the application for the enrollment of Fleming H. Wasson as a citizen by intermarriage of the Cherokee Nation.

Respectfully,

Enc. I-12   Commissioner.
RPI

◇◇◇◇◇

Cherokee 9999.   W.W. HASTINGS, ATTORNEY.   OFFICE OF   H.M. VANCE, SECRETARY.

Attorney for the Cherokee Nation,
MUSKOGEE, I. T.

January 18, 1907.

The Commissioner to the Five Civilized Tribes,
    Muskogee, Indian Territory.

Sir:

Receipt is acknowledged of the testimony and of your decision enrolling Fleming H. Wasson as a citizen by intermarriage of the Cherokee Nation. Time for protesting said decision is waived and I consent that said person may be placed upon the schedule immediately.

Yours very truly,
W. W. Hastings
Attorney for Cherokee Nation.

Cherokee Intermarried White 1906
Volume II

◇◇◇◇◇

Cherokee
9999

Muskogee, Indian Territory, January 23, 1907.

Catherine Wasson,
    Welch, Indian Territory.

Dear Madam:

    There is enclosed herewith a copy of the decision of the Commissioner to the Five Civilized Tribes, dated January 16, 1907, granting the application for enrollment of your husband, Fleming H. Wasson, as a citizen by intermarriage of the Cherokee Nation.

    You will be advised when the name of your husband has been placed upon a schedule of citizens of the Cherokee Nation and approved by the Secretary of the Interior.

                  Respectfully,

Encl. H-78   Commissioner.
JMH

Cher IW 55
Trans from Cher 10057 3-13-07

◇◇◇◇◇

                                                  E.C.M.

DEPARTMENT OF THE INTERIOR,

COMMISSIONER TO THE FIVE CIVILIZED TRIBES.

In the matter of the application for the enrollment of

MARY L. MORGAN

as a citizen by intermarriage of the Cherokee Nation.

CHEROKEE 10057.

Cherokee Intermarried White 1906
Volume II

DEPARTMENT OF THE INTERIOR.

COMMISSION TO THE FIVE CIVILIZED TRIBES.

Pryor Creek, I.T. September 13, 1900.

In the matter of the application of Gideon Morgan, for himself, his wife and children, for enrollment as Cherokee citizens. The said Gideon Morgan, being first duly worn by Commissioner C. R. Breckinridge, testified as follows:

Q What is your full name? [sic] Gideon Morgan.
Q How old are you? A Forty-nine.
Q What is your post office? A Gideon.
Q What is your district? A Tahlequah.
Q Who is it you wish to have put upon the roll?
A My wife and seven children and myself.
Q Your seven children are under twenty-one are they? A No, sir.
Q Well, give me those under twenty one and unmarried.
A Well, there are five under the age of twenty-one and unmarried.
Q Well, you can apply for the five; the others will have to apply for themselves. So you apply for your wife and yourself and five children? A Yes, sir.
Q Do you apply for yourself as a Cherokee by blood? A Yes, sir.
Q Do you apply for your wife as a Cherokee by blood? A Yes, sir.
Q How long have you lived in the Cherokee Nation? A Since 1871. About twenty nine years.
Q Where were you in 1880? A Sequoiah[sic] District.
Q Where were you in 1896? A Tahlequah District.
Q Give me the name of your father, please. A George W. Morgan.
Q White man or Cherokee? A Cherokee.
Q Is he dead or alive? A He is dead.
Q Give me the name of your mother, please. A Martha K. Morgan
Q Cherokee or white woman? A White.
Q Is she dead or alive? A Dead.
Q How long dead? A Nine years.
Q Give me the name of your wife please. A Mary L
Q How old is she? A She is forty-four.
Q What was her name when you married her? A Payne.
Q Was that her maiden name? A Yes, sir.
Q When were you married to her? A In 1874.
Q She is on the roll of 1880 and 1896? A Yes, sir.
Q She has lived with you in the Cherokee Nation ever since your marriage? A Yes, sir. I lived in Fort Smith about two years.
Q You were living there. What time was that.[sic] [sic] About 1880.
Q You were just living there for a short time? A Yes, sir.

Cherokee Intermarried White 1906
Volume II

Q Give me the name of your wife's father. A Samuel H. Payne.
Q Cherokee or white man? A White man.
Q Is he dead or alive? A Dead.
Q How long dead.[sic] A He died in 1877.
Q Your wife's mother, give me her name. A Martha A. Payne.
Q Cherokee or white woman? A A[sic] Well, a Cherokee.
Q Is she dead or alive? A Alive.
Q Now give us the names of your children. A Martha L. She is twenty years old.
Q The next. A Margaret E. A.
Q How old is she? A Seventeen.
Q The next? A Amanda P.
Q How old is she? A Fourteen years old.
Q The next child? A Sallie M.
Q How old is she? A Twelve years old.
Q The next child? A Ellen P. M.
Q How old? A Four years old.
Q Is the youngest child there on the roll of 1896? A Yes, sir.
Q These children are all living with you now are they? A Yes sir.

(On roll 1880, page 709, No. 853, Gideon Morgan, Sequoiah District. On roll 1880, page 709, No. 854, Mary Llewellyn Morgan. Native. On 1880 Roll, page 709, No. 857, Lelia Morgan, Sequoiah District.)

(On Roll 1896, page 1211, No. 2203, Gideon Morgan, Tahlequah. District. On Roll 1896, page 1211, No. 2204, Mary L. Morgan, Tahlequah District. On roll 1896, page 1211, No. 2207, Martha L. Morgan, Tahlequah District. On roll 1896, page 1211, No. 2208, Margarette E. A. Morgan, Tahlequah District. On roll 1896, page 1211, No. 2209, Amanda P. Morgan, Tahlequah District. On 1896 Roll, page 1211, No. 2210, Sallie M. Morgan, Tahlequah District. On Roll 1896, page 1211, No. 2211, Ellen P. M. Morgan, Tahlequah District.)

Q Mr. Morgan, did your wife in 1896 make application to the Dawes Commission for admission? A Her mother did.
Q What was the outcome of that? A The verdict of the Dawes Commission was that they were citizens, and the Nation took an appeal, and is showed my wife at Muskogee was not appealed with the balance, and the decision of the Court was that they were not citizens. It was reversed, but I have been told since she was not in the appeal.

The applicant applies for the enrollment of himself, his wife and five children. The applicant is identified on the rolls of 1880 and 1896, as a native Cherokee. He is living in the Cherokee nation[sic] and has lived there ever since his enrollment in 1880, and he will be enlisted now for enrollment as a Cherokee by blood.

His wife is identified on the rolls of 1880 and 1896 as a native Cherokee. She has lived with her husband in the Cherokee nation[sic] ever since her enrollment in 1880, but it appears from the records of the Dawes Commission, Docket B, page 400, Dawes case 5324, that by some means indicated by the present line of testimony the applicant's wife

Cherokee Intermarried White 1906
Volume II

was a party to an application for admission to Cherokee citizenship, in the application filed September 5th, 1896. That application was granted by the Dawes Commission. The case was appealed to the Federal Court, and the judgment of the Commission reversed. As far as the record discloses it appears that the applicant's wife was included in the action of the Federal Court, for the copy of the decision of the court refers to the petitions in block, and contains a statement that "it does not ppear[sic] that any of the claimants, or any of their ancestors have ever been enrolled as citizens of the Cherokee Nation," which is manifestly an error as the present examination of the original records show that the applicant's wife was enrolled in 1880 and 1896. For the further consideration of this case, however, the application for the enrollment of Mary L. Morgan, will be placed upon a doubtful card and the final decision will be communicated to the applicant at his post office address.

As to the five children here applied for, Martha L. Morgan is identified on the rolls of 1880, and 1896. The four remaining children Margaret A. E. Morgan, Amanda P., Sallie M. and Ellen P. M., are identified with their parents on the roll of 1896. They are all minors and they are all living with their parents at this time in the Cherokee Nation, and they will now be enlisted for enrollment as Cherokee's by blood.

The undersigned, being duly sworn, states that as stenographer to the Commission to the Five Civilized Tribes, he correctly recorded the testimony and other proceedings in the above cause, and that the foregoing is a correct and complete transcript of his stenographic notes thereof.

Wm S. Wellshear

Subscribed and sworn to before me this 18th day of September A. D. 1900.

C R Breckinridge
Commissioner.

◇◇◇◇◇

Cherokee D-280.

DEPARTMENT OF THE INTERIOR,

COMMISSION TO THE FIVE CIVILIZED TRIBES.

In the matter of the application for the enrollment of Mary L. Morgan as a citizen of the Cherokee Nation.

D E C I S I O N.

The record in this case shows that on September 13, 1900, Gideon Morgan appeared before the Commission at Pryor Creek, Indian Territory, and made application for the enrollment, among others, of his wife, Mary L. Morgan as a citizen by blood of the Cherokee Nation. Further proceedings were had in the matter of said application at

Cherokee Intermarried White 1906
Volume II

Muskogee, Indian Territory, on October 4, 1902. The other parties to the application are differently classified, and are not embraced in this decision.

The evidence shows that Mary L. Morgan is the daughter of Martha A. Payne, and it appears from an examination of the records of the Commission to the Five Civilized Tribes that the said Martha A. Payne filed an application, under the provisions of the Act of June 10, 1896 (29 Stats., 321), for the admission of the said Mary L. Morgan, among others, to citizenship in the Cherokee Nation, by reason of her Cherokee by blood. On November 23, 1896, the Commission admitted said Mary L. Morgan to citizenship, and that on appeal to the United States Court in the Indian Territory for the Northern District, said Court reversed the decision of the Commission and denied the application of all the parties including the said Mary L. Morgan.

It further appears from the evidence that the said Mary L. Morgan was married in 1874 to Gideon Morgan, a citizen by blood of the Cherokee Nation, who is duly identified on the authenticated tribal roll of 1880. Mary L. Morgan is identified on the authenticated tribal roll of 1880, and on the Cherokee Census roll of 1896.

The evidence further shows that the said Mary L. Morgan has resided with her husband in the Cherokee Nation continuously since the date of her marriage to him up to and including September 1, 1902.

It is the opinion of this Commission that the said Mary L. Morgan acquired rights as an intermarried Cherokee by her marriage to said Gideon Morgan, and that her right to enrollment as such is not prejudiced by the denial of her application for admission as a citizen by blood under the provisions of the said Act of June 10, 1896, and that the said Mary L. Morgan should therefore be enrolled as a citizen by intermarriage of the Cherokee Nation, in accordance with the provisions of Section twenty-one of the Act of Congress approved June 28, 1898, (30 Stat., 495), and it is so ordered.

       Tams Bixby
           Acting Chairman.

       TB Needles
           Commissioner.

       C. R. Breckinridge
           Commissioner.

Dated at Muskogee, Indian Territory,
this   DEC 10 1902

Cherokee Intermarried White 1906
Volume II

R.

DEPARTMENT OF THE INTERIOR.
Commission to the Five Civilized Tribes.
Muskogee, Indian Territory, October 4th, 1902.

In the matter of the application of Mary L. Morgan for the enrollment of herself as a citizen by intermarriage of the Cherokee Nation.

Supplemental to D-280.

Appearances:
Gideon Morgan for Applicant.
J. C. Starr for Cherokee Nation.

GIDEON MORGAN, being duly sworn, testified as follows:--
Examination by the Commission.

Q. What is your name? A. Gideon Morgan.
Q. What is your age? A. 51.
Q. What is your post office? A. Tahlequah.
Q. What is your wife's name? A. Mary L.
Q. What is your wife's age at this time? A. She was 47 the first of this month. Born in '55. I believe that would make her 47.
Q. Does your wife claim as an intermarried citizen or a citizen by blood? A. Well, she is an intermarried citizen according to that decision.
Q. Your wife applied to the Commission as a citizen by blood under the act of June 10th? A. Her mother put her down.
Q. She was denied as a citizen by blood by the Dawes Commission under the act of June 10th, 1896? A. I think so.
Q. She now applies as a citizen by adoption by virtue of her marriage to you? A. Yes, sir; adoption. That is the only way she could do it.
Q. When were you and your wife Marl[sic] L. married? A. June 25th, '74.
Q. Were you ever married prior to your marriage to this wife? A. No, sir.
Q. Was she ever married prior to her marriage to you? A. Yes, sir
Q. Have you and Mary L. lived together continuously since you were married?
A. Yes, sir.
Q. Never have been separated? A. No, sir.
Q. Living together on the first of September, 1902? A. Yes, sir.
Q. She has never been married to any other man except you? A. No, sir.
Q. How long has your wife lived in the Cherokee Nation? A. I think ever since '68. I am not certain about that.

Cherokee Intermarried White 1906
Volume II

Q. Has she lived in the Cherokee Nation since 1880? A. I believe we were in Fort Smith about a year; then moved to Tahlequah.

Q. In what year were you in Fort Smith? A. I think in '82 or 3.

Q. Since 1882 or 3 you and your wife have lived in the Cherokee Nation all the time? A. All the time. The date we were at Fort Smith, Arkansas it may be '83 or 4.

Q. Do you know whether you filed a marriage certificate showing when you and your wife were married? A. Never got any. Didn't need any. Didn't file any; swore to it myself. You know at that time we had no marriage laws.

Jesse O. Carr, being first duly sworn, states that as stenographer to the Commission to the Five Civilized Tribes he reported the above entitled case and that the foregoing is a true and complete transcript of his stenographic notes thereof.

Jesse O. Carr

Subscribed and sworn to before me this 27th day of October, 1902.

BC Jones
Notary Public.

◇◇◇◇◇

Cherokee D-280/[sic]

DEPARTMENT OF THE INTERIOR,

COMMISSION TO THE FIVE CIVILIZED TRIBES,

MUSKOGEE, I. T., NOVEMBER 4, 1902.

In the matter of the application for the enrollment of Mary L. Morgan as a citizen of the Cherokee Nation.

SUPPLEMENTAL STATEMENT.

From an examination had in the matter of the above application, it is found in Record B, Citizenship Cases, page 400, #5324, that the applicant, Mary L. Morgan, among others, filed her original application for admission as a citizen by blood of the Cherokee Nation on September 5, 1896, which application was granted by the Commission to the Five Civilized Tribes, and was later appealed to the United States Court for the Northern District, Indian Territory, and wherein the judgment of the Commission was reversed as shown by Court #246.

It is ordered that copies of this statement be filed with this case, and made a part of the record herein.

C. R. Breckinridge
Commissioner.

Cherokee Intermarried White 1906
Volume II

CHEROKEE-10057.

DEPARTMENT OF THE INTERIOR,
COMMISSIONER TO THE FIVE CIVILIZED TRIBES.
Muskogee, Indian Territory, January 5, 1907.

In the matter of making proof of the marriage of Mary L. Morgan to her Cherokee husband, prior to November 1, 1875.

Mary L. Morgan, being sworn by J. E. Tidwell, a Notary Public, testified as follows:

COMMISSIONER:

Q. What is your name? A. Mary L. Morgan.
Q. What is your age? A. 51.
Q. What is your post office address? A. Pryor Creek.
Q. Do you claim rights as a citizen by intermarriage of the Cherokee Nation the Cherokee Nation? A. Yes sir.
Q. Through whom do you claim such rights? A. Gideon Morgan.
Q. When were you married? A. June 25, 1874.
Q. Where were you married? A. Near Fort Smith in the Cherokee Nation -- in Sequoyah District.
Q. Who married you? A. E. W. King, a Methodist minister.
Q. Did he give you a certificate? A. No sir.
Q. Were you ever married before you married Gideon Morgan? A. No sir.
Q. Was Gideon Morgan ever married before he married you? A. No sir.
Q. Have you lived together continuously since 1874 up to the present time? A. Yes sir.

(Commissioner -- The applicant is identified upon the 1880 Roll, Sequoyah District, opposite No. 854. Her husband, through whom she claims her right to enrollment, is identified upon said roll, said District, opposite No. 853. He is also identified upon the final roll of citizens by blood of the Cherokee Nation, opposite No. 6761.)

Witness excused.

Connell Rogers, being sworn by J. E. Tidwell, a Notary Public, testified as follows:

Cherokee Intermarried White 1906
Volume II

<u>COMMISSIONER:</u>

Q. What is your name? A. Connell Rogers.
Q. How old are you? A. 56.
Q. What is your post office address? A. Fort Gibson.
Q. Are you a citizen by blood of the Cherokee Nation? A. Yes sir.
Q. Are you acquainted with Gideon Morgan? A. Yes sir.
Q. Do you know Mary L. Morgan? A. Yes sir.
Q. Do you know when they were married? A. Yes sir.
Q. When? A. In 1874.
Q. Were you present at the marriage? A. Yes sir.
Q. Have they lived together continuously as husband and wife since their marriage in 1874? A. Yes sir.

Witness excused.

Gunter M. Turner, being sworn by J. E. Tidwell, a Notary Public, testified as follows:

<u>COMMISSIONER:</u>

Q. What is your name? A. Gunter M. Turner.
Q. What is your age? A. 37.
Q. What is your post office address? A. Muskogee.
Q. Are you acquainted with Gideon Morgan? A. Yes sir.
Q. Do you know Mary L. Morgan? A. Yes sir.
Q. Do you know when they were married? A. No -- they were married, but I don't know the year.
Q. Were you present? A. Yes sir.
Q. What relation are you to Gideon Morgan? A. A sister-in-law.

Witness excused.

Eula Jeanes Branson, being sworn, states that she correctly reported the proceedings had in the above and foregoing, on the 5th. day of January, 1907.

Eula Jeanes Branson

Subscribed and sworn to before me this the 9th. day of January, 1907

Notary Public.

Cherokee Intermarried White 1906
Volume II

C.F.B.   Cherokee 10057.

DEPARTMENT OF THE INTERIOR,

COMMISSIONER TO THE FIVE CIVILIZED TRIBES.

In the matter of the application for the enrollment of MARY L. MORGAN as a citizen by intermarriage of the Cherokee Nation.

D E C I S I O N

THE RECORDS OF THIS OFFICE SHOW: That at Pryor Creek, Indian Territory, September 13, 1900, application was received by the Commission to the Five Civilized Tribes for the enrollment of Mary L. Morgan as a citizen of the Cherokee Nation. Further proceedings in the matter of said application were had at Muskogee, November 4, 1902, and January 5, 1907. The records further show that the applicant herein, Mary L. Morgan, is the daughter of Martha A. Payne, who filed an application, under the provisions of the Act of Congress approved June 10, 1896 (29 Stats., 321), for the admission of the said Mary L. Morgan, among others, to citizenship in the Cherokee Nation by reason of Cherokee blood; that on November 23, 1896, said Commission admitted said Mary L. Morgan to citizenship; and that appeal was taken to the United States Court for the Northern District of Indian Territory, where said decision was reversed, and said Mary L. Morgan denied the right of admission as a citizen by blood of the Cherokee Nation.

THE EVIDENCE IN THIS CASE SHOWS: That the applicant herein, Mary L. Morgan, married on June 25, 1874, one Gideon Morgan, who was at the time of said marriage a recognized citizen by blood of the Cherokee Nation, who is identified on the Cherokee authenticated tribal roll of 1880, Sequoyah District, N. 853, as a native Cherokee and whose name appears on the approved partial roll of citizens by blood of the Cherokee Nation, opposite No 6761. It is further shown that since said marriage said Gideon and Mary L. Morgan have resided together as husband and wife, and continuously lived in the Cherokee Nation up to and including September 1, 1902. Said applicant is identified on the Cherokee authenticated tribal roll of 1880, and the Cherokee census roll of 1896, as an intermarried citizen of the Cherokee Nation.

IT IS, THEREFORE, ORDERED AND ADJUDGED: That in accordance with the decision of the Supreme Court of the United States, dated November 5, 1906, in the cases of Daniel Red Bird et al. vs. the United States, Nos. 125, 126, 127 and 128, the said applicant, Mary L. Morgan, is entitled, under the provisions of Section twenty-one, of the Act of Congress approved June 28, 1898 (30 Stats., 495), to enrollment as a citizen by intermarriage of the Cherokee Nation, and her application for enrollment as such is accordingly granted.

Cherokee Intermarried White 1906
Volume II

Tams Bixby
Commissioner.

Dated at Muskogee, Indian Territory,
this   JAN 19 1907

◇◇◇◇◇

Cherokee
10057.

Muskogee, Indian Territory, January 18, 1907.

W. W. Hastings,
    Attorney for the Cherokee Nation,
        Muskogee, Indian Territory.

Dear Sir:

    There is enclosed herewith a copy of the decision of the Commissioner to the Five Civilized Tribes, dated January 18, 1907, granting the application for the enrollment of Mary L. Morgan, as a citizen by intermarriage of the Cherokee Nation.

Respectfully,

Incl. C-12
LMC

Commissioner.

◇◇◇◇◇

Cherokee 10057.   W.W. HASTINGS, ATTORNEY.   OFFICE OF   H.M. VANCE, SECRETARY.

Attorney for the Cherokee Nation,
MUSKOGEE, I. T.

January 18, 1907.

The Commissioner to the Five Civilized Tribes,
    Muskogee, Indian Territory.

Sir:

    Receipt is acknowledged of the testimony and of your decision enrolling Mary L. Morgan as a citizen by intermarriage of the Cherokee Nation. Time for protesting said decision is waived and I consent that said person may be placed upon the schedule immediately.

Respectfully,
W. W. Hastings
Attorney for Cherokee Nation.

◇◇◇◇◇

Cherokee Intermarried White 1906
Volume II

Cherokee
10057

Muskogee, Indian Territory, January 21, 1907.

Mary L. Morgan,
    Tahlequah, Indian Territory.

Dear Madam:

    There is enclosed herewith a copy of the decision of the Commissioner to the Five Civilized Tribes, dated January 19, 1907, granting the application for your enrollment as a citizen by intermarriage of the Cherokee Nation.

    You will be advised when your name has been placed upon a schedule of citizens of the Cherokee Nation and approved by the Secretary of the Interior.

                              Respectfully,

E.R.C.   Commissioner.
Enc. E.C. 6

◇◇◇◇◇

Cherokee
10057.

Muskogee, Indian Territory, December 27, 1906.

Mary L. Morgan,
    Tahlequah, Indian Territory.

Dear Madam:

    November 6, 1906, the United States Supreme Court held that white persons who intermarried with Cherokee citizens according to Cherokee law prior to November 1, 1875, are entitled to enrollment and allotments of land as citizens of the Cherokee Nation.

    You are advised that to properly determine your right to enrollment as a citizen by intermarriage of the Cherokee Nation, it will be necessary for you to appear before the Commissioner for the purpose of giving testimony as to the date of your marriage and whether or not your husband, by reason of your marriage to whom you claim the right to enrollment as a citizen by intermarriage of the Cherokee Nation, was a recognized Cherokee citizen at the time of your marriage to him.

Cherokee Intermarried White 1906
Volume II

You are therefore directed to appear before the Commissioner at Muskogee, Indian Territory, at 9 o'clock A. M., on Saturday, January 5, 1907, and give testimony as above indicated.

Respectfully,

GHL Acting Commissioner.

Cher IW 56
Trans from Cher 192 3-15-07

◇◇◇◇◇

E.C.M.

DEPARTMENT OF THE INTERIOR,

COMMISSIONER TO THE FIVE CIVILIZED TRIBES.

In the matter of the application for the enrollment of

FRANCIS M. CONNER

as a citizen by intermarriage of the Cherokee Nation.

CHEROKEE 192.

◇◇◇◇◇

Department of the Interior,
Commission to the Five Civilized Tribes,
Fairland, I.T., July 13, 1900.

In the matter lf[sic] the application of Francis M. Conner for the enrollment of himself by intermarriage, and his wife and children as Cherokees by blood; being duly sworn, and examined by Commissioner Breckenridge[sic], he testified as follows:

Q What is your name? A Francis M. Conner.
Q What is your age? A 48.
Q What is your post office address? A Fairland.
Q And your district? A Delaware district.
Q How long have you lived in this district? A About 30 years.
Q This has been your home continuously for the past 30 years? A Yes, sir.
Q Do you apply as a Cherokee by blood? A No, sir.

Cherokee Intermarried White 1906
Volume II

Q By intermarriage? A Yes, sir.
Q To whom were you married? A Rebecca J. Duncan.
Q When were you married? A In 1873.
Q Is her name on the roll of 1880 as Rebecca J. Conner? A Yes, sir.
(1880 roll, page 238, No. 589, Delaware district, Rebecca J. Conner; same roll, page 238, No. 598, Francis M. Conner, Delaware district.)
Q Is your wife still living? A Yes, sir.
(1896 roll, page 445, No. 454, Rebecca J. Conner. The name of Francis M. Conner on adopted white roll, page 567, No. 92, Delaware district, 1896.)
Q Do you apply for your children? A Yes, sir.
Q Give their names and ages please. A Two names on the 1880 roll, Lee Conner is dead.
Q Give me the names of your living children under 21 and unmarried?
A Crawford Conner, age 19.
(1896 roll, page 445, No. 456)
Q What is the name of your next one? A Lula May, age 15.
(On 1896 roll, page 445, No. 457.)
Q What is the next one? A Leonard Conner, 13 years old.
(On 1896 roll, page 445, No. 458.)
Q Those are all for whom you wish to make application? A Yes, sir; there is one of the 1896 roll that is dead.
Q Give the name of that child? A Maude Emmie.

   Mr. Conner, you and your wife being duly identified on the roll of 1880, she as a Cherokee by blood and you as a Cherokee by intermarriage, and your children, Crawford, Lula May and Leonard, being duly identified on the roll of 1896, you will all be enrolled upon the roll now being prepared, your wife and children as Cherokees by blood and you as a Cherokee by intermarriage.

------o------

   Bruce C. Jones, being duly sworn, says that as stenographer to the Commission to the Five Civilized Tribes he reported the testimony of the above named witness, and that the foregoing is a full, true and correct translation of his stenographic notes.

Bruce C Jones

Sworn to and subscribed before me this the 16th day of July, 1900.

Clifton R Breckinridge
Commissioner.

Cherokee Intermarried White 1906
Volume II

Cherokee 192.

Department of the Interior,
Commission to the Five Civilized Tribes,
Muskogee, I. T., September 22, 1902.

In the matter of the application of Francis M. Conner for the enrollment of himself as a citizen by intermarriage of the Cherokee Nation.

Cherokee Nation appears by W. W. Hastings.

Francis M. Conner, being sworn and examined by the Commission, testified as follows:

Q What is your name, age and postoffice address? A Francis M. Conner, postoffice Fairland, Indian Territory age fifty.
Q Are you the identical Francis M. Conner who applied to the Commission in July, 1900, for enrollment as a citizen by intermarriage? A Yes sir.
Q What is the name of the wife through whom you claim your right to enrollment?
A Rebecca J.
Q About when were you married to her? A '73.
Q Have you and she lived together continuously since that time as man and wife?
A Yes sir.
Q Are you living together at the present time? A We are.
Q Have you lived in the Cherokee Nation since that time? A Yes sir.
Q Are you living there at the present time? A Yes sir.

The undersigned, being duly sworn, states that as stenographer to the Commission to the Five Civilized Tribes he correctly recorded the testimony and proceedings in this case, and that the foregoing is a true and correct transcript of his stenographic notes thereof.

E.G. Rothenberger

Subscribed and sworn to before me this 24th day of September, 1902.

BC Jones
Notary Public.

Cherokee Intermarried White 1906
Volume II

C.F.B. Cherokee 192

DEPARTMENT OF THE INTERIOR,
COMMISSIONER TO THE FIVE CIVILIZED TRIBES.
MUSKOGEE, IND. TER. JANUARY 2, 1907

In the matter of the application for the enrollment of FRANCIS M. CONNER as a citizen by intermarriage of the Cherokee Nation.

-:-

APPEARANCES: Applicant appears in person:

Cherokee Nation represented by H. M. Vance, on behalf of W. W. Hastings, Attorney

FRANCIS M. CONNER being first duly sworn by B. P. Rasmus, a Notary Public: testified as follows:

ON BEHALF OF COMMISSIONER:

Q. What is your name? A. Francis M. Conner.
Q. What is your age? A. Fifty-four.
Q. What is your postoffice address? A. Fairland, I.T.
Q. You are an applicant for enrollment as a citizen by intermarriage of the Cherokee Nation? A. Yes sir.
Q. You possess no Cherokee blood? A. No sir.
Q. You claim your right to enrollment as a citizen of the Cherokee Nation by virtue of your marriage to a citizen by blood of the Cherokee Nation? A. Yes sir.
Q. What is the name of the person through whom you claim the right to enrollment as a citizen by intermarriage of the Cherokee Nation? A. Rebecca J. Duncan was her maiden name.
Q. When were you married to him?her[sic] A. December 24, 1873.
Q. Where were you married? A. In Delaware District, by the District Judge.
Q. Were you ever married prior to your marriage to her? A. No sir.
Q. Was she ever married prior to her marriage to you? A. No sir.
Q. Did you secure a license at the time of your marriage to her? A. Yes sir.
Q. From the Clerk of Delaware District, Cherokee Nation? A. Yes sir.
Q. Have you any documentary evidence to show your marriage? A. Yes sir; I have the marriage License and Certificate (Presents Marriage License and Certificate).

The applicant presents an original marriage license and certificate showing that on December 24, 1873, he was married in accordance with Cherokee law to Rebecca J. Duncan, Indian Territory a citizen of the Cherokee Nation. Said Marriage license and certificate is filed herewith and made a part of the record in this case.

Cherokee Intermarried White 1906
Volume II

Q. Since the marriage of yourself and wife, Rebecca J. Duncan, Indian Territory have you and she continuously lived together as husband and wife? A. Yes sir.

Q. And have lived continuously in the Cherokee Nation have you? A. Yes sir.

    The applicant, Francis M. Conner is identified on the Cherokee authenticated tribal roll of 1880 Delaware District, No. 588. His wife, Rebecca J. Conner is included in an approved partial roll of citizens by blood of the Cherokee Nation, opposite Number 621.

    The undersigned, being first duly sworn, states that as stenographer to the Commissioner to the Five Civilized Tribes she correctly recorded the testimony taken in this case, and that the above and foregoing is a full, true and correct transcript of her stenographic notes thereof.

                                                               Lucy M. Bowman

Subscribed and sworn to before me this 4th day of January, 1907

                                                      John E. Tidwell
                                                      Notary Public.

(The Marriage License and Certificate below typed as given.)

Cherokee Nation)   to any of the Judges of this Nation or to any Legal ordained
Del. District   )   Minister of the gospel having care of Souls in the Name of
                        the Cherokee Nation and By the power vested in me By law you are hereby authorized to Solemnize and Lawfuly Join together as man and wife Frank Coner a white man a Citizen of the United States and Rebeca Duncan- a female Cherokee woman known to Me to Be a Cherokee the above named Frank Conner having foiled in this office a lawful petition and Complyed with the other requirements of the Cherokee laws in regard to white men intermarriage in the Cherokee Nation I. thus issue this Licens you are further Command to attach a Certificate of Servis to this Licens and return to this office heren fail not at your peril

                                       S.A. Melton   Clerk of Dis Court in
December 18th 1873   Del D C C.N

Cherokee Nation   )
Delaware Dist   )   this is to certify By Me that the Marriage of cerremony Being
                           Deuly performed By Me with the Parties names In the within Licens this December the 24th 1873
                        T J McGhee Judge D C D D C N.

    Licens for Frank Conner to marry Rebeca Duncan

Cherokee Intermarried White 1906
Volume II

to Mr Conner I would rater you would go to the Judge as I know he is Judge and some of these preachers I do not know

Cherokee Nation)
Delaware District)
                          that I This is to certify By Me, T. J. McGhee Judge of the District Court married for said Delaware District Cherokee Nation. Have this day By virtue of the Authority vested in my By the Laws of the Cherokee Nation Have this Day under the authority of a Licens Isued By the Clerk of the District Court Baring Date December 18th A. D 1873 Have solmonize the Rights of Matrimony of Marriage Between Frank Conner and Rebecky Duncan obtain & fully complied with the Laws of the Cherokee Nation with accordance to the act past By the National Council Baring Date Oct-15-1855-Regulating Intermarriags with white men this December the 24 1873
)   T J McGhee Judge D C DD C N.
)

this Marriage Certificate of Frank Conner and Reu Becky Duncan Baring Date December 24th A. D 1873

            The undersigned being duly sworn states that as stenographer to the Commissioner to the Five Civilized Tribes, she made the above copy, and that the same is a true and correct copy of the instrument now on file in this office.

                                                            Mary Tabor Mallory

Subscribed and sworn to before me this the 17th. day of January 1907.

                                                            Chas E Webster
                                                            Notary Public.

◇◇◇◇◇

E.C.M.   Cherokee 192.

DEPARTMENT OF THE INTERIOR,

COMMISSIONER TO THE FIVE CIVILIZED TRIBES.

In the matter of the application for the enrollment of FRANCIS M. CONNER as a citizen by intermarriage of the Cherokee Nation.

D E C I S I O N

THE RECORDS OF THIS OFFICE SHOW: That at Fairland, Indian Territory, July 13, 1900, application was received by the Commission to the Five Civilized Tribes for

Cherokee Intermarried White 1906
Volume II

the enrollment of Francis M. Conner as a citizen by intermarriage of the Cherokee Nation. Further proceedings in the matter of said application were had at Muskogee, Indian Territory, September 22, 1902, and January 2, 1907.

THE EVIDENCE IN THIS CASE SHOWS: That the applicant herein, Francis M. Conner, a white man, was married in accordance with Cherokee law, December 24, 1873, to his wife, Rebecca J. Conner, nee Duncan, Indian Territory who was at the time of said marriage a recognized citizen by blood of the Cherokee Nation, who is identified on the Cherokee authenticated tribal roll of 1880, Delaware District, No. 589, as a native Cherokee, and whose name appears on the approved partial roll of citizens by blood of the Cherokee Nation, opposite No. 621. It is further shown that since said marriage the said Francis M. Conner and Rebecca J. Conner have resided together as husband and wife, and have continuously lived in the Cherokee Nation. Said applicant is identified on the Cherokee authenticated tribal roll of 1880, and the Cherokee census roll of 1896, as an intermarried citizen of the Cherokee Nation.

IT IS, THEREFORE, ORDERED AND ADJUDGED: That in accordance with the decision of the Supreme Court of the United States, dated November 5, 1906, in the cases of Daniel Red Bird et al. vs. the United States, Nos. 125, 126, 127 and 128, the said applicant, Francis M. Conner, is entitled, under the provisions of Section 21, of the Act of Congress approved June 28, 1898 (30 Stats., 495), to enrollment as a citizen by intermarriage of the Cherokee Nation, and his application for enrollment as such is accordingly granted.

           Tams Bixby
            Commissioner.

Dated at Muskogee, Indian Territory,
this JAN 21 1907

◇◇◇◇◇

Cherokee
 192

         Muskogee, Indian Territory, December 22, 1906.

Francis M. Conner,
  Fairland, Indian Territory.

Dear Sir:

  November 6, 1906, the United States Supreme Court held that white persons who intermarried with Cherokee citizens according to Cherokee law prior to November 1, 1875, are entitled to enrollment and allotments of land as citizens of the Cherokee Nation.

Cherokee Intermarried White 1906
Volume II

      You are advised that to properly determine your right to enrollment as a citizen by intermarriage of the Cherokee Nation, it will be necessary for you to appear before the Commissioner for the purpose of giving testimony as to the date of your marriage and whether or not your wife, by reason of your marriage to whom you claim the right to enrollment as a citizen of the Cherokee Nation, was a recognized citizen of the Cherokee Nation at the time of your marriage to her, and whether or not you were married to her in accordance with Cherokee laws.

      You are, therefore, directed to appear before the Commissioner at Muskogee, Indian Territory, at 9 o'clock A. M., on Wednesday, January 2, 1907, and give testimony as above indicated.

Respectfully,

J.M.H.   Acting Commissioner.

◇◇◇◇◇

Cherokee 192.

Muskogee, Indian Territory, 21, 1907.[sic]

W. W. Hastings,
      Attorney for the Cherokee Nation,
            Muskogee, Indian Territory.

Dear Sir:

      There is enclosed herewith copy of the decision of the Commissioner to the Five Civilized Tribes, dated January 21, 1907, granting the application for the enrollment of Francis M. Conner as a citizen by intermarriage of the Cherokee Nation.

Respectfully,

Enc I-28   Commissioner.
RPI

◇◇◇◇◇

Cherokee Intermarried White 1906
Volume II

Cherokee 192

W.W. HASTINGS.
ATTORNEY.

OFFICE OF

H.M. VANCE.
SECRETARY.

Attorney for the Cherokee Nation,
MUSKOGEE, I. T.

January 21, 1907.

The Commissioner to the Five Civilized Tribes,
Muskogee, Indian Territory.

Sir:

Receipt is acknowledged of the testimony and of your decision enrolling Francis M. Conner as a citizen by intermarriage of the Cherokee Nation. Time for protesting said decision is waived and I consent that said person may be placed upon the schedule immediately.

Respectfully,
W. W. Hastings
Attorney for Cherokee Nation.

◇◇◇◇◇

Cherokee 192

Muskogee, Indian Territory, January 24, 1907.

Francis M. Conner,
Fairland, Indian Territory.

Dear Sir:

There is enclosed herewith copy of the decision of the Commissioner to the Five Civilized Tribes, dated January 21, 1907, granting the application for your enrollment as a citizen by intermarriage of the Cherokee Nation.

You will be advised when your name has been placed upon a schedule of citizens of the Cherokee Nation.

Respectfully,

Enc I-100
RPI

Commissioner.

◇◇◇◇◇

Cherokee Intermarried White 1906
Volume II

Muskogee, Indian Territory, April 8, 1907.

Francis M. Conner,
    Fairland, Indian Territory.

Dear Sir:

    Your marriage license and certificate filed in connection with your application for enrollment as a citizen by intermarriage of the Cherokee Nation, is returned to you herewith, copies of the same being retained in this office.

    Respectfully,

Incl. P-4-14   Acting Commissioner.
MMP

Cher IW 57
Trans from Cher 210 3-15-07

◇◇◇◇◇

E.C.M.

DEPARTMENT OF THE INTERIOR,

COMMISSIONER TO THE FIVE CIVILIZED TRIBES.

In the matter of the application for the enrollment of

LOUIS L. DUCKWORTH

as a citizen by intermarriage of the Cherokee Nation.

CHEROKEE NO. 210.

◇◇◇◇◇

Cherokee Intermarried White 1906
Volume II

Department of the Interior,
Commission to the Five Civilized Tribes,
Westville, I.T., July 16, 1900.

In the matter of the application of Louis L. Duckworth for the enrollment of himself as a Cherokee by intermarriage, and for the enrollment of his wife and children as Cherokees by blood; being duly sworn and examined by Commissioner Breckenridge[sic], he testified as follows:

Q What is your name? A Louis L. Duckworth.
Q What is your post office? A Siloam Springs, Ark.
Q Do you live in the Cherokee Nation? A At the present my family is in Siloam Springs, I have been living in the Territory all the way through until right lately; my family is there in town at the schools.
Q What do you call your district in the Cherokee Nation? A Going Snake.
Q For whom do you make application? A For my wife and family; I am only an adopted citizen.
Q Do you apply for yourself, wife and children? A Yes, sir.
Q You say you are a Cherokee by intermarriage? A Yes, sir.
Q Are you on the roll of 1880? A Yes, sir.
(On 1880 roll, page 427, No. 559, G. L. Duckworth, Going Snake district. On 1896 roll, page 820, No. 61, Lewis L. Duckworth, Going Snake district.)
Q Mr. Duckworth, in regard to your present residence, you say your family at present in Siloam Springs? A Yes, sir, my home is in the Cherokee Nation; I moved to the town for the benefit of the schools temporarily; my home has been for 30 years in this district.
Q You have a residence on your farm? A Yes, sir, my home; I am looking after it some as I always did, and my family is simply going to school in town.
Q You are simply there temporarily for a temporary purpose? A Yes, sir.
Q How far is your farm from Siloam Springs? A I have one farm four miles, and then I have one farm seven miles.
Q Will you please give your wife's name? A Lavinia A.
Q How long have you been married? A I was married in 1867, 32 years ago I reckon.
(On 1880 roll, L. A. Duckworth, page 427, No. 560, Going Snake district. On 1896 roll, page 742, No. 669, Lavinia A. Duckworth, Going Snake district.)
Q What proportion of Cherokee blood does your wife claim? A I believe 1/16, I don't remember.
Q How many children have you that you wish to apply for? A Well, I have one daughter that is over age, can I enroll her?
Q Is she married? A No, sir.
Q Is she living with you? A Yes, her name is Nevada, she is 23 years old I think.
(On 1880 roll, page 427, No. 565, Going Snake district. On 1896 roll, page 742, No. 672, Going Snake district.)
Q She has lived continuously in the Territory? A Yes, sir.
Q Now your next child? A Effie.
Q What is her age? A She is 17, I believe she has got a middle name, Effie N. Perhaps; Laura E. I believe is the way she is on it.

Cherokee Intermarried White 1906
Volume II

(On 1896 roll, page 742, No. 673, Going Snake District, Laura E. Duckworth.)
Q Any other children? A Yes, sir, the next girl is named Nancy, she is 15.
Q Is that her full name? A I believe that is all the name she has.
(On 1896 roll, page 742, No. 674, Going Snake district.)
Q Any other children? A Yes, sir, a boy named Gunter, he is 12 years old.
(On 1896 roll, page 742, No. 675, Going Snake district.)
Q And[sic] more children? A Yes, sir, Robert, age 7.
(On 1896 roll, page 742, No. 676, Going Snake district.)
Q Are all of these children living with you? A Yes, sir.

Mr. Duckworth, you are duly identified on the roll off 1880, and likewise on the roll of 1896, your residence is satisfactorily established, and you will be enrolled as a citizen by adoption in accordance with your application. Your wife is duly identified on the rolls of 1880 and 1896, and she will be enrolled as a citizen by blood. Your children are all duly identified as indicated in the testimony, and they will be enrolled as Cherokees by blood.

Bruce C. Jones, being duly sworn, says that as stenographer to the Commission to the Five Civilized Tribes he reported the testimony of the above named witness, and that the foregoing is a full, true, and correct translation of his stenographic notes.

Bruce C. Jones

Sworn to and subscribed before me this the 16th day of July, 1900.

Clifton R Breckinridge
Commissioner.

◇◇◇◇◇

H.
Cher. 210.

Department of the Interior.
Commission to the Five Civilized Tribes.
Tahlequah, I. T., October 6, 1902.

SUPPLEMENTAL TESTIMONY AND PROCEEDINGS in the matter of the application for the enrollment of LOUIS L. DUCKWORTH as a citizen by intermarriage of the Cherokee Nation.

LOUIS L. DUCKWORTH, being first duly sworn, and being examined, testified as follows:

BY COMMISSION: What is your name? A Louis L. Duckworth.

Cherokee Intermarried White 1906
Volume II

Q How old are you? A Sixty.
Q What is your post office address? A Siloam Springs, Arkansas.
Q You are a white man? A Yes sir.
Q Have you heretofore made application to this Commission for enrollment as a citizen by intermarriage of the Cherokee Nation? A Yes sir.
Q What is the name of your wife? A Louvinia.
Q Is she living? A Yes sir.
Q Is she a Cherokee by blood? A Yes sir.
Q When were you and she married? A In 1867.
Q Have you and she lived together continuously since your marriage? A Yes sir.
Q You are living together now? A Yes sir.
Q Did you make satisfactory rpoof[sic] to this Commission of your marriage to her according to Cherokee law? A Yes sir.
Q Were you ever married before you married her? A No sir.
Q Was she ever married before she married you? A No sir.
Q Have you lived in the Cherokee Nation continuously since your application for enrollment? A My family is living now at Siloam Springs for the school, that is about two miles from the farm.
Q You are living in Arkansas, are you? A Yes, my family are there at present. A How long have you been living there? A Been living there about three years. A Were y[sic]
Q Were you living there at the time you made application for enrollment? A Yes sir, that was explained to the Dawes Commission and Mr. Hastings was there.
Q For what purpose did you move there? A For the school. My home is in the Territory, and has been ever since I have been here.
Q Have you any improvements in the Cherokee Nation? A Yes sir, all my improvements and everything I have got are here.

  This testimony will be filed with and made a part of the record in the matter of the application for the enrollment of Louis L. Duckworth as a citizen by intermarriage of the Cherokee Nation, Cherokee straight card field No. 210.

Wm. Hutchinson, being first duly sworn, states that as stenographer to the Commission to the Five Civilized Tribes he correctly recorded the testimony and proceedings in this case, and that the foregoing is a true and complete transcript of his stenographic notes thereof.

                    Wm Hutchinson

Subscribed and sworn to before me this 8th day of October, 1902.

                     John O Rosson
                     Notary Public.

Cherokee Intermarried White 1906
Volume II

Cherokee No. 210.

DEPARTMENT OF THE INTERIOR.
COMMISSIONER TO THE FIVE CIVILIZED TRIBES.

Muskogee, Indian Territory, January 3rd, 1907.

In the matter of the application for the enrollment of Louis L. Duckworth as a citizen by intermarriage of the Cherokee Nation.

Louis L. Duckworth, being first duly sworn and examined, testifies as follows:

BY THE COMMISSIONER:

Q What is your name? A Louis L Duckworth.
Q How old are you? A I am 64.
Q Where do you live? A Siloam Springs, Arkansas.
Q You claim to be a citizen by intermarriage to[sic] the Cherokee Nation, do you not? A Yes, sir.
Q Through whom do you claim your rights? A By my wife.
Q What is her name? A Lavina[sic] A. Gunter.
Q When were you married to Lavina A. Gunter? A In 1867.
Q Where were you married to her? A In Goingsnake District.
Q Did you get a licence[sic]? A Yes, sir.
Q Have you got your licence[sic] with you? A No, sir.
Q Where is it? A Lost it.
Q Where did you loose[sic] it? A It was misplaced. I supposed I had it until I commenced hunting for it for this business.
Q Were you ever married before you married Lavina A. Gunter? A No, sir.
Q Was she ever married before she married you? A No, sir.
Q Have you lived together continuously since your marriage in 1867 up to the present time? A Yes, sir.

The applicant is identified on the 1880 Cherokee Roll opposite No. 559. His wife through whom he claims his intermarriage rights is identified on siad[sic] roll opposite No. 560. She is also identified on the final roll of citizens by blood of the Cherokee Nation opposite No. 22335.

Q It will be necessary for you to furnish this office with evidence of the loss of your marriage licence[sic] issued to you by the Cherokee authorities, and also for establishing the fact that you obtained the licence[sic] under the Cherokee laws and was married according to said laws prior to 1875.

Cherokee Intermarried White 1906
Volume II

WITNESS EXCUSED.

F. Elma Lane, upon oath, states that she reported the proceedings in the above entitled cause and that the foregoing is a true and correct transcript of her stenographic notes taken therein.

F. Elma Lane

Subscribed and sworn to before me this 3rd day of January, 1907.

Chas E Webster
Notary Public.

◇◇◇◇◇

LGD

Cherokee 210.

DEPARTMENT OF THE INTERIOR,
COMMISSIONER TO THE FIVE CIVILIZED TRIBES.

———

Muskogee, Indian Territory, January 3, 1907.

Supplemental testimony in the matter of the application of LOUIS L. DUCKWORTH for enrollment as a citizen by intermarriage of the Cherokee Nation.

Annie Eliza Chandler, being first duly sworn by B. P. Rasmus, a notary public, testified as follows:

Q What is your name? A Annie Eliza Chandler.
Q What is your age? A 59 years old.
Q What is your postoffice address? A Vinita, I. T.
Q Are you a citizen of the Cherokee Nation? A Yes sir.
Q By blood? A Yes sir.
Q Do you know Louis L. Duckworth? A Yes sir.
Q Do you know where he was married? A Yes, in the Goingsnake District.
Q Who married them? A Preacher Williams.
Q Do you know whether he had a Cherokee license? A Yes.
Q Did you see the license? A Yes.
Q When were they married? A They were married in 1867.
Q What time in the year. A December 26.
Q Who was present at the time Louis L. Duckworth and Louvina Duckworth were married? A There was a big crowd present. I was married at the same time, by the same sermon.
Q Are you any relation to Louis L. Duckworth? A His wife is a sister of mine.
Q You both married white men? A Yes.

Cherokee Intermarried White 1906
Volume II

Q Both had to get Cherokee license? A Yes sir.
Q That is how you remember that he got a marriage license? A Yes sir.

Witness excused.

Demie T. Stubblefield, being duly sworn, on oath states that as stenographer to the Commissioner to the Five Civilized Tribes she reported the proceedings in the above case, and that the above and foregoing is a true and correct copy of her stenographic notes thereof.

Demie T. Stubblefield

Subscribed and sworn to before me this, January 4, 1907.

Edward Merrick
Notary Public.

◇◇◇◇◇

E C M   Cherokee 210.

DEPARTMENT OF THE INTERIOR,

COMMISSIONER TO THE FIVE CIVILIZED TRIBES.

In the matter of the application for the enrollment of LOUIS L. DUCKWORTH as a citizen by intermarriage of the Cherokee Nation.

D E C I S I O N

THE RECORDS OF THIS OFFICE SHOW: That at Westville, Indian Territory, July 16th, 1900 application was received by the Commission to the Five Civilized Tribes for the enrollment of Louis L. Duckworth as a citizen by intermarriage of the Cherokee Nation. Further proceedings in the matter of said application were had at Tahlequah, Indian Territory on October 6th, 1902 and at Muskogee, Indian Territory, January 3rd, 1907.

THE EVIDENCE IN THIS CASE SHOWS: That the applicant herein, Louis L. Duckworth, a white man, was married in accordance with Cherokee law December 26th, 1867, to his wife, Louvina A. Duckworth, nee Gunter, who was at the time of said marriage a recognized citizen by blood of the Cherokee Nation, who is identified on the Cherokee authenticated tribal roll of 1880, Going Snake District No. 560 as a native Cherokee, and whose name is included in the approved partial roll of citizens by blood of the Cherokee Nation, opposite No. 22335. It is further shown that from the time of said marriage the said Louis L. Duckworth and Louvina A. Duckworth resided together as husband and wife and lived continuously in the Cherokee Nation up to and including September 1st, 1902. Said applicant is identified on the Cherokee authenticated tribal

Cherokee Intermarried White 1906
Volume II

roll of 1880 and the Cherokee census roll of 1896 as an intermarried citizen of the Cherokee Nation.

IT IS, THEREFORE, ORDERED AND ADJUDGED: That in accordance with the decision of the Supreme Court of the United States, dated November 5, 1906, in the cases of Daniel Red Bird et al. vs. the United States, Nos. 125, 126, 127 and 128, the said applicant, Louis L. Duckworth is entitled, under the provisions of Section Twenty-one of the Act of Congress approved June 28, 1898 (30 Stats. 495), to enrollment as a citizen by intermarriage of the Cherokee Nation and his application for enrollment as such is accordingly granted.

Tams Bixby
Commissioner.

Dated at Muskogee, Indian Territory,
this   JAN 23 1907

◇◇◇◇◇

Cherokee
210

Muskogee, Indian Territory, December 21, 1906.

Louis L. Duckworth,
    Siloam Springs, Arkansas.

Dear Sir:

November 6, 1906, the United States Supreme Court held that white persons who intermarried with Cherokee citizens according to Cherokee law prior to November 1, 1875, are entitled to enrollment and allotments of land as citizens of the Cherokee Nation.

You are advised that to properly determine your right to enrollment as a citizen by intermarriage of the Cherokee Nation, it will be necessary for you to appear before the Commissioner for the purpose of giving testimony as to the date of your marriage and whether or not your wife, by reason of your marriage to whom you claim the right to enrollment as a citizen of the Cherokee Nation, was a recognized citizen of the Cherokee Nation at the time of your marriage to her, and whether or not you were married to her in accordance with Cherokee laws.

You are therefore directed to appear before the Commissioner at Muskogee, Indian Territory, at 9 o'clock A. M., on Thursday, January 3, 1907, and give testimony as above indicated.

Respectfully,

H.J.C.   Acting Commissioner.

◇◇◇◇◇

Cherokee Intermarried White 1906
Volume II

Cherokee 210

Muskogee, Indian Territory, January 23, 1907.

W. W. Hastings,
    Attorney for the Cherokee Nation,
        Muskogee, Indian Territory.

Dear Sir:

    There is enclosed herewith copy of the decision of the Commissioner to the Five Civilized Tribes, dated January 23, 1907, granting the application for the enrollment of Louis L. Duckworth as a citizen by intermarriage of the Cherokee Nation.

        Respectfully,

Enc I-76   Commissioner.
RPI

◇◇◇◇◇◇

Cherokee 210

| W.W. HASTINGS. | OFFICE OF | H.M. VANCE. |
| ATTORNEY. | | SECRETARY. |

Attorney for the Cherokee Nation,
MUSKOGEE, I. T.

        January 23, 1907.

The Commissioner to the Five Civilized Tribes,
    Muskogee, Indian Territory.

Sir:

    Receipt is acknowledged of the testimony and of your decision enrolling Louis L. Duckworth as a citizen by intermarriage of the Cherokee Nation. Time for protesting said decision is waived and I consent that said person may be placed upon the schedule immediately.

        Respectfully,
        W. W. Hastings
        Attorney for the Cherokee Nation.

◇◇◇◇◇◇

Cherokee Intermarried White 1906
Volume II

Cherokee 210

Muskogee, Indian Territory, January 23, 1907.

Louis L. Duckworth,
  Siloam Springs, Arkansas.

Dear Sir:

There is enclosed herewith copy of the decision of the Commissioner to the Five Civilized Tribes, dated January 17, 1907, granting the application for your enrollment as a citizen by intermarriage of the Cherokee Nation.

You will be advised when your name has been placed upon a schedule of citizens of the Cherokee Nation and approved by the Secretary of the Interior.

Respectfully,

Commissioner.

Enc I-94
RPI

Cher IW 58
Trans from Cher 518 3-13-07

◇◇◇◇◇

E.C.M.

DEPARTMENT OF THE INTERIOR,

COMMISSIONER TO THE FIVE CIVILIZED TRIBES.

In the matter of the application for the enrollment of

LEMUEL S. SAUNDERS

as a citizen by intermarriage of the Cherokee Nation.

CHEROKEE 518

◇◇◇◇◇

Cherokee Intermarried White 1906
Volume II

Department of the Interior,
Commission to the Five Civilized Tribes,
Stillwell[sic], I.T., July 24, 1900.

In the matter of the application of Lemual[sic] S. Saunders for enrollment as a Cherokee by intermarriage; being duly sworn and examined by Commissioner Breckenridge[sic], he testified as follows:

Q What is your name? A Lemuel S. Saunders.
Q What is your age? A 71.
Q What is your post office address? A Stillwell[sic].
Q What is your district? A Flint.
Q How long have you lived in this district? A About 30 years.
Q It is your home now, it is? A Yes, sir.
Q For whom do you make application for enrollment? A For myself, I have one son living with me 30 years old.
Q He must make application for himself. Anybody besides yourself you want to apply for now? A No, sir.
Q You apply as a Cherokee by blood? A No, sir, by adoption.
Q You are an intermarried Cherokee? A Yes, sir.
Q Your wife is dead, is she? A Yes, sir.
Q What was her name? A Viana Raper.
Q When were you married? A April 7, 1961.
Q Your wife was a Cherokee by blood? A Yes, sir.
Q Where were you married? A I was married in North Carolina and then remarried in the Nation according to the statute.
Q When did you wife, die? A I can't give the exact date.
Q About when? A About 22 years ago I think.
Q Are you on the roll of 1880? A Yes, sir.
(On 1880 roll, page 390, No. 1162, L. S. Saunders, Flint district.
On 1896 roll, page 716, No. 66, Lemul S. Sanders, Flint district.)

Mr. Aaunders[sic], you are duly identified on the roll of 1880, and also upon the roll of 1896, your residence is satisfactorily established, and you will be enrolled as a Cherokee by adoption.

-------o-------

Bruce C. Jones, being duly sworn, says that as stenographer to the Commission to the Five Civilized Tribes he reported the testimony of the above named witness, and that the foregoing is a full, true and correct translation of his stenographic notes.

Bruce C Jones

Cherokee Intermarried White 1906
Volume II

Sworn to and subscribed before me this the 24th day of July, 1900.

       Clifton R. Breckinridge
          Commissioner.

◇◇◇◇◇

H.
Cher. 518.

      Department of the Interior.
    Commission to the Five Civilized Tribes.
     Tahlequah, I. T., October 6, 1902.

  SUPPLEMENTAL TESTIMONY AND PROCEEDINGS in the matter of the application for the enrollment of LEMUEL S. SAUNDERS as a citizen by intermarriage of the Cherokee Nation.

  LEMUEL S. SAUNDERS, being first duly sworn, and being examined, testified as follows:

BY COMMISSION: What is your name? A Lemuel S. Saunders.
Q How old are you? A I will be seventy-four the 10th day of Next May.
Q What is your post office address? A Stilwell, I. T.
Q You are a white man, are you? A Yes sir.
Q Have you heretofore made application to this Commission for enrollment as a citizen by intermarriage of the Cherokee Nation? A Yes sir.
Q What is the name of your wife? A My first wife's name was Vianna Raper.
Q Is she living? A She is dead.
Q Was she a Cherokee by blood? A Yes sir.
Q Did you live with her until the time of her death? A Yes sir.
Q What is the name of your second wife? A Second wife's name was Mary Keys.
Q Is she living? A She is dead.
Q Was she a Cherokee by blood? A Yes sir.
Q Did you live with her until the time of her death? A Yes sir.
Q When did you second wife die? A She has been dead about fourteen years.
Q Do you claim your right to enrollment by reason of your Cherokee wife? A Yes sir.
Q Have you married since the death of your second wife? A No sir.
Q Have you lived in the Cherokee Nation continuously since you and she were married? A No sir.
Q Was your wife ever married before she married you? A No sir.

  This testimony will be filed with and made a part of the record in the matter of the application for the enrollment of Lemuel S. Saunders as a citizen by intermarriage of the Cherokee Nation, Cherokee straight card field No. 518.

Cherokee Intermarried White 1906
Volume II

Wm. Hutchinson, being first duly sworn, states that as stenographer to the Commission to the Five Civilized Tribes he correctly recorded the testimony and proceedings in this case, and that the foregoing is a true and complete transcript of his stenographic notes thereof.

Wm Hutchinson

Subscribed and sworn to before me this 7th day of October, 1902.

John O. Rosson
Notary Public.

◇◇◇◇◇

C.FB.   Cherokee 518

DEPARTMENT OF THE INTERIOR,
COMMISSIONER TO THE FIVE CIVILIZED TRIBES.
MUSKOGEE, IND. TER. JANUARY 3, 1907.

In the matter of the application for the enrollment of LEMUEL S. SAUNDERS as a citizen by intermarriage of the Cherokee Nation.

APPEARANCES:
Applicant appears in person:

Cherokee Nation represented by H. M. Vance on behalf of W. W. Hastings, Attorney.

LEMUEL S. SAUNDERS being first duly sworn by John E. Tidwell, a Notary Public, testified as follows:

On Behalf of Commissioner:

Q. What is our name? A. Lemuel S. Saunders.
Q. What is your age? A. I will be eighty- no seventy-eight, next May.
Q. What is your postoffice address? A. Stilwell, I. T.
Q. Are you an applicant for enrollment as a citizen by intermarriage of the Cherokee Nation? A. Yes sir.
Q. You have no Cherokee blood? A. No sir.
Q. You claim the right to enrollment solely by virtue of your marriage to a Cherokee by blood? A. Yes sir.
Q. What is the name of the person through whom you claim the right to enrollment? A. Vianna Raper was her maiden name.
Q. Is she living at the present time? A. No sir.
Q. When did she die? A. I think sir, it was in 1874.
Q. When were you and she married? A. My recollection is that we were married in December, 1869, or January or Feburary[sic] of 1870, but it may have been December of '70.

Cherokee Intermarried White 1906
Volume II

Q. Where were you living at the time you married her? A. I was living in Flint District?[sic]
Q. Cherokee Nation? A. Yes sir, Cherokee Nation.
Q. Was she living there also? A. Yes sir, she lived there all her life.
Q. Was she a recognized citizen of the Cherokee nation at the time you married her?
A. Yes sir, she was a recognized citizen at that time. I attended to that myself, I was a practicing attorney before their courts.
Q. Were you ever married before you married her? A. No sir.
Q. Was she ever married before she married you? A. No sir.
Q. Since your marriage to her have you always lived in the Cherokee Nation?
A. Yes sir.
Q. Did you and she continuously reside together as husband and wife until her death?
A. Yes sir.
Q. Have you since re-married? A. Since that?
Q. Yes sir? A. Yes sir.
Q. Is your second wife living? A. No sir.
Q. When did she die? A. My recollection of her death-- I believe it was in '76- I am not certain, since I had that stroke I have been feble[sic] and my recollection is not what it was.
Q. Your second wife died in '76 you think? A. Yes sir.
Q. You married you second wife shortly after your first wife's death?
A. I think I married my second wife in September, '75.
A. Was she a Cherokee by blood? A. Yes sr.
Q. Did you live with her as her husband until her death? A.[sic]
A. Yes sir.
Q. Since the death of your second wife have you married again? A. Since the death of my second wife, five or six years after that I married another Cherokee, her name was Nancy Carlile. Nancy Hampton was her name then.
Q. Is she living at this time? A. No sir.
Q. Did you and she live together as husband and wife until her death? A. Yes sir, we lived together as husband and wife, I cared for her all the way along; she died of consumption My second wife died of Pleurisy.
Q. Have you remarried since the death of your third wife? A. No sir, and never intend to.
Q. When you were married to your first wife did you comply with Cherokee law? A. I did, sir.
Q. You secured a Cherokee license did you? A. Yes sir; I will explain to you sir, if you want me to?
Q. Yes sir? [sic] Well, the law required that Emigrants from the East go before the Supreme Court of the Cherokee Nation and apply for re-admission. After we removed here I took out a license to practice law, and then I went before the Supreme Court and had my wife and her children admitted to citizenship, and they made up the record that she was admitted to citizenship, and when I complied with the law I would be admitted. Judge Vann said to me "Judge Saunders, these people seem to think there should be a marriage, or a record of your marriage." So I went and got a license and turned them into the Court, and told William Turner who was

Cherokee Intermarried White 1906
Volume II

the Supreme Court Clerk, that the record shows that L. S. Saunders has filed his marriage license and certificate and he is also a citizen of the Cherokee Nation, and it is there on the record, sir.

Q. Were you and your first wife married before you came to the Cherokee Nation?
A. Yes sir.
Q. You married in what State? A. I married in Cherokee County, North Carolina. I think it was in the month of April, 1861.
Q. What year did you come to the Nation? A. My recollection is now that I arrived in the Cherokee Nation in February, 1869.
Q. Your wife accompanied you, did she? A. Yes sir, all the way through.
Q. And you complied with the Cherokee law at the time your wife was admitted, or after her admission? A. Yes sir, just after her admission.
Q. You secured a marriage license and married her again in accordance with the laws of the Cherokee Nation? A. Yes sir, I complied with the law in every letter.

The applicant, Lemuel S. Saunders, is identified on the authenticated Cherokee Tribal Roll of 1880, Flint District, Number 1162.

Q. In what distgrict[sic] were you residing at the time of your marriage?
A. In Flint District, sir.
Q. Then your papers were recorded in Flint District?
A. I got the license from the Clerk, Warren Adair, by request of the Supreme Court and the license was executed by Reverend Wilson Morris, and I handed it in to the Supreme Court.
Q. By whom was your wife admitted to citizenship in the Cherokee Nation upon her coming here? A. My recollection is that the Supreme Court of the Cherokee Nation admitted her and her children, and they made up the record that they were citizens, and that when I complied with the law I would be a citizen also.
Q. Did they give her a Certificate of Admission to citizenship?
A. Yes sir, they did, and they requested me to get a marriage license and turn it in and then I would be admitted to citizenship.

The original Marriage Records of Flint District, Cherokee Nation are in the possession of this office and "Book B" containing said Records shows that on the 18th of March, 1871, license was issued in accordance with the laws of the Cherokee Nation, to Lemuel S. Saunders, a citizen of the United States, to marry Miss Nianna[sic] Raper, a Cherokee by birth, and that said parties were united in marriage in accordance with the terms of said license, March 23, 1871.

The undersigned, being first duly sworn, states that as stenographer to the Commissioner to the Five Civilized Tribes she correctly recorded the testimony had in this case, and that the above and foregoing is a full, true and correct transcript of her stenographic notes thereof.

Lucy M Bowman

Cherokee Intermarried White 1906
Volume II

Subscribed and sworn to before me this January 4th, 1907.

John E. Tidwell
Notary Public.

◇◇◇◇◇

E.C.M.   Cherokee 518.

DEPARTMENT OF THE INTERIOR,

COMMISSIONER TO THE FIVE CIVILIZED TRIBES.

In the matter of the application for the enrollment of LEMUEL S. SAUNDERS as a citizen by intermarriage of the Cherokee Nation.

D E C I S I O N

THE RECORDS OF THIS OFFICE SHOW: That at Stilwell, Indian Territory, July 24, 1900, Lemuel S. Saunders appeared before the Commission to the Five Civilized Tribes, and made application for the enrollment of himself as a citizen by intermarriage of the Cherokee Nation. Further proceedings in the matter of said application were had at Tahlequah, Indian Territory August 6, 1901, and at Muskogee, Indian Territory, January 3, 1907.

THE EVIDENCE IN THIS CASE SHOWS: That the applicant herein, Lemuel S. Saunders, a white man, was married in accordance with Cherokee law March 23, 1871, to his wife, Vianna (Nianna) Saunders nee Raper, since deceased, who was at the time of said marriage a recognized citizen by blood of the Cherokee Nation; that from the time of said marriage until the time of the death of the said Vianna (Nianna) Saunders, which occurred in the year 1874, the said Lemuel S. Saunders and Vianna Saunders resided together as husband and wife; that in the year 1875 said Lemuel S. Saunders married one Mary Saunders, nee Keys, since deceased, a recognized citizen by blood of the Cherokee Nation the Cherokee Nation; that from the time of said marriage until the time of the death of said Mary Saunders, which occurred in the year 1876, the said Lemuel S. Saunders and Mary Saunders resided together as husband and wife; that five or six years after the death of said Mary Saunders said Lemuel S. Saunders married one Nancy Saunders nee Hampton, a Cherokee by blood, since deceased, who is identified on the Cherokee authenticated tribal roll of 1880, Tahlequah District, number 882, as a native Cherokee; and from the time of said marriage until the time of the death of the said Nancy Saunders the said Lemuel S. and Nancy Saunders resided together as husband and wife and that since the death of said Nancy Saunders said Lemuel S. Saunders has remained unmarried and that he has continuously lived in the Cherokee nation since March 23, 1871. Said applicant was duly identified on the Cherokee authenticated tribal

Cherokee Intermarried White 1906
Volume II

roll of 1880 and the Cherokee census roll of 1896 as an intermarried citizen of the Cherokee Nation.

IT IS, THEREFORE, ORDERED AND ADJUDGED: That in accordance with the decision of the Supreme Court of the United States, dated November 5, 1906, in the cases of Daniel Red Bird et al. vs. the United States, Nos. 125, 126, 127 and 128, the said applicant, Lemuel S. Saunders, is entitled, under the provision of Section twenty-one of the Act of Congress approved June 28, 1898 (30 Stat. 495), to enrollment as a citizen by intermarriage of the Cherokee Nation, and his application for enrollment as such is accordingly granted.

Tams Bixby
Commissioner.

Dated at Muskogee, Indian Territory,
this JAN 23 1907

◇◇◇◇◇

Cherokee

518

Muskogee, Indian Territory, December 21, 1906.

Lemuel S. Saunders,
Stilwell, Indian Territory.

Dear Sir:

November 6, 1906, the United States Supreme Court held that white persons who intermarried with Cherokee citizens according to Cherokee law prior to November 1, 1875, are entitled to enrollment and allotments of land as citizens of the Cherokee Nation.

You are advised that to properly determine your right to enrollment as a citizen by intermarriage of the Cherokee Nation, it will be necessary for you to appear before the Commissioner for the purpose of giving testimony as to the date of your marriage and whether or not your wife, by reason of your marriage to whom you claim the right to enrollment as a citizen of the Cherokee Nation, was a recognized citizen of the Cherokee Nation at the time of your marriage to her, and whether or not you were married to her in accordance with Cherokee laws.

You are therefore directed to appear before the Commissioner at Muskogee, Indian Territory, at 9 o'clock A. M., on Thursday, January 3, 1907, and give testimony as above indicated.

Cherokee Intermarried White 1906
Volume II

Respectfully,

H.J.C.   Acting Commissioner.

◇◇◇◇◇

Cherokee 518

Muskogee, Indian Territory, January 23, 1907.

W. W. Hastings,
    Attorney for the Cherokee Nation,
        Muskogee, Indian Territory.

Dear Sir:

    There is enclosed herewith a copy of the decision of the Commissioner to the Five Civilized Tribes, dated January 23, 1907, granting the application for the enrollment of Lemuel S. Saunders as a citizen by intermarriage of the Cherokee Nation.

Respectfully,

Encl. H-69   Commissioner.
JMH

◇◇◇◇◇

Cherokee 518   W.W.HASTINGS.   OFFICE OF   H.M. VANCE.
                     ATTORNEY.   SECRETARY.

Attorney for the Cherokee Nation,
MUSKOGEE, I. T.

January 23, 1907.

The Commissioner to the Five Civilized Tribes,
    Muskogee, Indian Territory.

Sir:

    Receipt is acknowledged of the testimony and of your decision enrolling Lemuel S. Saunders as a citizen by intermarriage of the Cherokee Nation. Time for protesting said decision is waived and I consent that said person may be placed upon the schedule immediately.

Respectfully,
W. W. Hastings
Attorney for Cherokee Nation.

◇◇◇◇◇

Cherokee Intermarried White 1906
Volume II

Cherokee
518

Muskogee, Indian Territory. January 23, 1907.

Lemuel S. Saunders,
    Stilwell, Indian Territory.

Dear Sir:

    There is enclosed herewith a copy of the decision of the Commissioner to the Five Civilized Tribes, dated January 23, 1907, granting your application for enrollment as a citizen by intermarriage of the Cherokee Nation.

    You will be advised when your name has been placed upon a schedule of citizens of the Cherokee Nation and approved by the Secretary of the Interior.

                      Respectfully,

E.R.C.   Commissioner.
Enc. E.C. 90.

```
OK CFB

Cherokee 518
1 - I. W.

          Granted.
```

Cher IW 59
Trans from Cher 534 3-15-07

Cherokee Intermarried White 1906
Volume II

F. R.

DEPARTMENT OF THE INTERIOR,

COMMISSIONER TO THE FIVE CIVILIZED TRIBES.

In the matter of the application for the enrollment of

ANNA E. DANNENBERG

as a citizen by intermarriage of the Cherokee Nation.

Cherokee --- 534.

◇◇◇◇◇

Department of the Interior,
Commission to the Five Civilized Tribes,
Stilwell, I. T., July 24, 1900.

In the matter of the application of John H. Dannenberg for the enrollment of himself, his wife and children as Cherokees; being sworn and examined by Commissioner Needles he testifies as follows

Q What is your name? A John H. Dannenberg.
Q What is your age? A Fifty-eight.
Q What is your post-office address? A Stilwell.
Q What district do you live in? A Flint.
Q How long have you lived in the Cherokee Nation? A Fifty-eight years, all except four years.
Q Are you a Cherokee by blood? A I am.
Q For whom do you apply? A Myself, wife and one child? A What is the name of your father? A N. B. Dannenberg. He is dead.
Q He die before 1880? A Yes sir.
Q What is the name of your mother? A C. A. Dannenberg.
Q Is she living? A Yes sir.
Q Is she upon the rolls of the Cherokee Nation? A Yes sir.
 Note: 1880 roll examined for applicant: Page 363, #490, J. M. Dannenberg, Flint District. 1896 roll, Flint District, page 659, #565, John H. Dannenberg.
Q What proportion of blood do you claim? A One-sixteenth.
Q Are you married? A I am.
Q Married under the law of the Cherokee Nation? A Yes sir.

218

Cherokee Intermarried White 1906
Volume II

Q What is your wife's name? A Anna E.
Q When were you married? A in 1869.
   Note: 1880 roll examined for applicant's wife: page 363, #491, A. E. Dannenberg, Flint District. 1896 roll, page 712, #22, Annie E. Dannenberg, Flint District.
Q What is the name of your child at home? A Johnnie H., a girl about seventeen years old.
   Note: On 1896 roll, page 659, #567, as Johnnie H. Dannenberg, Flint District.
Q Your two boys are where they can't come? A Yes sir.
Q They are in prison? A Yes sir.
Q What are their names? A Louis B., about twenty-six years old. (On 1880 roll, page 363, #493, L. B. Dannenberg, Flint Dist) On 1896 roll, page 659, #571, Lewis B. Dannenberg, Flint District.)
Q What is the name of the other one? A Robert C., about twenty-three years old. (On 1880 roll, page 363, #494, R. C. Dannenberg, Flint District. 1896 roll, Flint District, page 659, #564, Robert C. Dannenberg.)
Q You have no marriage certificate? A No sir, I had one, but it is lost.
Q I didn't get the date of your marriage? A 16th day of June 1869.
Q Are these children all living at home? A Yes sir, all except the two boys; I haven't but one at home with me.
Q Had they been living continuously in the Territory? A Yes sir.
Q They make their home with you? A Yes sir.

   Com'r Needles: John H. Dannenberg's name appearing upon the authenticated roll of 1880 as well as upon the census roll of 1896, and his wife, Anna E.'s name also appearing upon the authenticated roll of 1880 and upon the census roll of 1896, she being a white woman, and his child, Johnnie H.'s name appearing upon the census roll of 1896, the said John H. Dannenberg and daughter, Johnnie H., are admitted to citizenship as Cherokees by blood, and his wife, Anna E., as a citizen by intermarriage.
   His son, Louis B., whose name appears upon the authenticated roll of 1880 as well as upon the census roll of 1896, and his son Robert C.'s name also appearing upon the authenticated roll of 1880 as well as the census roll of 1896; satisfactory poof being made that they are in prison and cannot present themselves in person, they are ordered enrolled as Cherokees by blood, and their names will appear upon the rolls now being made by the Commission.

   M.D. Green, being first duly sworn, states that as stenographer to the Commission to the Five Civilized Tribes he reported the foregoing case and that the above and foregoing is a full true and complete transcript of his stenographic notes in said case.

MD Green

Subscribed and sworn to before me this 25th day of July 1900.

TB Needles
Commissioner.

Cherokee Intermarried White 1906
Volume II

R.
Cher. 534.

Department of the Interior.
Commission to the Five Civilized Tribes.
Tahlequah, I. T., October 2, 1902.

SUPPLEMENTAL TESTIMONY AND PROCEEDINGS in the matter of the application for the enrollment of ANNIE E. DANNENBERG as a citizen by intermarriage of the Cherokee Nation.

JOHN H. DANNENBERG, being first duly sworn, and being examined, testified as follows:

BY COMMISSION: What is your name? A John Henry Dannenberg.
Q How old are you? A Sixty last May, the 10th day.
Q What is your post office address? A Salina.
Q Are you a recognized citizen by blood of the Cherokee Nation? A Yes sir.
Q What is the name of your wife? A Annie E.
Q Is she living? A Yes sir.
Q Is she a white woman? A So said to be.
Q Is she? A I think so.
Q Does she claim her right to enrollment by reason of her marriage to you? A Yes sir.
Q Application has been made to this Commission for her enrollment as a citizen by intermarriage of the Cherokee Nation? A Yes sir.
Q When were you married? A June 1869.
Q Have you and she lived together continuously ever since that time[sic] A Yes sir.
Q Are you living together now? A Yes sir.
Q Has she resided in the Cherokee Nation continuously since the date of her application for enrollment? A Yes sir.
Q Were you ever married before you married her? A No sir.
Q Was she ever married before she married you? A No sir.

This testimony will be filed with and made a part of the record in the matter of the application for the enrollment of Annie E. Dannenberg as a citizen by intermarriage of the Cherokee Nation, Cherokee straight card field No. 534.

Wm. Hutchinson, being first duly sworn, states that as stenographer to the Commission to the Five Civilized Tribes he correctly recorded the testimony and proceedings in this case, and that the foregoing is a true and complete transcript of his stenographic notes thereof.

Wm Hutchinson

Cherokee Intermarried White 1906
Volume II

Subscribed and sworn to before me this 2d day of October, 1902.

John O Rosson
Notary Public.

◇◇◇◇◇◇

Cherokee 534.

DEPARTMENT OF THE INTERIOR,
COMMISSIONER TO THE FIVE CIVILIZED TRIBES.
Muskogee, I. T., January 2, 1907.

In the matter of the application for the enrollment of Annie E. Dannenberg as a citizen by intermarriage of the Cherokee Nation.

Annie E. Dannenberg being first duly sworn by Frances R. Lane, a Notary Public for the Western District of Indian Territory, testified as follows:

By the Commissioner:
Q What is your name? A Annie E. Dannenberg.
Q How old are you? A Firty[sic]-three or fifty-four. I can't hardly tell positive.
Q What is your postoffice address? A Stilwell, I. T.
Q You claim to be an intermarried citizen of the Cherokee Nation? A Yes sir.
Q Through whom do you claim you derive your rights as such?
A John Henry Dannenberg.
Q When were you married to John Henry Dannenberg? A I was married in 1869.
Q What time? A June 6th.
Q Where were you married to John Henry Dannenberg? A In Flint District at the residence of Dr. T. R. Ferguson.
Q Did you get a certificate of marriage? A Yes, I did, but I havn't[sic] got it now.
Q Where is it? A I don't know; it is lost; I had a certificate.
Q It is lost at the present time? A Yes sir.
Q Have you hunted for it? A No, I havn't[sic]; I think I could not find it if I did.
Q When is the last time you saw it? A Good many years--several years.
Q As many as ten years? A No, I don't hardly think it has been that long, but I have been moving right smart, and building and changing, and I don't think I could find it.
Q Were you ever married before you married John H. Dannenberg? A No sir.
Q Was he ever married prior to his marriage to you? A No sir.
Q Have you lived together continuously in the Cherokee nation[sic] as husband and wife since your marriage in 1869? A Yes sir.
Q Was your husband a citizen of the Cherokee Nation at the time you were married to him? A He was.
Q Has his name been placed upon all the rolls since 1869? A Yes sir.

    Applicant is identified upon the 1880 Cherokee roll opposite No. 491. Her husband through whom she claims her right to enrollment is identified on said roll

Cherokee Intermarried White 1906
Volume II

opposite No. 490, and is also identified on the final roll of citizens by blood of the Cherokee Nation opposite No. 1539.
Q Are you and John Henry Dannenberg living together at the present time? A Yes sir.
Q Have you any other witness heret[sic] today that knew of your marriage to him in accordance with Cherokee laws. 1869? A Not that I know of.
Q Neither one of these ladies know about it? A No, I don't guess they do. They was not present that I know of.

It will be necessary for you to furnish the Commissioner evidence of your marriage to John Henry Dannenberg in 1869. If you have any witnesses you will have to bring them down here.

Q Haven't you anyone that can testify to your marriage? A No, I can't think of anyone that is here today.
Q Well, you will have to bring someone in. If you can get someone we will take up your case later on. If you could find the marriage certificate that would be the best evidence.
A I think I can get a duplicate from the man that married me.
Q Well, if you cannot do that bring two witnesses that can testify to the fact.

Witness excused.

Note. Addition[sic] evidence of the marriage required.

Frances R. Lane being first duly sworn states that as stenographer to the Commission to the Five Civilized Tribes she reported the testimony in the above entitled cause and that the above and foregoing is an accurate transcript of her shorthand notes in said cause.

Frances R Lane

Subscribed and sworn to before me this 4th day of January, 1907.

Edward Merrick
Notary Public.

◇◇◇◇◇

Cherokee Intermarried White 1906
Volume II

Cherokee No. 534.

DEPARTMENT OF THE INTERIOR.
COMMISSIONER TO THE FIVE CIVILIZED TRIBES.

Muskogee, Indian Territory, January 3, 1907.

Supplementary proceedings in the matter of the application of the enrollment of Anna E. Dannenburg[sic], as a citizen by intermarriage of the Cherokee Nation.

Josephine E. Rasmus, being first duly sworn and examined, testifies as follows:

BY THE COMMISSIONER:

Q What is your name? A Josephine E. Rasmus.
Q How old are you? A 66.
Q What is your Post Office address? A Talequah[sic].
Q Are you a citizen or non-citizen of the Cherokee Nation? A Citizen.
Q Are you acquainted with Anna E. Dannenburg? A Yes, sir.
Q Do you know John H. Dannenburg? A He is my brother.
Q Do you know when they were married? A Yes, sir.
Q When were they married? A In '69
Q Do you remember the date? A June 6th, 1869.
Q Were you present when they were married? A Yes, sir.
Q Where were they married? A In Flint District.
Q Have they lived together continuously since their marriage in 1869? A Yes, sir.
Q In the Cherokee Nation? A Yes, sir.

WITNESS EXCUSED.

F. Elma Lane, upon oath, states that she reported the proceedings in the above entitled cause and that the foregoing is a true and correct transcript of her stenographic notes taken therein.

F. Elma Lane

Subscribed and sworn to before me this 3rd day of January, 1907.

Chas E Webster
Notary Public.

Cherokee Intermarried White 1906
Volume II

F.R. Cherokee 534.

DEPARTMENT OF THE INTERIOR,
COMMISSIONER TO THE FIVE CIVILIZED TRIBES.

In the matter of the application for the enrollment of Anna E. Dannenberg as a citizen by intermarriage of the Cherokee Nation.

D E C I S I O N .

THE RECORDS OF THIS OFFICE SHOW: That on July 24, 1900, application was received by the Commission to the Five Civilized Tribes for the enrollment of Anna E. Dannenberg as a citizen by intermarriage of the Cherokee Nation. Further proceedings in the matter of said application were had at Tahlequah, Indian Territory, October 2, 1902, and at Muskogee, Indian Territory, January 2, 1907, and January 3, 1907.

THE EVIDENCE IN THIS CASE SHOWS: That the applicant herein, Anna E. Dannenberg, a white woman, was lawfully married on June 6, 1869, to John Henry Dannenberg, who was at the time of said marriage a recognized citizen by blood of the Cherokee Nation, and who is identified on the Cherokee authenticated tribal roll of 1880, Flint District, No. 490, as a Native Cherokee, and whose name is included in the approved partial roll of citizens by blood of the Cherokee Nation, opposite No. 1537. It is further shown that from the time of said marriage the said John Henry Dannenberg and Anna E. Dannenberg resided together as husband and wife, and continuously lived in the Cherokee Nation up to and including September 1, 1902. The applicant is identified on the Cherokee authenticated tribal roll of 1880, and on the Cherokee census roll of 1896, as an intermarried citizen of the Cherokee Nation.

IT IS, THEREFORE, ORDERED AND ADJUDGED: That in accordance with the decision of the Supreme Court of the United States, dated November 5, 1906, in the cases of Daniel Red Bird et al., vs. the United States, Nos. 125, 126, 127 and 128, the said applicant, Anna E. Dannenberg is entitled, under the provisions of Section 21 of the Act of Congress approved June 28, 1898 (30 Stats., 495), to enrollment as a citizen by intermarriage of the Cherokee Nation, and her application for enrollment as such is accordingly granted.

                                                    Tams Bixby
                                                    Commissioner.

Dated at Muskogee, Indian Territory,
this JAN 23 1907

Cherokee Intermarried White 1906
Volume II

REFER IN REPLY TO THE FOLLOWING:
Cherokee
534.

DEPARTMENT OF THE INTERIOR,
COMMISSIONER TO THE FIVE CIVILIZED TRIBES.

Muskogee, Indian Territory, December 21, 1906.

Anna E. Dannenberg,
    Salina, Indian Territory.

Dear Madam:

    November 6, 1906, the United States Supreme Court held that white persons who intermarried with Cherokee citizens according to Cherokee law prior to November 1, 1875, are entitled to enrollment and allotments of land as citizens of the Cherokee Nation.

    You are advised that to properly determine your right to enrollment as a citizen by intermarriage of the Cherokee Nation, it will be necessary for you to appear before the Commissioner for the purpose of giving testimony as to the date of your marriage and whether or not your husband, by reason of your marriage to whom you claim the right to enrollment as a citizen by intermarriage of the Cherokee Nation, was a recognized Cherokee citizen at the time of your marriage to him.

    You are therefore directed to appear before the Commissioner at Muskogee, Indian Territory, at 9 o'clock A. M., on Thursday, January 3, 1907, and give testimony as above indicated.

                    Respectfully,
                                                Wm O. Beall

H.J.C.   Acting Commissioner.

◇◇◇◇◇

Cherokee 534

                                        Muskogee, Indian Territory, January 23, 1907.

W. W. Hastings,
    Attorney for the Cherokee Nation,
        Muskogee, Indian Territory.

Dear Sir:

    There is enclosed herewith copy of the decision of the Commissioner to the Five Civilized Tribes, dated January 23, 1907, granting the application for the enrollment of Anna E. Dannenberg as a citizen by intermarriage of the Cherokee Nation.

Cherokee Intermarried White 1906
Volume II

Respectfully,

Enc I-66
RPI
                Commissioner.

◇◇◇◇◇

Cherokee 534   W.W. HASTINGS.   OFFICE OF   H.M. VANCE.
        ATTORNEY.   SECRETARY.

Attorney for the Cherokee Nation,
MUSKOGEE, I. T.

January 23, 1907.

The Commissioner to the Five Civilized Tribes,
  Muskogee, Indian Territory.

Sir:

  Receipt is acknowledged of the testimony and of your decision enrolling Anna E. Dannenberg as a citizen by intermarriage of the Cherokee Nation. Time for protesting said decision is waived and I consent that said person may be placed upon the schedule immediately.

           Respectfully,
           W. W. Hastings
           Attorneu[sic] for the Cherokee Nation

◇◇◇◇◇

REFER IN REPLY TO THE FOLLOWING:	
Cherokee 534	DEPARTMENT OF THE INTERIOR, COMMISSIONER TO THE FIVE CIVILIZED TRIBES.

         Muskogee, Indian Territory, January 23, 1907.

Anna E. Dannenberg,
  Salina, Indian Territory.

Dear Madam:

  There is enclosed herewith copy of the decision of the Commissioner to the Five Civilized Tribes, dated January 23, 1907, granting the application for your enrollment as a citizen by intermarriage of the Cherokee Nation.

  You will be advised when your name has been placed upon a schedule of citizens of the Cherokee Nation and approved by the Secretary of the Interior.

Cherokee Intermarried White 1906
Volume II

Respectfully,
Tams Bixby
Commissioner.

Enc I-85
RPI

Cher IW 60
Trans from Cher 558 3-15-07

◇◇◇◇◇◇

C.E.W.

DEPARTMENT OF THE INTERIOR,

COMMISSIONER TO THE FIVE CIVILIZED TRIBES.

In the matter of the application for the enrollment of

MATTIE J. DANNENBERG

as a citizen by intermarriage of the Cherokee Nation.

CHEROKEE 558.

◇◇◇◇◇◇

Department of the Interior,
Commission to the Five Civilized Tribes,
Stilwell, I. T., July 24, 1900.

In the matter of the application of Lewis L. Dannenberg for the enrollment of himself and wife as Cherokee citizens; being sworn and examined by Commissioner Needles he testifies as follows:

Q What is your name? A Lewis L. Dannenberg.
Q What is your age? A Forty-seven.
Q What is your post-office? A Stilwell.
Q What district do you live in? A Flint.
Q How long have you lived in Flint District? A About thirty years I guess.
Q Are you a Cherokee? A Yes sir.
Q You make application as a Cherokee by blood? A Yes sir.
Q Is your father living? A No sir.
Q Did he die before 1880? A Yes sir.

Cherokee Intermarried White 1906
Volume II

Q Is your mother living? A Yes sir.
Q Are you upon the authenticated roll of 1880? A Yes sir.
    Note: 1880 roll examined, page 363, #484, L.L. Dannenberg, Flint District. 1896 roll examined, page 659, #568, Lrwis[sic] L. Dannenberg, Fling District.
Q What proportion of Cherokee blood do you claim? A About one eighth I guess.
Q Are you married? A Yes sir.
Q What is your wife's name? A Mattie J.
Q Is she a Cherokee by blood[sic] A No sir.
Q What was her name before you married her? A Mattie Martin.
Q What is the date of your marriage? A 1874.
    Note: 1880 roll examined for applicant's wife: page 363, #485, M. J. Dannenberg. 1896 roll, page 712, #23, Martha J. Dannenberg.
Q Have you any children? A One.
Q You have none under twenty-one? A No sir.
Q You just want to enroll yourself and wife? A Yes sir.
Q She is living? A Yes sir.

    Com'r Needles: The name of Lewis L. Dannenberg appearing up on the authenticated roll of 1880 as well as the census roll of 1896, and his wife, Mattie J., appearing upon the authenticated roll of 1880 as well as the roll of 1896, identified according to page and number as specified in the testimony given, they are ordered enrolled as Cherokees by blood, and their names will be placed upon the rolls now being made by this Commission.

    M. D. Green, being first duly sworn, states that as stenographer to the Commission to the Five Civilized Tribes he reported the foregoing case and that the above is a full true and complete transcript of his stenographic notes in said case.

                                                                  MD Green

Subscribed and sworn to before me this 25th day of July 1900.

                                                  TB Needles
                                                  Commissioner.

Cherokee Intermarried White 1906
Volume II

JOR.
Cher. 558.

Department of the Interior.
Commission to the Five Civilized Tribes.
Tahlequah, I. T., October 20, 1902.

SUPPLEMENTAL TESTIMONY in the matter of the application for the enrollment of MATTIE J. DANNENBERG as a citizen by intermarriage of the Cherokee Nation.

MATTIE J. DANNENBERG, being first duly sworn, and being examined, testified as follows:

BY COMMISSION: What is your name? A Mattie J. Dannenberg.
Q How old are you? A Fifty.
Q What is your post office address? A Stilwell.
Q You are a white woman, are you? A Yes sir.
Q Has application been made to this Commission for your enrollment as a citizen by intermarriage of the Cherokee Nation? A Yes sir, when the Dawes Commission was at Stilwell two years ago.
Q What is the full name of your husband? A Lewis L. Dannenberg.
Q Is he living? A Yes sir, here he sists[sic].
Q Is he a Cherokee by blood? A Yes sir.
Q When were you and he married? A Married in 1874, September 27th
Q Do you claim your right to enrollment by reason of your marriage to him? A Yes sir.
Q Does your name appear upon the roll of 1880? A Yes sir.
Q Have you and he lived together continuously since that time? A Yes sir.
Q Were you living together on the 1st day of September, 1902? A Yes sir.
Q Never been separated at all? A No sir.
Q Were you ever married before you married him? A No sir.
Q Was he ever married before he married you? A No sir.
Q You are his first wife and he is your first husband? A Yes sir.
Q Have you resided in the Cherokee Nation continuously since your marriage?
A Always.
Q Has he resided here continuously since that time? A Yes sir.
Q You have no minor children? A No sir.

> This testimony will be filed with and made a part of the record in the matter of the application for the enrollment of Mattie J. Dannenberg as a citizen by intermarriage of the Cherokee Nation, Cherokee straight card field No. 558.

Wm. Hutchinson, being first duly sworn, states that as stenographer to the Commission to the Five Civilized Tribes he correctly recorded the testimony and proceedings in this

Cherokee Intermarried White 1906
Volume II

case, and that the foregoing is a true and complete transcript of his stenographic notes thereof.

Wm. Hutchinson

Subscribed and sworn to before me this 31st day of October, 1902.

John O Rosson
Notary Public.

◇◇◇◇◇

Cherokee No. 588

DEPARTMENT OF THE INTERIOR,
COMMISSIONER TO THE FIVE CIVILIZED TRIBES.
Muskogee, Indian Ter., January 2, 1907.

In the matter of the application for the enrollment of Mattie J. Dannenberg as a citizen by intermarriage of the Cherokee Nation.

Mattie J. Dannenberg being first duly sworn by Frances R. Lane, Notary Public for the Western District, Indian Territory, testified as follows:

By the Commissioner:
Q What is your name? A Mattie J. Dannenberg.
Q How old are you? A 54 years old.
Q What is your postoffice address? A Stilwell, I. T.
Q You xlaim[sic] to be an intermarried citizen of the Cherokee Nation? A Yes sir.
Q Through whom do you claim your right as such? A Louis Dannenberg.
Q When were you married to Louis Dannenberg? A I was married December 27, 1874.
Q Where were you married to him? A I was married in Flint District at his brothers[sic] in the Cherokee Nation.
Q Did you get a license? A No, I was married under Cherokee law.
Q Who married you? A Minister of the gospel, Dr. Ferguson.
Q Can you get a certificate from Dr. Ferguson? A No, he is dead.
Q How long has he been dead? A His daughter is in the other room; I can't tell you.
Q Was she present? A Yes, I was married in her house.
Q Had you ever been married prior to your marriage to Louis Dannenberg? A No sir.
Q Had he ever been married prior to his marriage to you? A No sir.
Q Have you lived together continuously as man and wife in the Cherokee nation[sic] ever since the date of your marriage in 1874? A Yes sir.
Q And you are still living together as husand[sic] and wife? A Yes sir.
Q Was your husband a citizen of the Cherokee Nation at the time of your marriage in 1874? A Yes sir.
Q Did he vote in the Cherokee elections at that time? A Yes sir.
Q And is on the 1880 roll? A Yes, I suppose he is.

Cherokee Intermarried White 1906
Volume II

The applicant is identified on the 1880 Cherokee roll opposite No. 485.
Her husband through whom she claims her right to enrollment is identified on said roll opposite No. 484, and also on the final roll of citizens by blood of the Cherokee Nation opposite No. 1644.

  Annie Danninberg[sic], being first duly sworn by Frances R. Lane, a Notary Public for the Western District of Indian Territory, testified as follows:

By the Commissioner:
Q What is your name? A Annie Dannenberg.
Q Are you any relation to Mattie J. Dannenberg? A Yes sir.
Q What relation? A Sister-in-law.
Q Were you present at the time Mattie J. Dannenberg was married to Louis Dannenberg? A I was.
Q When was she married to Louis Dannenberg? A In 1874.
Q What time of the year in 1874? A December 27th.
Q Where was she married to Louis Dannenberg? A She was married at my house in Flint District.
Q Who married her? A My father, Dr. T. R. Ferguson.
Witness excused.

Frances R. Lane, upon oath, states that as stenographer to the commissioner[sic] to the Five Civilized Tribes she reported the testimony in the above entitled cause and that the foregoing is a true and correct transcript of her stenographic notes thereof.

Frances R Lane

Subscribed and sworn to before me this 4th day of January, 1907.

Edward Merrick
Notary Public.

◇◇◇◇◇

Cherokee Intermarried White 1906
Volume II

C.E.W. Cherokee 558

DEPARTMENT OF THE INTERIOR,

COMMISSIONER TO THE FIVE CIVILIZED TRIBES.

In the matter of the application for the enrollment of Mattie J. Dannenberg, as a citizen by intermarriage of the Cherokee Nation.

D E C I S I O N

THE RECORDS OF THIS OFFICE SHOW: That at Stilwell, Indian Territory, July 24, 1900, application was received by the Commission to the Five Civilized Tribes for the enrollment of Mattie J. Dannenberg, as a citizen by intermarriage of the Cherokee Nation. Further proceedings in the matter of said application were had at Tahlequah, Indian Territory October 20, 1902, and at Muskogee, Indian Territory, January 2, 1907.

THE EVIDENCE IN THIS CASE SHOWS: That the applicant herein, Mattie J. Dannenberg, a white woman, was married in accordance with Cherokee law December 27, 1874, to one Lewis[sic] L. Dannenberg, who was at the time of said marriage a recognized citizen by blood of the Cherokee Nation, who is identified on the Cherokee authenticated tribal roll of 1880, Flint District, page 363 number 484, as a native Cherokee, and whose name appears upon the approved partial roll of citizens by blood of the Cherokee Nation, opposite number 1644, that since said marriage the said Mattie J. Dannenberg and Lewis L. Dannenberg have resided together as husband and wife and have continuously lived in the Cherokee Nation. Said Mattie J. Dannenberg is identified on the Cherokee authenticated tribal roll of 1880, and the Cherokee census roll of 1896 as an intermarried citizen of the Cherokee Nation.

IT IS, THEREFORE, ORDERED AND ADJUDGED: That in accordance with the decision of the Supreme Court of the United States, dated November 5, 1906, in the cases of Daniel Red Bird et al., vs. the United States, Nos. 125, 126, 127 and 128, the said applicant Mattie J. Dannenberg is entitled, under the provision of Section 21 of the Act of Congress approved June 28, 1898, (30 Stat., 495), to enrollment, as a citizen by intermarriage of the Cherokee Nation, and her application for enrollment as such is accordingly granted.

Tams Bixby
Commissioner.

Dated at Muskogee, Indian Territory,
this JAN 23 1907

Cherokee Intermarried White 1906
Volume II

Cherokee
558.

Muskogee, Indian Territory, December 21, 1906.

Mattie J. Dannenberg,
    Stilwell, Indian Territory.

Dear Sir:

    November 6, 1906, the United States Supreme Court held that white persons who intermarried with Cherokee citizens according to Cherokee law prior to November 1, 1875, are entitled to enrollment and allotments of land as citizens of the Cherokee Nation.

    You are advised that to properly determine your right to enrollment as a citizen by intermarriage of the Cherokee Nation, it will be necessary for you to appear before the Commissioner for the purpose of giving testimony as to the date of your marriage and whether or not your husband, by reason of your marriage to whom you claim the right to enrollment as a citizen by intermarriage of the Cherokee Nation, was a recognized Cherokee citizen at the time of your marriage to him.

    You are therefore directed to appear before the Commissioner at Muskogee, Indian Territory, at 9 o'clock A. M., on Thursday, January 3, 1907, and give testimony as above indicated.

                  Respectfully,

H.J.C.   Acting Commissioner.

⋄⋄⋄⋄⋄

Cherokee 558

Muskogee, Indian Territory, January 23, 1907.

W. W. Hastings,
    Attorney for the Cherokee Nation,
        Muskogee, Indian Territory.

Dear Sir:

    There is enclosed herewith a copy of the decision of the Commissioner to the Five Civilized Tribes, dated January 23, 1907, granting the application for the enrollment of Mattie J. Dannenberg as a citizen by intermarriage of the Cherokee Nation.

                  Respectfully,

Encl. H-61   Commissioner.
JMH

Cherokee Intermarried White 1906
Volume II

◇◇◇◇◇

Cherokee 558

W.W. HASTINGS.
ATTORNEY.

OFFICE OF

H.M. VANCE.
SECRETARY.

Attorney for the Cherokee Nation,
MUSKOGEE, I. T.

January 23, 1907.

The Commissioner to the Five Civilized Tribes,
           Muskogee, Indian Territory.

Sir:

     Receipt is acknowledged of the testimony and of your decision enrolling Mattie J. Dannenberg as a citizen by intermarriage of the Cherokee Nation. Time for protesting said decision is waived, and I consent that said person may be placed upon the schedule immediately.

                           Respectfully,
                           W. W. Hastings
                           Attorney for the Cherokee Nation.

◇◇◇◇◇

Cherokee 558

                      Muskogee, Indian Territory, January 23, 1907.

Mattie J. Dannenberg,
          Stilwell, Indian Territory.

Dear Madam:

     There is enclosed herewith a copy of the decision of the Commissioner to the Five Civilized Tribes, dated January 23, 1907, granting your application for enrollment as a citizen by intermarriage of the Cherokee Nation.

     You will be advised when your name has been placed upon a schedule of citizens of the Cherokee Nation and approved by the Secretary of the Interior.

                           Respectfully,

Encl. H-83   Commissioner.
JJH

Cherokee Intermarried White 1906
Volume II

Cher IW 61
Trans from Cher 718 3-15-07

C.E.W.

DEPARTMENT OF THE INTERIOR,

COMMISSIONER TO THE FIVE CIVILIZED TRIBES.

In the matter of the application for the enrollment of

JANE RIDER

As a citizen by intermarriage of the Cherokee Nation.

CHEROKEE No. 718.

DEPARTMENT OF THE INTERIOR,
COMMISSION TO THE FIVE CIVILIZED TRIBES,
STILWELL, IT., JULY 26, 1900.

In the matter of the application of Charles A. Rider et als., for enrollment as citizens of the Cherokee Nation, said Rider being sworn by Commissioner Needles, testified:

Q What is your name? A Charles A. Rider.
Q Your age? A 70.
Q Your postoffice. A Evansville, Ark.
Q Have you been recognized by the Cherokee tribal authorities as a citizen of the Cherokee Nation? A Yes.
Q Have you ever been enrolled by the Cherokee tribal authorities as a citizen of the Cherokee Nation? A I guess so.
Q What district do you live in? A Goingsnake.
Q How long have you lived there? A 65 or 66 years.
Q What is the name of your father? A Austin.
Q Is he living? A No sir.
Q Was his name on any of the rolls of the Cherokee Nation? A Not that I know of.
Q What's the name of your mother? A Polly.
Q Is she living? A No sir.
Q Is her name upon the rolls of the Cherokee Nation? A Not that I know of.
Q Does you name appear upon the '80 roll? A I guess so.
       On '80 roll, page 467, number 1427 as Guss;
       On '96 roll, page 780, number 1673 as Charles A. Rider.

Cherokee Intermarried White 1906
Volume II

  On '94 roll, page 703, number 1842 as Augustus C. Rider.
Q Are you married? A Yes.
Q Is your wife living? A Yes.
Q What is her name? A Jane.
Q When were you married to her? A '70.
Q Are you a Cherokee by blood? A Yes.
Q Is your wife a Cherokee by blood? A No sir.
  On '80 roll, page 467, number 1428;
   On '96 roll, page 827, number 157.
Q Have you any children under 21 years of age? A Yes.
Q What proportion of Cherokee blood do you claim? A About 1/16.
Q Are you married? A Yes.
Q Under what law? A Cherokee law.
Q What's the name of your children under 21 years of age? A Elizabeth, 18 years old.
  On '96 roll, page 780, number 1677;
  On '94 roll, page 703, number 1846.
Q What's the next one? A Myrtle May, 16 years old.
  On '96 roll, page 780, number 1678 as Myrta.
  On '94 roll, page 703, number 1847.
Q Next one? A Viola, 13 years old.
  On '96 roll, page 780, number 1679
  On '94 roll, page 703, number 1843 as Violet.
Q Are these children at home with you? A Yes.

  The name of Charles A. Rider appearing upon the authenticated roll of '80 as well as the census roll of '96 and the pay-roll of '94, and his children, Elizabeth, Myrtle May and Viola appearing upon the census roll of '96 and the pay-roll of '94, are ordered listed for enrollment by this Commission as Cherokees by blood, with the exception of his wife Jane, who will be enrolled as a citizen by marriage.

  Brown McDonald, being duly sworn, says as Stenographer to the Commission to the Five Civilized Tribes, he reported in full the testimony of the above named witness, and that the foregoing is a full, true and correct transcript of his notes.

Brown McDonald

Sworn to and subscribed before me this 2nd day of August, 1900, at Bunch, I.T.

TB Needles
Commissioner.

Cherokee Intermarried White 1906
Volume II

JOR.
Cher. 718.

Department of the Interior.
Commission to the Five Civilized Tribes.
Tahlequah, I.T., October 13, 1902.

SUPPLEMENTAL TESTIMONY AND PROCEEDINGS in the matter of the application for the enrollment of JANE RIDER as a citizen by intermarriage of the Cherokee Nation.

JANE RIDER, being first duly sworn, and being examined, testified[sic] as follows:

BY COMMISSION: What is your name? A Jane Rder[sic].
Q How old are you? A Fifty-five.
Q What is your post office address? A Evansville, Arkansas.
Q You are a white woman, are you? A Yes sir.
Q Has application heretofore been made to this Commission for your enrollment as a citizen by intermarriage of the Cherokee Nation? A No sir, we only enrolled. This is my first application here.
Q Application has been made before this? A Yes sir.
Q What is the name of your husband? A Charles Augustus Rider.
Q Is he living? A No sir, he has died since we enrolled.
Q How long has he been dead? A The 24th of last December.
Q Was he a Cherokee by blood? A Yes sir.
Q Do you claim your right to enrollment by reason of your marriage to him? A Yes sir.
Q When were you and he married? A In 1870, the 10th of November.
Q At the time application was made to the Commission for your enrollment, was satisfactory proof made of your marriage to him? A Yes sir.
Q Were you ever married before you married him? A Yes sir.
Q What was the name of your first husband? A Harvey D. Forrest, is the way he signs his name. I was his widow when I married Rider.
Q Was he living when you married your husband Charles A. Rder[sic]? A No sir.
Q Is that the only time you were ever married before? A Yes sir.
Q Was Charles A. Rider married before? A Yes sir.
Q What was the name of his wife? A Mary Bigby.
Q Was she living when you and Charles A. Rider were married.[sic]
A No sir, been dead ten years.
Q Was that the only time he was married before he married you? A Yes sir.
Q You are his second wife and he is your second husband? A Yes sir.
Q Did you and he live together continuously until the time of his death? A Yes sir.
Q Never been separated at all? A No sir.
Q Have you married since he died? A No sir.
Q Have you resided in the Cherokee Nation continuously since you and he were married? A Yes sir, for thirty-two years.

Cherokee Intermarried White 1906
Volume II

Q Did he reside in the Cherokee Nation continuously until the time of his death?
A Yes sir.
Q You have how many children that application was made for? A Seven
Q How many minor children that application was made for? A I had only two that were under age?[sic] Myrtle and Viola.
Q Was Elizabeth enrolled with your family? A Yes sir, but she married since.
Q Are all three of those children living at this time? A Yes sir, they are living.

    This testimony will be filed with and made a part of the record in the matter of the application for the enrollment of Jane Rider as a citizen by intermarriage of the Cherokee Nation, Cherokee straight card field No. 718.

Wm. Hutchinson, being first duly sworn, states that as stenographer to the Commission to the Five Civilized Tribes he correctly recorded the testimony and proceedings in this case, and that the foregoing is a true and complete transcript of the stenographic notes thereof.

                                              Wm Hutchinson

Subscribed and sworn to before me this 20th day of October, 1902.

                                                John O Rosson
                                                Notary Public.

◇◇◇◇◇

MFM

                                                Cherokee 718.

                    Department of the Interior,
            Commission to the Five Civilized Tribes,
                    Cherokee Land Office,
               Tahlequah, I.T., October 19, 1904.

    In the matter of the application of CHARLES A. RIDER for the enrollment of himself, his wife, JANE, and daughters, MYRTLE M. and VIOLA RIDER and ELIZABETH PALOBE[sic], nee Rider, as citizens by blood of the Cherokee Nation.

                    SUPPLEMENTAL TESTIMONY.

    STEVE PALONE, being duly sworn and examined by the Commission, testified as follows:

Q What is your name? A Steve Palone.

Cherokee Intermarried White 1906
Volume II

Q How old are you? A I'll be 25 the 30th of November.
Q What is your postoffice address? A Dutch Mills.
Q Are you a citizen of the Cherokee Nation? A Yes.
Q Are you married? A Yes.
Q When were you married? A I forget just when I was married; been married going on 3 years.
Q You were married in 1902? A Yes, I think that's when it was.
Q Do you remember what time of year it was? A I don't know exactly; right after New Years 2 or 3 weeks.
Q That would be in January, 1902? A Yes.
Q What is the name of your wife? A Elizabeth Rider she was.
Q She's a citizen of the Cherokee Nation? A Yes.
Q Are you and she living together now? A Yes.

Mabel F. Maxwell, being duly sworn, states that, as stenographer to the Commission to the Five Civilized Tribes, she correctly recorded the supplemental testimony in this case, and that the above and foregoing is an accurate and complete transcript of her stenographic notes thereof.

Mabel F. Maxwell

Subscribed and sworn to before me
this 21st day of October, 1904.

(Name Illegible)
Notary Public.

MFM

◇◇◇◇◇◇

Cherokee No. <u>718</u>

DEPARTMENT OF THE INTERIOR,
COMMISSIONER TO THE FIVE CIVILIZED TRIBES.
Muskogee, I. T., January 2, 1907.

In the matter of the application for the enrollment of Jane Rider as a citizen by intermarriage of the Cherokee Nation.

Jane Rider, being first duly sworn by Frances R. Lane, a Notary Public for the Western District Indian Territory, testified as follows:

By the Commissioner:
Q What is your name? A Jane Rider.
Q How old are you? A Sixty years old.
Q What is your postoffice address? A Evansville, Kan.
Q You claim to be an intermarried citizen of the Cherokee Nation? A Yes sir.

Cherokee Intermarried White 1906
Volume II

Q Through whom do you claim? A Charles Augustus Rider.
Q When were you married to Charles A. Rider? A The 10th of November, 1870.
Q Where were you married to him? A We were married in Going Snake District at the parson's house. We was married by a preacher.
Q What was his name? A Michael Gormley.
Q Did he give you a certificate? A No, I don't know whether he gave my husband on or not.
Q Were you ever married before you were married to him? A Yes, in Georgia.
Q Who did you marry there? A Forrest.
Q Was he living or dead at the time you married Chas. A. Rider? A Dead.
Q Was Charles A. Rider ever married before he married you? A Yes sir.
Q Who to? A Mary Bigby.
Q Was she living at the time you were married to him? A No, she was dead.
Q Neither one of you had any husband or wife at the time you were married? A No sir.
Q How long did you live with Charles A. Rider?[sic] after you married him? A Thirty-one years. He died in 1901.
Q Have you married since his death? A No sir.
Q Have you lived in the Cherokee nation[sic] all that time? A Yes, I have never lived anywhere else.
Q Was your husband a citizen of the Cherokee Nation at the time you were married in 1870? A Yes sir.
Q And voted at the Cherokee elections? A Yes, he was a recognized Cherokee.
Q Is there anyone here today besides yourself that knows that you were married to Charles A. Rider in 1870? A There sits Mr. Bigsby[sic].
Q Was he present? A No, he was not present, but he knows that I was married.

The applicant is identified on the 1880 Cherokee roll opposite No. 1428. Her husband, through whom she claims her right to enrollment is identified on said roll opposite No. 1429. It appears from the census card record that he is now dead.

Thomas W. Bigby, being first duly sworn by Frances R. Lane, a Notary Public for the Western District of Indian Territory, testified as follows:
Q What is your name? A Thomas W. Bigby.
Q Do you know Jane Rider? A Yes sir.
Q Did you know Charles A. Rider in his lifetime? A Yes sir.
Q Do you know when he was married? A No, I don't. I can't say just exactly what time it was. Sometime in the early part of 1870.
Q You know that they were married? A Yes sir.
Q Did you know them at that time? A Yes, I knew Charles A. Rider ever since he was born.
Q You know that she and Charles A. Rider held themselves out as man and wife from the early part of 1870 up to the time of his death.[sic] A Yes sir.

Witness excused.

Cherokee Intermarried White 1906
Volume II

Frances R. Lane upon oath states that as stenographer to the Commissioner to the Five Civilized Tribes she reported the testimony in the above entitled cause and that the foregoing is an accurate transcript of her stenographic notes thereof.

Frances R Lane

Subscribed and sworn to before me this January 4, 1906.

Edward Merrick
Notary Public.

◇◇◇◇◇◇

C.E.W.　　　　　　　　　　　　　　　　　　　　　　　　　　　　　Cherokee 718.

DEPARTMENT OF THE INTERIOR,

COMMISSIONER TO THE FIVE CIVILIZED TRIBES.

In the matter of the application for the enrollment of JANE RIDER as a citizen by intermarriage of the Cherokee Nation.

D E C I S I O N

THE RECORDS OF THIS OFFICE SHOW: That at Stillwell[sic], Indian Territory, July 26th, 1900, application was received by the Commission to the Five Civilized Tribes for the enrollment of Jane Rider as a citizen by intermarriage of the Cherokee Nation. Further proceedings in the matter of said application were had at Tahlequah, Indian Territory, October 13th, 1902, October 19th, 1904 and January 2nd, 1907.

THE EVIDENCE IN THIS CASE SHOWS: That the applicant herein, Jane Rider, a white woman, married November 10th, 1870, one Charles A. Rider, since deceased, who was at the time of said marriage a recognized citizen by blood of the Cherokee Nation, and who is identified on the Cherokee authenticated tribal roll of 1880, Going Snake District, Page 467 No. 1427, as a native Cherokee; that from the time of said marriage the said Charles A. Rider and Jane Rider resided together as husband and wife and continuously lived in the Cherokee Nation up to the time of his death, which occurred in the year 1901; and that said Jane Rider has remained unmarried and continuously lived in the Cherokee Nation since the death of Charles A. Rider. Said Jane Rider is identified on the Cherokee authenticated tribal roll of 1880 and the Cherokee census roll of 1896 as an intermarried citizen of the Cherokee Nation.

IT IS, THEREFORE, ORDERED AND ADJUDGED: That in accordance with the decision of the Supreme Court of the United States dated November 5th, 1906, in the cases of Daniel Red Bird et al. vs. the United States, Nos. 125, 126, 127 and 128, the said applicant, Jane Rider is entitled, under the provisions of Section Twenty-one of the Act of

Cherokee Intermarried White 1906
Volume II

Congress approved June 28th, 1898 (30 Stats. 495), to enrollment as a citizen by intermarriage of the Cherokee Nation, and her application for enrollment as such is accordingly granted.

             Tams Bixby
                Commissioner.

Dated at Muskogee, Indian Territory,
this   JAN 23 1907

◇◇◇◇◇

Cherokee 718

        Muskogee, Indian Territory, December 22, 1906.

Jane Rider,
  Oak Grove, Indian Territory.

Dear Madam:

  November 6, 1906, the United States Supreme Court held that white persons who intermarried with Cherokee citizens according to Cherokee law prior to November 1, 1875, are entitled to enrollment and allotments of land as citizens of the Cherokee Nation.

  You are advised that to properly determine your right to enrollment as a citizen by intermarriage of the Cherokee Nation, it will be necessary for you to appear before the Commissioner for the purpose of giving testimony as to the date of your marriage and whether or not your husband, by reason of your marriage to whom you claim the right to enrollment as a citizen by intermarriage of the Cherokee Nation, was a recognized Cherokee citizen at the time of your marriage to him.

  You are therefore directed to appear before the Commissioner at Muskogee, Indian Territory, at 9 o'clock A. M., on Thursday, January 3, 1907, and give testimony as above indicated.

             Respectfully,

H.J.C.   Acting Commissioner.

◇◇◇◇◇

Cherokee Intermarried White 1906
Volume II

Cherokee 718

Muskogee, Indian Territory, January 23, 1907.

W. W. Hastings,
    Attorney for the Cherokee Nation,
        Muskogee, Indian Territory.

Dear Sir:

    There is enclosed herewith a copy of the decision of the Commissioner to the Five Civilized Tribes, dated January 23, 1907, granting the application for the enrollment of Jane Rider as a citizen by intermarriage of the Cherokee Nation.

        Respectfully,

Encl. H-62   Commissioner.
JMH

◇◇◇◇◇◇

Cherokee 718   W.W. HASTINGS.   OFFICE OF   H.M. VANCE.
                    ATTORNEY.   SECRETARY.

Attorney for the Cherokee Nation,
MUSKOGEE, I. T.

                                                          January 23, 1907.

The Commissioner to the Five Civilized Tribes,
    Muskogee, Indian Territory.

Sir:

    Receipt is acknowledged of the testimony and of your decision enrolling Jane Rider as a citizen by intermarriage of the Cherokee Nation. Time for protesting said decision is waived and I consent that said person may be placed upon the schedule immediately.

                Respectfully,
                      W. W. Hastings
                      Attorney for Cherokee Nation.

◇◇◇◇◇◇

Cherokee Intermarried White 1906
Volume II

Cherokee 718

Muskogee, Indian Territory, January 23, 1907.

Jane Rider,
    Oak Grove, Indian Territory.

Dear Madam:

    There is enclosed herewith a copy of the decision of the Commissioner to the Five Civilized Tribes, dated January 23, 1907, granting the application for your enrollment as a citizen by intermarriage of the Cherokee Nation.

    You will be advised when your name has been placed upon a schedule of citizens of the Cherokee Nation and approved by the Secretary of the Interior.

                      Respectfully,

Encl. H-84   Commissioner.
JMH

Cher IW 62
Trans from Cher 811 3-15-07

◇◇◇◇◇

                                                          F.R.

DEPARTMENT OF THE INTERIOR,
COMMISSIONER TO THE FIVE CIVILIZED TRIBES.

In the matter of the application for the enrollment of

SARAH L. PRICE

as a citizen by intermarriage of the Cherokee Nation.

CHEROKEE 811.

◇◇◇◇◇

Cherokee Intermarried White 1906
Volume II

Department of the Interior,
Commission to the Five Civilized Tribes,
Bunch, I. T., July 30, 1900.

In the matter of the application of Sarah L. Price et al for enrollment as Cherokee citizens; being sworn and examined by Commissioner Needles she testifies as follows:

Q What is your name? A Sarah L. Price.
Q What is your age? A Sixty-three.
Q What is your post-office? A Evansville, Arkansas.
Q Have you ever been recognized by the Tribal authorities of the Cherokee Nation as a citizen? A Yes sir.
Q Does your name appear upon the rolls of the Cherokee Nation? A Yes sir.
Q What district do you live in? A Flint.
Q How long have you lived there? A Been living in the Nation thirty years, come here in 1870.
Q Been living in the Nation continuously? A Yes sir, never have been out of the Nation.
Q What is the name of your father? A Martin Williams. He died during the War.
Q What is your mother's name? A Frances Williams.
Q Is she living? A No sir, they were white, I am a white woman.
Q Does your name appear upon the 1880 roll? A Yes sir, and all my family except one daughter and grand-children.
Q Your name appear[sic] upon the 1896 rolls? A Yes sir.
Q What proportion of Cherokee blood do you claim to have? [sic] My husband claimed to have one-eighth.
Q Is your husband living? A No sir, he has been dead three years.
Q What was his name? A Samuel J. Price.
    Note: 1880 roll, page 384, #1003, as Joseph Price, Flint District.
Q Have you a marriage license or certificate? A We married back in the Old Nation.
Q Where were you living at the time of your marriage, in the Old Nation? A Yes sir, my husband lived here in the Nation before we were married, he was brought on here when he was a child, his mother and father brought him on here to the Nation when he was seven years old, and after he was twenty-one, he went back to the Old Nation to see his grand-father, and we were married while he was there.
Q Have you any children under age? A I have one daughter under twenty years old, and I have two grand-children that I am raising.
Q What is your daughter's name? A Ophelia B. Stephens, twenty years old.
Q Is her name upon the roll of 1880? A No sir, she was born in 1881.
Q What is the name of her husband? A James Stephens.
Q Was he a Cherokee? A No sir.
Q Is he living? A No sir, he is dead, he died last fall.
Q When was she married? A She was married in September, it will be two years this coming September.
    Note: 1896 roll, page 689, #1337, Ophelia B. Price, Flint District. 1894 roll, page 575, #1389, as Ophelia B. Price, Flint District. 1880 roll examined for applicant: Page

Cherokee Intermarried White 1906
Volume II

384, #1004, as S.L. Price, Flint District. 1896 roll, page 715 #62, as Sarah L. Price, Flint District.
Q You say you have some grand-children? A Yes sir.
Q Whose children are they? A Lewis C. Powhatan's.
Q Are they living with you? A Yes sir, I have had them ever since their mother died.
Q Is their father dead? A No sir, he is living, he married again in three or four months after their mother died.
Q Wont[sic] he enroll these children? A He didn't enroll them before. He is a white man and married a white woman.
Q What are the names of these children? A Norma P. Powhatan, she is eleven years old. Cordelia A. Powhatan, she is nine years old. Sarah L., she is seven.
Q What is the name of the mother of these children? A Sarrah F. E. Price before she was married.
Q She was your daughter? A Yes sir.
Q She is now dead? A She is dead.
Q These children are alive and living with you? A Yes sir, they are all alive and I have had them ever since her mother died, she died at my house.
     Note: 1880 roll, page 384, #1005, S. F. E. Price, Flint District.
Q You didn't draw the Strip money for them? A Their father drawed it.
     1896 roll: page 689, #1338, as Norma P. Powhatten (Delaware) Flint District. 1894 roll, page 982, #1045, as Norma E. Powhatton, Sequoyah District 1896 roll, page 689, #1339, as Cordella A. Powhatten, Flint District. 1894 roll, page 982, #1046, as Cordie A. Powhatton, Sequoyah District. 1896 roll, page 689, #1340, Sarah L. Powhatten, Flint District. 1894 roll, page 982, #1047, as Sarah L. Powhatton, Sequoyah District.
Q That is all you want to enroll is it? A Yes sir.
Q Are these children alive and living with you? A Yes sir.
Q They have been living with you since their mother died, since they were infants? A Yes sir, the youngest one was seven months old when their mother died, their father told me when their mother died that he would give me the children, and he would never take them away from me unless I wanted to give them up.

     Com'r Needles: The name of Sarah L. Price appearing upon the authenticated roll of 1880, as well as the census roll of 1896 and the name of her daughter, Ophelia V. Stephens, appearing upon the census roll of 1896 and the pay roll of 1894, she being a widow, and the names of Sarah F. E. Price, daughter of Sarah L. Price, being found upon the authenticated roll of 1880, satisfactory proof beig[sic] made as to her death, and the names of the children of th[sic] said Sarah F. E. Price to-wit: Norma P. Powhatan Cordelia A. Powhatan and Sarah L. Powhatan being found upon the census roll of 1896 and the pay roll of 1894, and they being lineal descendants of the said Sarah F. E. Price, who name appears upon the authenticated roll of 1880, proof of residence having been made, as to Sarah L. Price and her daughter Ophelia B. Stephens and her grand-children, Norma P. Powhatan, Cordelia A. and Sarah L. Powhatan, they are all ordered listed for enrollment by this Commission as citizens of the Cherokee Nation, the said Sarah L. Price as a citizen by intermarriage and the others as citizens by blood.

--

Cherokee Intermarried White 1906
Volume II

M.D. Green, being first duly sworn, states that as stenographer to the Commissioner to the Five Civilized Tribes he reported the foregoing case and that the above and foregoing is a full true and complete transcript of his stenographic notes in said case.

MD Green

Subscribed and sworn to before me this 1st day of August, 1900.

TB Needles
Commissioner.

◇◇◇◇◇

JOR.
Cher. 811.

Department of the Interior.
Commission to the Five Civilized Tribes.
Tahlequah, I. T., October 7, 1902.

SUPPLEMENTAL TESTIMONY AND PROCEEDINGS in the matter of the application for the enrollment of SARAH L. PRICE as a citizen by intermarriage of the Cherokee Nation.

SARAH L. PRICE, being first duly sworn, and being examined, testified as follows:

BY COMMISSION: What is your name? A Sarah L. Price.
Q How old are you? A Sixty-four.
Q What is your post office address? A Evansville, Arkansas.
Q You are a white woman, are you? A Yes sir.
Q Have you heretofore made application to this Commission for enrollment as a citizen by intermarriage of the Cherokee Nation? A Yes sir.
Q What is the name of your husband? A Joseph Price.
Q Is he living? A No sir.
Q Was he a Cherokee by blood? A Yes sir.
Q Do you claim your right to enrollment by reason of your marriage to him? A Yes sir.
Q When were you and he married? A We were married back in the old Nation, in Alabama.
Q When did you and he come to this country? A We moved into the Nation here in 1870, and have been here ever since.
Q How long has Joe Price been dead? A It is four years along next month since he died.
Q Did you ad[sic] he live together continuously from the date of your marriage until the time of his death? A Yes sir.
Q Were you ever married before you married him? A No sir.
Q Was he ever married before he married you? A No sir.
Q You were his first wife and he was your first husband? A Yes sir.
Q Have you married since the date of his death? A No sir.

Cherokee Intermarried White 1906
Volume II

Q Have you resided in the Cherokee Nation continuously from the time you and he came here in 1870 until the present time? A Never been out of the Nation since we came here in 1870.
Q Have you resided here continuously during that time? A Yes sir.
Q Did Joe Price reside here in the Cherokee Nation continuously until the time of his death after he came here in 1870? A Yes sir. He came on here before him and me were married, and stayed here three or four years, then he went back down to Alabama where his people lived, and we were married, and it was a few years before we came back to the Nation. But in 1870 we came back to the Nation and have been here ever since.
Q Was he readmitted to citizenship at that time? A Yes sir, he was admitted to citizenship. They told us when we came that we would have to be married again, but the finally said he was a Cherokee and wuld[sic] not have to do it, but we was admitted to citizenship.
Q Was he always recognized as a citizen by blood of the Cherokee Nation? A Yes sir.
Q You have not lived with any other man as his wife since the date of the death of Joe Price? A No sir, and never expect to.

    This testimony will be filed with and made a part of the record in the matter of the application for the enrollment of Sarah L. Price as a citizen by intermarriage of the Cherokee Nation, Cherokee straight card field No. 811.

Wm. Hutchinson, being first duly sworn, states that as stenographer to the Commission to the Five Civilized Tribes he correctly recorded the testimony and proceedings in this case, and that the foregoing is a true and complete transcript of his stenographic notes thereof.

                                                                                      Wm Hutchinson

Subscribed and sworn to before me this 11th day of October, 1902.

                                                                               John O Rosson
                                                                               Notary Public.

Cherokee Intermarried White 1906
Volume II

Cherokee No. 811.

DEPARTMENT OF THE INTERIOR.
COMMISSIONER TO THE FIVE CIVILIZED TRIBES.

Muskogee, Indian Territory, January 3, 1907.

In the matter of the application for the enrollment of Sarah L. Price as a citizen by intermarriage of the Cherokee Nation.

Sarah L. Price, being first duly sworn and examined, testifies as follows:

BY THE COMMISSIONER:

Q What is your name? A Sarah L. Price.
Q How old are you? A 57.
Q What is your postoffice address? A Evansville, Arkansas.
Q Do you claim to be a citizen by intermarriage of the Cherokee Nation? A Yes sir.
Q Through whom do you claim your rights? A Samuel Joseph Price.
Q When were you married to Samuel Joseph price? A In 1856.
Q Where were you married to him? A Married back in the old Nation.
Q Where abouts? A In Alabama.
Q In 1856? A December 23, 1856.
Q Did you get any cirtificate[sic] or anything of that kind? A No, sir.
Q Who married you? A A man by the name of Keys - Andy Keys.
Q Minister of the gospel? A No, sir, justice of the Peace.
Q Were you married under a licence[sic] ? A No, sir, I don't think we had any licence[sic]; I think our marriage was recorded as well as I remember.
Q When did you move to the Cherokee Nation? A Well my husband was partly raised in here. After he became his own man he went back to the old Nation to visit his relatives there and while he was there we were married. We then came back and we got here in the spring of '70.
Q When was your husband first admitted to citizenship in the Cherokee Nation? A He was brought on here when the emigrants first came oh here.
Q Was your husband first admitted to citizenship after you came out her in '70?
A Yes, sir.
Q When? A It was the same year we came out here.
Q Did he get a decree of the Court? A Yes, sir.
Q Have you got that? A No, sir, That told us that we would have to marry over when we came here thinking I was a Cherokee. When they found out that he was they told him that we wouldn't have to do it. They told him he would have to apply for a citizenship and he did that.

Cherokee Intermarried White 1906
Volume II

Q Did your husband always vote in the Cherokee elections? A Yes, sir.
Q Do you know when he first voted? A No, sir, I couldn't say.
Q Do you know if he voted prior to '75? A Yes, sir.
Q Is there any body here to-day that knew your husband? A Lots of peoply[sic], I reckon.
Q Were you ever married before you married Samuel Joseph Price? A No, sir.
Q Was he ever married before he married you? A No, sir.
Q How long did you live together as husband and wife? A From '56 till '80. He died in 1880.
Q Have you married again since his death? A No, sir.
Q You lived together continuously in the Cherokee Nation since your removal here in 1870? A Yes, sir. I haven't had any of my effects out of it.

The applicant is identified on the 1880 Cherokee Roll opposite No. 1004.

Q Can you get any body here to-day that knew your husband in his life-time that can testify as to his admission to citizenship in 1870? A I don't know whether I could or not.

WITNESS EXCUSED.

J. H. Morris being first duly sworn and examined, testifies as follows:

BY THE COMMISSIONER:

Q What is your name? A J. H. Morris.
Q How old are you? A About 51 years old.
Q What is your postoffice address? A Stillwell[sic], Indian Territory,.
Q Do you know Sarah L. Price? A Yes, sir.
Q Did you know her husband in his life-time? A Yes, sir.
Q What is his name? A Joseph Price.
Q When did you first get acquainted with Joseph Price? A Why it was when he first came to the County.
Q Are you a citizen of the Cherokee Nation? A Yes, sir.
Q Citizen by blood? A Yes, sir.
Q Was he recognized as a citizen by blood of the Cherokee Nation the Cherokee Nation? A Yes, sir, I suppose so. He voted there at the same precinct that I voted at.
Q When was the first time he ever voted in the Cherokee Nation, do you know? A No, sir, I don't.
Q Did he vote at the first election that was held after he moved out here? A I don't know whether he did or not.
Q Can you remember about the year the first time you ever saw him at a voting precinct? A No, sir.
Q When did you first vote. Who was the first man you ever voted for in the Cherokee Nation? A It was Charles Thompson. He was running for Chief.
Q What year was that he was running for Chief? A I couldn't tell you. It has been quite a while ago.

Cherokee Intermarried White 1906
Volume II

Q Did Joseph Price vote at that election, or do you know? A I don't know.
Q Do you know whether he was admitted to citizenship when he came out here? A I don't know.
Q Did you ever his rights to citizenship questioned? A No, sir.
Q When did he die, do you know? A No, sir, I don't remember when he died.

WITNESS EXCUSED.

F. Elma Lane, upon oath, states that she reported the proceedings in the above entitled cause and that the foregoing is a true and correct transcript of her stenographic notes taken therein.

F. Elma Lane

Subscribed and sworn to before me this 4th day of January, 1907.

Chas E Webster
Notary Public.

◇◇◇◇◇

F.R.   Cherokee 811.

DEPARTMENT OF THE INTERIOR,
COMMISSIONER TO THE FIVE CIVILIZED TRIBES.

In the matter of the application for the enrollment of Sarah L. Price as a citizen by intermarriage of the Cherokee Nation.

D E C I S I O N .

THE RECORDS OF THIS OFFICE SHOW: That on July 30, 1900, application was received by the Commission to the Five Civilized Tribes for the enrollment of Sarah L. Price as a citizen by intermarriage of the Cherokee Nation. Further proceedings in the matter of said application were had at Tahlequah, Indian Territory, October 7, 1902, and at Muskogee, Indian Territory, January 3, 1907.

THE EVIDENCE IN THIS CASE SHOWS: That the applicant herein, Sarah L. Price, a white woman, was lawfully married on December 23 1856, to Samuel Joseph Price, who was at the time of said marriage a recognized citizen by blood of the Cherokee Nation, who is identified on the Cherokee authenticated tribal roll of 1880, Flint District, No. 1002, as an adopted Cherokee, the said Samuel Joseph Price having been admitted to citizenship in 1870. It is further shown that from the time of said marriage the said Samuel Joseph Price and Sarah L. Price resided together as husband and wife until the death of the said Samuel Joseph Price in 1880. That since the death of said Samuel Joseph Price the applicant has not remarried, and has resided continuously in the

Cherokee Intermarried White 1906
Volume II

Cherokee Nation from 1870 up to and including September 1, 1902. The applicant is identified on the Cherokee authenticated tribal roll of 1880 and on the Cherokee census roll of 1896 as an intermarried citizen of the Cherokee Nation.

IT IS, THEREFORE, ORDERED AND ADJUDGED: That in accordance with the decision of the Supreme Court of the United States, dated November 5, 1906, in the cases of Daniel Red Bird et al., vs. the United States, Nos. 125, 126, 127 and 128, the said applicant, Sarah L. Price, is entitled, under the provision of Section 21 of the Act of Congress approved June 28, 1898 (30 Stats., 495), to enrollment as a citizen by intermarriage of the Cherokee Nation, and her application for enrollment as such is accordingly granted.

Tams Bixby
Commissioner.

Dated at Muskogee, Indian Territory,
this JAN 23 1907

◇◇◇◇◇

Cherokee
811.

Muskogee, Indian Territory, December 22, 1906.

Sarah L. Price,
    Evansville, Arkansas.

Dear Madam:

    November 6, 1906, the United States Supreme Court held that white persons who intermarried with Cherokee citizens according to Cherokee law prior to November 1, 1875, are entitled to enrollment and allotments of land as citizens of the Cherokee Nation.

    You are advised that to properly determine your right to enrollment as a citizen by intermarriage of the Cherokee Nation, it will be necessary for you to appear before the Commissioner for the purpose of giving testimony as to the date of your marriage and whether or not your husband, by reason of your marriage to whom you claim the right to enrollment as a citizen by intermarriage of the Cherokee Nation, was a recognized Cherokee citizen at the time of your marriage to him.

    You are therefore directed to appear before the Commissioner at Muskogee, Indian Territory, at 9 o'clock A. M., on Thursday, January 3, 1907, and give testimony as above indicated.

Respectfully,

H.J.C.   Acting Commissioner.

◇◇◇◇◇

Cherokee Intermarried White 1906
Volume II

Cherokee
811

Muskogee, Indian Territory, January 23, 1907.

W. W. Hastings,
    Attorney for the Cherokee Nation,
        Muskogee, Indian Territory.

Dear Sir:

    There is enclosed herewith a copy of the decision of the Commissioner to the Five Civilized Tribes, dated January 23, 1907, granting the application for the enrollment of Sarah L. Price as a citizen by intermarriage of the Cherokee Nation.

                  Respectfully,

Encl. H-56   Commissioner.
JMH

◇◇◇◇◇

Cherokee 811   W.W. HASTINGS.   OFFICE OF   H.M. VANCE.
                      ATTORNEY.   SECRETARY.

Attorney for the Cherokee Nation,
MUSKOGEE, I. T.

                                                      January 23, 1907.

The Commissioner to the Five Civilized Tribes,
        Muskogee, Indian Territory.

Sir:

    Receipt is acknowledged of the testimony and of your decision enrolling Sarah L. Price as a citizen by intermarriage of the Cherokee Nation. Time for protesting said decision is waived and I consent that said person may be placed upon the schedule immediately.

                                      Respectfully,
                                        W. W. Hastings
                                        Attorney for Cherokee Nation.

◇◇◇◇◇

Cherokee Intermarried White 1906
Volume II

Cherokee
    811

Muskogee, Indian Territory, January 23, 1907.

Sarah L. Price,
    Evansville, Arkansas.

Dear Madam:

    There is enclosed herewith a copy of the decision of the Commissioner to the Five Civilized Tribes, dated January 23, 1907, granting your application for enrollment as a citizen by intermarriage of the Cherokee Nation.

    You will be advised when your name has been placed upon a schedule of citizens of the Cherokee Nation and approved by the Secretary of the Interior.

Respectfully,

E.R.C.   Commissioner.
    Enc. E.C. 81

Cher IW 63
Trans from Cher 825 3-15-07

E.C.M.

DEPARTMENT OF THE INTERIOR,

COMMISSIONER TO THE FIVE CIVILIZED TRIBES.

In the matter of the application for the enrollment of

JOHN W. JOHNSON

As a citizen by intermarriage of the Cherokee Nation.

CHEROKEE NO. 825.

Cherokee Intermarried White 1906
Volume II

DEPARTMENT OF THE INTERIOR,
COMMISSION TO THE FIVE CIVILIZED TRIBES,
BUNCH, I. T. July 31st, 1900.

In the matter of the application of John W. Johnson et al for enrollment as Cherokee citizens, said Johnson being sworn by Commissioner Breckinridge, testified as follows:

Q Give your full name. A John W. Johnson.
Q What is your age? A sixty seven years old.
Q What is your postoffice? [sic] Stilwell.
Q What is your district? A Flint.
Q How long have you been living in Flint? A twenty eight years.
Q To whom do you make application for enrollment? A For muself[sic] wife and blind duaghter[sic].
Q Do you apply as a Cherokee full blood? A No sir.
Q It is intermarriage.[sic] A Yes sir..
Q Is your wife a Cherokee by blood? A Yes sir.
Q Now Mr. Johnson does your name appear on the roll as[sic] 1880 Flint District.[sic] A Yes sir.
Q You have made your home continuously there? A Lived first year in Talaquah[sic] and the rest in Flint.
Q You and your wife living together at this time? A Yes sir.
Q And have continuously? A Yes sir.
Q When were you married? A First time first of March---last time in 1863 February sometime.
Q Now give name of your wife? [sic] Alcey A. Johnson.
Q I suppose she appears on the roll of 1886.[sic] A I don't know.
Q Give name of child. A Julia A. Johnson.
Q How old is she? A twenty nine
Q Is she on the roll of 1896? A Yes sir.
Note 1880 Roll Page 374 #714 J.W. Johnson Flint District 1880 roll page 774 #715 A.A. Johnson daughter[sic]. 1880 roll page 374 #719 J.A. Johnson Flint. 1880 enrollment page 714 John W. Johnson Flint. 96 enrollment page 766 #1009 Alcey A. Johnson Flint 96 enrollment 766 1010 Julia A. Johnson Flint.
Q Is this daughter living with you? A Yes sir.
Q Has she made her home with you all her life? A Yes sir.
Q Your daughter is over age, but you say she is blind and you make application for her. Your wife and daughter will be enrolled as Cherokees by blood, and you by adoption.

W. J. Hastain, being first duly sworn, states that as stenographer to the Commission to the Five Civilized Tribes he reported the foregoing case and that the above and foregoing is a full true and complete transcript of his stenographic notes in said case.

Cherokee Intermarried White 1906
Volume II

Subscribed and sworn to before me this 30th day of July 1900.

Commissioner.

◇◇◇◇◇

WHA
Cher

Department of the Interior,
Commission to the Five Civilized Tribes,
Flint C. H., I. T., May 26, 1902.

In the matter of the application of John W. Johnson, for the enrollment of himself, his wife Alcey A. Johnson, and his blind daughter Julia A. Johnson, as citizens of the Cherokee Nation.

JOHN W. JOHNSON, being duly sworn, and examined by the Commission, testified as follows:

Q What is your name ? A John W. Johnson.
Q What is your age ? A 69.
Q What is your post office address ? A Stilwell, I. T.
Q In what district do you reside ? A Flint.
Q For whom do you make application ?
A For myself, my wife and daughter.
Q What is the name and age of your wife ?
A Alcey A. Johnson, age 60.
Q Is she living ? A Yes sir.
Q What is the name and age of your daughter ?
A Julia A. Johnson, age 31.
Q Is she blind ? A Yes sir.
Q Is she living ? A Yes sir.
Q Are you the identical John W. Johnson who made application to the Commission for the enrollment of yourself and your wife Alcey A. Johnson, and your daughter Julia A. Johnson, as citizens of the Cherokee Nation, at Bunch, I. T., on July 31, 1900 ?
A Yes sir.
Q Do you claim to be a Cherokee by blood ? A No sir.
Q You are an intermarried citizen A Yes sir.
Q How long have you been married to your present wife ?
A I married her the first time in 1863, and the last time in 1872.
Q Have you continuously lived with her since you married her the first time ?
A Yes sir.
Q Why did you re-marry her in 1872 ?
A Because the Cherokee law required it.

Cherokee Intermarried White 1906
Volume II

--The applicant asks leave to file his marriage certificate which explains his second marriage, which is allowed and filed herewith, and made a part of the record.

Q Is your wife a recognized citizen of the Cherokee Nation ?
A Yes sir.
Q Is she a Cherokee by blood ? A Yes sir she has always been recognized and treated as such.
Q What degree of Cherokee blood do you claim for her ?
Q I can't say; her grandmother was said to be a quarter breed. About 1/24 I reckon her degree of Cherokee blood would be.
Q Has she ever been recognized as a citizen by the tribal authorities of the Cherokee Nation ? A Yes sir.
Q Does her name appear upon the tribal rolls of the Cherokee Nation ? A Yes sir.
Q What was the name of her father ? A Charles Raper.
Q Was he a Cherokee by blood ? A Yes sir.
Q In what district did he reside ? A He never came to this Nation to live; he came here in his young days, but he went back and died in North Carolina.
Q What is the name of your wife's mother ? A Julia Ann Raper.
Q Is she living ? A No sir, she's dead.
Q Was she a Cherokee by blood ? A No sir, she was a white woman.
Q How long has your wife resided in the Cherokee Nation ?
A Thirty years.
Q Has she resided here in the Cherokee Nation continuously since that time ?
A Yes sir, all the time.
Q What is the name of your father ? A Joseph R. Johnson.
Q He was a white man ? A Yes sir.
Q Is he living ? A No sir.
Q He was not a citizen of the Cherokee Nation ?
A No sir, he never was here.
Q What is the name of your mother ? A Abigail Johnson.
Q Is she living ? A No sir.
Q Was she a white woman ? A Yes sir.

--The printed copy of the 1880 Cherokee roll examined and the name of John W. Johnson is found and identified thereon at No. 796, Flint District;
--The printed copy of the 1880 Cherokee roll examined and the name of Alcey A. Johnson is found and identified thereon as A. A. Johnson, at No. 797, Flint District;
--The printed copy of the 1880 Cherokee roll examined and the name of Julia A. Johnson is found and identified thereon as J. A. Johnson, at No. 801, Flint District;
--The 1896 Cherokee roll examined and the name of John W. Johnson is found and identified thereon at page 714, #_____, Flint District;
--The 1896 Cherokee roll examined and the name of Alcey A. Johnson is found and identified thereon at page 766, # 1009, Flint District;
--The 1896 Cherokee roll examined and the name of Julia A. Johnson is found and identified thereon at page 766, # 1010, Flint District;

Cherokee Intermarried White 1906
Volume II

E. C. Bagwell, on oath states that as stenographer to the Commission to the Five Civilized Tribes, he correctly recorded the testimony and proceedings had in the above entitled cause, and that the foregoing is an accurate transcript of his stenographic notes thereof.

E.C. Bagwell

Subscribed and sworn to before me this _____ JUL 15 1902 _____, 1902.

PG Reuter

◇◇◇◇◇

JOR.
Cher. 825.

Department of the Interior.
Commission to the Five Civilized Tribes.
Tahlequah, I. T., October 24, 1902.

SUPPLEMENTAL TESTIMONY in the matter of the application for the enrollment of JOHN W. JOHNSON as a citizen by intermarriage of the Cherokee Nation.

JOHN W. JOHNSON, being first duly sworn, and being examined, testified as follows:

BY COMMISSION: What is your name? A John W. Johnson.
Q How old are you? A Sixty-nine.
Q What is your post office address? A Stilwell.
Q Are you a white man? A Yes sir, I claim to be.
Q Have you heretofore made application to this Commission for enrollment as a citizen by intermarriage of the Cherokee Nation? A Yes sir.
Q What is the name of your wife? A Alcey A. Johnson.
Q Is she living? A Yes sir.
Q Is she a Cherokee by blood? A Yes sir, that is what she has always claimed.
Q Do you claim your right to enrollment by reason of your marriage to her? A Yes sir.
Q When were you and she married? A Married the first time in 1863 and the last time in 1872, here in Tahlequah District.
Q You were married the first time in 1863 according to the state law
A Married in the State of North Carolina the first time.
Q When did you come to the Cherokee Nation? A In the fall of 1871
Q Then in 1982 were you married according to the laws of the Cherokee Nation?
A According to the laws of the Cherokee Nation, in February, 1872.
Q Does your name appear upon the roll of 1880? A Yes sir.
Q Were you ever married before you married your present wife? A No sir.
Q Was she ever married before she married you? S[sic] No sir.

Cherokee Intermarried White 1906
Volume II

Q You are her first husband and she is your first wife? A Yes sir.
Q Have you and she lived together continuously since your marriage? A Yes sir.
Q Were you living together on the 1st day of September, 1902.[sic]
A She was up here at Nowata taking care of a sick daughter, she was up there on the 1st of September.
Q She was just away on a visit? A Just away taking care of a sick daughter.
Q You were not separated, had not quarreled or anything like that? A No sir.
Q Have you and she lived together continuously without any separation? A Never separated. I reckon as agreeable as any two ever got along.
Q Have you resided in the Cherokee Nation continuously since you married your wife in 1872? A Yes sir, never been out but very little.
Q Has she resided here continuously? A All the time.
Q You made application for the enrollment of one child? A For myself and wife and one child, a daughter.
Q Is that child living at this time? A Yes sir, she is living.

   This testimony will be filed with and made a part of the record in the matter of the application for the enrollment of John W. Johnson as a citizen by intermarriage of the Cherokee Nation, Cherokee straight card field No. 825.

Wm. Hutchinson, being first duly sworn, states as stenographer to the Commission to the Five Civilized Tribes he correctly recorded the testimony and proceedings in this case, and that the foregoing is a true and complete transcript of his stenographic notes thereof.

                       Wm Hutchinson

Subscribed and sworn to before me this 12th day of November, 1902.

                            BC Jones
                            Notary Public.

◇◇◇◇◇

Cherokee Intermarried White 1906
Volume II

Cherokee 825

DEPARTMENT OF THE INTERIOR,
COMMISSIONER TO THE FIVE CIVILIZED TRIBES.
MUSKOGEE, IND. TER. JANUARY 15, 1907.

In the matter of the application for the enrollment of JOHN W. JOHNSON as a citizen by intermarriage of the Cherokee Nation.

--:--

APPEARANCES: Applicant represented by Ailsey A. Johnson
Cherokee Nation not represented.

AILSEY A. JOHNSON, being first duly sworn by Charles E. Webster, a Notary Public, testified as follows:

On behalf of Commissioner:

Q. What is your name? A. Now? Johnson.
Q. Your full name? A. Ailsey A. Johnson.
Q. What is your age? A. Sixty-four or sixty-five.
Q. What is your postoffice address? A. Stilwell, Indian Territory.
Q. You are a citizen by blood of the Cherokee Nation, are you?
Q. Yes sir, I am recognized as that.
Q. You are on the final roll? A. I am on all of them.
Q. You appear here to-day for the purpose of giving testimony relative to the right of your husband, John W. Johnson, to enrollment as a citizen by intermarriage of the Cherokee Nation, do you? A. Yes sir.
Q. Is John W. Johnson living or dead? A. He is dead.
Q. When did he die? A. August 1, 1905 -- a year ago last August.
Q. Was he a white man? A. Yes sir.
Q. He claimed his right to enrollment as a citizen of the Cherokee Nation by reason of his marriage to you? A. Yes sir.
Q. When were you and he married? A. We were first married in 1863.
Q. Where were you living at that time? A. In Murphy, North Carolina, we was married in Murphy, North Carolina.
Q. You were living in North Carolina? A. Yes sir.
Q. When did you and he come to the Cherokee Nation? A. In the fall of '71.
Q. You came here with the Eastern Cherokees did you?
A. Well, we just came here by ourselves; I don't know.
Q. After coming to the Cherokee Nation were you admitted to citizenship in the Nation?
A. Yes sir.
Q. When were you admitted? A. Well; that paper I handed you will tell you, I don't just remember the date, it was in February, '72, I believe though.

Cherokee Intermarried White 1906
Volume II

Q. This paper which you handed me is a Marriage License?
A. Well, that will show; I haven't got my certificate of citizenship, but it is on all the rolls since '71.
Q. You were admitted before you were married--that is married here? A. We were here just about a month before we was married. We was admitted just a little bit before we was married.

An original marriage license and certificate is presented on behalf of the applicant, John W. Johnson, showing that on January 31, 1872, license was issued by W. H. Turner, Clerk District Court, Tahlequah District, acting in accordance with Cherokee laws, authorizing the marriage of John W. Johnson, a citizen of the United States and Alcy A. Johnson, formerly Raper, a Cherokee, and that said parties were united in marriage in accordance with the terms of said license, February 18, 1872, by John B. Jones, a Minister of the Gospel. Said marriage license and certificate will be filed herewith and made a part of the record herein.

Q. From the time of your marriage to your husband, John W. Johnson, February 18, 1872, did you and he continuously live together as husband and wife until his death?
A. Yes sir.
Q. And continuously live in the Cherokee Nation? A. Yes sir.
Q. Was he your first husband? A. Yes sir, and last one too.
Q. Were you his first wife? A. Yes sir.

The applicant, John W. Johnson, is identified on the Cherokee authenticated tribal roll of 1880, Flint District No. 714. His wife, Alsy A. Johnson is identified on said roll at No. 715, Flint District, and her name appears on an approved partial roll of citizens by blood of the Cherokee Nation opposite No. 2245.

The undersigned being first duly sworn states that as stenographer to the Commissioner to the Five Civilized Tribes she correctly recorded the testimony in the above case and that the above and foregoing is a full, true and correct transcript of her stenographic notes thereof.

                Lucy M Bowman

Subscribed and sworn to before me this 17th day of January, 1907.

                B.P. Rasmus
                Notary Public.

Cherokee Intermarried White 1906
Volume II

(Below was originally handwritten as given on the microfilm. The transcribed copy immediately followed and is given below and typed as given.)

Cherokee Nation)
)
Tahlequah Dist)   To any Ordained Minister of the Gospel, or Judge of any of the Courts of the Cherokee Nation This is to authorize you to Join in the Holy bonds of Matrimony Mr. John W. Johnson a white man & formerly a citizen of the U.S. and Alcey A. Johnson (formerly Raper) a Cherokee. He the said John W. Johnson having complied with the Cherokee Laws "Regulating Intermarriage with White men" & return this Instrument to my office for record with your Certificate of service

Jany 31st 1872   W.H Turner Clk

                                                        Dist Ct Tah Dist C.N.

   This is to certify that in accordance with the above license, I have this day solemnized the rite of marriage between John W. Johnson a citizen of the United States, & Alcy A. Johnson (formerly Raper) of the Cherokee Nation Mr. & Mrs. Johnson having already been married according to the laws of the U.S. the bands of marriage were reaffirmed in conformity to the laws of this Nation, recognizing the former marriage.
Tahlequah Dist. C.N.)
Feb. 18 1872   )   John B Jones
                                                 Minister of the Gospel.

Jno W. Johnson's Marriage Certificate by Rev Jno B. Jones.
         Recorded   W.H. Turner Clk

   The undersigned being duly sworn states that as stenographer to the Commissioner to the Five Civilized Tribes, she made the above copy, and that the same is a true and correct copy of the instrument now on file in this office.

                                            Mary Tabor Mallory

Subscribed and sworn to before me this he 19th. day of January 1907.

                                            Chas E Webster
                                               Notary Public.

◇◇◇◇◇

Cherokee Intermarried White 1906
Volume II

E C M   Cherokee 825.

DEPARTMENT OF THE INTERIOR,

COMMISSIONER TO THE FIVE CIVILIZED TRIBES.

In the matter of the application for the enrollment of JOHN W. JOHNSON as a citizen by intermarriage of the Cherokee Nation.

_ D E C I S I O N _

THE RECORDS OF THIS OFFICE SHOW: That on July 31st, 1900 application was received by the Commission to the Five Civilized Tribes for the enrollment of John W. Johnson as a citizen by intermarriage of the Cherokee Nation. Further proceedings in the matter of said application were had at Flint, C. H., Indian Territory, May 26th, 1902 and Tahlequah, Indian Territory, October 24th, 1902 and January 15th, 1907.

THE EVIDENCE IN THIS CASE SHOWS: That the applicant herein, John W. Johnson, a white man, was married in accordance with Cherokee law on February 18th, 1982 to his wife, Alsy A. Johnson, nee Raper, who was at the time of said marriage a recognized citizen by blood of the Cherokee Nation, who is identified on the Cherokee authenticated tribal roll of 1880, Flint District No. 715 as an adopted Cherokee, and whose name is included in the approved partial roll of citizens by blood of the Cherokee Nation, opposite No. 2245. It is further shown that from the time of said marriage the said John W. Johnson and Alsy A. Johnson resided together as husband and wife and continuously lived in the Cherokee Nation up to and including September 1st, 1902. Said applicant is identified upon the Cherokee authenticated tribal roll of 1880 and the Cherokee census roll of 1896 as an intermarried citizen of the Cherokee Nation.

IT IS, THEREFORE, ORDERED AND ADJUDGED: That in accordance with the decision of the Supreme Court of the United States dated November 5, 1906 in the cases of Daniel Red Bird et al. vs. the United States, Nos. 125, 126, 127 and 128, the said applicant, John W. Johnson is entitled, under the provisions of Section Twenty-one of the Act of Congress approved June 28th, 1898 (30 Stats. 495), to enrollment as a citizen by intermarriage of the Cherokee Nation and his application for enrollment as such is accordingly granted.

Tams Bixby
Commissioner.

Dated at Muskogee, Indian Territory,
this   JUN 23 1907

Cherokee Intermarried White 1906
Volume II

Cherokee
825

Muskogee, Indian Territory, December 22, 1906.

John W. Johnson,
    Stilwell, Indian Territory.

Dear Sir:

    November 6, 1906, the United States Supreme Court held that white persons who intermarried with Cherokee citizens according to Cherokee law prior to November 1, 1875, are entitled to enrollment and allotments of land as citizens of the Cherokee Nation.

    You are advised that to properly determine your right to enrollment as a citizen by intermarriage of the Cherokee Nation, it will be necessary for you to appear before the Commissioner for the purpose of giving testimony as to the date of your marriage and whether or not your wife, by reason of your marriage to whom you claim the right to enrollment as a citizen of the Cherokee Nation, was a recognized citizen of the Cherokee Nation at the time of your marriage to her, and whether or not you were married to her in accordance with Cherokee laws.

    You are therefore directed to appear before the Commissioner at Muskogee, Indian Territory, at 9 o'clock A. M., on Thursday, January 3, 1907, and give testimony as above indicated.

                                    Respectfully,

H.J.C.   Acting Commissioner.

Cherokee Intermarried White 1906
Volume II

Cherokee
825.

Muskogee, Indian Territory, December 31, 1906.

James M. Johnson,
    Stilwell, Indian Territory.

Dear Sir:

    In reply to your letter of December 27, 1906, you are advised that as it appears from your letter that your father, John W. Johnson, an applicant for enrollment as an intermarried citizen of the Cherokee Nation, is dead, your mother should appear before the Commissioner on the date his case is set for hearing in order to give testimony as to your father's marriage to his Cherokee wife, by reason of his marriage to whom he claims the right to enrollment as a citizen by intermarriage of the Cherokee Nation, and as to whether or not he was married to her according to Cherokee law.

                              Respectfully,

S.W.   Commissioner.

⋄⋄⋄⋄⋄

Cherokee
825

Muskogee, Indian Territory, January 23, 1907.

W. W. Hastings,
    Attorney for the Cherokee Nation,
        Muskogee, Indian Territory.

Dear Sir:

        There is enclosed herewith copy of the decision of the Commissioner to the Five Civilized Tribes, dated January 23, 1907, granting the application for the enrollment of John W. Johnson as a citizen by intermarriage of the Cherokee Nation.

                              Respectfully,

Enc I-60   Commissioner.

RPI

⋄⋄⋄⋄⋄

Cherokee Intermarried White 1906
Volume II

Cherokee 825

W.W. HASTINGS.
ATTORNEY.

OFFICE OF

H.M. VANCE.
SECRETARY.

Attorney for the Cherokee Nation,
MUSKOGEE, I. T.

January 23, 1907.

The Commissioner to the Five Civilized Tribes,
    Muskogee, Indian Territory.

Sir:

    Receipt is acknowledged of the testimony and of your decision enrolling John W Johnson as a citizen by intermarriage of the Cherokee Nation. Time for protesting said decision is waived and I consent that said person may be placed upon the schedule immediately.

                    Respectfully,
                      W. W. Hastings
                      Attorney for the Cherokee Nation.

◇◇◇◇◇

Cherokee 825

                    Muskogee, Indian Territory, January 24, 1907.

Alsy A. Johnson,
    Stilwell, Indian Territory.

Dear Madam:

    There is enclosed herewith copy of the decision of the Commissioner to the Five Civilized Tribes, dated January 23, 1907, granting the application for the enrollment of your husband, John W. Johnson, as a citizen by intermarriage of the Cherokee Nation.

    You will be advised when his name has been placed upon a schedule of citizens of the Cherokee Nation and approved by the Secretary of the Interior.

                    Respectfully,

Enc I-80   Commissioner.

RPI

Cherokee Intermarried White 1906
Volume II

Cher IW 64
Trans from Cher 999 3-15-07

E.C.M.

DEPARTMENT OF THE INTERIOR,

COMMISSIONER TO THE FIVE CIVILIZED TRIBES.

In the matter of the application for the enrollment of

EMMA C. WHEELER

as a citizen by intermarriage of the Cherokee Nation.

CHEROKEE 999.

Department of the Interior,
Commission to the Five Civilized Tribes,
Sallisaw, I. T., August 6, 1900.

In the matter of the application of William W. Wheeler et al for enrollment as Cherokee citizens; being sworn and examined by Commissioner Needles he testifies as follows:

Q What is your name? A William W. Wheeler.
Q What is your age? A Fifty-three.
Q What is your post-office? A Sallisaw.
Q Are you a recognized citizen of the Cherokee Nation by blood? A Yes sir.
Q What district do you live in? A Sequoyah District.
Q How long have you lived there? A I have lived in Sequoyah District off and on ever since 1870.
Q Have you been a permanent resident of the Cherokee Nation since 1870?
A Well you might say yes. I have been backwards and forwards; mt[sic] property has always been here.
Q Where have you lived yourself for the last ten years? A I have been here since 1892 continuously.
Q What is the name of your father? A John F. Wheeler.
Q Is he living? A No sir, he died in 1880.
Q Is his name on the 1880?/[sic] roll? A No sir.
Q What is the name of your mother? A Nancy.
Q Is she living? A No sir, she died in 1852.

Cherokee Intermarried White 1906
Volume II

Q Are you married? A Yes sir.
Q What is the name of your wife? A Emma C.
Q Is she a Cherokee citizen by blood? A No sir, she is a white woman.
Q When did you marry her? A In 1868.
Q Have you a marriage certificate? A Yes sir, but not with me
Q Under what law were you married? A Married in the State of Arkansas.
Q Your wife was a non-citizen? A Yes sir.
Q And her father and also her mother were non-citizens? A Yes sir, they was white.
Q Have you any children under twenty-one years of age? A Yes sir.
Q What is the name of the oldest one under twenty-one? A Jessie V., twenty years old; Carnall[sic], fourteen; Theodore, eleven;
Q Are these children alive and living with you? A Yes sir.
Q Is your wife living? A Yes sir.

    Noe[sic]: 1880 roll examined for applicant: page 728 #1402 as Will Wheeler, Sequoyah District.
1896 roll, page 1193 #1521 as Will W. Wheeler, Sequoyah District.
1894 roll, page 1007 #1499 as William W. Wheeler, Sequoyah Dist.
    1880 roll examined for applicant's wife: page 728 #1403 E. C. Wheeler, Sequoyah District.
1896 roll, page 1119 #185 as Emma C. Wheeler, Sequoyah District.
    1880 roll examined for children: page 728 #1409 as Jessie V. Wheeler, Sequoyah District.
1896 roll, page 1108 #1526 as Jessie V. Wheeler, Sequoyah District.
1894 roll, page 1007 #1496 as Jessie V. Wheeler, Sequoyah Dis't.
1896 roll, page 1108 #1527 Carnell Wheeler, Sequoyah District.
1894 roll, page 1007 #1497 as Cammel[sic] Wheeler, Sequoyah District.
1896 roll, page 1108 #1528 as Theodore Wheeler, Sequoyah District.
1894 roll, page 1007 #1498 as Theodore Wheeler, Sequoyah District.

    Com'r Needles: The name of William W. Wheeler appearing upon the authenticated roll of 1880 as well as the census roll of 1896 and the pay roll of 1894, and his wife, Emma C. Wheeler, also appearing upon said rolls, being fully identified according to page and number as indicated in the testimony; and his daughter Jessie V. and Carnall and Theodore, their names also appearing upon the rolls of 1880 as well as the census roll of 1896 and the pay roll of 1894 respectively, proof of their residence being made satisfactory, they are all ordered listed for enrollment by this Commission as Cherokee citizens by blood, except his wife, Emma C., who is ordered listed for enrollment as a citizen by intermarriage.

    M.D. Green, being first duly sworn, states that as stenographer to the Commission to the Five Civilized Tribes he reported the foregoing case and that the above and foregoing is a full true and complete transcript of his stenographic notes in said case.

                                                          MD Green

Cherokee Intermarried White 1906
Volume II

Subscribed and sworn to before me this 7th day of August 1900.

TB Needles
Commissioner.

◇◇◇◇◇◇

File with Cherokee straight No. 999.

Department of the Interior,
Commission to the Five Civilized Tribes,
Tahlequah, I.T., November 8, 1901.

In the matter of the application of William W. Wheeler et al for enrollment as Cherokee citizens.

Commissioner Needles: In the field judgment it is stated that the names of Carnall and Theodore Wheeler appear on the roll of 1880; this is error. They are too young to be on that roll, and their names do not appear thereon.

It is ordered that a copy of the foregoing be attached to and filed with each copy of the testimony in this case.

M.D. Green, being first duly sworn, states that as stenographer to the Commission to the Five Civilized Tribes he corrected recorded the testimony and proceedings in this case and that the foregoing is a true and complete transcript of his stenographic notes thereof.

MD Green

Subscribed and sworn to before me this November 8, 1901.

TB Needles
Commissioner.

◇◇◇◇◇◇

Cherokee 999.

Department of the Interior,
Commission to the Five Civilized Tribes.
Muskogee, I. T., October 7, 1902.

In the matter of the application of William W. Wheeler for the enrollment of himself and children, Jessie V. Mayo, Carnall Wheeler and Theodore Wheeler, as citizens by blood, and for the enrollment of his wife, Emma C. Wheeler, as a citizen by intermarriage of the Cherokee Nation; said Emma C. Wheeler, being sworn and examined by the Commission, testified as follows:

Cherokee Intermarried White 1906
Volume II

Q What is your name? A Emma C. Wheeler.
Q What is your age at this time? A Fifty-four.
Q What is your postoffice? A Sallisaw.
Q Are you the same Emma C. Wheeler for whom application was made for enrollment as an intermarried citizen on August 6, 1900? A Yes sir.
Q What is your husband's name? A W. W. Wheeler.
Q Is he a citizen by blood of the Cherokee Nation? A Yes.
Q When were you married to your husband, William W. Wheeler? A In 1868.
Q Were you ever married prior to your marriage to him? A No sir.
Q Was he ever married prior to his marriage to you? A No sir.
Q He was your first husband and you his first wife? A Yes sir.
q Have you and he lived together as husband and wife from 1880 up until the present time? A Yes sir.
Q You never had been separated? A No sir.
Q And you never have been married to any other man? A No sir.
Q You and he living together as husband and wife on the first day of September, 1902? A Yes sir.
Q Have you and your husband lived in the Cherokee Nation all the time since 1880?
A He has been here the greater portion of the time; I haven't been here all the time.
Q Where has your home been? A At Fort Smith.
Q When did you go to Fort Smith? A We first bought property in here in '71.
Q I want to know what you have done since '80? A We lived here since '80 for two years, and then we have been here for ten years this last time.
Q Have you and your husband been in the Cherokee Nation for the last ten years?
A Yes sir.
Q Haven't lived out in the last ten years? A No sir
Q Now have these children, Jessie V., Carnall and Theodore lived in the Cherokee Nation for the last ten years? A Yes sir.
Q They haven't lived out of the nation for the last ten years? A No sir.
Q Are all these three children I have just named living at this time? A Yes.
Q Jessie V. is now married is she? A Yes sir.
Q What is her name at this time? A Mrs. W. D. Mayo.

The undersigned, being duly sworn, states that as stenographer to the Commission to the Five Civilized Tribes he correctly recorded the testimony and proceedings in this case, and that the foregoing is a true and correct transcript of his stenographic notes thereof.

E.G. Rothenberger

Subscribed and sworn to before me this 31st day of October, 1902.

BC Jones
Notary Public.

Cherokee Intermarried White 1906
Volume II

Cherokee 999.

DEPARTMENT OF THE INTERIOR,
COMMISSION TO THE FIVE CIVILIZED TRIBES.
Muskogee, Indian Territory, January 3, 1907.

In the Matter of the Application for the Enrollment of Emma C. Wheeler as a citizen by intermarriage of the Cherokee Nation.

APPEARANCES: Applicant appears in person.

Cherokee Nation represented by H. M. Vance, in behalf of W. W. Hastings, Attorney.

Emma C. Wheeler being first duly sworn by B. P. Rasmus, Notary Public, testified as follows:

ON BEHALF OF COMMISSIONER.

Q What is your name? A Emma C. Wheeler.
Q What is your age? A 58.
Q What is your post office address?
A Sallisaw, Indian Territory.
Q Are you an applicant for enrollment as a citizen by intermarriage of the Cherokee Nation?
A I am.
Q You have no Cherokee blood:
A No.
Q The only claim you have to enrollment is by virtue of your marriage to a citizen by blood of the Cherokee Nation, is it?
A Yes sir.
Q What is the name of the citizen through whom you claim the right to enrollment?
A William W. Wheeler.
Q Is he living at the present time?
A Yes.
Q When were you married to your husband, Wm. W. Wheeler?
A In 1868.
Q He was at that time a recognized citizen of the Cherokee Nation, was he?
A Yes sir.
Q Was he at that time living in the Cherokee Nation?
A Not at that time but in 1870.
Q Where were you married?
A In fort Smith, Arkansas.
Q He was living in Fort Smith at the time you were married?
A Yes.

Cherokee Intermarried White 1906
Volume II

Q Was he making that his permanent home or was his presence there a temporary absence from the Cherokee Nation?
A That was his home at that time but in 1870 we bought land in the territory and moved over.
Q Had he prior to your marriage ever been a resident of the Cherokee Nation?
A He had not but his name was on the roll ever sine[sic] 1851.
Q When you and he came to the Cherokee Nation, was he immediately recognized as a citizen of the Nation?
A Yes, he has always been.
Q They didn't require him to go before the Cherokee authorities and be admitted to citizenship in the Cherokee Nation?
A I can't tell you that; I don't remember.
Q You say that you and he removed to the Cherokee Nation in 1870?
A Yes sir.
Q And since that time have you continuously resided in the Cherokee Nation?
A This has been our home all the time.
Q Any absene[sic] from the Cherokee Nation since then has been of a temporary character?
A Yes sir.
Q The Cherokee Naton[sic] has been your permanent home?
A Yes; he has been here continuously himself.
Q Was he ever married prior to his marriage to you?
A No.
Q Were you ever married prior to your marriage to him?
A No.
Q And since your marriage you have continuously lived together as husband and wife?
A Yes.

The applicant, Emma C. Wheeler, is identified on the Cherokee authenticated Tribal Roll of 1880, Sequoyah District, No. 1403. Her husband, William W. Wheeler is included in the approved partial roll of citizens by blood of the Cherokee Nation at No. 2703.

BY H. M. VANCE FOR W. W. HASTINGS, ATTORNEY.

Q Do you live in the vicinity of Salisaw[sic] now, Mrs. Wheeler?
A Yes; about three-quarters of a mile.
Q Have you lived in Fort Smith since 1870?
A Yes, I have lived there; my children went to school there but my husband has been in the territory all the time.
Q How long have you lived here?
A I have been here continuously 12 years but prior to that time I would be out at different times during the school terms.
Q How long was the longest period you lived at Fort Smith at any one time since 1870?

Cherokee Intermarried White 1906
Volume II

A   I can't tell you; I would come over here and stay a few years and go back and stay there a few years, until my children were old enough to send away to school.
Q   While you were residing in Fort Smith for the purpose of sending your children to school, your husband resided in the territory?
A   Yes; he was here at Salisaw.

ON BEHALF OF COMMISSIONER.

Q   Your residence in Fort Smith since 1870 has been for the sole purpose of educating the children?
A   Yes, that was all.
Q   You would return to the Cherokee Nation to your home during vacations, would you?
A   Yes sir.

William W. Wheeler being first duly sworn by B. P. Rasmus, Notary Public, testified on behalf of Emma C. Wheeler as follows:

ON BEHALF OF COMMISSION.

Q   What is your name?   A William W. Wheeler.
Q   What is your age?   A Going on 60.
Q   What is your post office address?
A   Salisaw[sic], Indian Territory.
Q   Are you a Cherokee by blood?
A   Half blood.
Q   Where were you born Mr. Wheeler?
A   Fort Smith, Arkansas.
Q   How long did you reside in Arkansas before coming to the Cherokee Nation?
A   I came to the Cherokee Nation during the war. I went South with the troops and at the close of the war I came back and stayed around here for quite a while in Canadian District, and then went back to Fort Smith and stayed there for sometime, married my wife and came back to the Cherokee Nation.
Q   What is your wife's name?
A   Emma C. Wheeler.
Q   She is an applicant for enrollment as a citizen by intermarriage of the Cherokee Nation?
A   Yes sir.
Q   When were you married to her?
A   5th day of November, 1868.
Q   Shortly after your marriage to her, did you and she remove to the Cherokee Nation for the purpose of making this your permanent home?
A   Yes sir.
Q   At what time did you come to the Cherokee Nation?
A   In 1869 or 1870; I don't remember which.

Cherokee Intermarried White 1906
Volume II

Q And you have since continuously made your permanent home in the Cherokee Nation?
A Yes, this has been our permanent home; we have gone backwards and forwards but this has been our permanent home here at Salisaw[sic]. We lived several years in the Arkansas River bottom above Fort Smith; then we came to Salisaw and have been there since.
Q On your coming to the Cherokee Nation, were you recognized as a citizen of the Cherokee Nation or was it necessary for you to go before the authorities of the Cherokee Nation and be admitted?
A We were recognized but I think in 1868 or 69, we were admitted by the Cherokee authorities.
Q You were admitted at that time?
A Yes sir, or they re-admitted me. My father left here on account of the fued[sic] between the Cherokees and at the time, all my kin were killed; my father took his wife and children and went to Arkansas and there they remained and my mother died there; and as soon as we got of age, we came back here.
Q You think it was about the year 1868 that you were admitted?
A Either 1868 or '69. My impression is 1869.
Q That was the only time that you ever had to make application for admission,-- your citizenship was never questioned since?
A No sir.

BY H. M. VANCE FOR W. W. HASTINGS, ATTORNEY.

Q Mr. Wheeler, were you re-admitted before or after you removed from Fort Smith?
A I am not positive; probably it was before.
Q You don't know then how long it was before you came back to the Cherokee Nation after you were admitted, if admitted before you removed from Fort Smith?
A If it was before, we had to comply with the law by being back here in six months.
Q And did you comply with that provision?
A Yes sir; if we were admitted in November, we were here in February or March. All of our property has been here since.

The undersigned being first duly sworn states that as stenographer to the Commission to the Five Civilized Tribes, she correctly recorded the testimony taken in this case and that the foregoing is a full, true and correct transcript of her stenographic notes thereof.

Myrtle Hill

Subscribed and sworn to before me this the 4th day of January, 1907.

B. P. Rasmus
Notary Public.

Cherokee Intermarried White 1906
Volume II

Tahlequah, C. N., Dec. 12, 1870.

J. L. Adair,
   Clk Senate pro tem.

Eli Smith,
   President Senate pro tem.

Consurred[sic] in, with the following amendment, viz:

This Act shall not go into effect so far as relates to White men, until they shall have complied with the laws of this Nation governing intermarriage of white men with Cherokee women.

Stephen Foreman,
   Clerk Council.

Jumper Mills,
   Speaker of Council.

Dec. 16, 1870.

The amendment concurred in.

J. L. Adair,
   Clerk Senate pro tem.

Arch Scraper,
   President of Senate.

Approved,
   Lewis Downing,
      Principal.

(SEAL)

I, C. J. Harris, Assistant Executive Secretary of the Interior the Cherokee Nation, certify that the above and foregoing is a true and correct copy of the Act of the Cherokee National Council entitled "An Act to re admit to citizenship the persons therein named" as appears of record in this office.

Executive Department, Cherokee Nation.
Tahlequah, Ind. Ter.,
Jan. 5, 1907.

C.J. Harris
Assistant Executive Secy.
Cherokee Nation.

    Homer J. Councilor, being first duly sworn states that as stenographer to the Commissioner to the Five Civilized Tribes he made the above and foregoing from the original thereof and that the same is a true and correct copy.

Homer J Councilor

Subscribed and sworn to before me this fourteenth day of Jan. 1907

Chas E. Webster
Notary Public.

Cherokee Intermarried White 1906
Volume II

(COPY)

AN ACT TO RE ADMIT TO CITIZENSHIP THE PERSONS THEREIN NAMED.

    Be it enacted by the National Council: That the following named persons be admitted to the enjoyments of the rights and proviledges[sic] of citizenship to the Cherokee Nation: to-wit--

    E. Jane Edwards, Cherokee
    John B. Edwards her husband, white
    Herbert Thompson, Cherokee
    E. J. Hensley, children and husband
    Mary E. Numby and husband
    George Bible
    Lewis Bible
    Wm. Bible
    Susan Jane Perry, children and husband
    Hariet B. Quesenbury " " "
    John C. Wheeler, children and wife.
   xWilliam Wheeler " " "
    Sarah P. Wheeler,
    Jesse Bright
    Mary Bright
    Caroline E. Howell, and children
    Mary Jane Porter " "
    Mary E. Hall, formerly M. E. Davis.
    Sabra Clark, Formerly Sabra England
    Elizabeth J. Cowen
    Jane Christie, and children
    Mrs. Rebecca Haggerty and family, consisting of daughter Mrs. Louisa N. Scott, grand daughters Rebecca L. Scott Fannie Scoot[sic], Grandsons John B. Scott and William Scott, daughter Fanny Haggarty[sic], son L. M. Haggarty, grand daughter Fannie L. McFarland, grandson Sam'l McFarland.

    Mrs. Delila Drew and family considting[sic] of daughter Mertha A. Scott, son-in-law, white Jas. N. Scott, grandsons George W. Scott, S. H. Scott, and Thomas H. Scott, son-in-law, white man, W. B. Rogers, daughters Kate D. Rogers, and Jesse Drew.

    Mrs. Peggy Bumgarner, Maud Bumgarner, daughter and Bumgarner, son.

    Elizabeth A. Ridge
    Still B. Beatty
    Aenias Ridge

Cherokee Intermarried White 1906
Volume II

Andrew J. Ridge, wife and 5 children.
Nancy Dial and husband Martin Dial, children: Nathaniel Dial and Rebecca Dial.
Catherine Blair, and husband
John Priest
Madoria Priest
Sarah Welch
John C. Welch
Albert Harlin
Ann A. Welch

Provided that no rights or privileges conferred by this Act shall accrue to any of the individuals before named until they shall have settled within the limits of this Nation and become bonafide residents thereof.

E.C.M.
Cherokee 999.

DEPARTMENT OF THE INTERIOR,

COMMISSIONER TO THE FIVE CIVILIZED TRIBES.

In the matter of the application for the enrollment of EMMA C. WHEELER as a citizen by intermarriage of the Cherokee Nation.

D E C I S I O N

THE RECORDS OF THIS OFFICE SHOW: That at Salisaw[sic], Indian Territory, August 6, 1900, William W. Wheeler appeared before the Commission to the Five Civilized Tribes, and made application for the enrollment of himself, et al., as citizens by blood, and for the enrollment of his wife, Emma C. Wheeler, as a citizen by intermarriage of the Cherokee Nation. The application for the enrollment of the said William W. Wheeler, et al., as citizens by blood of the Cherokee Nation has been heretofore disposed of, and their rights to enrollment will not be considered in this decision. Further proceedings in the matter of said application were had at Tahlequah, Indian Territory, November 8, 1901, and at Muskogee, Indian Territory, October 7, 1902 and January 3, 1907.

THE EVIDENCE IN THIS CASE SHOWS: That the applicant herein, Emma C. Wheeler, a white woman, married in the year 1868 one, William W. Wheeler, a Cherokee by blood; that shortly after said marriage, by an Act of the Cherokee National Council dated "Tahlequah C. N. Dec. 12, 1870", said William W. Wheeler, whose name appears upon the approved partial roll of citizens by blood of the Cherokee Nation opposite No. 2703, was admitted to citizenship in the Cherokee Nation as a citizen by blood of said

Cherokee Intermarried White 1906
Volume II

Nation; that from the time of said admission said William W. Wheeler and Emma C. Wheeler resided together as husband and wife and continuously lived in the Cherokee Nation up to and including September 1, 1902. Said Emma C. Wheeler is identified upon the Cherokee authenticated tribal roll of 1880 and the Cherokee Census roll of 1896 as an intermarried citizen of the Cherokee Nation.

IT IS, THEREFORE, ORDERED AND ADJUDGED: That in accordance with the decision of the Supreme Court of the United States, dated November 5, 1906, in the case of Daniel Red Bird et al. vs. the United States under the provision of Section 21, of the Act of Congress approved June 28, 1898 (30 Stat., 495), Emma C. Wheeler is entitled to enrollment as a citizen by intermarriage of the Cherokee Nation, and her application for enrollment as such is accordingly granted.

                                  Tams Bixby
                                        Commissioner.

Dated at Muskogee, Indian Territory,
this   JAN 23 1907

◇◇◇◇◇

Cherokee
999

                              Muskogee, Indian Territory, December 24, 1906.

Emma C. Wheeler,
    Sallisaw, Indian Territory.

Dear Madam:

November 6, 1906, the United States Supreme Court held that white persons who intermarried with Cherokee citizens according to Cherokee law prior to November 1, 1875, are entitled to enrollment and allotments of land as citizens of the Cherokee Nation.

You are advised that to properly determine your right to enrollment as a citizen by intermarriage of the Cherokee Nation, it will be necessary for you to appear before the Commissioner for the purpose of giving testimony as to the date of your marriage and whether or not your husband, by reason of your marriage to whom you claim the right to enrollment as a citizen by intermarriage of the Cherokee Nation, was a recognized Cherokee citizen at the time of your marriage to him.

You are, therefore, directed to appear before the Commissioner at Muskogee, Indian Territory, at 9 o'clock A. M., on Thursday, January 3, 1907, and give testimony as above indicated.

                                  Respectfully,

L.M.C.   Acting Commissioner.

Cherokee Intermarried White 1906
Volume II

◇◇◇◇◇

Cherokee - 999

Muskogee, Indian Territory, January 23, 1907.

W. W. Hastings,
    Attorney for the Cherokee Nation,
        Muskogee, Indian Territory.

Dear Sir:

    There is enclosed herewith a copy of the decision of the Commissioner to the Five Civilized Tribes, dated January 23, 1907, granting the application for the enrollment of Emma C. Wheeler as a citizen by intermarriage of the Cherokee Nation.

        Respectfully,

Encl. H-63   Commissioner.
JMH

◇◇◇◇◇

Cherokee 999   W.W.HASTINGS.   OFFICE OF   H.M. VANCE.
                    ATTORNEY.   SECRETARY.

Attorney for the Cherokee Nation,
MUSKOGEE, I. T.

                                            January 23, 1907.

The Commissioner to the Five Civilized Tribes,
    Muskogee, Indian Territory.

Sir:

    Receipt is acknowledged of the testimony and of your decision enrolling Emma C. Wheeler as a citizen by intermarriage of the Cherokee Nation. Time for protesting said decision is waived and I consent that said person may be placed upon the schedule immediately.

                    Respectfully,
                    W. W. Hastings
                    Attorney for Cherokee Nation.

◇◇◇◇◇

Cherokee Intermarried White 1906
Volume II

Cherokee 999

Muskogee, Indian Territory, January 23, 1907.

Emma C. Wheeler,
    Sallisaw, Indian Territory.

Dear Madam:

There is enclosed herewith a copy of the decision of the Commissioner to the Five Civilized Tribes, dated January 23, 1907, granting the application for your enrollment as a citizen by intermarriage of the Cherokee Nation.

You will be advised when your name has been placed upon a schedule of citizens of the Cherokee Nation and approved by the Secretary of the Interior.

Respectfully,

Encl. H-85
JMH

Commissioner.

Cher IW 65
Trans from Cher 1338 3-15-07

◇◇◇◇◇

F.R.

DEPARTMENT OF THE INTERIOR,

COMMISSIONER TO THE FIVE CIVILIZED TRIBES.

In the matter of the application for the enrollment of

JAMES H. RALEY

as a citizen by intermarriage of the Cherokee Nation.

CHEROKEE 1338.

◇◇◇◇◇

Cherokee Intermarried White 1906
Volume II

Department of the Interior,
Commission to the Five Civilized Tribes,
Muldrow, I. T., August 14, 1900.

In the matter of the application of James M. Raley for the enrollment of himself by intermarriage and his wife as a Cherokee by blood: being sworn and examined by Commissioner Breckenridge[sic], he testified as follows:

Q What is your full name? A James M. Raley.
Q What is your age? A 54.
Q What is your post office address? A Muldrow.
Q What is your district? A Sequoyah.
Q For whom do you apply now to have enrolled? A Myself and wife.
Q You apply for yourself as a Cherokee by blood? A No, sir.
Q Do you apply for your wife as a Cherokee by blood? A Yes, sir.
Q What is your wife's name? A Mary L. Raley.
Q How old is she? A 49.
Q Is she on any of the rolls of the Cherokee Nation? A Yes, sir.
Q What was her name before you married her? A Starr.
Q Was that her maiden name? A Yes, sir.
Q When did you marry her? A I married her in 1871.
Q Then you are also on the roll of 1880? A Yes, sir, I am on every roll from 1870[sic].
Q Have you and your wife lived in the Cherokee Nation since 1880? A Yes, sir.
Q And lived together? A Yes, sir.
Q Have you lived in Sequoyah district all the time? A Yes, sir.

(James M. Raley on 1880 roll, page 715, No. 1041, Sequoyah district. Mary L. Raley on 1880 roll, page 715, No. 1042, Mary Raley, Sequoyah district. James L. Raley on 1896 roll, page (118), No. 145, Sequoyah (Page 1118) district. Mary L. Raley on 1896 roll, page 1094, No. 1188, Mary L. Raley, Sequoyah district.)

Mr. W. W. Hastings, representative of Cherokee Nation: Where did you come from to this country? A I came from Arkansas.
Q How old were you when you came over here? A When I came in here I was about 25 years old.
Q You lived here ever since? A Yes, sir, I married in Flint district and been here ever since the enrollment of 1870.

Commissioner Breckenridge[sic]: This applicant is identified on the roll of 1880 and the roll of 1896, and his wife is identified on both of said rolls. It is shown that he and his wife have lived together continuously in the Cherokee Nation since the roll of 1880. She will now be enrolled as a Cherokee by blood and he will be enrolled as a Cherokee by adoption.

---------o---------

Bruce C. Jones, being duly sworn, says that as stenographer to the Commission to the Five Civilized Tribes he reported the testimony of the above named witness, and that the foregoing is a full, true and correct translation of his stenographic notes.

Cherokee Intermarried White 1906
Volume II

Bruce C Jones

Sworn to and subscribed before me this the 20th day of August, 1900.

C.R. Breckinridge

Commissioner.

◇◇◇◇◇

DEPARTMENT OF THE INTERIOR.
Commission to the Five Civilized Tribes.
Muskogee, Indian Territory, October 13th, 1902.

In the matter of the application of James M. Raley for the enrollment of himself as a citizen by intermarriage and his wife, Mary L. Raley, as a citizen by blood of the Cherokee Nation.

Supplemental to #1338.

JAMES M. RALEY, being duly sworn, testified as follows.
Examination by the Commission.

Q. What is your name? A. James M. Raley.
Q. How old are you? A. I am 56, in my 56th year.
Q. What is your post office? A. Muldrow.
Q. You are a white man? A. Yes, sir.
Q. You are on the eighty roll as an intermarried white?
A. Yes, sir.
Q. What is your wife's name? A. Mary L.
Q. Was she your wife in 1880? A. Yes, sir.
Q. Have you and your wife been living together ever since 1880?
A. Yes, sir.
Q. Never been separated? A. No, sir.
Q. Never made your home elsewhere than the Cherokee Nation? A. No, sir.
Q. Have you any children? A. No, sir.

IIIIIIIIIIIIIIIIIIIIIIIIIIII

Jesse O. Carr, being first duly sworn, states that as stenographer to the Commission to the Five Civilized Tribes he reported the above entitled case and that the foregoing is a true and complete transcript of his stenographic notes thereof.

Jesse O. Carr

Cherokee Intermarried White 1906
Volume II

Subscribed and sworn to before me this 26th day of December, 1902.

BC Jones
Notary Public.

◇◇◇◇◇

Cherokee No. 1338.

DEPARTMENT OF THE INTERIOR.
COMMISSIONER TO THE FIVE CIVILIZED TRIBES.

Muskogee, Indian Territory, January 3, 1907.

In the matter of the application for the enrollment of James M. Raley as a citizen by intermarriage of the Cherokee Nation.

James M. Raley, being first duly sworn and examined, testifies as follows:

BY THE COMMISSIONER:

Q What is your name? A James M. Raley.
Q How old are you? A 61.
Q What is your Post Office address? A Muldrow.
Q Do you claim to be an intermarried citizen of the Cherokee Nation? A Yes, sir.
Q Through whom do you claim your rights as an intermarried citizen? A My wife, Mary A. Raley.
Q When were you married to Mary A. Raley? A February 16th, 1871.
Q Were you ever married before you married Mary A. Raley? A No, sir.
Q Was she ever married before she married you? A No, sir.
Q Where were you married? A Flint District.
Q Have you lived together continuously since your marriage up to the present time?
A Yes, sir.
Q Did you get a licence[sic] under the Cherokee Law to get married? A Yes, sir.
Q Have you got a copy of that licence[sic]? A Yes, sir.

The applicamt[sic] offers in evidence a licence[sic] issued to him to marry Miss. Mary Star on the 14th day of February, 1871, said licence[sic] being signed by James W. Adair, Clerk of the District Court of Flint District, Cherokee Nation, together with a cirtificate[sic] of Rev. W. A. Duncan, that he performed said marriage ceremony on February 16th, 1871. The same will be filed with and made a part of the record in this case.

Cherokee Intermarried White 1906
Volume II

The applicant is identified on the 1880 Cherokee Roll opposite No. 1041. His wife through whom he claims his intermarriage rights is identified on said roll opposite No. 1042. She was also identified on the final roll of the citizens by blood of the Cherokee Nation opposite No. 3683.

Q Was your wife recognized as a citizen of the Cherokee Nation at the time you married her in 1871? A Yes, sir.

WITNESS EXCUSED.

F. Elma Lane, upon oath, states that she reported the proceedings in the above entitled cause and that the foregoing is a true and correct transcript of her stenographic notes taken therein.

F. Elma Lane

Subscribed and sworn to before me this 3rd day of January, 1907.

Chas E Webster
Notary Public.

◇◇◇◇◇

CERTIFIED COPY.

Cherokee Nat.)
Flint District.)

By the authority in me vested by the laws of the Cherokee Nation I do hereby grant License of marriage unto James M. Raley, a citizen of the United States and a man of good moral character, of industrious habits, to marry Miss Mary Starr, a Cherokee by birth and a daughter of Leroy Starr (He James M. Raley) having complied with the requirements of the law regulating intermarriage with white men. Given from under my hand in office This the 14 day of Feby. 1871.

James W. Adair Clk.
Dist. Ct. Flint C. N.

License Fee $5.00

I hereby certify that I solemnized the marriage of the above named James M. Raley and Mary Starr according to requirement of Law Flint Dist. C.N., Feby 16, 1871.

W. A. Duncan,
Preacher M. E. C. South

I hareby[sic] certify that the above license and certificate is correct according to record.

John B. Lynch,
(SEAL) Clk. Flint C.N. Oct. 9, 1896.

Cherokee Intermarried White 1906
Volume II

I, Frances R. Lane, a stenographer to the Commissioner to the Five Civilized Tribes, do hereby certify that the above and foregoing is a true and complete copy of a marriage license and certificate issued to James M. Raley to marry Miss Mary Starr, now on file with the records of this office in the matter of the application of James M. Riley for enrollment as a citizen by intermarriage of the Cherokee Nation-- Cherokee 3972.

Frances R Lane

Subscribed and sworn to before me this January 21, 1907.

Edward Merrick
Notary Public.

◇◇◇◇◇

F.R.   Cherokee 1338.

DEPARTMENT OF THE INTERIOR,
COMMISSIONER TO THE FIVE CIVILIZED TRIBES.

In the matter of the application for the enrollment of James M. Raley as a citizen by intermarriage of the Cherokee Nation.

D E C I S I O N .

THE RECORDS OF THIS OFFICE SHOW: That on August 14, 1900, application was received by the Commission to the Five Civilized Tribes for the enrollment of James M. Raley as a citizen by intermarriage of the Cherokee Nation. Further proceedings in the matter of said application were had at Muskogee, Indian Territory, on October 13, 1902, and January 3, 1907.

THE EVIDENCE IN THIS CASE SHOWS: That the applicant herein, James M. Raley, a white man, was married in accordance with the laws of the Cherokee Nation, on February 16, 1871, to Mary L. Raley (nee Starr), who was at the time of said marriage a recognized citizen by blood of the Cherokee Nation, who is identified on the Cherokee authenticated tribal roll of 1880, Sequoyah District, No. 1042, as a native Cherokee, and whose name is included in the approved partial roll of citizens by blood of the Cherokee Nation opposite No. 3683. It is further shown that from the time of said marriage the said James M. Raley and Mary L. Raley resided together as husband and wife and continuously lived in the Cherokee Nation up to and including September 1, 1902. The applicant is identified on the Cherokee authenticated tribal roll of 1880, and on the Cherokee census roll of 1896, as an intermarried citizen of the Cherokee Nation.

Cherokee Intermarried White 1906
Volume II

IT IS, THEREFORE, ORDERED AND ADJUDGED: That in accordance with the decision of the Supreme Court of the United States, dated November 5, 1906, in the cases of Daniel Red Bird et al., vs. the United States, Nos. 125, 126, 127 and 128, the said applicant, James M. Raley, is entitled, under the provision of Section 21 of the Act of Congress approved June 28, 1898 (30 Stats., 495), to enrollment as a citizen by intermarriage of the Cherokee Nation, and his application for enrollment as such is accordingly granted.

Tams Bixby
Commissioner.

Dated at Muskogee, Indian Territory,
this   JAN 23 1907

◇◇◇◇◇◇

Cherokee
1338.

Muskogee, Indian Territory, December 24, 1906.

James M. Raley,
    Muldrow, Indian Territory.

Dear Sir:

November 6, 1906, the United States Supreme Court held that white persons who intermarried with Cherokee citizens according to Cherokee law prior to November 1, 1875, are entitled to enrollment and allotments of land as citizens of the Cherokee Nation.

You are advised that to properly determine your right to enrollment as a citizen by intermarriage of the Cherokee Nation, it will be necessary for you to appear before the Commissioner for the purpose of giving testimony as to the date of your marriage and whether or not your wife, by reason of your marriage to whom you claim the right to enrollment as a citizen of the Cherokee Nation, was a recognized citizen of the Cherokee Nation at the time of your marriage to her, and whether or not you were married to her in accordance with Cherokee laws.

You are, therefore, directed to appear before the Commissioner at Muskogee, Indian Territory, at 9 o'clock A. M., on Thursday, January 3, 1907, and give testimony as above indicated.

Respectfully,

LMC   Acting Commissioner.

◇◇◇◇◇◇

Cherokee Intermarried White 1906
Volume II

Cherokee 1338

Muskogee, Indian Territory, January 23, 1907.

W. W. Hastings,
    Attorney for the Cherokee Nation,
        Muskogee, Indian Territory.

Dear Sir:

    There is enclosed herewith copy of the decision of the Commissioner to the Five Civilized Tribes, dated January 23, 1907, granting the application for the enrollment of James M. Raley as a citizen by intermarriage of the Cherokee Nation.

Respectfully,

Enc I-69
RPI

Commissioner

◇◇◇◇◇

Cherokee 1338   W.W.HASTINGS. ATTORNEY.   OFFICE OF   H.M. VANCE. SECRETARY.

Attorney for the Cherokee Nation,
MUSKOGEE, I. T.

January 23, 1907.

The Commissioner to the Five Civilized Tribes,
    Muskogee, Indian Territory.

Sir:

    Receipt is acknowledged of the testimony and of your decision enrolling James M. Raley as a citizen by intermarriage of the Cherokee Nation. Time for protesting said decision is waived and I consent that said person may be placed upon the schedule immediately.

Respectfully,
W. W. Hastings
Attorney for the Cherokee Nation.

◇◇◇◇◇

Cherokee Intermarried White 1906
Volume II

Cherokee 1338

Muskogee, Indian Territory, January 23, 1907.

James M. Raley,
    Muldrow, Indian Territory.

Dear Sir:

    There is enclosed herewith a copy of the decision of the Commissioner to the Five Civilized Tribes, dated January 23, 1907, granting the application for your enrollment as a citizen by intermarriage of the Cherokee Nation.

    You will be advised when your name has been placed upon a schedule of citizens of the Cherokee Nation and approved by the Secretary of the Interior.

                      Respectfully,

Encl. H-105   Commissioner.
  JMH

◇◇◇◇◇

Cherokee I.W. 65

Muskogee, Indian Territory, April 8, 1907.

James M. Raley,
    Muldrow, Indian Territory.

Dear Sir:

    Your marriage license and certificate filed in connection with your application for enrollment as a citizen by intermarriage of the Cherokee Nation, is returned to you herewith, copies of the same being retained in this office.

                        Respectfully,

Incl. P-4-15   Acting Commissioner.
  MMP

Cherokee Intermarried White 1906
Volume II

Cher IW 66
Trans from Cher 1584 3-15-07

◇◇◇◇◇

C.F.B.

DEPARTMENT OF THE INTERIOR,

COMMISSIONER TO THE FIVE CIVILIZED TRIBES.

In the matter of the application for the enrollment of

FLORIAN H. NASH

as a citizen by intermarriage of the Cherokee Nation.

CHEROKEE 1584.

Department of the Interior,
Commission to the Five Civilized Tribes,
Fort Gibson, I. T., August 20, 1900.

In the matter of the application of Florian H. Nash for the enrollment of himself and children as Cherokee citizens; being sworn and examined by Commissioner Needles, he testified as follows:
Q What is your name? A Florian H. Nash.
Q What is your age? A 63.
Q What is your post office address? A Gibson.
Q Are you a recognized citizen of the Cherokee Nation? A I am.
Q What district do you belong to? A Illinois.
Q How long have you lived in Illinois district? A 47 years.
Q For whom do you apply, Mr. Nash? A For myself and four children under 21.
Q Your father and mother are not living? A No sir.
Q They died before 1800? A Yes, sir.
Q What is the names of the children? A Lucy M., age 19.
Q What is the name of the next one? A Corinne, age 15.
Q What is the name of the next one? A Hilda, 13 years old.
Q What is the name of the next one? A Edwin O., 10 years old.
Q What is the next one? A That is four.
Q Are these children alive and living with you? A Yes, sir, they are at home.
(On 1880, roll, page 561, No. 1300, F. H. Nash, Illinois district.)
Q Any of the others of your family on the 1880 roll? A Yes, sir, some that are dead.

Cherokee Intermarried White 1906
Volume II

(On 1896 roll, page 933, No. 148, Florian Nash, Illinois district. Lucy M. Nash on 1896 roll, page 886, No. 1351, Lucy M. Nash, Illinois district. Corinne Nash on 1896 roll, page 886, No. 1352, Corinne Nash, Illinois district. Hilda Nash on 1896 roll, page 886, No. 1353, Hilda Nash, Illinois district. Edwin O. Nash on 1896 roll, page 886, No. (1353), Illinois district.)(#1354)

Q The mother of these children not living? A No, sir.
Q Do you claim as a citizen by blood or intermarriage? A By intermarriage.

The name of Florian H. Nash appears upon the authenticated roll of 1880, and the names of himself and his children, Lucy M., Corinne, Hilda, and Edwin O., also appear upon the census roll of 1896, and they being fully identified according to page and number as indicated in the testimony, and having made satisfactory proof as to their residence, they will be duly listed for enrollment by this Commission, himself as a citizen by intermarriage, and his children as citizens by blood.

-------o-------

Bruce C. Jones, being duly sworn, says that as stenographer to the Commission to the Five Civilized Tribes he reported the testimony of the above named witness, and that the foregoing is a full, true and correct translation of his stenographic notes.

Bruce C. Jones

Sworn to and subscribed before me this the 25th day of August, 1900.

TB Needles
Commissioner.

◇◇◇◇◇

Cher
Supp'l to # 1584

Department of the Interior,
Commission to the Five Civilized Tribes,
Muskogee, I. T., October 20, 1902.

In the matter of the application of FLORIAN H. NASH, for the enrollment of himself as a citizen by intermarriage, and his children, LUCY M., CORINNE, HILDA and EDWIN O. NASH, as citizens by blood, of the Cherokee Nation.

FLORIAN H. NASH, being duly sworn and examined by the Commission, testified as follows:

Q What is your name ? A Florian H. Nash.
Q What is your age at this time ? A Sixty five years.
Q What is your post office ? A Fort Gibson.

Cherokee Intermarried White 1906
Volume II

Q Are your he same Florian H. Nash that applied to the Commission for enrollment as an intermarried citizen in August, 1900 ? A I am.
Q What is your wife's name ? A She's dead; Lucy M. Nash was my last wife. She was reported dead on the rolls at the time.
Q Was she a Cherokee by blood ? A Yes sir.
Q When were you married to your wife Lucy ? A I was married in 1874, I believe it was.
Q You are on the 1880 roll ? A I am.
Q Did you and your wife Lucy M., live together as husband and wife from 1880 up to her death ? A We did.
Q Were you ever separated ? A No sir.
Q Were you still single and a widower on the first day of September, 1902 ? A Yes sir.
Q have you lived in the Cherokee Nation from the time you were married to your wife up to the present time ? A Yes sir.
Q Are these children, Lucy M., Corinne, Hilda and Edwin O., your children by your wife Lucy M. Nash ? A Yes sir.
Q Are they living now ? A Yes sir.
Q Have they lived in the Cherokee Nation all their lives ? A Yes sir.

E. C. Bagwell, on oath states that, as stenographer to the Commission to the Five Civilized Tribes, he correctly recorded the testimony and proceedings had in the above entitled cause, and that the foregoing is an accurate transcript of his stenographic notes thereof.

E.C. Bagwell

Subscribed and sworn to before me this November 21, 1902.

BC Jones
Notary Public.

◇◇◇◇◇

Cherokee 1584.

DEPARTMENT OF THE INTERIOR,
COMMISSION TO THE FIVE CIVILIZED TRIBES.
Muskogee, Indian Territory, January 3, 1907.

In the Matter of the Application for the Enrollment of Florian H. Nash as a citizen by intermarriage of the Cherokee Nation.

APPEARANCES: Applicant appears in person.

Cherokee Nation represented by H. M. Vance, in behalf of W. W. Hastings, Attorney.

Cherokee Intermarried White 1906
Volume II

Florian H. Nash being first duly sworn by B. P. Rasmus, Notary Public, testified as follows:

ON BEHALF OF COMMISSIONER.

Q What is your name?   A Florian H. Nash.
Q What is your age?   A 69 Last November.
Q What is your post office address?
A Fort Gibson.
Q You are an applicant for enrollment as a citizen by intermarriage of the Cherokee Nation?
A Yes sir.
Q You have no Cherokee blood?   A No sir.
Q The only claim you make to the right of enrollment as a citizen of the Cherokee Nation is by the virtue of your marriage to a citizen by blood of the Cherokee Nation, is it?
A Yes sir.
Q What is the name of the citizen through whom you claim the right of enrollment?
A I have been married twice; my first wife was Fannie Ross Vann.
Q Was she a citizen by blood of the Cherokee Nation?
A She was.
Q Is she living or dead?   A Dead.
Q When were you married to her?   A May 29, 1862.
Q Where was she living at the time you married her?
A Paris Hill, Cherokee Nation.
Q You married her in the Cherokee Nation, did you?
A Yes sir.
Q Did you and she continuously live together as husband and wife until the time of her death?
A Yes sir.
Q When did she die?   A September, '73.
Q When were you married to you second wife?
A November, '74.
Q A citizen of the Cherokee Nation?
A Yes sir.
Q Is she living or dead?   A Dead.
Q When did she die?
A She died the 28th of December, 1890.
Q You and she continuously lived together as husband and wife did you, from the date of your marriage until the time of her death?
A We did.
Q Since the death of your second wife, you have not re-married?
A No sir.

Cherokee Intermarried White 1906
Volume II

Q Since your marriage to your first wife, have you continuously resided in the Cherokee Nation?
A I have except for a short time during the war when they were all driven away.
Q Any absence that you may have had from the Cherokee Nation since your marriage to your wirst[sic] wife has been of a temporary character?
A Yes sir.
Q The Cherokee Nation has been your home?
A Yes sir, I have lived continuously in Fort Gibson.
Q But you married both your wifes[sic] in accordance with the Cherokee laws?
A Yes sir.
Q In what district did you secure license to marry your first wife?
A Tahlequah District.
Q The license was secured in due form, was it?
A Yes sir
Q In what district did you secure the license to marry your second wife?
A It was not required; my second wife being a Cherokee and myself being a Cherokee citizen, we did not get any license.
Q Have you any documentary evidence showing your marriage to your first wife?
A I have not; they were all lost during the war; lost everything I had.

The applicant, Florian H. Nash, is identified on the Cherokee authenticated Tribal Roll of 1880, Illinois District No. 1300.

Percy W. Hicks being duly sworn by B. P. Rasmus, Notary Public, testified as follows:

Q What is your name?   A Percy W. Hicks.
Q What is your age?   A 54.
Q What is your post office address?
A Fort Gibson.
Q You appear here for the purpose of giving testimony relative to the right of enrollment of Florian H. Nash as a citizen by intermarriage of the Cherokee Nation, do you?
A Yes sir.
Q How long have you known Florian H. Nash?
A Since he was married in '62.
Q Were you present at the marriage ceremony?
A Yes sir.
Q Was he married in accordance with the laws of the Cherokee Nation
A I think so; I didn't see the license. I know it was so understood by every one.
Q It has always been the understanding then that he was married to a Cherokee by blood in accordance with the Cherokee laws?
A Yes sir.
Q Do you know when his first wife died?
A No, I don't know the date; I live near him though and I knew at the time.
Q After her death, he married a Cherokee by blood did he?
A Yes sir.

Cherokee Intermarried White 1906
Volume II

Q And he has always lived in the Cherokee Nation since his marriage to his first wife, has he?
A Yes sir.

Joshua Ross being duly sworn by B. P. Rasmus, Notary Public, testified as follows:

Q What is your name?   A Joshua Ross.
Q What is your age?   A 73.
Q What is your post office?   A Muskogee.
Q You appear here for the purpose of giving testimony relative to the right of enrollment of Florian H. Nash as a citizen by intermarriage of the Cherokee Nation, do you?
A Yes.
Q How long have you known Florian H. Nash?
A About 50 years.
Q What was the name of his first wife?
A Fannie Vann.
Q Was she a citizen by blood?
A Yes sir.
Q When was he married to her?
A May, 1862.
Q Were you present at the ceremony?
A Yes.
Q Was he married in accordance with the laws of the Cherokee Nation?
A Yes.
Q And continuously lived with his wife did he, from the time of his marriage until the time of her death?
A Yes sir.
Q After her death, he married a Cherokee by blood and lived with her until the time of her death?
A Yes sir.
Q Has he continuously resided in the Cherokee Nation from the time of his marriage to his first wife until the present time?
A Yes sir.

The undersigned being first duly sworn states that as stenographer to the Commission to the Five Civilized Tribes, she correctly recorded the testimony taken in this case and that the foregoing is a full, true and correct transcript of her stenographic notes thereof.

Myrtle Hill

Subscribed and sworn to before me this the 4th day of January, 1907.

B.P. Rasmus
Notary Public.

Cherokee Intermarried White 1906
Volume II

F. R. Cherokee 1584.

DEPARTMENT OF THE INTERIOR,

COMMISSIONER TO THE FIVE CIVILIZED TRIBES.

In the matter of the application for the enrollment of FLORIAN H. NASH as a citizen by intermarriage of the Cherokee Nation.

_D_E_C_I_S_I_O_N_

THE RECORDS OF THIS OFFICE SHOW: That at Fort Gibson, Indian Territory, August 20th, 1900, application was received by the Commission to the Five Civilized Tribes for the enrollment of Florian H. Nash as a citizen by intermarriage of the Cherokee Nation. Further proceedings in the matter of said application were had at Muskogee, Indian Territory, October 20th, 1902 and January 3rd, 1907.

THE EVIDENCE IN THIS CASE SHOWS: That the applicant herein, Florian H. Nash, a white man, was married in accordance with Cherokee law May 29th, 1862 you Fannie Ross Nash, nee Vann, who was at the time of said marriage a recognized citizen by blood of the Cherokee Nation; that said Florian H. Nash and Fannie Ross Nash resided together as husband and wife from the time of said marriage until the death of said Fannie Ross Nash, which occurred in September, 1873; that thereafter, in 1874 said Florian H. Nash was married to his wife, Lucy M. Nash, since deceased, who was at the time of said marriage a recognized citizen by blood of the Cherokee Nation, and who is identified on the Cherokee authenticated tribal roll of 1880, Illinois District No. 1301, as a native Cherokee; that said Florian H. Nash and Lucy M. Nash resided together as husband and wife from the time of their marriage in 1874 until the death of said Lucy M. Nash, which occurred December 28th, 1890; that since the death of said Lucy M. Nash said Florian H. Nash has not married, and that he has resided continuously in the Cherokee Nation since 1862. Said applicant is identified on the Cherokee authenticated tribal roll of 1880 and the Cherokee census roll of 1896 as an intermarried citizen of the Cherokee Nation.

IT IS, THEREFORE, ORDERED AND ADJUDGED: That in accordance with the decision of the Supreme Court of the United States dated November 5, 1906 in the cases of Daniel Red Bird et al. vs. the United States, Nos. 125, 126, 127 and 128, the said applicant, Florian H. Nash is entitled, under the provisions of Section Twenty-one of the Act of Congress approved June 28, 1898 (30 Stats. 495), to enrollment as a citizen by intermarriage of the Cherokee Nation, and his application for enrollment as such is accordingly granted.

Tams Bixby
Commissioner.

Dated at Muskogee, Indian Territory,
this   JAN 21 1907

Cherokee Intermarried White 1906
Volume II

Cherokee
1584.

Muskogee, Indian Territory, December 24, 1906.

Florian H. Nash,
    Fort Gibson, Indian Territory.

Dear Sir:

November 6, 1906, the United States Supreme Court held that white persons who intermarried with Cherokee citizens according to Cherokee law prior to November 1, 1875, are entitled to enrollment and allotments of land as citizens of the Cherokee Nation.

You are advised that to properly determine your right to enrollment as a citizen by intermarriage of the Cherokee Nation, it will be necessary for you to appear before the Commissioner for the purpose of giving testimony as to the date of your marriage and whether or not your wife, by reason of your marriage to whom you claim the right to enrollment as a citizen of the Cherokee Nation, was a recognized citizen of the Cherokee Nation at the time of your marriage to her, and whether or not you were married to her in accordance with Cherokee laws.

You are, therefore, directed to appear before the Commissioner at Muskogee, Indian Territory, at 9 o'clock A. M., on Thursday, January 3, 1907, and give testimony as above indicated.

                Respectfully,

LMC   Acting Commissioner.

◇◇◇◇◇

Cherokee 1584

Muskogee, Indian Territory, January 21, 1907.

W. W. Hastings,
    Attorney for the Cherokee Nation,
        Muskogee, Indian Territory.

Dear Sir:

There is enclosed herewith copy of the decision of the Commissioner to the Five Civilized Tribes, dated January 21, 1907, granting the application for the enrollment of Florian H. Nash as a citizen by intermarriage of the Cherokee Nation.

Cherokee Intermarried White 1906
Volume II

Respectfully,

Enc I-29 Commissioner.
RPI

◇◇◇◇◇◇

Cherokee 1584   W.W. HASTINGS.   OFFICE OF   H.M. VANCE.
                ATTORNEY.   SECRETARY.

Attorney for the Cherokee Nation,
MUSKOGEE, I. T.

January 21, 1907.

The Commissioner to the Five Civilized Tribes,
　　Muskogee, Indian Territory.

Sir:

　　Receipt is acknowledged of the testimony and of your decision enrolling Florian H. Nash as a citizen by intermarriage of the Cherokee Nation. Time for protesting said decision is waived and I consent that said person may be placed upon the schedule immediately.

Respectfully,
W. W. Hastings
Attorney for the Cherokee Nation.

◇◇◇◇◇◇

Cherokee 1584

Muskogee, Indian Territory, January 24, 1907.

Florian H. Nash,
　　Fort Gibson, Indian Territory.

Dear Sir:

　　There is enclosed herewith copy of the decision of the Commissioner to the Five Civilized Tribes, dated January 21, 1907, granting the application for your enrollment as a citizen by intermarriage of the Cherokee Nation.

　　You will be advised when your name has been placed upon a schedule of citizens of the Cherokee Nation and approved by the Secretary of the Interior.

Respectfully,

Enc I-98 Commissioner.
RPI

Cherokee Intermarried White 1906
Volume II

Cher IW 67
Trans from Cher 1682 3-15-07

◇◇◇◇◇

E.C.M.

DEPARTMENT OF THE INTERIOR,

COMMISSIONER TO THE FIVE CIVILIZED TRIBES.

In the matter of the application for the enrollment of

SOLOMON BRAGG

as a citizen by intermarriage of the Cherokee Nation.

CHEROKEE 1682

◇◇◇◇◇

Department of the Interior,
Commission to the Five Civilized Tribes,
Ft. Gibson, I.T., August 21, 1900.

In the matter of the application of Solomon Bragg for the enrollment of his wife and self as Cherokee citizens; being sworn and examined by Commissioner Needles he testifies as follows:

Q What is your name? A Solomon Bragg.
Q What is your age? A Seventy-two.
Q What is your post-office addres[sic]? A Braggs.
Q Are you a recognized citizen of the Cherokee Nation? A Yes sir.
Q By blood? A By adoption.
Q What district do you live in? A Illinois.
Q How long have you lived in Illinois District? A I have lived here since 1867.
Q Since 1867 continuously? A Yes sir.
Q For whom do you apply for enrollment? A For myself and wife.
Q Your father living A YNo/sir[sic].
Q He was a non-citizen? A Yes sir.
Q Your mother was also a non-citizen? A Yes sir.
Q What is your wife's name? A Elizabeth Bragg.
Q What is her age A Seventy-three.
Q She a recognized citizen? A Yes sir.
Q Her father and mother not living? A No sir.

Cherokee Intermarried White 1906
Volume II

Q Did they die, either of the,[sic] since 1880, or before?
A Before.
1880 roll page 510 #273 Solomon Bragg, Illinois District.
1880 roll page 510 #274 Elizabeth Bragg Illinois District.
  1896 roll page 925 #10 Solomon Bragg Illinos[sic] District.
1896 roll page 838 #105 Elizabeth Bragg Illinois District.
Q You have no children with you under twenty-one? A No sir.

Com'r Needles: The name of Solomon Bragg appearing upon the authenticated roll of 1880 as well as the census roll of 1896, and being duly identified according to page and number of the said rolls as indicated in testimony, and the name of his wife also being found upon the authenticated roll of 1880 as well as the census roll of 1896 and being duly identified, and they having made satisfactory proof as to their residence, they will be duly listed for enrollment by this Commission as Cherokee citizens, Solomon Bragg as a Cherokee citizen by intermarriage and his wife, Elizabeth Bragg as a Cherokee citizen by blood.

M.D. Green, being first duly sworn, states that as stenographer to the Commission to the Five Civilized Tribes he reported the foregoing case, and that the above and foregoing is a full true and complete transcript of his stenographic notes of the testimony and proceedings therein.

MD Green

Subscribed and sworn to before me this 27 day of August 1900.

TB Needles
Commissioner.

◇◇◇◇◇

Cherokee 1682.

DEPARTMENT OF THE INTERIOR,
COMMISSION TO THE FIVE CIVILIZED TRIBES.
Muskogee, I. T., October 11, 1902.

In the matter of the application of Solomon Bragg for the enrollment of himself as a citizen by intermarriage, and for the enrollment of his wife, Elizabeth Bragg, as a citizen by blood, of the Cherokee Nation.

SUPPLEMENTAL PROCEEDINGS.

SOLOMON BRAGG, being sworn, testified as follows:

By the Commission,

Q What is your name? A Solomon Bragg.

Cherokee Intermarried White 1906
Volume II

Q How old are you at this time, Mr. Bragg? A Seventy-five years old.
Q What is your postoffice? A Edna, Kansas.
Q Are you the same Solomon Bragg that appeared before the Commission and applied for enrollment as an intermarried citizen in August, 1900? A Yes, sir.
Q What's your wife's name? A Elizabeth Bragg.
Q Is she living at this time? A Yes, sir.
Q Were you married to your wife, Elizabeth, prior to 1880?
A Yes, sir, we was married in 1867.
Q Have you ever been married to any other woman than Elizabeth since 1880?
A No, sir.
Q Have you and she lived together all the time as husband and wife since 1880 up to the present time? A Yes, sir.
Q Were you living together as husband and wife on the first day of September, 1902?
A Yes, sir.
Q Living in the Cherokee Nation at the present time? A Yes, sir.
Q Has your wife, Elizabeth, lived with you in the Cherokee Nation all the time since 1880? A Yes, sir.

Retta Chick, being first duly sworn, states that, as stenographer to the Commission to the Five Civilized Tribes, she recorded the testimony and proceedings in the matter of the foregoing application, and that the above is a true and complete transcript of her stenographic notes thereof.

Retta Chick

Subscribed and sworn to before me this 22nd day of October, 1902.

BC Jones
Notary Public.

◇◇◇◇◇

McG. Cherokee 1682.

DEPARTMENT OF THE INTERIOR,
COMMISSIONER TO THE FIVE CIVILIZED TRIBES.
Muskogee, I. T., January 5, 1907.

In the matter of the application for the enrollment of Solomon Braggs[sic] as a citizen by intermarriage of the Cherokee Nation.

Elizabeth Braggs[sic] being first duly sworn by Walter W. Chappelle, a Notary Public for the Western District, Indian Territory, testified as follows:

By the Commissioner:
Q What is your name? A Elizabeth Braggs.
Q What is your age? A I will be 80 the 4th of the coming June.
Q What is your postoffice address? A Braggs, I. T.

Cherokee Intermarried White 1906
Volume II

Q Is that in the Cherokee nation? A Yes, that was named after Mr. Braggs[sic]; we lived there and kept the railroad men.
Q What is your citizenship Mrs. Braggs? A I am a Cherokee. I was born at what is now called Clarksville, Ark.
Q You are a Cherokee by blood are you? A Yes, I am second cousin to Chief Rogers.
Q Did you come from the old nation to the present Cherokee nation? A My people did. I was born at Clarksville, Ark. in the year 1827. My people were the first Cherokees that ever come to this country, and we lived over there awhile.
Q What time did you parents first come to the Cherokee nation? A I don't know. They was here when I was born.
Q Have you lived here continuously since that time? A Only when I was in Virginia at school. My father's people were Brants.
Q Your home has always been here in the Cherokee nation ever since you arrived here as a child? A Yes, I went to school at Richmond. I was in Virginia when Van Buren was President.
Q Are you married Mrs. Braggs? A Yes, I was married to Mr. Braggs the 17th day of March, 1867.
Q Doed[sic] Mr. Braggs claim to be a citizen by intermarriage of the Cherokee nation? A Yes, he married according to Cherokee law; had ten signers and got his license and was married by the judge, and the judge took the license and said he would have it recorded. And I saw it on the record myself in looking for somebody else.
Q Where were you and Mr. Braggs married? A At my home within five miles of where we live now at Braggs.
Q You were married in 1867? A Yes sir.
Q You say you were married under a Cherokee license? A Yes.
Q Do you know where Mr. Braggs procured that license? Which District? A In Tahlequah, and got it from Dobson Reece.
Q He got the license in Tahlequah District from Dobson Reece? A Yes sir.
Q What office was Reece filling at that time? A He was clerk of the Supreme Court I think, and Albert Barns was clerk I think down at Ft. Gibson, and he is the one that recorded it at Gibson.
Q Have you a certified copy of the license under which you were married? A No sir.
Q Did you have a certified copy of this license? A I don't know that I did. We turned the license over to Judge Taylor and he said he would have it recorded at Ft. Gibson, and I guess he did.
Q Who performed the marriage ceremony between you and Mr. Braggs?
A Judge Sam Taylor.
Q Was he a Cherokee Judge? A Yes sir.
Q Had either you or Mr. Braggs been married prior to your marriage in 1867? A Yes, I had been married to a gentleman in New York by the name of Theodore Cummins.
Q Was your first husband dead when you married Mr. Braggs A Yes, he was killed in the commencement of the war.
Q He was dead at the time you married the second time? A Yes sir. Q Have you and Mr. Braggs lived together continuously as husband and wife since your marriage in 1867? A Yes, we never had no trouble in the world.
Q He is living at the present time is he? A Yes, but he is very sick.

Cherokee Intermarried White 1906
Volume II

Q Is he able to appear before this office and testify in this case? A No, he is not able to get out of bed.
Q He is confined to his room? A Yes sir?[sic] If he hadn't have been I wouldn't have come here, and we have no children.

> The marriage record for Tahlequah district furnished this office by the Cherokee nation does not cover the year 1867, ~~and no record of a license covering the year 1867~~, and no record of a license having been issued by the authorities of Tahlequah District authorizing the marriage of the applicant Solomon Braggs[sic] can be found.
> The marriage record for Illinos[sic] District furnished this office by the Cherokee nation fails to show that any such license as above described was recorded in that district.
> The marriage records for the districts above named are in very bad shape, many leaves being missing from the several books.

Q Were any witnesses present when you and Mr. Braggs were married? A The judge brought a young man from Webbers Falls by the name of Cherley[sic] Drew, and Kate North, that made her home with me, and George Elders, my nephew. He was a policeman under Colonel Wisdom, but he died last May. He is our only witness and he is dead.
Q There are witnesses to the marriage ceremony are there not? A Yes, George Elders, was the last and he died last May.
Q Are any of the citizens who signed your husband's petition to secure a license living at the present time? A Not one, and that seems so strange.
Q Is the clerk who issued the license living? A No sir.
Q Is the person who performed the ceremony living? A No, that was Judge Samuel Taylor.
Q Then all those persons who would be in a position to know that you and Mr. Braggs were married under Cherokee law are dead? A Yes, and all that we have to depend upon is our own word and our neighbors that had an idea we was married. We couldn't have lived here without we were.
Q Are any of your neighbors present here today who knew that you and Mr. Braggs were living together in the latter '60's? A No, my neighbors are scarce; nobody living nearer than ten miles; that was a barren country at that time
Q Could you produce any witnesses that could testify that you and Mr. Braggs have been living together as husband and wife since the year 1870? A Yes, I can find plenty of them right there at Braggs.
Q You have none of those present now, have you? A No sir.

> The witness, Elizabeth Braggs, wife of the applicant, Solomon Braggs, is included in the approved partial roll of Cherokees by blood of the Cherokee Nation, opposite No. 4490.

Cherokee Intermarried White 1906
Volume II

The applicant Solomon Braggs[sic] is identified on the authenticated Cherokee tribal roll 1880, and Cherokee census roll 8196[sic] Illinois District, opposite Nos. 273 and 10 respectively, as an intermarried white.

As you have no witnesses present this is all that can be done in your case today, and you will be notified later by this office whether or not it will be necessary to produce witnesses to establish that you and Mr. Braggs have lived together for the past thirty-five years as husband and wife.

A We can get plenty of them.

Frances R. Lane upon oath states that as stenographer to the Commissioner to the Five Civilized Tribes she reported the testimony in the above entitled cause and that the foregoing is an accurate transcript of her stenographic notes thereof.

Frances R. Lane

Subscribed and sworn to before me this January 7, 1907.

Edward Merrick
Notary Public.

◇◇◇◇◇

F. R.   Cherokee 1682

DEPARTMENT OF THE INTERIOR,
COMMISSIONER TO THE FIVE CIVILIZED TRIBES.
Muskoge[sic], I. T., January 15, 1907.

In the matter of the application for the enrollment of Solomon Bragg as citizen by intermarriage of the Cherokee Nation.

Nancy McDaniel, being first duly sworn by Frances R. Lane, a Notary Public for the Western District of Indian Territory, testified as follows:

By the Commissioner:
Q What is your name? A Nancy McDaniel.
Q How old are you? A Seventy-two.
Q What is your post office address? A Muskoge[sic], I. T.
Q Do you know Solomon Bragg? A Yes sir.
Q How long have you known him? A Ever since the war, after I came from the south.
Q Did you know his wife, Elizabeth? A Yes sir.
Q Do you know when they were married? A No, they were man and wife before I knew them.

Cherokee Intermarried White 1906
Volume II

Q After you knew them were they married in accordance with the Cherokee law? A I never did hear whether they was or not.
Q They resided together as husband and wife? A Yes, up until his death.
Q About when did he die? A I think it has been a week ago yesterday since I saw it in the paper. It is a few days ago.
Q It was your understanding, was it, that they had been married in accordance with the Cherokee law? A Yes, I always understood it that way.
Q But of your own personal knowledge you don't know anything with the reference to the date? A No sir.
Q Where did Solomon Bragg and his wife live? A When I first knew them they lived about four miles from Gibson.
Q They have lived continuously in the Cherokee nation from the time of their marriage until his death a short time ago? A Yes sir.

By Mr. Hastings:
Q They were living there as husband and wife immediately after you returned after the war in 1866-7? A Yes sir.
Q You knew them as early as 1867? A Yes sir.
Q And knew them as husband and wife at that time? A Yes sir.
Q And they lived together continuously as husband and wife until his death? A Yes sir.
Q Did you know Mrs. Bragg before the war? A yes, I wasn't to say acquainted with her well; I knew of her; she was a Rogers. Q Was it your understanding that this marriage to Mr. Bragg was her first marriage? A No, she was married to Mr. Rogers before that time.
Q Do you know whether her husband was dead? A Yes, he died before the war.
Q Do you know whether Mr. Bragg was ever married previously or not? A No sir.

Frances R. Lane upon oath states that as stenographer to the Commissioner to the Five Civilized Tribes she reported the testimony in the above entitled cause and that the foregoing is an accurate transcript of her stenographic notes therein.

                   Frances R. Lane

Subscribed and sworn to before me this January 17, 1907.

                   Edward Merrick
                   Notary Public.

Cherokee Intermarried White 1906
Volume II

E C M   Cherokee 1682

DEPARTMENT OF THE INTERIOR,
COMMISSIONER TO THE FIVE CIVILIZED TRIBES.

In the matter of the application for the enrollment of Solomon Bragg as a citizen by intermarriage of the Cherokee Nation.

D E C I S I O N .

THE RECORDS OF THIS OFFICE SHOW: That at Fort Gibson, Indian Territory, application was received by the Commission to the Five Civilized Tribes for the enrollment of Solomon Bragg as a citizen by intermarriage of the Cherokee Nation. Further proceedings in the matter of said application were had at Muskogee, Indian Territory, October 11, 1902, January 5, 1907 and January 15, 1907.

THE EVIDENCE IN THIS CASE SHOWS: that the applicant herein, Solomon Bragg, a white man, was married in accordance with Cherokee law on March 17, 1867 to his wife Elizabeth Bragg, nee Brant, and who was at the time of said marriage a recognize citizen by blood of the Cherokee Nation, who is identified on the Cherokee authenticated tribal roll of 1880, Illinois District No. 274 as a native Cherokee, and whose name is included in the approved partial roll of citizens by blood opposite No. 4490. It is further shown that from the time of said marriage the said Solomon Bragg and Elizabeth Bragg resided together as husband and wife and continuously lived in the Cherokee Nation up to and including September 1, 1902. Said applicant is identified on the Cherokee authenticated tribal roll of 1880 and the Cherokee census roll of 1896 as an intermarried citizen of the Cherokee Nation.

IT IS THEREFORE ORDERED AND ADJUDGED: That in accordance with the decision of the Supreme Court of the United States, dated November 5, 1906, in the case of Daniel Red Bird et al. vs. the United States, numbers 125, 126, 127, 128, the said applicant, Solomon Bragg is entitled, under the provisions of Section 21, of the Act of Congress approved June 28, 1898 (30th. Stats. 495), to enrollment as a citizen by intermarriage of the Cherokee Nation, and his application for enrollment as such is accordingly granted.

                                                            Tams Bixby
                                                                    Commissioner.

Dated at Muskogee, Indian Territory,
this   JAN 23 1907

◇◇◇◇◇◇

Cherokee Intermarried White 1906
Volume II

Department of the Interior,
COMMISSION TO THE FIVE CIVILIZED TRIBES.

In the matter of the death of **Solomon Bragg** a citizen of the **Cherokee** Nation, who formerly resided at or near **Braggs**, Ind. Ter., and died on the **9th** day of **January**, 1907.

AFFIDAVIT OF RELATIVE.

UNITED STATES OF AMERICA, }
INDIAN TERRITORY,
Western District.

I, **Elizabeth Bragg**, on oath state that I am **79** years of age and a citizen by **blood**, of the **Cherokee** Nation; that my postoffice address is **Braggs**, Ind. Ter.; that I am **the widow** of **Solomon Bragg** who was a citizen, by **Adoption**, of the **Cherokee** Nation and that said **Solomon Bragg** died on the **9th** day of **January**, 1907

her
Elizabeth x Bragg
mark

Witnesses To Mark:
{ E L King
{ Edwin B Smith

Subscribed and sworn to before me this **5** *day of* **April**, 190 **7**

Edward McLain
Notary Public.

AFFIDAVIT OF ACQUAINTANCE.

UNITED STATES OF AMERICA, }
INDIAN TERRITORY,
Western District.

I, **Luther Hopkins**, on oath state that I am **29** years of age, and a citizen by ~~adopted~~ of the **U. S.** Nation; that my postoffice address is **Braggs**, Ind. Ter.; that I was personally acquainted with **Solomon Bragg** who was a citizen, by **Adoption**, of the **Cherokee** Nation; and that said **Solomon Bragg** died on the **9th** day of **January**, 1907

Luther Hopkins

Witnesses To Mark:
{

Cherokee Intermarried White 1906
Volume II

Subscribed and sworn to before me this   5   *day of*   **April**   , 190 7

Edward McLain
Notary Public.

◇◇◇◇◇◇

Cherokee
1682.

Muskogee, Indian Territory, January 10, 1907.

Soloman Braggs[sic],
    Braggs, Indian Territory.

Dear Sir:

    After an examination of the records of your application for enrollment as a citizen by intermarriage of the Cherokee Nation, this office is unable to find any documentary evidence of your marriage to Elizabeth Braggs, Indian Territory in accordance with Cherokee laws. You are advised that in order to be enrolled as a citizen by intermarriage of the Cherokee Nation it will be necessary for you to furnish this office with the original or a certified copy of your marriage license, or the evidence of witnesses who know of your marriage to Elizabeth Braggs.

    The evidence must be furnished at this office on or before January 17, 1907. This matter is important and you are requested to give it your immediate attention.

                  Respectfully,

HJC   Commissioner.

◇◇◇◇◇◇

Cherokee
1682

Muskogee, Indian Territory, January 12, 1907.

Solomon Bragg,
    Braggs, Indian Territory.

Dear Sir:

    This office is in receipt of your recent letter, without date, stating that on account of illness neither you nor your wife are able to appear before the Commissioner in connection with your application for enrollment as a citizen by intermarriage of the Cherokee Nation.

Cherokee Intermarried White 1906
Volume II

In reply you are advised that the record in the matter of your application will be carefully examined, and if it is found necessary that further evidence be introduced, you will be duly advised thereof and given an opportunity to introduce the same.

If you have a marriage license or a certificate of marriage, you should forward same to this office by return mail to be used in connection with your case.

Respectfully,

L M B   Commissioner.

◇◇◇◇◇

Cherokee 1682

Muskogee, Indian Territory, January 23, 1907.

W. W. Hastings,
    Attorney for the Cherokee Nation,
        Muskogee, Indian Territory.

Dear Sir:

There is enclosed herewith a copy of the decision of the Commissioner to the Five Civilized Tribes, dated January 23, 1907, granting the application for the enrollment of Solomon Bragg as a citizen by intermarriage of the Cherokee Nation.

Respectfully,

Encl. H-72   Commissioner.
    JMH

◇◇◇◇◇

Cherokee 1682   W.W.HASTINGS.   OFFICE OF   H.M. VANCE.
                 ATTORNEY.   SECRETARY.

Attorney for the Cherokee Nation,
MUSKOGEE, I. T.

January 23, 1907.

The Commissioner to the Five Civilized Tribes,
    Muskogee, Indian Territory.

Sir:

Receipt is acknowledged of the testimony and of your decision enrolling Solomon Bragg as a citizen by intermarriage of the Cherokee Nation. Time for protesting said decision is waived and I consent that said person may be placed upon the schedule immediately.

Cherokee Intermarried White 1906
Volume II

                Respectfully,

                     W. W. Hastings
                     Attorney for Cherokee Nation.

◇◇◇◇◇

Cherokee
1682

                Muskogee, Indian Territory, January 23, 1907.

Elizabeth Bragg,
    Braggs, Indian Territory.

Dear Madam:

    There is enclosed herewith copy of the decision of the Commissioner to the Five Civilized Tribes, dated January 23, 1907, granting the application for the enrollment of your husband as a citizen by intermarriage of the Cherokee Nation.

    You will be advised when his name has been placed upon a schedule of citizens of the Cherokee Nation and approved by the Secretary of the Interior.

                Respectfully,

E.R.C.   Commissioner.

Enc E.C.93

Cher IW 68
Trans from Cher 2052 3-15-07

◇◇◇◇◇

Cherokee Intermarried White 1906
Volume II

C.E.W.

DEPARTMENT OF THE INTERIOR,

COMMISSIONER TO THE FIVE CIVILIZED TRIBES.

In the matter of the application for the enrollment of

GEORGE W. WILLIAMS

as a citizen by intermarriage of the Cherokee Nation.

CHEROKEE 2052.

DEPARTMENT OF THE INTERIOR,
COMMISSION TO THE FIVE CIVILIZED TRIBES,
FORT GIBSON, I.T., AUGUST 27, 1900.

In the matter of the application of George W. Williams for enrollment of himself and wife as citizens of the Cherokee Nation, said Williams being sworn by Commissioner Needles, testified as follows:

Q What is your name? A George W. Williams.
Q Your age? A 55.
Q Are you a recognized citizen of the Cherokee Nation? A Yes, by adoption.
Q What is your postoffice address? A Muskogee.
Q What district do you live in? A Canadian.
Q For whom do you apply? A Myself and wife.
Q How long have you lived in the Cherokee Nation continuously? A 34 years.
Q Do you lived[sic] in the Cherokee Nation now? A Yes.
Q Your father and mother are non-citizens? A Yes.
Q Are hey living? A No sir.
Q What is the name of your wife? A Nancy.
Q When did you marry her? A On the 28th day of November, '69.
Q Is she an Indian by blood? A Yes.
Q Is her father and mother living? A No sir, they both died before the war.

      Applicant on '80 roll page 53 number 1472, as G. W. Williams.
      Applicant on '96 roll, page '95, number 318, as George.
      Applicant's wife on '80 roll, page 53, number 1473.
      Applicant's wife on '96 roll, page 81, number 2264.

Cherokee Intermarried White 1906
Volume II

The name of George W. Williams appears upon the authenticated roll of '80 as G. W. Williams amd[sic] on the census roll of '96 as George Williams. The name of his wife, Nancy, appears upon the authenticated roll of '80 as well as the census roll of '96.; They being fully identified thereby and having made satisfactory proof as to their residence, they will be duly listed by this Commission for enrollment as Cherokee citizens – she by blood, and he by intermarriage

The undersigned, being first duly sworn, states that as stenographer to the Commission to the Five Civilized Tribes, he correctly recorded the testimony and proceedings in this case and that the foregoing is a true and complete transcript of his stenographic notes thereof.

Brown McDonald

Subscribed and sworn to before me this 12th day of September, 1900, at Pryor Creek, I.T.

CR Breckinridge

Commissioner.

◇◇◇◇◇

Cherokee 2052.

DEPARTMENT OF THE INTERIOR,
COMMISSION TO THE FIVE CIVILIZED TRIBES.
Muskogee, I. T., October 11, 1902.

In the matter of the application of George W. Williams for the enrollment of himself as a citizen by intermarriage, and for the enrollment of his wife, Nancy Williams, as a citizen by blood of the Cherokee Nation.

SUPPLEMENTAL PROCEEDINGS.

GEORGE W. WILLIAMS, being sworn, testified as follows:

By the Commission,

Q What's your name, Mr. Williams? A G. W. Williams is my name.
Q What's your age at this time, Mr. Williams? A I was fifty-seven years old the twenty-second day of last August.
Q What's your postoffice? A Muskogee.
Q Are you the same George W. Williams that made application to this Commission for enrollment as an intermarried citizen in August, 1900?
A I enrolled at Fort Gibson but I guess so, I married Nancy Ratlingourd[sic].
Q You are an applicant for enrollment as an intermarried citizen?
A Yes, sir, I have already enrolled.
Q Now, what's your wife's name? A Nancy Ratlingourd before I married her, she was a widow.

Cherokee Intermarried White 1906
Volume II

Q Is she living at this time? A Yes, sir.
Q Is she a citizen by blood of the Cherokee Nation? A Yes, sir, she's an old settler Cherokee.
Q When were you married to Nancy? A 29th of November, 1869.
Q Have you and your wife, Nancy, lived together as husband and wife ever since 1880 up to the present time? A Ever since 1869 up to the present time.
Q You have not been separated since 1880? A No, sir, never did separate.
Q You and she living together as husband and wife on the first day of September, 1902? A Yes, sir.
Q And you never married any other woman since 1880? A No, sir.
Q Have you and your wife lived together in the Cherokee Nation as husband and wife since 1880? A Yes, sir.

Retta Chick, being first duly sworn, states that, as stenographer to the Commission to the Five Civilized Tribes, she recorded the testimony and proceedings in the matter of the foregoing application, and that the above is a true and complete transcript of her stenographic notes thereof.

Retta Chick

Subscribed and sworn to before me this 23rd day of October, 1902.

PG Reuter
Notary Public.

◇◇◇◇◇

C.F.B. Cherokee 2052.

DEPARTMENT OF THE INTERIOR,
COMMISSIONER TO THE FIVE CIVILIZED TRIBES.
MUSKOGEE, I. T., JANUARY 7, 1907.

In the matter of the application for the enrollment of George W. Williams as a citizen by intermarriage of the Cherokee Nation.

APPEARANCES: Applicant appears in person.
Cherokee Nation represented by H.M. Vance,
for W. W. Hastings, Attorney.

GEORGE W. WILLIAMS, being first duly sworn by John E. Tidwell, Notary Public, testified as follows:

ON BEHALF OF THE COMMISSIONER:

Q What is your name? A George W. Williams.

Cherokee Intermarried White 1906
Volume II

Q What is your age? A 59, the 22d of last August.
Q What is your post office address? A Muskogee.
Q Are you an applicant for enrollment as a citizen by intermarriage of the Cherokee Nation? A Yes sir.
Q You have no Cherokee blood? A No sir.
Q You claim the right to enrollment as a citizen of the Cherokee Nation solely by virtue of your marriage to a citizen by blood of the Cherokee Nation, do you? A Yes sir.
Q What is the name of your wife, through whom you claim the right to enrollment? A Nancy Rattlingourd.
Q Is she living? A No sir, she died two years ago.
Q You have not married since her death? A No sir.
Q Were you ever married prior to your marriage to her? A No sir.
Q Was she ever married prior to her marriage to you? A Yes sir, she had been married three times.
Q Were her former husbands living or dead at the time you married her? A All dead; I have seen her last husband.
Q But he was dead when you married her? A Yes sir.
Q Was your wife a recognized citizen of the Cherokee Nation at the time of your marriage to her? A Yes sir, she was an old settler.
Q And living in the Cherokee Country, was she? A Yes sir.
Q Have you any documentary evidence to show your marriage to your wife? A Nothing more than that; that is what the Cherokee Nation says.
Q Your license was issued in Canadian District, was it? A Yes, sir, I was married by the Chief Justice of the Supreme Court of the Cherokee Nation.

"The applicant presents a certified copy of marriage record, Canadian District, Cherokee Nation, showing that on November 29, 1869, license was issued by J. A. Scales, Acting Clerk, authorizing the marriage of G. W. Williams, a white man, citizen of the United States, and Mrs. Nancy Ratlingord[sic]; and that said parties were united in marriage in accordance with the terms of said license on the 29th day of November, 1869, by John D. Vann, Associate Justice, Supreme Court.
"This certified copy of marriage record will be filed with and made a part of the record in this case."

"The applicant, George W. Williams, is identified on the Cherokee authenticated tribal roll of 1880, Canadian District, No. 1472. His wife, Nancy Williams, is identified on said roll at No. 1473, and her name is also included in the approved partial roll of citizens by blood of the Cherokee Nation, opposite No. 5334."

The undersigned, being first duly sworn, states that as stenographer to the Commissioner to the Five Civilized Tribes, she correctly reported the above and foregoing testimony, and that the same is a full, true and correct transcript of her stenographic notes thereof.

Cherokee Intermarried White 1906
Volume II

Sarah Waters

Subscribed and sworn to before me this 7th day of January, 1907.

John E. Tidwell
Notary Public.

◇◇◇◇◇

(The Marriage License and Certificate below typed as given.)

COPY

A copy of the mariage license and certificate of mariage of G. W. Williams and Nancy Ratlingoard.

To any Judge or other authorized person:

You are hereby autherized to solemnize the rights of matrimony between G. W. Williams a white man a citizen of the United States and Mrs. Nancy Ratlingord in accordance with the act regulating intermariage with white men. Mr. Williams has been qualified as the law directs.

Given November 29th 1869.

J. A. Scales,
Acting Clerk.

This is to certify that on the twenty-ninth day of November A. D. one thousand eight hundred and sixty-nine, before me John S. Vann associate justice of the supreme court, G. W. Williams a white man citizen of the U. S. and Nancy Ratlingoard were legally joined in mariage according to the within authorized license.

In witness whereof I hereunto set my hand officially,

John S. Vann
A. J. S. Court

I hereby certify that the above is a correct copy from the original and recorded on this the 15th of January A. D. 1870.

J. L. McCorkle,
Clerk D. C. C. D. C. N.

Executive Office, Taahlequah Cherokee Nation.

I B. W. Alberty assistant Executive secretary of the Cherokee Nation do hereby certify that the foregoing is a correct copy of the marriage license and certificate of marriage of G. W. Williams and Nancy Ratlingoard as appears from the marriage record

Cherokee Intermarried White 1906
Volume II

page 201 of Canadian District Cherokee Nation, the said record book now being in accordance with an act of the Cherokee-------------------Council, a part of the records of this office.

------------------This the 9th day of April 1900

(SEAL) (Signed) B. W. Alberty.

Assistant Executive Secre.

The undersigned being first duly sworn states that as stenographer to the Commissioner to the Five Civilized Tribes she made the above and foregoing copy and that the same is a true and correct copy of the copy of the marriage record now on file in this office.

Lola M. Champlin

Subscribed and sworn to before me this 17 day of January 1907.

Chas E Webster
Notary Public.

◇◇◇◇◇

C.E.W. Cherokee 2052.

DEPARTMENT OF THE INTERIOR,

COMMISSIONER TO THE FIVE CIVILIZED TRIBES.

In the matter of the application for the enrollment of George W. Williams, as a citizen by intermarriage of the Cherokee Nation.

D E C I S I O N

THE RECORDS OF THIS OFFICE SHOW: That at Fort Gibson, Indian Territory, August 27, 1900, application was received by the Commission to the Five Civilized Tribes for the enrollment of George W. Williams, as a citizen by intermarriage of the Cherokee Nation. Further proceedings in the matter of said application were had at Muskogee, Indian Territory, October 11, 1902, and January 7, 1907.

THE EVIDENCE IN THIS CASE SHOWS: That the applicant herein, George W. Williams, a white man, was married in accordance with Cherokee law November 29, 1869, to his wife, Nancy Williams, nee Ratlingourd, who was at the time of said marriage a recognized citizen by blood of the Cherokee Nation, and who is identified on the Cherokee authenticated tribal roll of 1880, Canadian District, page 53, number 1473, as a native Cherokee, and whose name appears upon the approved partial roll of citizens by

Cherokee Intermarried White 1906
Volume II

blood of the Cherokee Nation, opposite number 5334; that since said marriage the said George W. Williams and Nancy Williams have resided together as husband and wife and have continuously lived in the Cherokee Nation. Said applicant is identified on the Cherokee authenticated tribal roll of 1880, and the Cherokee census roll of 1896 as an intermarried citizen of the Cherokee Nation.

IT IS, THEREFORE, ORDERED AND ADJUDGED: That in accordance with the decision of the Supreme Court of the United States, dated November 5, 1906, in the cases of Daniel Red Bird et al., vs. the United States, Nos. 125, 126, 127 and 128, the said applicant George W. Williams is entitled, under the provision of Section 21 of the Act of Congress approved June 28, 1898, (30 Stat., 495), to enrollment, as a citizen by intermarriage of the Cherokee Nation, and his application for enrollment as such is accordingly granted.

Tams Bixby
Commissioner.

Dated at Muskogee, Indian Territory,
this   JAN 21 1907

◇◇◇◇◇

Cherokee
2052

Muskogee, Indian Territory, December 24, 1906.

George W. Williams,
Muskogee, Indian Territory.

Dear Sir:

November 6, 1906, the United States Supreme Court held that white persons who intermarried with Cherokee citizens according to Cherokee law prior to November 1, 1875, are entitled to enrollment and allotments of land as citizens of the Cherokee Nation.

You are advised that to properly determine your right to enrollment as a citizen by intermarriage of the Cherokee Nation, it will be necessary for you to appear before the Commissioner for the purpose of giving testimony as to the date of your marriage and whether or not your wife, by reason of your marriage to whom you claim the right to enrollment as a citizen of the Cherokee Nation, was a recognized citizen of the Cherokee Nation at the time of your marriage to her, and whether or not you were married to her in accordance with Cherokee laws.

You are, therefore, directed to appear before the Commissioner at Muskogee, Indian Territory, at 9 o'clock A. M., on Thursday, January 3, 1907, and give testimony as above indicated.

Cherokee Intermarried White 1906
Volume II

Respectfully,

J.M.H.   Acting Commissioner.

◇◇◇◇◇◇

Cherokee 2052

Muskogee, Indian Territory, January 21, 1907.

W. W. Hastings,
    Attorney for the Cherokee Nation,
        Muskogee, Indian Territory.

Dear Sir:

      There is enclosed herewith copy of the decision of the Commissioner to the Five Civilized Tribes, dated January 21, 1907, granting the application for the enrollment of George W. Williams as a citizen by intermarriage of the Cherokee Nation.

Respectfully,

Enc I-45   Commissioner.
RPI

◇◇◇◇◇◇

| Cherokee 2052 | W.W. HASTINGS. ATTORNEY. | OFFICE OF | H.M. VANCE. SECRETARY. |

Attorney for the Cherokee Nation,
MUSKOGEE, I. T.

January 21, 1907.

The Commissioner to the Five Civilized Tribes,
    Muskogee, Indian Territory.

Sir:

      Receipt is acknowledged of the testimony and of your decision enrolling George W. Williams as a citizen by intermarriage of the Cherokee Nation. Time for protesting said decision is waived and I consent that said person may be placed upon the schedule immediately.

Respectfully,
W. W. Hastings
Attorney for the Cherokee Nation

◇◇◇◇◇◇

Cherokee Intermarried White 1906
Volume II

Cherokee 2052

Muskogee, Indian Territory, January 24, 1907.

George W. Williams,
    Muskogee, Indian Territory.

Dear Sir:

There is enclosed herewith copy of the decision of the Commissioner to the Five Civilized Tribes, dated January 21, 1907, granting the application for your enrollment as a citizen by intermarriage of the Cherokee Nation.

You will be advised when your name has been placed upon a schedule of citizens of the Cherokee Nation and approved by the Secretary of the Interior.

Respectfully,

Commissioner.

Enc I-96

RPI

◇◇◇◇◇

Cherokee I.W. 68

Muskogee, Indian Territory, April 8, 1907.

George W. Williams,
    Muskogee, Indian Territory.

Dear Sir:

Your marriage license and certificate, filed in connection with your application for enrollment as a citizen by intermarriage of the Cherokee Nation, is returned to you herewith, copies of the same being retained in this office.

Respectfully,

Incl. P-4-16

Acting Commissioner.

MMP

Index

ADAIR
  J H 89
  J L 275
  James W 283,284
ADAMS, Rev W N 46
ALBERTY, B W 172,173,314,315
ARGENT, William 45
BAGWELL, E C 34,164,258,291
BAKER
  Annie E 112
  Eliza 111
  Elizabeth 111,112,113,115
  John 112
  John F 117
  John H 111,112,113,114,115, 116,117,118
  John Harvey 113,114
  Lizzie 112
  Sarah A E 112
  Sarah Anna Eliza 111
  Webster C 112,113
  Webster Cleveland 111
BALENTINE
  Hamilton 67,69
  J A A 69
  Rev Hameltin 68
  Rev Hameltine 67
BALLARD, Randolph 167
BARNS, Albert 301
BATES, A J 159
BAUGH, Mr J L 167
BEALL, Wm O 225
BEATTY, Still B 276
BIBLE
  George 276
  Lewis 276
  Wm 276
BIGBY
  Mary 237,240
  Thomas W 240
BIGSBY, Mr 240
BIXBY, Tams 8,18,26,40,49,57,70, 82,91,100,108,116,125,132,140,151,160, 174,175,182,188,196,206,215,224,227, 232,242,252,263,278,286,295,305,316
BLAIR, Catherine 277
BLY, Mary 172

BOWMAN, Lucy M 194,213,261
BRAGG
  Elizabeth 298,299,300,303,305, 306,309
  Mrs 304
  Solomon 298,299,300,303,304,305, 306,307,308
BRAGGS
  Elizabeth 300,302,307
  Mr 301
  Mrs 301
  Soloman 307
  Solomon 300,302,303
BRANSON, Eula Jeanes 131,186
BRANT, *(Unknown)* 301
BRECKENRIDGE, Commissioner 165, 167,168,190,281
BRECKINRIDGE
  C R ... 2,12,21,22,31,33,64,87,104,112, 120,145,155,168,179,181,182,184,282 ,311
  Clifton R 191,201,210
  Commissioner 52,119,128,255
  Com'r 21,53,128
BRIGHT
  Jesse 276
  Mary 276
BROWN
  Ann Henry 100
  Annie H 94
  Annie Henry 98
  John 53
  Julia 55,56,57
  Pinkey 56
  Sarah 53
BUCKNER
  Cynthia 86
  Minnie 85,86
  Minnie B 86
BUFFINGTON
  Elizabeth 114
  Lizzie 115
BUMGARNER
  Maud 276
  Peggy 276
CAKER, Rev Dempy 56
CARLILE, Nancy 212

Index

CARR, Jesse O 106,121,130,184,282
CHAMPLIN, Lola M 81,315
CHANDLER, Annie Eliza 204
CHANDY, Mr 59
CHANEY
    Della 53,54
    Eliza 53,54
    Ethel 53,54
    Florence 54
    Florence E 54
    George W 53,54
    I M 56
    J M 54
    Jame M 61
    James 53
    James M 52,53,54,55,56,57,58,60,62
    James W 52
    Julia 52,53,54,56,57
    Julia A 55
    Lou E 54
    Lou Ella 53
    Louella 53
    Mama 53
    Mamie 53,54
    Mr 59
    Pinkey 53,56
    Pinkie 52,53
    Pinky 53
CHAPPELL
    W W 170
    Walter W 4,5,6,34,36,46,47,55,98, 99,122,131,172
CHAPPELLE, Walter W 300
CHICK, Retta 55,113,300,312
CHOATE, Charlotte 87,88,89
CHRISTIE, Jane 276
CLARK, Sabra 276
COCHRAN
    Betsy 103
    Elizabeth 107
    Jesse 103
COKER
    Demps 74
    Dempsey 56
    Dempy F 74
    John 74
CONER, Frank 194

CONNER
    Crawford 191
    Francis M 22,27,190,192,193,194, 195,196,197,198,199
    Frank 194,195
    Lee 191
    Leonard 191
    Lula May 191
    Maude Emmie 191
    Rebecca J 191,192,194,196
COUNCILOR, Homer J 275
COWEN, Elizabeth J 276
CUMMINS, Theodore 301
DANIEL
    Cyntha J 74
    Cyntha Jane 74
DANNENBERG
    Anna E 218,219,224,225,226
    Annie 231
    Annie E 219,220,221
    C A 218
    A E 219
    J H 218
    J M 218
    John H 218,219,220,221
    John Henry 220,221,222,224
    Johnnie H 219
    L B 219
    L L 228
    Lewis B 219
    Lewis L 227,228,229,232
    Louis 230,231
    Louis B 219
    Lrwis L 228
    M M 228
    Martha J 228
    Mattie J 227,228,229,230,231, 232,233,234
    N B 218
    R C 219
    Robert C 219
DANNENBURG
    Anna E 223
    John H 223
DANNINBERG, Annie 231
DAVIS, M E 276
DIAL

Martin	277
Nancy	277
Nathaniel	277
Rebecca	277
Rebecca J	158,159
DOWNING, Lewis	275

DRAKE
Amma L	121
Bessie W	120,121,123
Bessie Walker	119
Betsy W	120
Emily J	119,120,121
Emily Jane	119,125
Emma	119
Emma J	121
Emma L	120,123
Emma Lane	119
J P	122,124
Joanna	125
John E	120,121,123
John Ella	119,120
John P	119,120,121,122
John Polk	118,119,124,125,126,127
Mary B	123
Nannie E	119,120,121,123

DREW
Cherley	302
Delila	276
Jesse	276

DUCKWORTH
Effie	200
Effie N	200
Gunter	201
L A	200
Laura E	200,201
Lavinia A	200
Lewis L	200
Louis L	199,200,201,202,203, 204,205,206,207,208
Louvina	204
Louvina A	205
Louvinia	202
Nancy	201
Robert	201

DUNCAN
Becky	195
Rebeca	194
Rebecca J	191,193,194,196
Rebecky	195
Rev W A	283
W A	284

EDWARDS
E Jane	276
John B	276
ELDERS, George	302

ENGLAND
Catherine	173
Elizabeth	166
Sabra	276
William	166
ESTES, A J	158
EVERETT, Cynthia	86
FALKNER, Franklin	89
FAULKER, Franklin	88

FERGUSON
Dr	230
Dr T R	221,231
FIEDS, Ezekial	12

FIELDS
Bud	12
Ella Z	11,12
Ella Zoe	11
Ezecial	12
Ezekial	11
Ezekial, Jr	11
Ezekiel	6,11,12,14,15,16,17
Lula Pearl	11
Lule P	12
Maggie	11
Maggie M	12
Maggie May	11
Margaret	6,10,11,12,13,14,15,16, 17,18,19,20
Margarette	11
Martha J	11
Martha Jane	11,12

FOIL
Alfred	86
Charlotte	86

FOREMAN
H L	56
Link	56
Samuel	97
Stephen	275

Index

Steven 139
FORREST, Harvey D 237
FOYIL
   Alford 86
   Alfred 85,86,87,88,90,91,92,93
   Charlotte 85,86,87,88,90
   Milo 85,86,87,90
FOYL, Alfred 89
GODDARD, Catherine 163
GORMLEY, Michael 240
GREEN, M D 2,53,54,87,95,104,129,
145,155,165,219,228,247,268,269,299
GUNTER, Lavina A 203
HAGGARTY
   Fanny 276
   L M 276
HAGGERTY, Rebecca 276
HALL, Mary E 276
HAMPTON
   Cindy 86
   Cynthia 86
   Nancy 212,214
HANNA, Gertrude 47,99
HARLAND, Jim 171
HARLIN, Albert 277
HARLM, J E 25
HARRIS, C J 275
HASTAIN, W J 255
HASTINGS
   Mr 202,304
   W W 9,10,19,22,29,41,50,51,
60,62,65,71,72,83,92,101,109,110,117
,125,126,133,134,142,153,161,162,
164,175,177,188,192,193,197,198,207
,211,216,225,226,233,234,243,253,
265,266,271,272,274,279,281,287,291
,296,297,308,309,312,317
HEFFERFINGER
   Lizzie 104
   Pace 104
HEFFLEFINGER
   Elizabeth 103,105,106,108
   G P 107
   Greenville 103
   Greenville P 102,105,106,107,
108,109,110
   Greenville Pace 103

Lizzie 104
Nancy 103
Pace 103,104
HEFLEFINGER, Elizabeth 107
HENRY, Annie 96
HENSLEY, E J 276
HICKS, Percy W 293
HILL, Myrtle 67,123,274,294
HOPKINS, Luther 306
HOWELL, Caroline E 276
HUDSON
   James 21
   Mary 25
   Mary E 23
   Mary E A 21,23,26
   May 24
   Sallie 21
HUTCHINSON, Wm 4,13,137,147,
202,211,220,229,230,238,248,259
IRONS
   Almira 35,37,38
   Almyra 32,35
   William 32
IRONSIDE, Robt P 90
JACKSON
   Nat 113
   Nathan 113
   Sarah A E 112,113
JAMES
   C G 27,28
   Garett 25
   Garret 21
   Garret G 22
   Garrett 21,24
   Garrett G 20,21,23,24,26,27,
28,29,30
   Houston 21
   Houston W 22
   Houston Wyley 21
   Jesse P 22,23,27
   Jesse Price 21
   Mary Ann Elizabeth 21
   Mary E 23
   Mary E A 21,22,23,24,26
JOHNSON
   A A 255,257
   Abigail 257

Ailsey A 260
Alcey A 255,256,257,258,262
Alcy A 261,262
Alsy A 261,263,266
J A 255,257
J W 255
James M 265
Jno W 262
John W 254,255,256,257,258, 259,260,261,262,263,264,265,266
Joseph R 257
Julia A 255,256,257
JONES
   B C .... 4,23,34,45,65,78,88,96,106, 113,122,130,147,157,164,184,192,259 ,270,283,291,300
   Bruce C 120,168,191,201,209, 281,282,290
   James K 59,60,61
   Jno B 80
   John 79
   John B 79,80,98,261,262
   Rev Jno B 262
KEELER
   C R 38,39
   Geo B 38
   George B 35,36,38
KEYS
   Andy 249
   Mary 210
KING
   E L 306
   E W 185
LAHAY, Joe M 47,48
LANE
   F Elma 172,204,223,251,284
   Frances L 150
   Frances R 45,68,96,107,149, 221,222,230,231,240,241,285,303,304
LAWSON
   E B 58
   Mr 59
LIPE
   C C 67,68
   D W 66,67,68,69,115
LOFLAN
   Beckey 155

   H A 155
   A J 155
LOFLIN
   Ada 154
   Ada A 154,155
   Chester C 154,155,156
   Clarence 155
   Clarence R 155,156
   Clarence Robert 155
   Harris A 154,155,156,157,158, 159,161,162
   Harris A, Jr 155,156
   Harris Asberry 154
   Harris Asbury 157
   Harris L 160
   Oscar M 155,156
   Rebecca 157
   Rebecca J 155,156,158,160
   Rebecca Jane 154
   Vaul D 154,155,156
   Vol D 155
LOTTA
   Anna J 81
   Wm R 81
LUSK, Mary C 1,5,6
LYNCH, John B 284
MACK, Parson 149
MALLORY, Mary Tabor . 25,124,195,262
MAN
   Catherine 144
   Charlotte 145
   Robert 144
   Robert J 144
MANN
   Bertha 146
   Bertha E 146
   Charlotta G 149
   Charlotte 144,145
   Charlotte C 143,144,145,146, 147,148,149,150,151,152,153
   Charlotte G 144,145,146
   Charlotte Galilee 144,146
   Dave 148
   David 149
   Effie 146
   Effie V 149
   Effie Viola 146

Index

Galilee 144
Gertrude 144,149
Gertrude E 145
John D 145,149
John Davis 144
Julia 147
Narcissa 144,145,149
Robert J 144,145,146,148, 149,150,151
Robert L 144,145,149
Robert L, Jr 144
Ruth 144
Ruth L 144,145,149
MARTIN
  Bill 43,44
  Eillism 44
  James Robert 45
  Joel 43,45
  Joel T 43,44,45
  Mattie 228
  Sarah 43,44,45
  Sarah E 43,44,45,46,49
  William 42,43,44,46,47,48,49,50,51
  William P 44,45
  Wm 46,47
  Wm P 43
MAXWELL, Mabel F 97,239
MAYES
  J B 74
  John 47,107
MAYO
  Jessie V 269,270
  Mrs W D 270
MCCLOUD, Murdoc 94
MCCORKLE, J L 314
MCDANIEL, Nancy 303
MCDONALD, Brown 236,311
MCFARLAND
  Fnnie L 276
  Sam'L 276
MCGEE
  Ambrose 2
  David 2
  David A 1,2,4,5,6,7,15,16
  Dennis B 2
  Dennis Busheyhead 2
  Eliza J 2
  Elizabeth B 2
  Esther L 2
  Florene 2
  Jeff 167
  John R 2
  Mary C 1,2,4,5,6,7
  Mr 5
  T J 24
MCGHEE
  Ambrose 1,2
  David A 2,3,7,8
  Dennis B 1,2
  Eliza J 1,2
  Elizabeth B 1,2
  Esther 1
  Esther L 2
  Florence 1
  Florence E 2
  Jeff 171
  John R 2
  John Ross 1
  Mary 1
  Mary C 2,3,7,8,9,10
  T J 25,194,195
MCLAIN, Edward 306,307
MCLEOD
  Ann Henry 100
  Murdoch 95,97,98,99,100,101,102
  Murdock 94,95,96
  Nellie Catherine 99
MCLEON, Murdoch 96
MCLEORD, M 94,95
MCNAIR
  Joanna 122,125
  Joannah 124
MEHLIN
  Elizabeth 76,77,81,82
  Ja,es G 76
  James 80
  James C 77
  James E 78
  James G 76,77,80,81,82,83,84
  James T 78
MELTON, S A 194
MERRICK, Edward 7,15,37,38,56,68, 107,139,150,158,159,205,222,231,241, 285,303,304

Index

MGHEALEN
   Elizabeth 76
   James 76,77
MIELENZ, Ella 173
MILLS, Jumper 275
MORGAN
   Amanda P 180,181
   Ellen P M 180,181
   George W 179
   Gideon 179,180,182,183,185, 186,187
   Lelia 180
   Margaret A E 181
   Margaret E A 180
   Margarette E A 180
   Marl L 183
   Martha K 179
   Martha L 180,181
   Mary L 178,179,180,181,182, 183,184,185,186,187,188,189
   Mary Llewellyn 180
   Sallie M 180,181
MORRIS
   J H 250
   Reverend Wilson 213
MYERS
   (Unknown) 107
   John 46
NASH
   Corine 291
   Corinne 289,290
   Edwin O 289,290,291
   F H 289
   Fannie Ross 295
   Florian 290
   Florian H 289,290,291,292,293, 294,295,296,297
   Hilda 289,290,491
   Lucy 291
   Lucy M 289,290,291,295
NEEDLES
   Commissioner 235,269,298,310
   Com'r 2,12,85,86,112,145,155, 219,228,246,268
   Comr 299
   T B 11,44,54,63,77,136,165,182, 219,228,236,247,269,290,299

NORTH, Kate 302
NUMBY, Mary E 276
PACE, Mattie M 69
PALOBE, Elizabeth 238
PALONE, Steve 238
PARRISH
   Cyntha Jane 74
   Holland L 73,74,75
PAYNE
   Marth A 187
   Martha A 180,182
   Mary L 179
   Samuel H 180
PERRY, Susan Jane 276
PORTER, Mary Jane 276
POWHATAN
   Cordelia A 246
   Norma P 246
POWHATTAN
   Cordelia A 246
   Lewis C 246
   Norma P 246
   Sarah L 246
POWHATTEN
   Cordella A 246
   Norma P 246
   Sarah L 246
POWHATTON
   Cordie A 246
   Norma E 246
   Norma P 246
   Sarah L 246
PRICE
   Joe 247,248
   Joseph 245,247,250,251
   Ophelia B 245
   S F E 246
   S L 246
   Samuel J 245
   Samuel Joseph 249,250,251
   Sarah F E 246
   Sarah L 244,245,246,247,248,249, 250,251,252,253,254
   Sarrah F E 246
PRIEST
   John 277
   Madoria 277

Index

QUESENBURY, Hariet B.................. 276
R GOARD, Elizabeth 80
R GOURD
   Betsy.. 80
   Eliza beth.. 79
   Elizabeth......................................79,81
RALEY
   James H 280
   James L....................................... 281
   James M............ 281,282,283,284,285, 286,287,288
   Mary.. 281
   Mary A 283
   Mary L..................................281,282,285
RAMUS, B P...................................... 157
RAPER
   Alcey A 262
   Alcy A 261,262
   Alsy A 263
   Charles.. 257
   Julia 138,140
   Julia A 139
   Julia Ann 257
   Nianna 213,214
   Viana 209
   Vianna 210,211,214
RASMUS
   B P .... 14,15,23,24,69,80,89,106, 115,124,130,193,204,261,271,273,274 ,292,293,294
   Josephine E.................................. 223
RATLINGOARD, Nancy................... 314
RATLINGORD, Nancy...................... 313
RATLINGOURD, Nancy.......311,312,315
RATTELING-GOARD, Elizabeth 76
RATTLENGOARD, Elizabeth............. 76
RATTLINGOURD
   Elizabeth....................................... 77
   Nancy 313
RDER
   Charles A..................................... 237
   Jane.. 237
RED BIRD, Daniel........8,17,26,40,49,57, 70,82,91,100,108,116,125,132,140,151, 160,174,187,196,206,215,224,232,241, 252,263,278,286,295,305,316
REECE, Dobson 301

REUTER, P G 55,258,312
RIDER
   Augustus C 236
   Austin 235
   Charles A.....235,236,237,238,240,241
   Charles Augustus.....................237,240
   Chas A 240
   Elizabeth...........................236,238,239
   Guss 235
   Jane............. 235,237,238,239,240,241, 242,243,244
   Myrta 236
   Myrtle 238
   Myrtle M 238
   Myrtle May 236
   Polly 235
   Viola 236,238
   Violet.. 236
RIDGE
   Aenias.. 276
   Andrew J 277
   Elizabeth A 276
ROGERS
   Chief.. 301
   Connell 185,186
   Elizabeth...................................... 304
   Kate D 276
   Mr.. 304
   W B 276
ROSS
   J M 158,159
   Joshua 294
   Nellie 99
   Nellie C 97
   Robert.. 98
ROSSON
   J O 12,22,33,112,128,129,169
   John O 13,138,202,211,221,230, 238,248
ROTHENBERGER, E G 23,64,65,78, 87,157,192,270
RYNER, R R 37
SAUNDERS
   Judge.. 212
   L S 209,213
   Lemual S 209
   Lemuel A..................................... 209

Index

Lemuel S 208,210,211,213,214, 215,216,217
Lemul S 209
Mary 214
Nancy 214
Nianna 214
Vianna 214
SCALES, J A 313
SCOOT, Fannie 276
SCOTT
George W 276
Jas N 276
John B 276
Mertha A 276
Mrs Louisa N 276
Rebecca L 276
S H 276
Thomas H 276
William 276
SCRAPER, Arch 275
SEIBOLT, Delila 32
SHELTON, Claud 167
SHORTHILL, J J 4
SLOAN, B E 16
SMITH
Edwin B 306
Eli 275
J A 129
John 128,129
John A 127,128,129,130,131, 132,133,134
John Addison 128
Susan 128,129
Susan C 128,129,132
STANFIELD, W S 48
STAR, Mary 283
STARR
J C 105,121,129,183
Leroy 284
Mary 284,285
Mary L 281,285
STEPHENS
James 245
Ophelia B 245,246
Ophelia V 246
STUBBLEFIELD, Demie T 15,205
TAYLOR

Judge 301
R R 88,89
Sam 301
Samuel 302
TEACHER
Jim 106
Rev James 107
THOMPSON
Charles 250
Herbert 276
THORNBROUGH
Hortense 63
James 63,67,68
THORNBRUGH
Hortense 65,70
Hortense D 64
Hortensia B 67
James 63,64,65,66,69,70,71,72,73
THORNBURGH
Hortense 64
Hortenuse 63
James 63
THORNTON
Amos 35,36,37
Judge 32
TIDWELL
J E 185,186
John E 67,73,74,148,194,211, 214,312,314
TURNER
Gunter M 186
W H 122,124,261,262
William 79,212
William H 79,80
TYAN, Thos 60
TYNER
Almira 37
Almira V 32
Almyra 32,33,38
Almyra V .. 31,33,34,35,36,39,40,41,42
Almyre 31
Elmira 38,39
Emira 38
Emma 37
Fannie 37
Flora May 37
Frank P 38

Index

G E 37
Geo W 39
George 38
George W 35
Jackson 32
James B W 38
Laura 31,32,33
Laura A 38
Leaw W 33
Leonard P 37
Lew Wallace 31,33,34,38
Lula Maud 38
Maud 31,32,33
R R 35,37,38,39
Reuben 32
Reuben R 31,33,34,35,36,39
Rheubin 32
T J 37
A V 32
Weaver 31,32,33
VAN ARMON, Mary 172
VAN BUREN, President 301
VAN NORMAN, Millie 163
VAN NORMIAN, Mary 172
VANCE, H M 65,193,211,271,272, 274,291,312
VANN
   Fannie 294
   Fannie Ross 292,295
   John D 313
   John S 314
   Judge 212
VARNERMAN, Mary 172
VARNORMAN, Mary 175
VON WEISE, Chas 44,77,94,136
WALKER
   E M 119
   Emily J 123
   Emily Jane 119,125
   George 46
   Hortense 63
   Hortensia 66,67,68
   Hortensia D 69
   Judge T M 122,124
   Sarah 46,47
   Sarah E 46,49
   T M 119,131

WALLACE
   Ailsy 136
   Alcie E 136
   Anna Alice E 136
   Grace 135,136
   Julia 136,137,139,140
   Julia A 138,139
   Julie 135
   Julius M 136
   Lu Lu 135,136
   Lulu 136
   M A 139
   Martain A 136
   Martha 135,136
   Martin 136
   Martin A 135,136,137,138,139, 140,141,142,143
   Monroe 136
WARSAN, Fleming H 166
WASSAN, Nattie May 166
WASSON
   Catherine 165,166,167,169,173, 174,175,176,178
   F H 172
   Fleming H ....162,163,164,165,166, 169,170,171,172,173,174,175,176,177 ,178
   Katherine 170,171
   Mr 172
   Mrs 167
   Nettie May 166,168
WATERS, Sarah 48,74,80,314
WEBSTER
   Charles E 260
   Chas E 17,25,48,81,90,124,195, 204,223,251,262,275,284,315
WELCH
   Ann A 277
   John C 277
   Sarah 277
WELLSHEAR, Wm S 181
WETSEL, Daniel K 15
WHEELER
   Cammel 268
   Carnall 268,269,270
   Carnell 268
   E C 268

    Emma C 267,268,269,270,271,
    272,273,277,278,279,280
    Jessie V 268,270
    John C 276
    John F 267
    Mr 274
    Nancy 267
    Sarah P 276
    Theodore 268,269,270
    W W 270
    Will 268
    Will W 268
    William 276
    William W 267,268,269,270,
    271,272,273,277,278
    Wm W 271
WILLIAMS
    Dillon 131
    Frances 245
    G W 310,311,313,314
    George 310
    George W 310,311,312,313,315,
    316,317,318
    L B 128
    Martin 245
    Nancy 310,311,312,313,315,316
    Sallie 128
    Susan C 130,131,132
WILSON, Ella 147
WINSTEAD
    Ada A 156
    Florence E 156
WISDOM, Colonel 302
WOOD, Clara Mitchell 16,24,79,89,115
WOODS, *(Unknown)* 14
WRIGHT, S T 7,36,37,38,56,139,
158,159

www.ingramcontent.com/pod-product-compliance
Lightning Source LLC
Chambersburg PA
CBHW020244030426
42336CB00010B/608